The Apocryphal
Acts of the Apostles

Harvard University
Center for the Study of World Religions

Religions of the World

General Editor:
Lawrence E. Sullivan

Cambridge, Massachusetts

THE APOCRYPHAL ACTS OF THE APOSTLES

HARVARD DIVINITY SCHOOL STUDIES

edited by

François Bovon, Ann Graham Brock,
and Christopher R. Matthews

Distributed by
Harvard University Press
for the
Harvard University Center for the
Study of World Religions

The LaserCoptic font used in the printing of this work is available from Linguist's Software, Inc., PO Box 580, Edmonds, WA 98020-0580 USA tel (425) 775-1130.

Library of Congress Cataloging-in-Publication Data

The apocryphal acts of the Apostles : Harvard Divinity School studies /
  edited by François Bovon, Ann Graham Brock, and Christopher R.
  Matthews.
      p.   cm. — (Religions of the world)
   Includes bibliographical references and index.
   ISBN 0-945454-17-1 (hardcover : alk. paper)
   ISBN 0-945454-18-X (pbk. : alk. paper)
   1. Apocryphal Acts of the Apostles—Criticism, interpretation, etc.
I. Bovon, François. II. Brock, Ann, Rev. III. Matthews, Christopher R.
IV. Series: Religions of the world (Cambridge, Mass.)
BS2871.A66 1999
229'.92506—DC21
                                        98-43460
                                         CIP

Contents

Language

Literary and Religious Studies

Appendices

Foreword

The apostles occupy a special place in Christian belief and practice throughout the world. Around them has grown up a rich lore; and with good reason. Some of the apostles knew Christ in the flesh. Already in the second and third centuries it was believed that they were among the first ones chosen by Christ when he began his public life, along with such women disciples as Mary Magdalene. Their knowledge of Christ was sensory and fully embodied—a valuable quality of experience in a religion grounded in a theology of incarnation. The apostles were called by Christ in his own voice, often by name. They witnessed with their own eyes the power of his miracles. They were touched by him and fed by him. And they were the first ones sent and empowered by him to bring the good news of salvation. No wonder that in the Christian communities of Asia, Oceania, Africa, and Latin America, the apostles play special roles in rituals of divination and cure as well as in the mythologies and liturgies created in the encounter between Christian revelation and local cultures over the centuries.[1]

Christ's disciples par excellence, the apostles form a carnal bridge between the heavenly and earthly realms; they are living links between divine and human life. This explains why Saint James and Saint Peter, for example, are venerated as major cosmic forces in the religious life of many South American peoples, controlling lightning and fertility, warding off the forces of extermination, and bringing clairvoyant illumination to the obscure mysteries of life. Reflection on the life and

---

[1] Lawrence E. Sullivan, "Christianity: Christian Myth and Legend," *New Encyclopaedia Britannica*, 15th ed., 16:335–40, 365–66.

significance of the apostles sheds important light on the meaning of Christianity. This is one reason why this volume is so valuable.

This volume unearths the very roots of the widespread traditions about the apostles that exfoliate throughout the Christian world. It examines some of the first accounts about the apostles as well as subsequent sources, drawing on the early Christian apocryphal literature that stands on the border between biblical account and hagiography. For this reason, *The Apocryphal Acts of the Apostles* is a book of special importance to historians of religions. By lining up the series of variant themes, styles, and structures treated in this apocryphal literature, one understands better the broad cultural impact of Christian ideas and practices in history, an impact felt even in the repercussions and expressions not fully condoned by the Christian authorities of the day.

François Bovon, his fellow editors, Ann Graham Brock and Christopher R. Matthews, and his contributors call attention to the ample heritage of early Christianity. In doing so, they begin to heal a rift that has opened in the world of scholarship over the past century. The study of the history of religions that started in universities during the nineteenth century integrated biblical archaeology and textual study of scripture with the study of classical antiquity and the investigation of what were then called "oriental religions." Over the intervening decades, the *allgemeine Religionswissenschaft*, or general history of religions, fragmented into subspecialties and analytic discourses largely unacquainted with one another's discoveries. Much of this disintegration was propelled by the forces of good reason, such as the need for adequate language study, prolonged field experience, and thorough knowledge of particular historical contexts. Nevertheless, the appearance of this volume on early Christian apocryphal literature in the Religions of the World series is a welcome counterbalance to the centrifugal forces felt throughout the study of religion. Though the facile hope for a totalizing science of religion has been chastened, it is more clear than ever that an understanding of religious life in diverse times and places is necessary to gain a satisfactory account of the religious history of humankind and that the study of that history, both in particular contexts and as a whole, raises important general questions about how we interpret symbols, rites, and texts in any single place. Excellent studies of specific religious expressions that can be dated and placed advance our understanding of the general history of religions and, indeed, of the nature of religion and religious experience, and vice versa. The studies in this volume point to the specific context of early Christianity and, at the same time, raise a number of important questions and hypotheses concerning the formation of texts, the transformation of religious experience into oral and narrative expression, and the meaning and interpretation of specific symbolic complexes and practices. Indeed, the volume makes the case that understanding how these apocryphal texts originated and developed offers a model for understanding the formation of canonical Christian scripture:

> [For students of the gospels] the process of development should sound eerily familiar: various narratives about first-century figures are told and retold, in written and oral form, over a period of time long enough to result in several multiforms of many of the narrative units, in the attribution of Christian motivations to characters who are polytheist in other sources, in the fixed attribution of roles in the plots to various secondary characters, in the gradual erasure of non-essential details, and in the telescoping of chronology. The narrative at this point exists in oral tradition and in a number of small written units. . . . [An] author/ compiler begins to collect the. . .sources and to shape them into a coherent, extended narrative. . . . Later redactions begin with this base text and are even more modest. . . . (Christine M. Thomas, p. 61)

The volume studies not only how the texts were written but above all how these apocryphal writings were read. The purposes of reading these apocryphal acts of the apostles were varied and fascinating. They were taken as literal history, as allegories of the changes that occur within the soul, as inspirational material for sermons, as devotional readings for private piety, as librettos for dramatic spectacles and visual art, as enchantments during the liturgy, and as sources for doctrinal debate. All of these sorts of reading are detailed. The spectrum of uses alone testifies to the importance and fecundity of the acts of the apostles. In yet another transformation that tells us about our own cultural situation, these ancient texts now appear before us in this volume as documents retrieved for the purpose of scholarly study, having fallen from public view for centuries or even millennia. Their restoration to the realm of public reading, however, may reintroduce them to other creative spheres of culture as well.

These documents seldom presented themselves as detached historical chronicles but rather as efficacious words that powerfully effect and participate in the mystical union of saints with those on earth who commemorate them on their feast days. Commingling as a single mystical body, made one in the liturgy celebrating the communion of saints in heaven and on earth, led by the apostle, the words of the apostle carried extraordinary power and drew the devotee into the kingdom of grace through the power of anamnesis. The commemoration of the apostle-saint was not just an act of historical recollection but a vital and necessary participation in God's grace made manifest in the virtues embodied in the saint. The apostle, after all, lived a fleshly life in the miraculous age of Christ's bodily life. These acts of the apostles base their power on a theology of history and fleshly existence in time. The words of the apostles recorded in their acts possess efficacious power—to heal, to exorcise demons, to call down the spirit, to link earth with heaven, and to unite the soul with Christ. "The words of the apostle in the *Acts of Thomas*," for example, "are as crucial to the sacramental rituals as the utterances of the *magos* are to the efficacy of the spells" (Caroline Johnson, pp. 203–4). Many of the acts of the apostles reflect a pattern of perfection in their saintly hero that echoes not only Christian incarnational theology but also the models of divine humanity exemplified in the divine philosophers and sages of Roman and Greek antiquity. They do not, however, claim godhead for their apostles, but only that they are godlike (Laura S. Nasrallah, p. 239).

What does it mean to attend to and understand the meaning and intentions of these texts? If the words present themselves as efficacious, then what is their transformative effect on readers (Nasrallah)? Do the powerful words and deeds of the apostles create a community of disciples out of the readers? It remains to be seen. For now, it seems clear that François Bovon presents this book as an invitation to create a new area of study, for he offers a step-by-step guide on how best to do it. Based on his experience as a leading expert, his concrete suggestions are invaluable; they illustrate the entire process of research, from selection and identification of subjects and texts, to editing, translation, and commentary. Bovon argues that the process he outlines can apply to the study of scriptures and apocrypha in any number of languages. For this reason also the volume makes a fitting contribution to the Religions of the World book series, published by the Harvard University Center for the Study of World Religions. The Center fosters the historical and comparative study of religion. The book series encourages multiple disciplinary approaches to the full range of religious expression: in art, medicine, law, literature, music, liturgy, economy, anthropology, and the cosmological sciences. I wish to thank François Bovon and his colleagues Ann Graham Brock and Christopher R. Matthews for offering their work to the Center series and Kathryn Dodgson and Eric Edstam for their excellent work in preparing the publication.

Lawrence E. Sullivan, Director
Harvard University Center for the
Study of World Religions

Preface

Early Christian apocryphal literature has for a long time been neglected.[1] Few have considered it their main concern. Only those New Testament scholars interested by the question of the biblical canon, the survival of New Testament forms, or the oral transmission of Jesus' sayings have paid attention to it. The discovery of the *Gospel of Thomas* aroused some scholarly attention, but the attention was very selective. Gender-oriented studies provided another reason for returning to the apocryphal literature. In order to understand the tensions among the first Christian communities concerning the role of women, as prophets or ministers, historians have had to reconsider such texts as the *Acts of Thecla* or the *Gospel of Mary*. Again, such interest in the texts was occasioned by a specific agenda and only selected texts were helpful.

It is actually not so much the relation between canonical and apocryphal literature which should be attended to, but the question of the early Christian heritage. If we bear in mind this general question, the early Christian apocryphal literature does not belong to New Testament scholars only but to all historians of ancient Christianity.

---

[1] Part of this literature was generated before the canonization of the New Testament writings, therefore before the New Testament existed as a book. Further, a large portion of this literature is not dependent on the text of the New Testament. Finally, most of these apocryphal documents do not imitate the style, the forms, or the content of the New Testament, nor do they try to fill the gaps of the biblical texts. For all these reasons it is better to abandon the traditional title Apocrypha of the New Testament and to substitute the more adequate designation early Christian apocryphal literature.

Such scholars will soon discover that these many texts were not always considered to be apocryphal, nor were they always in opposition to the biblical canon. Some of the texts, it is true, were written in and for communities which would not become part of the victorious Orthodox or Catholic Churches. As we know, heresy and orthodoxy, like apocryphal and canonical, are categories that were applied later by the dominant religious movement to delineate and justify its own identity and boundaries. Other texts were, to begin with, neutral—if one can use this term—or available to an orthodox or heterodox understanding. Origen, for example, could still consider the *Acts of Peter* or the *Acts of Paul* worthy to be read and quoted. The fact, however, that the Manichaeans attributed a strong authority to the Apocryphal Acts of the Apostles dealt these acts a fatal blow as far as the Catholic and Orthodox Churches were concerned. Very often these texts were revised to remove them from unclean hands and to render them better suited to a new situation, a new taste, a new doctrinal discourse. It is, therefore, more appropriate to consider these documents to be part of the Christian heritage and to read them as an expression of the tradition, alongside the scriptures.

Scholars sensitive to nuance will realize that ancient Christians knew many ways to incorporate such a corpus of literature into their beliefs and practices. A bishop of the second century C.E., Serapion of Antioch, first accepted the value of the *Gospel of Peter*, because he believed its readers were orthodox Christians.[2] Later, the Byzantine Church considered the *Protevangelium of James* (the *Story of Mary* or the *Birth of Mary*, as it was originally named) a historical document and used it to shape liturgical celebrations in honor of the Virgin Mary.[3] Latin authors of the Middle Ages, as well as Byzantine preachers, were in need of stories for the feasts of the apostles and first disciples and rearranged apocryphal stories to fit these new demands. Gregory of Tours, to offer

---

[2] See Eusebius of Caesarea *Hist. eccl.* 6.12.2–6.

[3] See Émile Amann, *Le Protévangile de Jacques et ses remaniements latins. Introduction, textes, traduction et notes* (Les Apocryphes du Nouveau Testament; Paris: Letouzey et Ané, 1910), 108–37.

just one example, wrote a life of the apostle Andrew,[4] noting explicitly that he had access to the old apocryphal acts of this apostle and that he preferred to omit the long speeches (no doubt—although he does not say so—because he considered them to be heretical in nature).

The early Christian apocryphal literature is, therefore, a vital source for historians of Christianity as well as for New Testament scholars, patristics scholars, and theologians. It is the hope of the contributors to this volume, which is devoted to a long-neglected branch of this literature, the Apocryphal Acts of the Apostles, that the reading of this book will awaken interest among these scholarly groups. It is also fitting that this particular volume appears not in an explicitly biblical series, but in one open to the many manifestations of religion.

The first doctoral seminar that I led at Harvard Divinity School was devoted to the Apocryphal Acts of the Apostles. This was during the 1993–94 academic year. The zeal and enthusiasm of the students was so impressive that I proposed that a book be planned as an outcome of the seminar. Several participants—Ann Graham Brock, David H. Warren, Caroline Johnson, Laura S. Nasrallah, David W. Pao, Richard N. Slater, Yuko Taniguchi, and Athanasios Antonopoulos—accepted the task of preparing their research papers for publication. One of my colleagues at the Divinity School, Allen D. Callahan, was naturally associated with the seminar topic because he had worked on the *Acts of Mark* for his dissertation. The same was true of Christine M. Thomas and Christopher R. Matthews, both recipients of doctorates from Harvard, whom I invited to give lectures during the seminar. Evie Zachariades-Holmberg, a colleague at Holy Cross Greek Orthodox School of Theology, regularly attended the seminar. Because of her rich knowledge of ancient and modern Greek, I asked her to read the Apocryphal Acts of the Apostles with attention to their language. During the next two years each participant rewrote her or his paper and revised it in discussion with other contributors to the volume.

This volume begins with a general introduction, not so much to the Apocryphal Acts of the Apostles as such—fine examples of which exist

---

[4] Gregory, *Epitome* of the *Acts of Andrew*.

already in encyclopedias and collections of translations[5]—but to the concrete task of editing, translating, and commenting on apocryphal and hagiographic narratives on the apostles and the first Christians.

Because of the important question of the transmission of such stories, three articles are devoted to the relationship between tradition and redaction, between the first narratives and their ulterior rewritings. Beginning with the realization that the Apocryphal Acts of the Apostles offer a model for understanding the genesis and development of Christian narratives more generally, including the canonical gospels, Christine Thomas constructs a continuum between oral and written transmission. She underlines the flexibility of the traditional stories about the apostle Peter, the importance of each performance, oral or written, and the different functions that the same stories could fulfill according to time and space. A second article, a rigorous analysis of the several versions of the *Acts of Mark*, allows Allen Callahan to propose the hypothesis that there was a Coptic *Vorlage* of the *Acts of Mark*, now lost, anterior to all the preserved versions, even to the Greek recensions. This hypothesis, which is confirmed by the very nature of the Arabic version, provides strong support for the Egyptian origin of the story. A third article is a sounding of the Byzantine homiletic literature: I show that Byzantine preachers—even when hostile to apocryphal texts—used and quoted some of them. By doing so they participated in the phenomenon of rewriting and transforming apocryphal stories.

Too few scholars have scrutinized the language of the Apocryphal Acts of the Apostles. Still fewer have been interested in their style (a chapter also missing or underdeveloped in New Testament grammars).[6] Two chapters here deal with the Greek of the apocryphal acts and attempt to fill part of this lacuna. Using different procedures and methodologies, they nevertheless reach similar conclusions. David Warren has crafted an exercise on stylometry by looking at the level of complexity in

---

[5] See the articles by Eckhard Plümacher and Robert McL. Wilson mentioned in the general bibliography as well as the introductions in *NTApoc*[5].

[6] The exception being Nigel Turner's *Style*; see David H. Warren, "The Greek Language of the Apocryphal Acts of the Apostles: A Study in Style," p. 101 below.

sentence structure, at the type of preface the author wrote, and at the position of the verb in the phrase. Evie Zachariades-Holmberg examines the quality and social level of the Greek in the *Acts of Andrew*, the *Acts of Peter*, and the *Acts of Paul*: she establishes their relationship to the Koine Greek in general and to the New Testament in particular.

The border between literary criticism and motif analysis is not so rigid. Ann Graham Brock examines the differences between the *Acts of Peter* and the *Acts of Paul* with respect to political authorities, female and male characters, family and social responsibilities, and ecclesiological organization. She succeeds in differentiating the conservative attitude of the author of the *Acts of Peter* and the subversive orientation of the author of the *Acts of Paul*. The *Acts of Thomas* contains two epicleses, similar to one another, but different from the other prayers and hymns of the work. After a thorough investigation, Caroline Johnson insists on the incantational character of these texts. These calls for the Spirit have a structural kinship with magical texts of antiquity. Christopher R. Matthews explores the intriguing appearance of speaking animals in the Apocryphal Acts of the Apostles. He argues that this topos represents a complex appropriation of widespread literary, philosophical, and religious motifs. Thus, the effective employment of talking animals as characters in the apocryphal acts was made possible by their availability in the cultural repertoire of the ancient world.

By analyzing its epilogue, Laura Nasrallah throws light on the *Acts of Andrew* as a text that offers to initiate the reader and on the emergence of the authorial subject by the presence of the grammatical first person, singular and plural. David Pao reads the miracle stories contained in the same *Acts of Andrew* and explores how these healing stories serve the theological program of the author. At the end of this section, Richard Slater explains the encratite orientation of the first act of the *Acts of Philip* as well as the literary function of the tour of hell, preserved in one of the two witnesses of the text but banished from the other.

The last part of the book consists of two appendices, which should provide vivid proof that it is still possible to discover unedited documents related to the apostles. Two texts are published here for the first time. Evie Zachariades-Holmberg and I have edited one form of the *Martyrdom of the Holy Apostle Ananias*, the Christian of Damascus who welcomed, healed, and baptized the apostle Paul according to the canonical book of Acts. Yuko Taniguchi, Athanasios Antonopoulos, and I have edited one of the neglected prologues to the gospels, the *Memorial of Saint John the Theologian*. This memoir is not oriented toward the text of the gospel but toward the person of the beloved disciple.

Preparing this volume was an exciting experience of collegiality, a common effort to achieve a quality of scholarship within a framework of friendship and collaboration that does not exclude intellectual rigor and mutual involvement. My gratitude extends to each contributor for her or his willingness to persevere in the common task and to complete each step on time. My special and warm thanks go to the two people who agreed to help me with editorial tasks during the last part of the road: Ann Graham Brock and Christopher R. Matthews have done marvelous work. I would like also to express my deep appreciation to Kathryn Dodgson, who is responsible for the publications of the Harvard University Center for the Study of World Religions, and to her colleague, Eric Edstam. Lawrence E. Sullivan, director of the Center for the Study of World Religions, accepted this work for inclusion in the series "Religions of the World." I thank him for his hospitality. It has been a pleasure to collaborate with all these friends during the past few years.

François Bovon

Abbreviations

AAn	*Acts of Andrew*
AAnMt	*Acts of Andrew and Matthias*
AAnPt	*Acts of Andrew and Peter*
ABarn	*Acts of Barnabas*
AJn	*Acts of John*
AJnPr	*Acts of John* by Pseudo-Prochorus
AMk	*Acts of Mark*
APh	*Acts of Philip*
APl	*Acts of Paul*
APlAn	*Acts of Paul and Andrew*
APt	*Acts of Peter*
APtAn	*Acts of Peter and Andrew*
APtPl	*Acts of Peter and Paul*
APtTwelve	*Acts of Peter and the Twelve Apostles*
ATh	*Acts of Thomas*
AThad	*Acts of Thaddeus*
AThec	*Acts of Thecla*, part of the *Acts of Paul*, also called *Acts of Paul and Thecla*
ATim	*Acts of Timothy*
ATit	*Acts of Titus*
AVer	*Actus Vercellenses*
Epit.	Gregory's *Epitome* of the *Acts of Andrew*
MartPh	*Martyrdom of Philip*
MartPl	*Martyrdom of Paul*
MartPt	*Martyrdom of Peter*
PHam	Hamburg Greek Papyrus of the *Acts of Paul*
PHeid	Heidelberg Coptic Papyrus of the *Acts of Paul*
Ps-Clem Hom	*Pseudo-Clementine Homilies*
Ps-Clem Rec	*Pseudo-Clementine Recognitions*

* * *

AAA	*Acta Apostolorum Apocrypha*, ed. R. A. Lipsius and M. Bonnet, 1891–1903, reprint 1959
ABD	*Anchor Bible Dictionary,* ed. D. N. Freedman
ActaSS	*Acta Sanctorum*
AnBoll	*Analecta Bollandiana*
ANRW	*Aufstieg und Niedergang der römischen Welt*
BDF	F. Blass, A. Debrunner, and R. W. Funk, *A Greek Grammar of the New Testament*
BGBE	Beiträge zur Geschichte der biblischen Exegese
BHG	F. Halkin, *Bibliotheca Hagiographica Graeca*, 3d ed., 1957
BHG: Auctarium	F. Halkin, *Bibliotheca Hagiographica Graeca*, 3d ed., *Auctarium*, 1969
BHG: Novum Auctarium	F. Halkin, *Novum Auctarium Bibliothecae Hagiographicae Graecae*, 1984
BHL	H. Fros, *Bibliotheca Hagiographica Latina Antiquae et Mediae Aetatis*, 1986
BHO	*Bibliotheca Hagiographica Orientalis*, 1910, reprint 1970
CChrSA	Corpus Christianorum, Series Apocryphorum
CChrSG	Corpus Christianorum, Series Graeca
CChrSL	Corpus Christianorum, Series Latina
CSEL	Corpus Scriptorum Ecclesiasticorum Latinorum
EEC	*Encyclopedia of the Early Church*, ed. A. di Berardino, English translation by A. Walford
EEChr	*Encyclopedia of Early Christianity*, ed. E. Ferguson et al., 2d ed.
HTR	*Harvard Theological Review*
IDB	*The Interpreter's Dictionary of the Bible*, ed. G. A. Buttrick et al.
JR	*Journal of Religion*
JTS	*Journal of Theological Studies*
LCL	Loeb Classical Library
NHC	Nag Hammadi Codex
NHL	Nag Hammadi Library
NHLE	*The Nag Hammadi Library in English*, ed. J. M. Robinson, 3d ed., 1988
NHS	Nag Hammadi Studies
NTApoc[3]	*New Testament Apocrypha*, 3d ed., English translation ed. by R. McL. Wilson, 1963, 1965, reprint 1973, 1974
NTApoc[5]	*New Testament Apocrypha*, 5th ed., English translation ed. by R. McL. Wilson, 1991, 1992

NTApok[1]	*Neutestamentliche Apokryphen in deutscher Übersetzung,* ed. E. Hennecke, 1904
NTApok[2]	*Neutestamentliche Apokryphen in deutscher Übersetzung,* 2d ed., ed. E. Hennecke, 1924
NTApok[3]	*Neutestamentliche Apokryphen in deutscher Übersetzung,* 3d ed., ed. E. Hennecke and W. Schneemelcher, 2 vols. 1959–64
NTApok[4]	*Neutestamentliche Apokryphen in deutscher Übersetzung,* 4th ed., ed. E. Hennecke and W. Schneemelcher, 1968
NTApok[5]	*Neutestamentliche Apokryphen in deutscher Übersetzung,* 5th ed., ed. W. Schneemelcher, 1989–1990
NTS	*New Testament Studies*
OCD	*Oxford Classical Dictionary,* ed. S. Hornblower and A. Spawforth, 3d ed.
ODB	*Oxford Dictionary of Byzantium,* ed. A. P. Kazhdan et al.
PG	J. P. Migne, *Patrologia Graeca*
PL	J. P. Migne, *Patrologia Latina*
PO	*Patrologia Orientalis*
RHE	*Revue d'histoire ecclésiastique*
RThPh	*Revue de théologie et de philosophie*
SC	Sources chrétiennes
TDNT	*Theological Dictionary of the New Testament,* ed. G. Kittel and G. Friedrich, 10 vols.
TU	Texte und Untersuchungen zur Geschichte der altchristlichen Literatur
ZKG	*Zeitschrift für Kirchengeschichte*
ZNW	*Zeitschrift für die neutestamentliche Wissenschaft*

Short Titles

Actes apocryphes des apôtres
  Bovon, François, et al. *Les Actes apocryphes des apôtres. Christianisme et monde païen.* Publications de la Faculté de théologie de l'Université de Genève 4. Geneva: Labor et Fides, 1981.

Amsler, Bovon, and Bouvier, *Actes de l'apôtre Philippe*
  Amsler, Frédéric, François Bovon, and Bertrand Bouvier, eds. *Actes de l'apôtre Philippe. Introduction, traductions et notes.* Apocryphes 8. Turnhout: Brepols, 1996.

Bieler, *ΘΕΙΟΣ ANHP*
  Bieler, Ludwig. *ΘΕΙΟΣ ANHP. Das Bild des "göttlichen Menschen" in Spätantike und Frühchristentum.* 2 vols. 1935 36. Reprint, 2 vols. in 1. Darmstadt: Wissenschaftliche Buchgesellschaft, 1976.

Blumenthal, *Formen und Motive*
  Blumenthal, Martin. *Formen und Motive in den apokryphen Apostelgeschichten.* Texte und Untersuchungen zur Geschichte der altchristlichen Literatur 48/1. Leipzig: Hinrichs, 1933.

Bremmer, *Apocryphal Acts of John*
  Bremmer, Jan N., ed. *The Apocryphal Acts of John.* Studies on the Apocryphal Acts of the Apostles 1. Kampen: Kok Pharos, 1995.

Bremmer, *Apocryphal Acts of Paul and Thecla*
  Bremmer, Jan N., ed. *The Apocryphal Acts of Paul and Thecla.* Studies on the Apocryphal Acts of the Apostles 2. Kampen: Kok Pharos, 1996.

Brown, *Cult of the Saints*
   Brown, Peter. *The Cult of the Saints: Its Rise and Function in Latin Christianity*. Haskell Lectures on History of Religions, n.s., 2. Chicago: University of Chicago Press, 1981.

Budge, *Contendings of the Apostles*
   Budge, E. A. Wallis. *The Contendings of the Apostles*. 2 vols. 1899–1901. Reprint, Amsterdam: APA, Philo, 1976.

Burrus, *Chastity as Autonomy*
   Burrus, Virginia. *Chastity as Autonomy: Women in the Stories of the Apocryphal Acts*. Studies in Women and Religion 23. Lewiston, N.Y.: Mellen Press, 1987.

Davies, *Revolt of the Widows*
   Davies, Stevan L. *The Revolt of the Widows: The Social World of the Apocryphal Acts*. Carbondale: Southern Illinois University Press; London: Feffer and Simons, 1980.

Dvornik, *Idea of Apostolicity*
   Dvornik, Francis. *The Idea of Apostolicity in Byzantium and the Legend of the Apostle Andrew*. Dumbarton Oaks Studies 4. Cambridge, Mass.: Harvard University Press, 1958.

Elliott, *Apocryphal New Testament*
   Elliott, James K., ed. *The Apocryphal New Testament: A Collection of Apocryphal Christian Literature in an English Translation*. Oxford: Clarendon Press, 1993.

Fabricius, *Codex Apocryphus*
   Fabricius, Johann Albert. *Codex Apocryphus Novi Testamenti*. 2d ed. 3 vols. in 2. Hamburg: Schiller, 1719–43.

Ficker, *Die Petrusakten*
   Ficker, Gerhard. *Die Petrusakten. Beiträge zu ihrem Verständnis*. Leipzig: Barth, 1903.

Geerard, *Clavis Apocryphorum*
   Geerard, Maurice. *Clavis Apocryphorum Novi Testamenti*. Corpus Christianorum. Turnhout: Brepols, 1992.

Hennecke, *Handbuch*
    Hennecke, Edgar, ed. *Handbuch zu den neutestamentlichen Apokryphen.* Tübingen: Mohr (Siebeck), 1904.

Junod and Kaestli, *Acta Iohannis*
    Junod, Éric, and Jean-Daniel Kaestli. *Acta Iohannis.* 2 vols. Corpus Christianorum. Series Apocryphorum 1–2. Turnhout: Brepols, 1983.

Junod and Kaestli, *L'histoire des Actes apocryphes des apôtres*
    Junod, Éric, and Jean-Daniel Kaestli. *L'histoire des Actes apocryphes des apôtres du IIIe au IXe siècle. Le cas des Actes de Jean.* Cahiers de la Revue de théologie et de philosophie 7. Geneva/Lausanne/Neuchâtel: Revue de théologie et de philosophie, 1982.

Klijn, *Acts of Thomas*
    Klijn, Albertus Frederik Johannes. *The Acts of Thomas.* Supplements to Novum Testamentum 5. Leiden: Brill, 1962.

Leloir, *Écrits apocryphes sur les apôtres*
    Leloir, Louis. *Écrits apocryphes sur les apôtres. Traduction de l'édition arménienne de Venise.* 2 vols. Corpus Christianorum: Series Apocryphorum 3–4. Turnhout: Brepols, 1986–92.

Lipsius, *Die apokryphen Apostelgeschichten*
    Lipsius, Richard Adelbert. *Die apokryphen Apostelgeschichten und Apostellegenden. Ein Beitrag zur altchristlichen Literaturgeschichte.* 2 vols. in 3 and supplement. 1883–90. Reprint, Amsterdam: Philo, 1976.

MacDonald, *Acts of Andrew*
    MacDonald, Dennis Ronald. *The Acts of Andrew and the Acts of Andrew and Matthias in the City of the Cannibals.* Society of Biblical Literature. Texts and Translations 33; Christian Apocrypha 1. Atlanta: Scholars Press, 1990.

MacDonald, *Apocryphal Acts of Apostles*
    MacDonald, Dennis Ronald, ed. *The Apocryphal Acts of Apostles. Semeia* 38. Decatur, Ga.: Scholars Press, 1986.

MacDonald, *Legend and the Apostle*
    MacDonald, Dennis Ronald. *The Legend and the Apostle: The Battle for Paul in Story and Canon.* Philadelphia: Westminster Press, 1983.

Norelli, *Ascensio Isaiae*
Norelli, Enrico, et al. *Ascensio Isaiae*. 2 vols. Corpus Christianorum. Series Apocryphorum 7–8. Turnhout: Brepols, 1995.

Plümacher, "Apokryphe Apostelakten"
Plümacher, Eckhard. "Apokryphe Apostelakten." In *Paulys Realencyclopädie der classischen Altertumswissenschaft*, edited by Georg Wissowa et al., cols. 11–70. Supplementband 15. Munich: Druckenmüller, 1978.

Prieur, *Acta Andreae*
Prieur, Jean-Marc. *Acta Andreae*. 2 vols. Corpus Christianorum. Series Apocryphorum 5–6. Turnhout: Brepols, 1989.

Schmidt, *Acta Pauli*
Schmidt, Carl. *Acta Pauli aus der Heidelberger koptischen Papyrushandschrift Nr. 1*. 2d ed. 1905. Reprint, Hildesheim: Olms, 1965.

Schmidt, *Die alten Petrusakten*
Schmidt, Carl. *Die alten Petrusakten im Zusammenhang der apokryphen Apostelliteratur. Nebst einem neuentdeckten Fragment*. Texte und Untersuchungen zur Geschichte der altchristlichen Literatur 24/1. Leipzig: Hinrichs, 1903.

Schmidt, *ΠΡΑΞΕΙΣ ΠΑΥΛΟΥ*
Schmidt, Carl. *ΠΡΑΞΕΙΣ ΠΑΥΛΟΥ. Acta Pauli nach dem Papyrus der Hamburger Staats- und Universitäts-Bibliothek*, unter der Mitarbeit von Wilhelm Schubart. Veröffentlichen aus der Hamburger Staats- und Universitäts-Bibliothek 2. Glückstadt/Hamburg: Augustin, 1936.

Söder, *Die apokryphen Apostelgeschichten*
Söder, Rosa. *Die apokryphen Apostelgeschichten und die romanhafte Literatur der Antike*. 1932. Reprint, Stuttgart: Kohlhammer, 1969.

Thomas, "Acts of Peter"
Thomas, Christine M. "The Acts of Peter, the Ancient Novel, and Early Christian History." Ph.D. diss., Harvard University, 1995.

Vouaux, *Actes de Paul*
Vouaux, Léon. *Les Actes de Paul et ses lettres apocryphes. Introduction, textes, traduction et commentaire*. Les Apocryphes du Nouveau Testament. Paris: Letouzey et Ané, 1913.

Vouaux, *Actes de Pierre*
  Vouaux, Léon. *Les Actes de Pierre. Introduction, textes, traduction et commentaire*. Les Apocryphes du Nouveau Testament. Paris: Letouzey et Ané, 1922.

Wilson, "Apokryphen"
  Wilson, Robert McL. "Apokryphen II: Apokryphen des Neuen Testaments." In *Theologische Realenzyklopädie* 3, pp. 316–62. Berlin/New York: de Gruyter, 1978.

Wright, *Apocryphal Acts of the Apostles*
  Wright, William, ed. *Apocryphal Acts of the Apostles. Edited from Syriac Manuscripts in the British Museum and Other Libraries*. 2 vols. 1871. Reprint, 2 vols. in 1. Hildesheim/New York: Olms, 1990.

Editing the Apocryphal
Acts of the Apostles

François Bovon

Introduction

I would like to invite you to join me on a journey. This journey, from the selection of a particular apostolic figure to the production of a commentary, carries the scholar through ancient texts, Byzantine quotations, manuscripts in Greek, Latin, and other foreign languages, and compels him or her to consult indices spanning centuries of ancient, medieval, and even modern history. In the course of the work, the scholarly traveler will uncover a wealth of resources for inquiry into texts and traditions surrounding the early Christian apostles.[1]

Perhaps you are wondering if the journey I suggest is worthwhile. You may ask, "Is there anything new that can be written about the early apostles?" Let me reply that there is much that waits to be discovered! I believe that there are still unedited texts (not the oldest witnesses, perhaps, but other, later texts) connected with the apostles and the first Christians which await further examination. There are also Greek manuscripts of well-known documents that should be reexamined.

I would like to offer my warm thanks to Valerie C. Cooper, a doctoral student at the Harvard Divinity School, and Steven J. Larson, a former M.T.S. student at the Harvard Divinity School, now a doctoral student at Brown University, who helped with the editing of this paper. I appreciate both their sense of language and their enthusiasm.

[1] François Bovon, "Vers une nouvelle édition de la littérature apocryphe chrétienne. La *Series Apocryphorum* du *Corpus Christianorum*," *Augustinianum* 33 (1983): 373–78. The article describes the work and origin in the 1970s of an international group of scholars, the Association pour l'étude de la littérature apocryphe chrétienne.

Further, I believe that new editions are needed to replace some older and outdated editions. All this is true because the so-called apocryphal literature has been neglected in favor of the canonical texts, patristic literature, the Dead Sea Scrolls, and the Nag Hammadi Codices.

To start us on our journey, I shall share what I learned while investigating the apostolic figure Philip. The examples given here are drawn from my own experiences, which grew out of the preparation of a critical edition of the *Acts of Philip* in Greek.[2] This edition, now ready for publication, has been prepared from its early stages with the assistance of Bertrand Bouvier and, later, with the help of Frédéric Amsler.[3] Teamwork is particularly useful because it allows talents rarely found in one person alone—not only scholarly competence, but also endurance—to benefit a single text. Although the work I describe here concerns Greek texts, the same steps would also apply to work involving other apocryphal materials composed in or translated into other languages, such as Latin, Syriac, Coptic, Armenian, Georgian, Arabic, Ethiopic, Irish, or Slavonic.

Before Visiting a Library and Meeting Your Manuscripts

The Choice of an Apostle and the Reference Works of Richard Adelbert Lipsius

Most scholars have been interested in the five so-called major Apocryphal Acts of the Apostles: the *Acts of John*, the *Acts of Andrew*, the *Acts of Peter*, the *Acts of Paul*, and the *Acts of Thomas*.[4] This selection was influenced by the subsequent history of these texts, their *Wirkungs-*

---

[2] François Bovon, "Les Actes de Philippe," *ANRW* II 25/6:4431–527.

[3] The critical edition is on its way to the publisher. See the French translation: *Actes de l'apôtre Philippe. Introduction, traductions et notes*, ed. Frédéric Amsler, François Bovon, and Bertrand Bouvier (Apocryphes 8; Turnhout: Brepols, 1996).

[4] See *AAA*; Éric Junod and Jean-Daniel Kaestli, *Acta Iohannis* (CChrSA 1–2; Turnhout: Brepols, 1983); Jean-Marc Prieur, *Acta Andreae* (CChrSA 5–6; Turnhout: Brepols, 1989); Carl Schmidt, *Acta Pauli aus der Heidelberger koptischen Papyrushandschrift Nr. 1,* mit Tafelband, 2d ed. (Leipzig: Hinrichs, 1905; reprint, Hildesheim: Olms, 1965); Léon Vouaux, *Les Actes de Paul et ses lettres apocryphes. Introduction, textes, traduction et commentaire* (Les Apocryphes du Nouveau Testament; Paris: Letouzey et Ané, 1913); Carl Schmidt with Wilhelm Schubart, *ΠΡΑΞΕΙΣ*

geschichte. Used by the Manichaeans as early as the third century C.E.,[5] perhaps as a corpus, and then by several Christian sects, these texts were progressively dismissed by the Orthodox and Roman Catholic Churches in the East and in the West. However, there are other apocryphal acts outside of this group of five. These other texts, such as the *Martyrdom of Matthew*, the *Acts of Philip*, or the *Acts of Barnabas*, have been neglected, as is seen by the fact that the famous collection of translations by Edgar Hennecke and Wilhelm Schneemelcher, in its third edition, has very little on these so-called later acts.[6] The reason still given for the lack of interest in these other texts is that they are no longer apocryphal, but hagiographic, that is, they pertain to the saints of the church.[7] This, however, is not entirely convincing. Indeed, before publishing his last edition, Schneemelcher acknowledged the scholarly value of all the stories on all the apostles. He asked Aurelio de Santos Otero to give a longer description of most of them, with the result that instead of only six pages, the fifth edition has over fifty pages on the later Apocryphal Acts of the Apostles.[8]

The distinction between hagiographic and apocryphal writings may be useful in some instances, but for the texts under scrutiny here, it is

---

ΠΑΥΛΟΥ. *Acta Pauli nach dem Papyrus der Hamburger Staats- und Universitäts-Bibliothek* (Veröffentlichungen aus der Hamburger Staats- und Universitäts-Bibliothek 2; Glückstadt/Hamburg: Augustin, 1936); Léon Vouaux, *Les Actes de Pierre. Introduction, textes, traduction et commentaire* (Les Apocryphes du Nouveau Testament; Paris: Letouzey et Ané, 1922); Maximilien Bonnet, "Acta Thomas," in *AAA* 2/2:99–291.

[5] See Knut Schäferdiek, "Die Leukios Charinos zugeschriebene manichäische Sammlung apokrypher Apostelgeschichten," in *NTApok*[5] 2:81–93. This work is also available in an English translation, *NTApoc*[5] 2:87–100. See also *A Manichaean Psalmbook, Part II*, ed. Charles Robert Cecil Allberry, with a contribution from Hugo Ibscher (Manichaean Manuscripts of the Chester Beatty Collection 2; Stuttgart: Kohlhammer, 1938).

[6] *NTApok*[3] 2:399–404; English translation, *NTApoc*[3] 2:571–78.

[7] Wilhelm Schneemelcher, "Haupteinleitung," in *NTApok*[5] 1:51; English translation, *NTApoc*[5] 1:61. On the question of defining Christian apocryphal literature, see the discussion between Schneemelcher and Éric Junod in Éric Junod, "Apocryphes du Nouveau Testament: une appellation erronée et une collection artificielle. Discussion de la nouvelle définition proposée par W. Schneemelcher," *Apocrypha* 3 (1992): 17–46.

[8] See Aurelio de Santos Otero, "Jüngere Apostelakten" in *NTApok*[5] 2:381–438; English translation, *NTApoc*[5] 2:426–82.

not particularly relevant. Apart from some exceptional discoveries of papyri,[9] the apocryphal literature on the apostles has been preserved in hagiographic and liturgical manuscripts. Such is the paradox: Although the church condemned this literature, it also preserved part of it, as its memory of the apostolic age, in collections on the lives of the saints. After all, the apostles were also saints! My personal curiosity and interests have tended to push me to investigate neglected figures; almost arbitrarily, I chose the apostle Philip.

The first steps in my investigation were, of course, to discover where Philip fits into the New Testament, and particularly how he fits into the Gospel of John. A concordance of the New Testament and a good New Testament dictionary are very useful tools to begin this inquiry. Next, the new *Encyclopedia of the Early Church* (translated from the Italian) indicates the presence of two Philips in the patristic and Gnostic texts, and their occasional fusion into a single individual.[10] A century ago, Richard Adelbert Lipsius published an impressive work on all the traditions related to the apostles. Before beginning research on any of these figures, scholars should consult Lipsius's volumes as well as the *Ergänzungsheft*, which contains—as its title indicates—supplementary valuable material.[11] The indices of these volumes also prove to be quite helpful.

Examining Texts concerning an Apostle in the Lipsius-Bonnet Edition

To find texts related to an apostle such as Philip, we have more and better resources than were available even twenty years ago. Collections

---

[9] For example, the discovery of the oldest manuscript of the *Protevangelium of James* among the Bodmer Papyri. Michel Testuz, *Papyrus Bodmer V. Nativité de Marie* (Papyrus Bodmer 5; Cologny-Geneva: Bibliotheca Bodmeriana, 1958).

[10] For example, for Polycrates of Ephesus, see Eusebius of Caesarea *Hist. eccl.* 3.31.3. See also Ramón Trevijano, "Philip, apostle," and "Philip, the Deacon," in *EEC* 2:680, 682.

[11] Richard Adelbert Lipsius, *Die apokryphen Apostelgeschichten und Apostellegenden. Ein Beitrag zur altchristlichen Literaturgeschichte* (2 vols. in 3; Braunschweig: Schwetschke, 1883–87); idem, *Die apokryphen Apostelgeschichten und Apostellegenden. Ergänzungsheft* (Braunschweig: Schwetschke, 1890); reprint of the two works: idem, *Die apokryphen Apostelgeschichten und Apostellegenden. Ein Beitrag zur altchristlichen Literaturgeschichte und zu einer zusammenfassenden Darstellung der Neutestamentlichen Apokryphen* (2 vols.; Amsterdam: Philo Press, 1976).

of apocryphal literature, such as those published by Hennecke-Schneemelcher, James K. Elliott after Montague Rhodes James, or, in Italian, Mario Erbetta and Luigi Moraldi, indicate the editions on which their translations or summaries are based.[12] This is also true of the recent *Clavis Apocryphorum Novi Testamenti*, which Maurice Geerard produced under the auspices of the Association pour l'étude de la littérature apocryphe chrétienne (AELAC).[13] James Charlesworth's bibliography is also useful with regard to these materials.[14]

All these tools lead, in the case of Philip, to the edition of the Greek text by Maximilien Bonnet, included in the outstanding three volumes by Richard Adelbert Lipsius and Maximilien Bonnet, *Acta apostolorum apocrypha*,[15] volumes which remain the true bible for scholars in the field of the apocrypha. Published a century ago, they are still indispensable even if they are slowly replaced and expanded by the volumes prepared by members of the AELAC and published in the Series Apocryphorum of the Corpus Christianorum.[16] The Lipsius-Bonnet edition of the *Acts of Philip* comprises ninety pages of Greek text without translation; the only complete translation in a modern language is Erbetta's Italian version.[17]

When I started my investigation of Philip, Hennecke-Schneemelcher[18] gave only two brief remarks about this text: one, that it was "bruch-

---

[12] See *NTApok*[5]; *The Apocryphal New Testament: A Collection of Apocryphal Christian Literature in an English Translation*, ed. James K. Elliott (Oxford: Clarendon Press, 1993); Luigi Moraldi, *Apocrifi del Nuovo Testamento* (Classici delle Religioni, Sezione 5: Le Altre Confessioni Cristiane; Turin: Unione Tipografico-Editrice Torinese, 1971); Mario Erbetta, *Gli Apocrifi del Nuovo Testamento*, 2d ed. (4 vols.; Turin: Marietti, 1975–81).

[13] Maurice Geerard, *Clavis Apocryphorum Novi Testamenti* (Corpus Christianorum; Turnhout: Brepols, 1992).

[14] James H. Charlesworth, *The New Testament Apocrypha and Pseudepigrapha: A Guide to Publications, with Excurses on Apocalypses* (ATLA Bibliography Series 17; Chicago: American Theological Library Association; Metuchen, N.J.: Scarecrow, 1987).

[15] Maximilien Bonnet, "Acta Philippi," in *AAA* 2/2:1–90.

[16] In addition to the editions of the *Acts of John* and the *Acts of Andrew* mentioned above in n. 4, one should read the French translation of the Armenian apocryphal stories about the apostles by Louis Leloir, *Écrits apocryphes sur les apôtres. Traduction de l'édition arménienne de Venise* (2 vols.; CChrSA 3–4; Turnhout: Brepols, 1986–92).

[17] Erbetta, *Gli Apocrifi del Nuovo Testamento*, 2:457–90.

[18] *NTApok*[3] 2:404; English translation, *NTApoc*[3] 2:577.

stückhaft," or only partly preserved, and, two, that the date of composition was not prior to the end of the fourth century C.E. But, I thought, "Even the end of the fourth century is rather ancient," and, "If it is 'bruchstückhaft,' I can at least try to find the missing part!"

How is one to find the rest of a missing text? Even before that, how is one to get acquainted with this apocryphal literature on the apostles? The New Testament scholar or the historian of ancient Christianity may be at a loss because of the artificial divisions of the fields: Bible, patristics, apocryphal literature, and hagiography. Fortunately, in recent years bridges have been built between these disciplines. Several works[19] have brought the Apocryphal Acts of the Apostles under the same sort of scrutiny that the canonical texts receive.[20] The AELAC in Europe and the Christian Apocrypha Section of the Society of Biblical Literature in the United States have demonstrated a renewed interest in the apocryphal literature and are providing general studies, such as a search for the intellectual and spiritual background of the Apocryphal Acts of the Apostles in the world of late antiquity.[21] Papers from symposia on the apocryphal acts have been published (Rome, 1982; Paris, 1986; Groningen, 1991 and following; Lausanne-Geneva, 1995),[22] as have *status quaestionis* (for example, the large collection *Aufstieg und Niedergang der römischen Welt*[23] contains a series of articles on the apocryphal acts, including a piece on the *Acts of Philip*[24]).

---

[19] MacDonald, *Apocryphal Acts of Apostles*; and Richard I. Pervo, *Profit with Delight: The Literary Genre of the Acts of the Apostles* (Philadelphia: Fortress Press, 1987).

[20] For information on the apocryphal acts, see Plümacher, "Apokryphe Apostelakten," cols. 11–70; Wilson, "Apokryphen," 316–62, especially 341–48; *Actes apocryphes des apôtres*; MacDonald, *Apocryphal Acts of Apostles*. On the Gospels, see "The Historical Jesus and the Rejected Gospels," ed. Charles W. Hedrick, *Semeia* 44 (1988); Helmut Koester and François Bovon, *Genèse de l'écriture chrétienne* (Mémoires premières; Turnhout: Brepols, 1991).

[21] *Actes apocryphes des apôtres*.

[22] *Gli Apocrifi cristiani e cristianizzati*, *Augustinianum* 23 (1983); *La fable apocryphe*, *Apocrypha* 1-2 (1990–91), ed. Pierre Geoltrain, Jean-Claude Picard, and Alain Desreumaux; Bremmer, *Apocryphal Acts of John*; Bremmer, *Apocryphal Acts of Paul and Thecla*. The papers of the Lausanne-Geneva meeting have been published in *Apocrypha* 7-8 (1996–97).

[23] See particularly *ANRW* II 25/6.

[24] Bovon, "Actes de Philippe," 4431–527.

The Bollandists and François Halkin's Bibliotheca Hagiographica Graeca

I remember Henri Meylan, professor of church history at the University of Lausanne, telling us that in the Middle Ages the creed was thought to have been pronounced sentence-by-sentence by each apostle. He also mentioned that some frescoes of Romanesque churches show each of the twelve apostles carrying a phylactery with his own portion of the creed written on it. He added that for more than three hundred years, a group of highly qualified Jesuits, called the Bollandists after their founder Bollandus, had studied the lives of the saints.[25] From their research center, located within the walls of the College of Saint-Michel in Brussels and containing a large, specialized library, they publish a periodical, the *Analecta Bollandiana*, and a collection of monographs, the *Subsidia Hagiographica*.[26]

Particularly useful for the study of apocryphal literature are three resource books produced by the Bollandists: the *Bibliotheca Hagiographica Graeca* (*BHG*), the *Bibliotheca Hagiographica Latina* (*BHL*), and the *Bibliotheca Hagiographica Orientalis* (*BHO*).[27] In these books you can look up the name of the saint you are researching, such as the apostle Philip, and find references to several texts preserved in Greek, Latin, Syriac, Coptic, Armenian, Georgian, Arabic, or

---

[25] Paul P. Peeters, *L'œuvre des Bollandistes*, enlarged ed. (Subsidia Hagiographica 24; Brussels: Société des Bollandistes, 1961).

[26] The Bollandists can be contacted via the Internet (http://www.kbr.be/~socboll).

[27] François Halkin, *Bibliotheca Hagiographica Graeca*, 3d ed. (Subsidia Hagiographica 8a; Brussels: Société des Bollandistes, 1957); François Halkin, *Bibliotheca Hagiographica Graeca: Auctarium* (Subsidia Hagiographica 47; Brussels: Société des Bollandistes, 1969); François Halkin, *Novum Auctarium Bibliothecae Hagiographicae Graecae* (Subsidia Hagiographica 65; Brussels: Société des Bollandistes, 1984); *Bibliotheca Hagiographica Latina Antiquae et Mediae Aetatis*, ed. Socii Bollandiani (Subsidia Hagiographica 6; Brussels: Société des Bollandistes, 1949); Henryk Fros, *Bibliotheca Hagiographica Latina Antiquae et Mediae Aetatis* (Subsidia Hagiographica 70; Brussels: Société des Bollandistes, 1986); *Bibliotheca Hagiographica Orientalis*, ed. Socii Bollandiani (Subsidia Hagiographica 10; Brussels: Société des Bollandistes, 1910; reprint, Brussels: Société des Bollandistes, 1970).

Ethiopic.[28] Not only are the edited texts mentioned, but also the documents known only by manuscripts.

Since we are working on the Greek *Acts of Philip*, let us look at the *Bibliotheca Hagiographica Graeca*. This volume was compiled by the famous Bollandist François Halkin, who worked on it until his recent death. He produced the third edition of the *BHG*, an *Auctarium*, and a *Novum Auctarium*. In the *Bibliotheca Hagiographica Graeca*, all the saints of the Greek Orthodox Church are listed alphabetically. Since the life and martyrdom of each saint is often recorded in various Greek texts of different periods, each of these texts, whether edited or not, has been listed and assigned a number. Sometimes, as is the case with the *Acts of Philip*, which is divided into fifteen different episodes, the *BHG* has given a number to each episode. The original *Acts of Philip* comprises *BHG* 1516–26.[29] The title of the text (ancient or modern) is given, as well as the *incipit* (the first words) or the *desinit* (the last words, but not the final doxology). If the text is edited, the best available edition is mentioned. If the document is not yet edited, a reference is made to one or two manuscripts which contain it. In Brussels, the Bollandists have a manuscript catalog of all the hagiographic texts and of all the manuscripts they know to contain this document.

On the page concerning Philip in the third edition of the *BHG*, one can see what has already been published, such as *BHG* 1525, a recension of the Martyrdom, and one can also see what has not yet been published, such as *BHG* 1526m, a shorter version of the Martyrdom. The *Novum Auctarium* of the *BHG* has integrated the discovery of the new witness, the manuscript Athos, *Xenophontos 32*, according to the description I sent to François Halkin.[30]

---

[28] For the Slavonic tradition, there are the volumes by Aurelio de Santos Otero, *Die handschriftliche Überlieferung der altslavischen Apokryphen* (2 vols.; Patristische Texte und Studien 20 and 23; Berlin: de Gruyter, 1978–81). For the Irish Apocrypha, see the valuable, short work, Martin McNamara, *The Apocrypha in the Irish Church* (Dublin: Dublin Institute for Advanced Studies, 1975). See also *Irish Biblical Apocrypha: Selected Texts in Translation*, ed. Máire Herbert and Martin McNamara (Edinburgh: Clark, 1989).

[29] *BHG* 2:202–3.

[30] *BHG: Novum Auctarium*, 177–78.

The Search for New Manuscripts: Albert Ehrhard, Marcel Richard, and Jean-Marie Olivier

Once you have chosen your apostle (here, Philip) and the texts concerning him, such as *BHG* 1516–26, you may wish to find new manuscripts. The first thing to know is the date of the feast of your saint/apostle in the liturgical year of the Orthodox Church, because to locate manuscripts you have to look not only at the alphabetical listings of the *BHG*, but also at liturgical books connected with the date of your apostle's feast. In the Orthodox Church, the apostle Philip's feast day is the fourteenth of November. For the Western, or Roman Catholic, Church, Philip's feast day was, until recently, the first of May.

It should be said here that such stories about the apostles are usually preserved, if they are preserved at all, in one type of liturgical book, the *Menologion*. There are several types of liturgical books used by the Orthodox Church to this day: *Liturgikon*, *Euchologion*, Lectionary, *Tetraevangelion* (the four Gospels), *Apostolos* (the New Testament Epistles), *Menaion*, *Typikon*, *Synaxarion*, *Menologion*, collection of homilies, and so on.[31] If the *Menaia* contain some prayers with allusions to the life and martyrdom of a saint, the *Synaxarion* for each day gives a very short summary, in narrative style, of the saint of that day.[32] The two most famous Greek *Synaxaria*, both probably from the tenth century, are the one of the Church of Constantinople[33] and the one written by the emperor Basil.[34]

---

[31] On the several kinds of books used in Orthodox churches, see *Petit dictionnaire de l'Orient chrétien*, ed. Julius Assfalg and Paul Krüger (trans. and adapted by the Centre Informatique et Bible; Turnhout: Brepols, 1991), 327–47, and Hans Georg Beck, *Kirche und theologische Literatur im byzantinischen Reich*, 2d ed. (Byzantinisches Handbuch im Rahmen der Altertumswissenschaft 2/2; Munich: Beck, 1977).

[32] On the distinction between *Menaion, Synaxarion,* and *Menologion*, see Jacques Noret, "Ménologes, Synaxaires, Ménées. Essai de clarification d'une terminologie," *AnBoll* 86 (1968): 21–24.

[33] Hippolyte Delehaye, *Propylaeum ad Acta Sanctorum Novembris. . .Synaxarium Ecclesiae Constantinopolitanae. . .* (Brussels: Société des Bollandistes, 1902; reprint, Brussels: Société des Bollandistes, 1954).

[34] Easily accessible in *PG* 117 (under the title *Menologion*).

For our study, the *Synaxaria* have some relative importance, since these notices summarize longer and older stories. One can rely on them to reconstruct or imagine what was known and accepted in the Byzantine Church a thousand years ago. (*Synaxaria* exist also in many other languages, with other dates for the saints according to the local calendars.) Much more important are the so-called *Menologia*. These more extensive lives of the saints are read in the monasteries in either the church or in the refectory during meals.[35] For his monumental and unfinished study of Byzantine sermons, the German scholar Albert Ehrhard[36] examined the *Menologia* extensively, because, for the feast of a certain saint, the *Menologion* often communicates a sermon by a church father and not the usual life and martyrdom of the saint. Ehrhard was, therefore, interested in such books, and he classified them according to length, context, and age. Some of them contain the lives of the saints for one month, others the lives of the saints as they would be celebrated over three months. An exceptional volume includes the saints whose feasts would be celebrated over a period of six months or even a full year. In the case of our search for the apostle Philip, whose feast is the fourteenth of November, we must, therefore, look at the *Menologia* of November, or at the *Menologia* of September-November (the ecclesiastical year begins in September).

In order to prevent possible disappointment, a remark must be made concerning Symeon Metaphrastes,[37] a Byzantine author of the tenth century. As his nickname attests, he was a rewriter. Over time, the old, so-called premetaphrastic lives of the saints fell into disfavor, either because of the evolution of the Greek language or because of changes

---

[35] A colophon in the manuscript Athos, *Xenophontos 32*, on 29ᵛ, indicates that the travels, acts, and miracles of the apostle Philip are to be read aloud in the refectory during the meals and that the martyrdom should be read in the church; see Bovon, "Actes de Philippe," 4469.

[36] Albert Ehrhard, *Überlieferung und Bestand der hagiographischen und homiletischen Literatur der griechischen Kirche von den Anfängen bis zum Ende des 16. Jahrhunderts* (3 vols.; TU 50–52; Leipzig: Hinrichs, 1937–52).

[37] On his person and his work, see "Syméon Métaphraste," in *Dictionnaire des auteurs grecs and latins de l'Antiquité et du Moyen Âge*, ed. Wolfgang Buchwald, Armin Hohlweg, and Otto Print, trans. from the German and updated by Jean Denis Berger and Jacques Billen (Turnhout: Brepols, 1991), 802–4.

in religious tastes, or even because of the theology of some of the oldest documents. In this context, Symeon considerably reworked the older sources and composed new documents for the feast of each saint of the calendar. Therefore, if you open a *Menologion* to the date of your saint/ apostle, approximately nine times out of ten you will find the metaphrastic text (in the case of Philip, the call number *BHG* 1527) and you will be disappointed. Fortunately, the liturgy is conservative in its essence and the monks have been less strict than the bishops regarding orthodoxy. This explains the fact that out of ten texts, you will never-theless find one premetaphrastic text. Usually, as in the case of Philip, it is the story of the martyrdom (in one of its three forms: *BHG* 1525, 1526, or 1526c).[38]

It should be noted that the oldest Apocryphal Acts of the Apostles were very long. Fighting against the Manichaean, Priscillianist, or any other heretical use of them, the church, since it needed apostolic stories for the various feasts of the twelve disciples, adapted parts of these documents. Usually the last part—the Martyrdom—was adopted, but not without some form of orthodox rewriting, particularly of the apostle's prayers and sermons.[39] What Symeon did in the tenth century, then, was not at all new but already was a rather common practice at a much earlier time. On occasion, the early form of the martyrdom of the apostle was preserved without much change. This is so for the Greek *Martyrdom of Peter*,[40] the Armenian version of the *Martyrdom of Andrew* (this Armenian translation was made from a text older than the oldest form of the Greek text in our possession),[41] the *Metastasis of John* (John did not die as a martyr),[42] and so on. Another note of caution must be given. For the most famous apostles, many stories and legends circulated:[43] for example, the Pseudo-Linus, Pseudo-Marcellus, or even

---

[38] *BHG: Novum Auctarium,* 177–78.

[39] See Junod and Kaestli, *L'histoire des Actes apocryphes des apôtres.*

[40] See Vouaux, *Actes de Pierre,* 398–466.

[41] See Leloir, *Écrits apocryphes sur les apôtres,* 1:225–57; and Prieur, *Acta Andreae,* 1:30–39, 125, 236–65, 317–43, and 2:735–45.

[42] See Junod and Kaestli, *Acta Iohannis.*

[43] See Thomas, "The Acts of Peter."

Pseudo-Clementine literature for Peter[44] and the Pseudo-Prochorus for John.[45] It also happened that parts of the early apocryphal acts of these famous apostolic figures have been preserved, not only in the *Menologia*, but also in independent manuscripts devoted to one single apostle and containing one or several texts devoted to him.

In one of the three recensions of the *Acts of Philip*, the title of the document is exciting. It does not just read *Martyrdom of the Apostle Philip*; instead, it is entitled *[Extracted] from the Travels of Philip the Apostle from the fifteenth act till the end in which there is the Martyrdom*.[46] This title confirms what I have just indicated: that the church excerpted a section, usually the last section of an apocryphal act, to serve as a liturgical reading. What happened to the other parts? Again, patience and good luck are necessary to find out. If one of ten *Menologia* of November has a premetaphrastic text, then approximately one of ten of these premetaphrastic texts contains another story besides the martyrdom.[47] We presently are aware of approximately fifty Greek manuscripts with the premetaphrastic martyrdom of Philip, and of those, five or six contain other elements. And herein lies the immense importance of the search for manuscripts. In the case of Philip, one manuscript in Paris, one in the Vatican, and one in Milan contain *Acts of Philip* 2.[48] One manuscript in Athens has a large and original portion of *Acts of Philip* 8.[49] *Vaticanus graecus 824*, an extraordinary manuscript which includes the first nine acts of the *Acts of Philip* plus the Martyrdom, was found nearly a century ago by Maximilien Bonnet. In 1974 Bertrand Bouvier and I discovered *Acts of Philip* 1–15 (with the

---

[44] *Die Pseudoklementinen*, vol. 1, *Homilien*, ed. Bernhard Rehm, 3d ed., edited by Georg Strecker (Die griechischen christlichen Schriftsteller 42; Berlin: Akademie Verlag, 1992); *Die Pseudoklementinen*, vol. 2, *Rekognitionen in Rufins Übersetzung*, ed. Bernhard Rehm, 2d ed., rev., edited by Georg Strecker (Die griechischen christlichen Schriftsteller 51; Berlin: Akademie Verlag, 1994).

[45] See *Acta Joannis*, ed. Theodor Zahn (Erlangen: Deichert, 1880; reprint, Hildesheim: Gerstenberg, 1975).

[46] Version Γ of the *Acts of Philip* of Maximilien Bonnet, "Acta Philippi," in *AAA* 2/2:41. The title may vary slightly from one manuscript to the next.

[47] See Bovon, "Actes de Philippe," 4468–75, and the soon-to-be published edition in the Series Apocryphorum.

[48] *Parisinus graecus 881*; *Vaticanus graecus 866*; Milan, Ambrosiana, *graecus 405 (G 63 sup.)*.

[49] Athens, National Library, *346*.

unfortunate exception of *Acts of Philip* 10 and the first part of act 11) on Mount Athos in the monastery of Xenophontos (Athos, *Xenophontos 32*) in one of these manuscripts devoted to a single apostle.

Someone may ask, "Are not all of the world's Greek manuscripts well known?" While practically all have been seen, not all have been examined thoroughly or well described. The science of codicology is rather recent and many older catalogues do not contain correct, complete, or up-to-date descriptions of any given collection. Some libraries do not have trained librarians able to give complete descriptions. Others, like the largest libraries, the Vatican Library or the National Library in Paris, are so rich in Greek manuscripts that the publication of scholarly catalogues is still under way.[50] To these external difficulties one has to add an internal problem: the evolution of scholarly interests and tastes. For many centuries, humanists looked for classical texts in the Greek manuscripts; many then searched for biblical and eventually for patristic texts. The liturgical manuscripts, collections of sermons, and hagiographic literature did not interest many scholars in the past. One may excuse them their lack of enthusiasm, for such manuscripts are a headache for scholars. With their many documents in a single book, it is difficult to see exactly where one text ends and another begins.

For a long time the Bollandists and a few scholars such as Albert Ehrhard[51] have been the exceptions, trying to publish a list of hagiographic documents according to their location. Through the indices of their works, it is possible to see quickly if they know where a certain text is preserved (for example, the *Acts of Philip*, *BHG* 1516–26). François Halkin was very active and had published, in the form of books and articles, several "inventaires hagiographiques," which he organized according to libraries.[52] Unfortunately, such books do not exist for all

---

[50] For more information, see *Répertoire des bibliothèques et des catalogues de manuscrits grecs de Marcel Richard*, ed. Jean-Marie Olivier (Corpus Christianorum; Turnhout: Brepols, 1995).

[51] See above nn. 25, 27, and 36.

[52] See, for example: François Halkin, *Manuscrits grecs de Paris. Inventaire hagiographique* (Subsidia Hagiographica 44; Brussels: Société des Bollandistes, 1968); idem, "Les manuscrits grecs de la Bibliothèque Laurentienne à Florence. Inventaire hagiographique," *AnBoll* 96 (1978): 5–50; idem, *Catalogue des manuscrits hagiographiques de la Bibliothèque nationale d'Athènes* (Subsidia Hagiographica 66; Brussels: Société des Bollandistes, 1983).

libraries. Ehrhard's *Überlieferung und Bestand* also has numerous lists of hagiographic texts grouped according to the many manuscripts he perused. Ehrhard's work, however, is not complete and lacks indices. An Italian scholar, Lidia Perria, has since created an index by manuscript and location.[53] When looking for a specific saint, you still will need to go through all the pages of these large volumes, taking care not to miss anything. I did not realize this twenty years ago, and it was only after the discovery of *Xenophontos 32* that I found a footnote by Albert Ehrhard mentioning that he had seen this manuscript and even indicating his interest; nobody, however, had pursued the matter since then.[54] Another tool offered by the Bollandists should not be overlooked. On the occasion of the one hundredth anniversary of the *Analecta Bollandiana*, in 1982,[55] the Jesuits from Brussels published an index of their periodical in which you can look up your apostle by name. In this inventory you can find information about the volume of the periodical where an article—if any—has been devoted to your saint.

Your task is only just beginning. You now face a long quest. Theoretically, you have to look through all the catalogues of Greek manuscripts (or as many as possible) to find references to *Menologia* with interesting texts on your apostle. But how does one find such catalogues? In the Vatican Library's reading room, in the Institut d'histoire des textes in Paris, and in Widener Library at Harvard University, there are very large, if not exhaustive, collections of these catalogues. At this point I must mention a tool compiled by Marcel Richard and updated by Jean-Marie Olivier, two great experts of Greek manuscripts.[56] To help their fellow scholars they have produced a catalogue of all the catalogues of Greek manuscripts. In their book you can browse locations from Ann Arbor to Zakynthos and discover the

[53] Lidia Perria, *I manoscritti citati da Albert Ehrhard* (Testi e studi Bizantino-Neoellenici 4; Rome: Istituto di Studi Bizantini e Neoellenici, Università di Roma, 1979).

[54] Ehrhard, *Überlieferung und Bestand*, 3:971; cf. Bovon, "Les Actes de Philippe," 4471.

[55] "Inventaire hagiographique des tomes 1–100 (1882–1982)," *AnBoll* 100 (1982): 1–444.

[56] Olivier, *Répertoire des bibliothèques et des catalogues*.

titles of all the existing catalogues, each of which has been given a number. Consult the catalogues according to the "Richard"—now the "Richard-Olivier"—noting any catalogue that you have not yet consulted. Also, thanks to the *Analecta Bollandiana*, and particularly to Xavier Lequeux, many new catalogues have been read recently with special interest given to saints and apostles.[57] The most recent catalogues correspond to the most demanding expectations of codicology[58] and can yield information concerning new witnesses of your text. Catalogues of papyri should also not be neglected, for they have recently provided information on new fragments of apocryphal Gospels.[59] At this point, even before finishing the time-consuming task of consulting the catalogues, you can start collecting material.[60]

The Athonian manuscript, *Xenophontos 32*, caught my attention while I was using the above-mentioned tools. In 1974 a group of Swiss scholars was preparing a study tour of Mount Athos. Our main interest then was the *Acts of John*, but I had already decided to work on the *Acts of Philip*. I looked in Marcel Richard's catalogue,[61] under Athos, and learned that the main catalogue (no. 184 in Richard's list) had been published by Spyridon P. Lambros.[62] After going through all the pages of the index for these volumes, I found in four or five places mention of a πρᾶξις or μαρτύριον of Philip (one of the titles for the normal conclusion of the primitive *Acts of Philip*). This was nothing sensational because those texts had been known and published by Maximilien Bonnet. Suddenly, however, I noticed a plural: πράξεις τοῦ ἁγίου ἀποστόλου Φιλίππου.

---

[57] Xavier Lequeux, "Glanures d'hagiographie dans quelques catalogues de manuscrits récemment parus," *AnBoll* 110 (1992): 373–92; 112 (1994): 159–76; 113 (1995): 156–78; 115 (1997): 208–302.

[58] For example, those of the National Library of Vienna, the monasteries of Meteora (Greece), or the second volume of the National Library of Athens.

[59] This is particularly true for the Oxyrhynchus Papyri.

[60] It is better to order microfilm, which is less expensive than photographs and more readable than photocopies of microfilm.

[61] I used the second edition: Marcel Richard, *Répertoire des bibliothèques et des catalogues de manuscrits grecs*, 2d ed. (CNRS: Publications de l'Institut de recherche et d'histoire des textes; Paris: Centre National de la Recherche Scientifique, 1958), 41.

[62] Spyridon P. Lambros, *Catalogue of the Greek Manuscripts on Mount Athos* (2 vols.; Cambridge: Cambridge University Press, 1885–90; reprint, Amsterdam: Hakkert, 1966), 1:64.

There was no other information, except that this work, not exactly a *Menologion* but rather a book devoted entirely to a single saint, namely Philip, belongs to the Monastery of Xenophontos on Mount Athos and is designated there by the number 32.

Before approaching the Holy Mountain, however, you should first visit the Institute of Patristic Studies at the Monastery of Vlatadon in Thessaloniki.[63] One of the goals of this institute has been to obtain a complete collection on microfilm of the Mount Athos holdings, and their hope has largely been realized.[64] So, with Bertrand Bouvier, I had a preliminary look at the microfilm of *Xenophontos 32* and discovered the importance of the manuscript. Through *Vaticanus graecus 824*, nine of the fifteen acts had been preserved. Here, a totally new series of the acts of Philip, including the end of *Acts of Philip* 11 and *Acts of Philip* 12, 13, 14, and 15, appeared on the microfilm before our very eyes. What we did not realize at first glance was that for the nine acts known through Bonnet's edition of *Vaticanus graecus 824*, the text of *Xenophontos 32* was considerably larger and less expurgated. Still, it would have been wrong merely to order a copy of this microfilm without going to see (and touch!) the manuscript itself, because nothing replaces contact with the original. According to a strict rule, women are prohibited from entering Mount Athos. Fortunately, in the other Greek monastaries, as well as in the public libraries, there are no restrictions based on gender, religion, or nationality. The sequence of steps proposed here, based on my experience on Mount Athos, is valid for any other place as well.

Personal Contact with the Manuscript

You enter a library, perhaps a little shyly the first time, and ask for manuscripts. Of course, the situation in a great occidental library (such as the British Library or the Ambrosiana in Milan) is very different

---

[63] Address: Patriarchal Institute for Patristic Studies, Vlatadon Monastery, Thessaloniki (Greece). Telephone: 30 (202) 301 303.

[64] There is another project, sponsored by the National Bank of Greece and directed by Agamemnon Tsélikas, to make a complete collection of the microfilms of the Monastery of Iviron on Mount Athos.

from that of the small library of a Greek monastery (like Leimonos at Lesbos). You should always know beforehand which manuscript you would like to see, because you certainly cannot examine more than two or three during a half-day visit. You should also know that there is a rule in Greek monasteries that one monk (usually the librarian) must sit near you during your entire time working. (Monks still recall how often Western "scholars" cut leaves from manuscripts, particularly those with illuminations, and stole them.) So do not be surprised if you are permitted to work only when the librarian is free from other duties and can remain with you.

When you introduce yourself (a letter of recommendation may be helpful) and request to see your manuscripts, ask also for the catalogues the library has of its own collections. Very often there is, in addition to the published catalogues, a manuscript catalogue for internal usage. Such a catalogue is usually more exhaustive than the others because it integrates new manuscripts that have been found in the monastery or additional manuscripts gathered there from other monasteries or abandoned hermitages in recent years. I came upon several surprises when consulting internal catalogues, both in the Bodleian Library at Oxford[65] and in Megali Lavra on Mount Athos. At the latter location, for example, a local catalogue gave me access to a strange manuscript, a very recent one of the nineteenth century. It was a life of all the apostles, written in calligraphy but in a rather simple modern Greek, by a monk of Saint Sabas (in Palestine), called Joasaph. The oldest monks of Megali Lavra remembered that he came from Saint Sabas to spend his last days on the Holy Mountain. His work is interesting because it is a rewriting of ancient lives of the apostles that this monk must have known from the same type of manuscripts that interested such Western scholars of that period as Constantin Tischendorf.[66]

---

[65] In an old catalogue of the Bodleian Library I discovered a new witness of the Martyrdom of the *Acts of Philip* (J. E. Grabe Adversaria 9). See Henry O. Coxe, *Catalogi Codicum Manuscriptorum Bibliothecae Bodleianae*, vol. 1, *Recensionem Codicum Graecorum Continens* (Oxford: Oxford University Press, 1853), 858.

[66] Athos, *Lavra Z 59*; see François Bovon, "The Synoptic Gospels and the Noncanonical Acts of the Apostles," *HTR* 81 (1989): 19 n. 3.

Take care to indicate the correct call number when you ask for your manuscript. I once lost a great deal of time in the monastery of Karakallou (Athos) because I was mistaken about the call number of the manuscript I wished to study. It is important to know that each library has given a call number to each of its manuscripts and that many libraries have changed their systems over the years. That is the case in Karakallou,[67] as well as in the Ambrosiana of Milan, where you must indicate the old call number in brackets after the new one (for example, Milan, Ambrosiana, *graecus 405 [G 63 sup.]*). A further source of confusion are the call numbers sometimes given by authors of catalogues that include *several* libraries. Lambros,[68] for example, indicates first a general number of his own (his catalogue includes many monasteries on Mount Athos) and then the call number of a particular library (which itself may have changed since Lambros published his catalogue). The same is true for the New Testament: the so-called *Vaticanus* is known usually as B or O3, but in the Vatican Library it is *Vaticanus graecus 1209*.[69]

At last, filled with mixed feelings of joy, anxiety, and excitement, you sit at a small table with the manuscript, a pad of paper, a magnifier, and a pencil. First, you have to make sure you have the right manuscript and that it contains the document for which you have been looking. To identify your text, you need to examine the folios for its beginning and end and read and write down the title (often written in red uncials under a modest heading), the *incipit*, and the *desinit*. A glance at the text shows you whether the writing is difficult to read and whether the manuscript has suffered from humidity. (In such cases, it is less difficult to read the damaged part from the original than from microfilm. Be sure to allow enough time for this possibility.) There are certain elementary rules to follow when working with a manuscript. Use a pencil, not a pen, to write your notes in order to avoid getting any ink

---

[67] The manuscript Athos, Karakallou, *6* was numbered *8* in the previous catalogue of the library. The monastery has recently produced a new shelf list: it is now Athos, Karakallou, *48*.

[68] Lambros, *Catalogue of the Greek Manuscripts on Mount Athos*.

[69] *Novum Testamentum Graece*, 27th ed. (Stuttgart: Deutsche Bibelgesellschaft, 1994), 689.

stains on the manuscript. Even if you are only examining the material state of the manuscript, carry it gently and open it with care. Finally, do not rub your fingers or arms over the written part of the page.

This may seem like strange advice, but I would suggest that now is not the time to read your text and still less the occasion to make a complete collation. There is not sufficient time at this point, and you have other pressing matters to attend to in the next two or three hours (it is rare to have more time at your disposal, at least in a monastery). What you should do is everything that is not possible to accomplish with a microfilmed copy, which means making your own codicological description of the manuscript. It may help you to learn where the manuscript comes from, when it was copied, to whom it belonged, and so on. Answers to some or all of these questions may be provided in the catalogue of the library. If so, all the better, for you will not need to repeat the work. But often—and let us assume this is the case—the catalogue is not sufficient. Incidently, your manuscript might have been used and described already by another scholar who may, however, have been interested in another part of the same manuscript. It is useful, therefore, before leaving for the country where your manuscript is located, to look up the editions of the texts present in the same manuscript. For example: Philip is venerated, as I mentioned before, on the fourteenth of November. On the fifteenth of the same month the Orthodox Church celebrates Gourias and other saints. I once discovered by chance in Texte und Untersuchungen zur Geschichte der altchrist-lichen Literatur a study by Oskar Leopold von Gebhardt[70] on these saints of the fifteenth of November, with good descriptions of several manuscripts in which I was interested.

An example will show you why such a description is useful and why we should resist being interested only in the text contained in the manuscript. The manuscript *Vaticanus graecus 866* is important for the *Acts of Philip*. The excellent catalogue of the Vatican Library[71] tells us

---

[70] Oskar Leopold von Gebhardt, *Die Akten der edessenischen Bekenner Gurjas, Samonas und Abibos* (TU 37/2; Leipzig: Hinrichs, 1911).

[71] See Robert Devreesse, *Codices Vaticani Graeci*, vol. 3, *Codices 604–866* (Vatican City: Biblioteca Apostolica Vaticana, 1950), 440.

that this manuscript was brought to Rome from southern Italy by a famous sixteenth-century cardinal, himself a humanist, Gugliemo Sirleto. This piece of information confirms what a description of the manuscript suggests—that it was copied, not in Greece, but in southern Italy (a so-called Italo-Greek manuscript). Such information is important in order to establish the history of the manuscript tradition of a text. And it is true that the Italo-Greek manuscripts are particularly relevant for the apocryphal acts.

You should take the time to create your own checklist. Paul Canart, a librarian, or *scriptor*, from the Vatican Library, has given his own checklist in one of the volumes of the catalogues of that library.[72] Such a checklist may vary slightly from one scholar to another or from one catalogue to another, but, on the whole, the following are the questions you must try answer in the few hours you have at your library table.

The Size and Support of the Manuscript: First, you must record the dimensions of your manuscript in millimeters, starting with the width (for example, 240 x 350). Next, you need to note whether your manuscript is written on parchment (papyrus is exceptional) or on paper. What is the quality of the parchment? What is the origin of the paper? Does it contain watermarks? If so, by using a piece of tracing paper, you can copy samples of the watermarks on your manuscript (look at several places to see how many forms of watermarks are used and record the numbers of the folios where the watermarks appear). Later, at home, you can look at the lists of watermarks given by Charles Moïse Briquet[73] and, more recently, by Dieter and Johanna Harlfinger[74] to learn more about the paper of your manuscript, its origin, and its approximate date.

---

[72] Paul Canart, *Codices Vaticani Graeci, Codices 1745–1962*, vol. 1, *Codicum Enarrationes* (Vatican City: Biblioteca Apostolica Vaticana, 1970), ix.

[73] Charles Moïse Briquet, *Les filigranes. Dictionnaire historique des marques du papier dès leur apparition vers 1282 jusqu'en 1600*, Jubilee ed. (Amsterdam: Paper Publications Society, 1968).

[74] Dieter and Johanna Harlfinger, *Wasserzeichen aus griechischen Handschriften*, 2 vols. to date (Berlin: Mielke, 1974 and 1980); see also *International Standard for the Registration of Watermarks IPH*, ed. Association internationale des historiens du papier (Marburg: IPH Secretariat, 1992).

The External Structure of the Manuscript:[75] In the upper right corner of each folio—a folio is one sheet with a recto and a verso (two of what we call pages)—a page number is indicated. These are generally a modern addition, sometimes with mistakes, so check the sequence and the final number, because you will need to indicate how many folios a manuscript contains. Look also for loose leaves and, if there are any, indicate them.

A codex is not so different from a modern book; each is a collection of "quires" sewn together. These quires are usually arranged as "quaternions" (four double leaves, eight folios each), but you can occasionally find "binions," "ternions," or "quinions." Sometimes one sheet of paper, a folio, may have been added to a quire and you will notice this irregularity by the presence of a stub inside the quire. Each of these quires was usually given a number when the manuscript was copied to ensure that when bound—the next step—it had the correct sequence of quires, folios, and texts. These numbers are given in the Greek numeric system, with an acute accent following the Greek letter, thus indicating that this is a number and not a letter: Γ' or γ', for example, for the third quire. This number, called a "signature," may be placed at the beginning of the quire, or sometimes at the beginning and at the end. It is not always easy to find. On the page it is normally placed in the lower margin of a recto, at the left corner, in the middle, or at the right corner (which is exactly the place where the reader's hand would hold the manuscript, so it may have been worn away). You can also find the middle of a quire by opening the codex and looking for the seam of stitches holding the pages together. It is best if you can be sure of your quire by the signature and its seam. It is through this knowledge of the quire (and not of the modern sequence of the folios) that you can discover whether your manuscript is missing parts and, if so, the length of these lacunae. (In this way, we discovered a great deal

---

[75] On the following, see Jacques Lemaire, *Introduction à la codicologie* (Université catholique de Louvain: Institut d'études médiévales: textes, études, congrès 9; Louvain-la-Neuve: Université catholique de Louvain, 1989); Bernhard Bischoff, *Latin Palaeography: Antiquity and the Middle Ages*, trans. Dáibhí ó Cróinín and David Ganz (Cambridge: Cambridge University Press, 1990), 5–47.

about *Xenophontos 32*: twenty-four folios were missing from the beginning of act 8 of the *Acts of Philip* to the end of act 11. Deducing from the parts known from other manuscripts of acts 8 and 9, we could estimate the length of act 10 and the length of the first part of act 11.)[76]

This may also be the right moment to look at the binding. The most important question is this: Is the current binding the original or not? If not, there may have been some alteration because of the new bindings (two manuscripts bound together or some quires misplaced or some folios of another manuscript bound together with the original manuscript). Experts can discover many things from bindings. (You can, for example, distinguish between Eastern and Western bindings just by looking at the back to see if the seam is rounded or if it is as flat as possible.)[77] Such details, you must remember, cannot be ascertained from studying microfilm. Let me repeat: nothing can replace direct contact with the manuscript.

The Written Text: It is necessary to examine the layout of the page, and the eventual division of the text into two columns, to measure the written portion of a page, the dimensions of the vertical and horizontal margins, the number of lines per page, and the type and system of ruling. (Again, it is likely that a page from the same scriptorium used the same type of ruling for a certain period: a good knowledge of ruling can help you determine whether your manuscripts were copied in Constantinople, on Mount Athos, or in Southern Italy.) Julien Leroy and, more recently, Jacques-Hubert Sautel[78] have published tools to help in understanding these external features.

The writing is also interesting: for example, is the writing below the line, sitting directly on the line, or just above it? These questions are important for the date of your manuscript, because older writing often rests on the line while more recent script hangs below it. This change

---

[76] See Bovon, "Actes de Philippe," 4472.

[77] On bindings, see Bischoff, *Latin Palaeography*, 30–32.

[78] Julien Leroy, *Les types de réglure des manuscrits grecs* (Bibliographies, Colloques, Travaux Préparatoires—Institut de recherche et d'histoire des textes; Paris: Éditions du Centre National de la Recherche Scientifique, 1976); Jacques-Hubert Sautel, *Répertoire de réglures dans les manuscrits grecs sur parchemin. Base de données* (Bibliologia 13; Turnhout: Brepols, 1995).

occurred sometime in the tenth century.[79] The quality of the ink is also of some importance. (It may be more or less dark brown or black, red being normally used for titles and initials.)

The writing is very important; fortunately, once you are home, you can examine it more closely and describe it from your microfilm copy. Paleography[80] is a difficult science and art, but it is decisive for judging the *age* of a manuscript. From the shape of certain letters, the *ductus* (the general shape and formation of letters and their combinations in manuscripts), the quality of the orthography, and the geographic origin of the scribe, you can sometimes deduce the *education* of the scribe.[81] Most of our manuscripts are minuscules, which means they were written after the change from uncials to minuscules that took place around 830 C.E.[82] We may, however, have the privilege of uncovering an apocryphal text transmitted in uncials (as is the case for a witness of the *Acts of Thecla* recently discovered at St. Catherine's Monastery on Mount Sinai)[83] or the difficulty of dealing with a palimpsest, where the original writing that is partly rubbed out and covered over by a second writing contains apocryphal material (as is the case for a manuscript of the *Acts of John*).[84]

---

[79] See Robert Devreesse, *Introduction à l'étude des manuscrits grecs* (Paris: Imprimerie nationale, Klincksieck, 1954), 35.

[80] Edward Maunde Thompson, *An Introduction to Greek and Latin Palaeography* (Oxford: Clarendon Press, 1912; reprint, New York: Franklin, 1965 and 1973); *La paléographie grecque et byzantine* (Colloques internationaux du CNRS 559; Paris: Éditions du Centre National de la Recherche Scientifique, 1977); Alphonse Dain, *Les manuscrits*, 3d ed., rev. (Collection d'études anciennes; Paris: Belles Lettres, 1975), 191–205 (bibliography).

[81] Robert Devreesse, *Les manuscrits grecs de l'Italie méridionale. Histoire, classement, paléographie* (Studi e Testi; Vatican City: Biblioteca Apostolica Vaticana, 1955).

[82] See Dain, *Les manuscrits*, 62–63, 126–27.

[83] See Willy Rordorf, "Terra Incognita: Recent Research on Christian Apocryphal Literature, Especially on Some Acts of Apostles," in *Studia Patristica XXV: Papers Presented at the Eleventh International Conference on Patristic Studies Held in Oxford 1991: Biblica et Apocrypha, Orientalia, Ascetica*, ed. Elizabeth A. Livingstone (Leuven: Peeters, 1993), 148.

[84] The Palimpsest of Halki, *Mon. Trin. 102*; cf. Junod and Kaestli, *Acta Iohannis*, 1:13–15. The superior writing is from 1435 C.E., the inferior from the eleventh century; both are minuscules.

The best way to learn about paleography is to find a university or an institution which offers a course in it.[85] But you can also learn on your own with a handbook or a good collection of plates, such as that of Enrica Follieri, which includes a diplomatic transcription, a critical edition of the plates, and a description of the photographed manuscripts, all of which can be found in the Vatican Library.[86] What you must become familiar with—in part by reading—are the abbreviations, particularly the *nomina sacra* (Jesus Christ, Son, God, Lord, Jerusalem) and the most common terms (heaven, human beings, blessed).[87]

The Decoration: The manuscripts containing stories about the apostles are usually not beautiful manuscripts intended for aristocratic lay readers; rather, they are austere manuscripts for modest monks. Therefore, they generally do not possess miniatures (diverging from their cousins the Byzantine Tetraevangelia, the canonical four Gospels, which often display a portrait of the evangelist at work at the beginning of each Gospel).[88] This does not mean that the scholar does not have some decorative elements to describe: first, the headings placed just above the title of a new story are noteworthy; second, scribes sometimes used very elegant initial letters, which may help you to date or to localize a scribe, and therefore a manuscript;[89] and third, the scribe or a reader may have placed small drawings either in the margin or in one of the few empty spaces between two texts. (Parchment, as well as paper, was rare and expensive in those times, so very little free space was left unused; when it was, a later reader would often cut off the blank segment

---

[85] The Vatican Library organizes a course every second year. John Duffy, professor of Byzantine studies, Harvard University, teaches Greek paleography.

[86] See Enrica Follieri, *Codices Graeci Bibliothecae Vaticanae Selecti Temporum Locorumque Ordine Digesti, Commentariis et Transcriptionibus Instructi* (Exempla Scripturarum 4; Vatican City: Biblioteca Apostolica Vaticana, 1969).

[87] One can find a list of abbreviations in Viktor Gardthausen, *Griechische Palaeographie*, 2d ed. (2 vols.; Leipzig: Veit, 1911–13; reprint, Leipzig: Zentralantiquariat der Deutschen Demokratischen Republik, 1978), 2:319–52.

[88] For example, the one with the ὑπόμνημα on John, examined by Yuko Taniguchi, François Bovon, and Athanasios Antonopoulos in "The *Memorial of Saint John the Theologian* (*BHG* 919fb)," in this volume.

[89] Normally the decoration was the responsibility of some person other than the scribe, and it was carried out after the copy was completed (we possess manuscripts where the titles and the decoration were never finished).

of the parchment for his personal use.) These small drawings may represent birds, small human beings (male or female, and sometimes recognizable as monks), crosses, or blessing hands.[90] The blessing hand is particularly useful because the pose of the hands in blessing is distinctive in the East and in the West. So, a Greek manuscript with a Western blessing hand is likely to be an Italo-Greek manuscript, from southern Italy or Sicily, which, remember, were largely Greek-speaking regions until the Renaissance.[91]

Colophon, Dates, Marginal Notes, and Marks of Property: These are very important elements. Remember that a manuscript is like a human being you would like to know: you are eager to learn as much as possible about his or her life. In the case of a manuscript, you sometimes have the equivalent of the date of birth, namely, the date of the manuscript (such dates are not so easy to interpret because of the dating system of the Byzantines, but there are bibliographic aids to convert Byzantine dates to those of a standard, modern calendar).[92] Sometimes the scribe also signed his name on the work, combined with a prayer or a complaint.[93] Make sure to transcribe this colophon properly and later try to discover if your scribe is known by comparing the name and way of writing with scribes of the same name.[94] More difficult are the marginal notes that one often finds, written by some later readers. They are more of a challenge to read and understand because later writing (of, for example, the fifteenth through the

[90] See André Grabar, *Les manuscrits enluminés de provenance italienne, IXᵉ–XIᵉ siècles* (Bibliothèque des Cahiers archéologiques 8; Paris: Klincksieck, 1972).

[91] See Devreesse, *Manuscrits grecs de l'Italie méridionale.* An uncial manuscript as important as the famous codex Bezae (D or 05 = Cambridge University Library, Nn. 2.41) is bilingual (Greek-Latin) and perhaps of Italo-Greek origin. See *Codex Bezae: Studies from the Lunel Colloquium, June 1994*, ed. D. C. Parker and C. B. Amphoux (Leiden: Brill, 1996).

[92] On the so-called indiction and its equivalent to our dates, see Devreesse, *Introduction à l'étude des manuscrits grecs*, 51–53.

[93] In the manuscript Athos, *Xenophontos 32*, we find, on f. 109ᵛ: χειρ(ὶ) ταπεινοῦ Ἰακώβου τάλανος καὶ ῥακενδύτου, "by the hand of the humble James, miserable and in tattered rags."

[94] For a list of scribes, see Marie Vogel and Victor Gardthausen, *Die griechischen Schreiber des Mittelalters und der Renaissance* (Leipzig: Harrassowitz, 1909; reprint, Hildesheim: Olms, 1966).

eighteenth centuries) is difficult to read and because these notes were not written for an official reading but for personal recollection. Depending on the space, it may be a rough draft of a letter (as is the case with *Xenophontos 32*), a proverb, a biblical quotation (for example, a long passage from Romans 6), or even a fable of Aesop (the classical tradition was partly preserved by the monks), or something else entirely.[95]

Also worth noticing are the so-called property marks. In the same way that you write your name in a book of your own, ancient owners sometimes wrote down their names or the names of their monasteries. But, unlike our own custom, they often did not write it on the front page but on an internal page (or in several places): in *Atheniensis 346* the name of the same man, probably a monk, appears at least three times.

The Content of the Manuscript: It is time now to note the content of your manuscript. This may well have been done already by the editor of the catalogue, but in the case of older catalogues it is necessary to check the material. It is also useful to see whether the manuscript itself has a table of contents either at the beginning or at the end (in Greek called a πίναξ or κεφάλαια as a list of chapters). For each document, write where it starts and where it ends (e.g., ff. 36^v–43^r). In a *Menologion*, this can take some time because of the number of days in a month and the number of saints remembered.

Photography: Knowing that your time is limited, plan from the start how you will obtain a microfilm of your document. If your description of the codex is well done, you need only a microfilm of the folios which interest you. In a well-equipped library, you merely have to fill out an order form and the microfilm of your document will be sent to you. In a Greek monastery, you may ask to make your own photographs (permission is usually given). The best way is to photograph the document outside of the reading room of the library but not in direct sunlight. Place the manuscript on the ground in a shady corner of a courtyard, perhaps using a napkin or a towel to protect it. One person needs to hold the book and turn the pages (taking care not to omit a

---

[95] See Bovon, "Actes de Philippe," 4472.

double page by turning two folios).[96] Another person, using a tripod, with the camera directed downward, meticulously takes the pictures with the help of an extension cable, regularly measuring the intensity of the light. Professional photographers advised us to use black-and-white 400 ASA film. As a first shot, photograph a leaf of paper on which you have written the name, location, and call number of the manuscript and the folios you are photographing.[97]

Back Home at Your Desk

The Collation

Once you are home with the microfilm of your manuscript, you can start to work. You may find yourself in one of two possible situations. In the first, you have discovered a single witness of the text of your choice. I would advise first making a strict transcription of the text. For your own use, produce a so-called diplomatic edition, which will help you to see the difficulties of the text and to be better prepared to generate the critical edition.

In the second, you have several witnesses of your text and microfilms of all of them. Before collating all the manuscripts, it is advisable to compare your witnesses at three or four passages (at the beginning, at the end, and at the same places in the middle of the story). Through such a comparative check, you will be able to judge whether the witnesses are similar to one another and, therefore, if it is possible to make a single edition of all of them. After such an investigation, you will also have reached a certain opinion about the worth of your several witnesses and will be in a position to choose one of them as the base, or reference, text. This is the one you can copy properly, line by line, with only one line on the top of each page, leaving the rest of the page for the apparatus (this can be done on a computer; see, for example, the program Collate, which, according to Zbigniew Izydorczyk, can be

---

[96] On the troubles she encountered while photographing Arabic manuscripts, see Agnes Smith Lewis, *The Mythological Acts of the Apostles* (Horae Semiticae 4; London: Clay, 1904), vii–viii.

[97] On working in a library and describing a manuscript, I still recommend Dain, *Les manuscripts*, and Devreesse, *Introduction à l'étude des manuscrits grecs*.

found at http://www.dlib.dmu.ac.uk/projects/Collate/). The choice of this reference witness does not mean that its text will be the final text of your edition. It is just a convenient and stable reference. After this you can collate your other witnesses. This solution is convenient when you do not have more than ten to fifteen witnesses. In the case where you have more than one hundred manuscripts, as happens with apocryphal stories which have not been condemned by the Church (like the *Protevangelium of James* in the East or the *Gospel of Nicodemus* in the West),[98] the situation is much more complex. You must first search for families of witnesses, then select the best manuscripts of each family, and finally produce an edition, not of all, but only of the best witnesses.

The Critical Edition

It is not necessary to give here all the rules for establishing a critical edition.[99] A few remarks and a bit of advice will be sufficient. First, it is a difficult job that requires concentration, honesty, good philological training, and not too much imagination. Second, you should not judge everything according to the standards of classical Greek. You will find later forms, such as γενάμενος instead of γενόμενος. You should also hesitate before correcting a strange construction, for example, ἵνα followed by the indicative future and not the subjunctive aorist. Third, do not be surprised by the orthography; scribes usually did not care much for orthography, but most of the time they were correct with regard to accentuation (occasionally, the type of accent may be wrong, but very rarely is its position incorrect). Fourth, a knowledge of modern Greek pronunciation is indispensable if you do not want to be surprised when a scribe writes ἐβαγγέλλιον for "gospel" (εὐαγγέλιον). Fifth, be aware of the abbreviations scribes employed. For example, Ἰησοῦς is

---

[98] See Émile de Strycker, "Die griechischen Handschriften des Protevangeliums Iacobi (Originalbeitrag 1971/1975)," in *Griechische Kodikologie und Textüberlieferung*, ed. Dieter Harlfinger (Darmstadt: Wissenschaftliche Buchgesellschaft, 1980), 577–612; Zbigniew Izydorczyk, *Manuscripts of the Evangelium Nicodemi: A Census* (Subsidia Mediaevalia 21; Toronto: Pontifical Institute of Mediaeval Studies, 1993).

[99] See *Directives pour la préparation des manuscrits* (Sources chrétiennes; Paris: Éditions du Cerf, 1971); *Règles et recommandations pour les éditions critiques (Série grecque)*, ed. Jean Irigoin (Collection des Universités de France; Paris: Belles Lettres, 1972); Dain, *Les manuscrits*, 204–5 (bibliography).

usually written ἱ͞ς. Sixth, because you will be dealing mostly with manuscripts from the tenth to the fourteenth centuries, you will notice in these minuscules accents, breathing marks, and some punctuation, which provide hints as to how to understand the syntax of the phrases. Seventh, do not decide too rapidly the text you will choose for your critical edition. Sometimes you have to wait, particularly until you have completed the translation, before making a final decision on the choice of variant readings.

As an example, let us consider one page of *Parisinus graecus 881*, f. 342ᵛ (an old *Menologion* of the tenth century c.e.) (fig. 1) and propose an edition of the top of the right column, the title, and the beginning of the martyrdom of Philip (fig. 2).

The left column of the preceding story ends with a series of dots and a small ornament. Our text starts with a cross at the top left of the right column, but in many manuscripts, instead of the cross, or along with the cross, one finds a heading over the title. As usual, the title is written in uncials, but with breathing marks and accents. The phenomenon of itacism is apparent already in the first two lines: Φιλίππου is written φιλήππου (η being pronounced like ι). Here is the title: πρᾶξις τοῦ ἁγίου Φιλίππου τοῦ ἀποστόλου, ὅτε εἰσῆλθεν εἰς τὴν Ἑλλάδα τὴν ἄνω. Put exactly what you read in the manuscript into the apparatus when your proposed text is different from the manuscript. For example, record the incorrect (according to our standard) πράξις (because of itacism, the primitive title may have been πράξεις [plural] or πρᾶξις [singular]), but do not mention that Φιλίππου is written without a capital (this is the normal way of writing names at that time), nor that it is written with an η in place of the second ι. Normally, you add the missing accents (on τὴν, for example) without mentioning it in the apparatus. Mention the unusual spelling for Hellas (ἐλάδα) in the apparatus and prepare to write a note on the strange τὴν ἄνω ("the superior one").

Between the title and the beginning of the text you read in full capital letters: κύριε, εὐλόγησον ("Lord, give your blessing"). This prayer is not properly part of the text and should be put into the apparatus in this way: *post titulum*: κυριε ευλογησον P (P is the abbreviation given to the Parisian manuscript, and you write κυριε because the word is not accented). In a *Menologion*, practically all the texts contain a prayer at

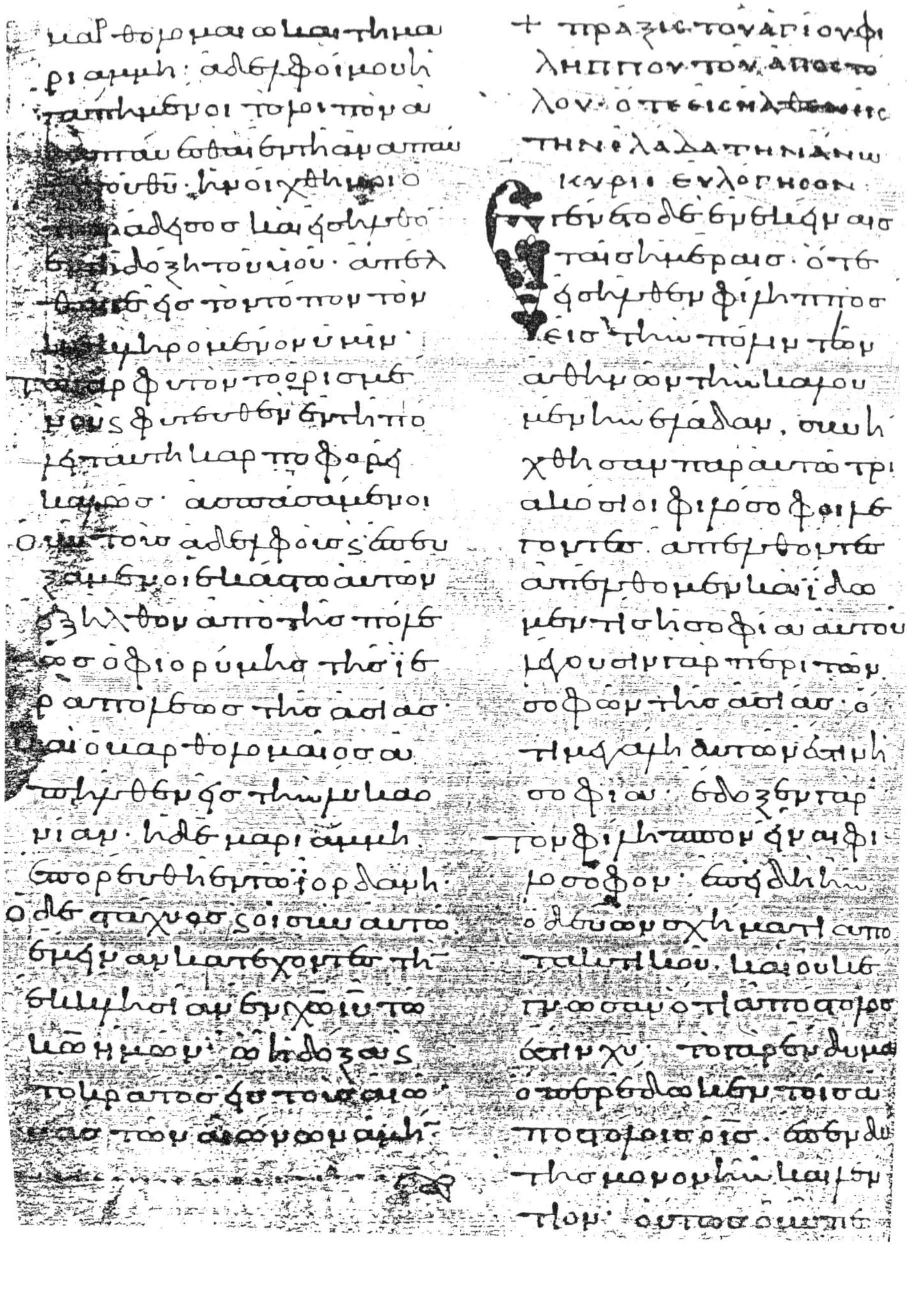

FIGURE 1. *PARISINUS GRAECUS 881*, F. 342[v]

the beginning (more often, εὐλόγησον, πάτερ ["give your blessing, Father"]), usually in an abbreviated form. If the "Lord" refers to Jesus Christ, the "Father" may be the abbot or God. It is interesting to meditate upon this short prayer. It means that the framework of this text is religious, even liturgical, even if it is not specified whom the Lord is asked to bless: the scribe, the reader, or the auditors. In any case, the liturgical background is clear: the very existence of such a prayer suggests the reason for the preservation and transmission of our text, not as a piece of secular history, but as a part of the sacred origins of the church—origins which have to be remembered by the praying community (the community of the monastery).

The text itself begins with an ornamented initial letter (an epsilon) which extends halfway into the margin. Its purpose is not only aesthetic, but also practical. It is an aid for the monk responsible for reading the text out loud. Here is the way the text begins (with rectified orthography):

ἐγένετο δὲ ἐν ἐκείναις ταῖς ἡμέραις, ὅτε εἰσῆλθεν Φιλίππος εἰς τὴν πόλιν τῶν Ἀθηνῶν τὴν καλουμένην Ἑλλάδα, συνήχθησαν παρ᾽ αὐτῷ τριακόσιοι φιλόσοφοι λέγοντες. . . .

It occurred in those days, when Philip entered the city of Athens, called Hellas, three hundred philosophers met together with him saying. . . .

It may be useful to demonstrate how to produce one page of a critical edition. As a sample, a part of the edition of *Acts of Philip* 1, according to *Xenophontos 32*, follows.[100]

In this edition of the text the number of each manuscript folio is recorded in the left margin (here, f. 31^r, then f. 31^v). The transition from one page to another (recto to verso of the same folio or verso of one folio to recto of the following) is indicated by the sign | (see line 17). The numbering "2[2]" and "[3]" in the left margin marks the division of the text into paragraphs (the first "2" being the new division, the second "2" and the "3" in brackets being the old division). Every fifth

---

[100] Bertrand Bouvier and François Bovon, "Actes de Philippe, I, d'après un manuscrit inédit," in *Œcumenica et Patristica. Festschrift für Wilhelm Schneemelcher zum 75. Geburtstag*, ed. Damaskinos Papandreou, Wolfgang A. Bienert, and Knut Schäferdiek (Stuttgart: Kohlhammer, 1989), 372–73.

372

moi aussi, semblable à ces imposteurs, pour lesquels j'ai dépensé en vain
mes biens, étant attentive à de vaines idoles? J'y ai perdu mon âme et, avec
elle, mon argent. Maudit soit celui qui adore les idoles ou consulte les
devins! Hélas, à qui vais-je réclamer l'argent que j'ai dépensé en vain,
attentive aux idoles et aux prédictions? J'ai méprisé les chrétiens; et voilà
que j'ai perdu mon fils, qui était mon seul bien.»

2|2| L'apôtre répondit: «Tu n'as rien subi d'étrange, ô mère, en étant égarée
de la sorte par l'ennemi qui ruine les âmes. C'est ainsi que le Diable égare
les hommes et les prive de la vie éternelle. Mais toi, cesse ta plainte, car à
l'instant je vais ressusciter ton enfant par la puissance de mon Dieu, Jésus-
Christ, lui qui fut crucifié et enseveli, et qui ressuscita et qui règne sur les
siècles; celui qui croit en lui reçoit la vie éternelle.» La vieille répondit:
«Puissent tes paroles m'être salutaires, étranger, et aussi vrai que tu es
l'envoyé de Dieu, viens en aide à ma misérable vieillesse. Après toutes les
épreuves que j'ai subies, j'ai souhaité mourir et je n'ai point été exaucée.

[3] Peut-être vaut-il mieux pratiquer le célibat et ne point manger ce qui
ensuite excite le corps, comme le vin et la viande, mais plutôt du pain et de
l'eau. Sinon on n'y gagne que des chagrins, mille maux et des deuils
amers.» L'apôtre répondit: «En vérité, ma mère, ce n'est pas de toi-même
que tu prononces ces mots, mais c'est le Sauveur qui, déjà, par ta bouche
parle de pureté. Que te semble la pureté? C'est précisément aux purs que
Dieu se manifeste et c'est pourquoi la pureté provoque tant de jalousie
parmi les hommes. Car incapables de vivre dans la pureté et de se conten-
ter d'eau, ils s'acharnent à calomnier ceux qui vivent dans la pureté. C'est
eux, en effet, que Dieu a proclamés bienheureux. Car Dieu a dit: 'Bienheu-

lin. 4: μαντεύεται: «consulte les devins»; on pourrait aussi traduire ici «rend des oracles», de
même que, ci-dessus (p. 371, lin. 2) μαντεῖαι aurait pu désigner l'activité des
devins plutôt que celle des consultants.

lin. 18: μὴ γαμεῖν: suggère à la fois le renoncement au mariage et la continence sexuelle.
lin. 23: περὶ ἁγνείας: le mot ἁγνεία, qui désigne aujourd'hui la chasteté, est difficile à traduire, car il
englobe la pureté, la continence, l'abstinence et l'ascèse. Il définit une attitude
et une éthique, celles que propage et exige la communauté à laquelle l'auteur
appartient (cf. infra, p. 393).

lin. 23,24: αὐτῇ τῇ ἁγνείᾳ τῇ ἁγνείᾳ ὁ θεὸς ὁμιλεῖ: le contact avec la divinité est assuré par l'ἁγνεία; ὁμιλῶ
paraît cumuler ici le sens classique de «fréquenter» et le sens moderne de
«converser». Quant au datif αὐτῇ τῇ ἁγνείᾳ, il doit exprimer à la fois le complément indirect, suivant la syntaxe classique (d'où notre traduction «aux
purs»), et le complément instrumental («par la pureté»).

373

f.31ʳ φλομένου. τάχα γὰρ καὶ ἐγὼ ὁμοία εἰμὶ τούτοις τοῖς πλάνοις, οἷς
εἰς μάτην ἀπώλεσα τὰ ἐμὰ προσέχουσα ματαίοις εἰδώλοις; ἀπό-
λεσά μου τὴν ψυχήν, σὺν αὐτῇ καὶ τὰ χρήματα. ἐπικατάρατος γὰρ
ὅστις εἰδώλοις λατρεύει ἢ μαντεύεται. οἴμοι, τίνα ἀπαιτήσω τὰ
χρήματα, ἅτινα εἰς μάτην ἀπώλεσα προσέχουσα εἰδώλοις καὶ   5
μαντείαις; τοῖς χριστιανοῖς; ἐξουθένησα ἀπώλεσά μου καὶ τὸν
υἱόν, ὃς μου μόνος ὑπῆρχεν.»

2|2| ὁ δὲ ἀπόστολος εἶπεν· «οὐδὲν ξένον πέπονθας, ὦ μῆτερ,
τοιαῦτα πλανηθεῖσα ὑπὸ τοῦ ἐχθροῦ τοῦ ἀπόλλοντος τὰς ψυχάς·
οὗτος γὰρ ὁ διάβολος πλανᾷ τοὺς ἀνθρώπους καὶ ὑστεροῦνται   10
τῆς αἰωνίου ζωῆς. σὺ δὲ κατάστειλον τὸν κοπετόν, καὶ ἄρτι σου
τὸ τέκνον ἀναστήσω τῇ τοῦ θεοῦ μου δυνάμει Ἰησοῦ Χριστοῦ τοῦ
σταυρωθέντος καὶ ταφέντος καὶ ἀναστάντος καὶ βασιλεύοντος
τῶν αἰώνων, ᾧ εἴ τις πιστεύει λαμβάνει ζωὴν αἰώνιον.» ἡ δὲ γραῦς
εἶπεν· «εἴη τὰ λεγόμενά μοι [...] σωτηρίας, ξένε ἄνθρωπε, καὶ ὡς   15
ἀληθῶς θεοῦ ἀπόστολος, εἰ βοήθησόν μου τῷ γήρᾳ τῷ κακῶς γε-

f.31ᵛ γηρακότι. ηὐξάμην οὖν ἀπολθανεῖν καὶ οὐκ εἰσηκούσθην· τοσαῦτα
κακὰ παθοῦσα. τάχα μᾶλλον συμφέρει μὴ γαμεῖν ἢ καὶ μηδὲν ἐ-
σθίειν· τὰ εἰς ὕστερον δονοῦντα τὸ σῶμα, οἶνον καὶ κρέα, ἀλλὰ
μᾶλλον ἄρτον καὶ ὕδωρ, καὶ λύπας κερδαίνειν καὶ πολλὰ κακὰ   20
καὶ πένθη πικρά;» ὁ δὲ ἀπόστολος εἶπεν αὐτῇ «ἀληθῶς, μῆτερ,
ταῦτα οὐκ ἀπὸ σεαυτῆς φθέγγῃ, ἀλλὰ ταῦτά σοι ὁ σωτὴρ ἤδη διὰ σοῦ
φθέγγεται τὰ περὶ ἁγνείας, τί γάρ σοι δοκεῖ ἡ ἁγνεία; ὅτι αὐτή τῇ
ἁγνείᾳ ὁ θεὸς ὁμιλεῖ, καὶ φθόνον ἔχει πολὺν παρὰ τοῖς ἀνθρώποις·
μὴ δυνάμενον γὰρ ἁγνεύειν ἢ ὑδροποτῆσαι σπουδάξουσί τι κατα-   25
ψεύσασθαι τοῖς ἁγνῶς διάγουσι. ὅθεν καὶ ὁ θεὸς τούτους ἐμακάρι-

1 ὁμοία· δμοια A || 10 οὗτος· οὖτος A || 15 post λεγόμενά μοι duo vel tria verba erasa sunt in A.
fort. ὑπὸ σοῦ ἀπαρχῆ || 16 βοήθησόν μου· βοηθήσον A || ᾗ γήρᾳ· γηρας A || 19 οἶνον· οἶνος A.

FIGURE 2. AN EDITION OF ACTS OF PHILIP 1, ACCORDING TO XENOPHONTOS 32

line of the text is numbered. Such line numbering may begin again on each page of your edition (which is more elegant) or the numbering may be continuous throughout the entire text (which is more practical). Sentences do not normally begin with capitals, which are reserved for proper names. It is permissable, however, to begin a sentence with a capital and is a matter of personal preference.

In this particular edition of the *Acts of Philip*, the meaning of the abbreviation (A = Athos, *Xenophontos 32*), the so-called *siglum*, has been indicated in the introduction. It would be better to indicate the manuscript(s) used in this section at the beginning of the apparatus on each page.

To make the apparatus more readable, you should describe the consistent tendencies of the manuscript in the introduction, particularly its orthographic habits. You must also indicate in the apparatus whether there is any possible ambiguity in the orthography of the manuscript, as here at line 10: οὕτως (the edition), οὗτος (the manuscript). οὗτος is ambiguous, as it can stand for οὗτος or for οὕτως, as the pronunciation is the same.

If you are not working with many manuscripts, it is better to present a so-called positive apparatus. A positive apparatus shows all the readings of all the manuscripts at each instance. That means that the sigla of all the manuscripts have to be presented for each variant reading or textual problem between two pairs of bars (‖ . . . ‖) or separated by a larger blank space.

For the apparatus, start by indicating the line, then put the lemma (the relevant portion of text) followed by a colon, then the readings of your manuscript(s), duplicating its orthography exactly, then the sigla of the manuscript(s) supporting the reading, followed by the symbol ‖ or a blank space. The ‖ or blank space is always given between the variant readings but is not used before the first problem of the page or after the last (the apparatus is usually completed with a period). It is good to have a biblical and an apocryphal index either directly under the text or under the *apparatus criticus*.

It is necessary to provide a translation of your text for those who cannot read Greek easily and to indicate your own understanding of the text.

The notes serve to explain the points where you are unsure of the translation or where there is ambiguity and to give some clarification about the meaning of a term or a name. It is often convenient to put the notes under the translation.

The Introduction

The last part you will write is the first that the reader will see: the introduction. The following items are indispensable in an introduction: 1) some mention of the object of your research (a critical edition of the *Acts of Philip*, for example) and a description of your principles for the edition; 2) a history of the research in this narrow field; 3) a description of your manuscripts (according to the checklist given above) and, if possible, a history of the manuscript tradition; 4) some remarks on the Greek language of your text, including its orthography, and an explanation of the principles of translation you have followed; 5) a summary of the content of your text and an evaluation of its significance within the corpus of apocryphal literature; 6) an analysis of the structure of the work (synchronic analysis); 7) the history of the text's composition (diachronic analysis), if you surmise that it is not unitary and you can detect sources; 8) the possible patristic or Byzantine quotations of your text; 9) ancient translations of your text, particularly into oriental languages; 10) the relation of your text to other Greek texts related to the same apostle; 11) your opinion on the date and geographic and social settings of the text; and 12) an annotated bibliography of the older or parallel editions, translations, and monographs.

The Commentary

It would be wrong to delay the publication of your edition so that you might simultaneously publish a commentary on it. It is better to present your text to the scholarly public and then work on the commentary. When you do produce a commentary, avoid writing along the lines of a New Testament commentary. The time is not ripe for such an enterprise. Only explain that which is difficult. Take one topic after another, not one paragraph after another. You may wish to characterize successively the structure of work (in a more sophisticated way than in the introduction), the social world of the author, the ideological function of the work, and its theological motive (through the image of the apostle, the shape and vocabulary of the prayers or sermons, and the encratite morality it proposes). Write a commentary which opens doors and invites other scholars into a dialogue with their own views and hypotheses. And remember the advice I received from Eduard Schweizer: an existing commentary with weaknesses is better than a perfect commentary which does not exist.[101]

[101] There will be a commentary by Frédéric Amsler in the critical edition of the *Acts of Philip* to be published in the Series Apocryphorum of the Corpus Christianorum. See his "Les *Actes de Philippe*. Aperçu d'une compétition religieuse en Phrygie," in *Le mystère apocryphe. Introduction à une littérature méconnue*, ed. Jean-Daniel Kaestli and Daniel Marguerat (Geneva: Labor et Fides, 1995), 125–40; and his "The Apostle Philip, the Viper, the Leopard, and the Kid: The Masked Actors of a Religious Conflict in Hierapolis of Phrygia (*Acts of Philip* VIII–XV and *Martyrdom*)," in *Society of Biblical Literature 1996 Seminar Papers* (Atlanta: Scholars Press, 1996), 432–37. For general information on the *Acts of Philip*, see François Bovon, "Philip, The Acts of," *ABD* 5:312; and Amsler, Bovon, and Bouvier, *Actes de l'apôtre Philippe*.

Performance and Rewriting

The "Prehistory" of
the *Acts of Peter*

Christine M. Thomas

The *Acts of Peter* has numerous versions in two distinct trajectories, the Eastern tradition, in Syriac, and the Western tradition, in Greek and Latin.[1] The texts of the Western tradition date to the late second through sixth centuries;[2] these various versions are a treasure trove, providing rich documentation of the textual processes of change undergone by these narratives. For students of earliest Christianity, however, does the *Acts of Peter* offer any generally valuable evidence for the manner in which early Christian texts were collected and redacted in the first and second centuries? Do the earliest available texts offer information on

---

[1] Joseph Flamion provides a thorough investigation of these texts into the early middle ages in both the East and West. His study comprises narrative reworkings and patristic citations, and is chiefly church-political in orientation, showing which parts of the narrative were being used as normative texts in which locations and times ("Les actes apocryphes de Pierre," *RHE* 9 [1908]: 233–54, 465–90; 10 [1909]: 5–29, 245–77; 11 [1910]: 5–28, 223–56, 447–70, 675–92; 12 [1911]: 209–30, 437–50).

[2] Many are available in vol. 1 edited by Richard Adelbert Lipsius (in the edition of Lipsius and Maximilien Bonnet): *Actus Petri cum Simone, AAA* 1:45–103; *Martyrium beati Petri apostoli a Lino episcopo conscriptum, AAA* 1:1–22; μαρτύριον τῶν ἀγίων ἀποστόλων Πέτρου καὶ Παύλου, *AAA* 1:118–77. An alternate Greek text of this work appears in the same volume as πράξεις τῶν ἀγίων ἀποστόλων Πέτρου καὶ Παύλου, *AAA* 1:178–222. See, for the *Acts of Nereus and Achilleus*, Hans Achelis, *Acta SS. Nerei et Achillei: Text und Untersuchung* (TU 11/2; Leipzig: Hinrichs, 1893). The brief text of Pseudo-Hegesippus can be found in *Hegesippi Qui Dicitur Historiae Libri V*, ed. Vincenzo Ussani (CSEL 66; Vienna: Hoelder-Pichler-Tempsky; Leipzig, Akademische Verlagsgesellschaft, 1932), 1:183–87. Pseudo-Abdias is available in Fabricius, *Codex apocryphus*, 2:390–92, 402–41.

the "prehistory" of the *Acts of Peter*, the form of the text in the first and early second centuries?

Any attempts to answer these questions will necessarily be fraught with difficulties, for the earliest evidence available for the *Acts of Peter* consists of a hybrid Latin text, the *Actus Vercellenses*, so named after the sixth- to seventh-century uncial Vercelli codex, which contains the sole copy. The Greek text is only preserved extensively in the martyrdom, which is a brief excerpt from the end of the *Acts of Peter* found in two independent ninth- to eleventh-century codices.[3] The *Actus Vercellenses* represents a sixth- to seventh-century truncation of a third- or fourth-century Latin translation of a somewhat earlier Greek narrative;[4] even on the surface level, then, the text has already undergone both translation and edition. Any evidence for the earlier history of the document must derive chiefly from source criticism, that is, analysis of the text that searches for discontinuities in plot, style, vocabulary, or theological perspective. Conclusions based on source criticism are not falsifiable; any success in constructing a cogent argument will depend on the explanatory force of the entire hypothesis.

Source criticism, though for centuries the trusty tool both of New Testament scholars and classical philologists, has of late fallen out of fashion. In part, this represents justified criticism against its overenthusiastic application, in which every clumsy word begets yet another hypothetical source. A further cause for reticence in the application of source criticism is the laudable recognition that texts offer evidence primarily for the time of their composition: they should therefore be considered holistically as meaningful acts of communication, rather than as quarries for the isolation of ever-earlier sources.

In the case of the *Acts of Peter*, however, the only existing early witness is a document that, even on *prima facie* evidence, represents

---

[3] A third Greek manuscript has been found in Ochrid (in the former Yugoslavia), *Bibl. mun. 4*; see Geerard, *Clavis Apocryphorum*, no. 190.4. It remains unedited.

[4] Cuthbert Hamilton Turner dates the manuscript to the sixth or seventh century on the basis of paleography, and the Latin translation to the third or fourth century ("The Latin Acts of Peter," *JTS* 32 [1931]: 119–33).

multiple distinct acts of redaction spanning a number of centuries. A strict application of the principle that the time of (last) composition is the truly operative date would leave us with only a sixth- to seventh-century *Actus Vercellenses*, for the latest act of composition in this document derives from the point in time at which this manuscript was copied.

In view of this methodological conundrum, the first section of this essay will briefly present, in reverse chronological order, the various stages of the redaction of this document. The second section will present the successive acts of *composition* for the *Actus Vercellenses* in normal chronological order—methodologically the reverse of the process of actual research—beginning at a point anterior to the first act of *redaction*. Not only the theological position evidenced by each successive redaction, but far more, the nature of the act of composition, will be the focus. The process, in brief, is one of crystallization of first-century stories into blocks of narrative, later united into a continuous work, which then underwent further interpolations, thoroughgoing rewritings, and, finally, became an excerpt. This example of the growth of an early Christian narrative is offered in hopes of shedding light on the compositional procedures employed for other such documents, including but not limited to the canonical literature.[5]

The *Acts of Peter*, Retro[6]

The *Acts of Peter* as presented in the *Actus Vercellenses* does not represent the entire text. It begins with the activities of Paul at Rome and the subsequent arrival of Peter in the capital city. Carl Schmidt first noticed numerous back references to a part of the narrative taking place

---

[5] See a treatment of the same issues, with important methodological observations, in François Bovon, "The Synoptic Gospels and the Noncanonical Acts of the Apostles," *HTR* 81 (1988): 19–36. His examples are taken from the *Acts of Philip*. The processes illustrated are selection, elimination, citation, imitation, and adaptation of written texts.

[6] Detailed argumentation for the various stages of redaction will be suppressed in the interest of space. Only previously unpublished observations are presented in full; the reader is directed to consult cited publications for the rest.

in Jerusalem, which has not been preserved.[7] Theodor Zahn also pointed
out that the stichometry of Nicephorus gives the length of his *Acts of
Peter* text as 2750 stichoi, about the length of the Gospel of Luke; we
would therefore be missing about one-third of the complete narrative.[8]
This one-third, among other things, must have contained an account of
Peter's activities in Jerusalem.

One of the extended back references in the *Actus Vercellenses*, in
chapter 17, recounts the saga of a certain Eubula, a character that is a
counterpart to the senatorial Marcellus, the other prominent polytheist
convert in the *Acts of Peter* narrative; like Marcellus, Eubula is also
deceived by the false miracles of Simon Magus, mistakenly offers him
the hospitality of her home, and later regrets it. A redactional seam at
the beginning of *AVer* 17 suggests that this chapter was excised from
the Judaean section and moved to its present location to provide
background information on Peter's prior activities and, most likely, to
avoid losing the entertaining Eubula story altogether. Peter sees a vision
in which Christ encourages him and predicts his victory in the coming
contest with Simon. He then reports this to the Christian congregation
(*AVer* 16–17):[9]

> luce{m} itaque facta{m}, narrauit fratribus quod sibi apparuisset
> dominus et quid illi praecepisset. credite autem mihi, o uiri fratres, ego
> hunc Simonem a Iudea fugaui multa mala facientem magico carmine,
> morantem in Iudaea ad quandam mulier Eubola, honesta nimis in saeculo
> hoc, adiacente ei auro copioso et margaritis non minimo praetio.[10]

---

[7] In addition to chapter 17, treated here at length, chapters 5, 9, and 23 also allude to
Peter's conflict with Simon in Judaea; see Carl Schmidt, "Studien zu den alten
Petrusakten: II. Die Komposition," *ZKG* 45 (1926): 481–513. A Syriac history of Peter
(*BHO* 935), identified by Poupon as using the *Acts of Peter* among its sources, explicitly
situates the Eubula episode in Jerusalem (Gérard Poupon, "Les 'Actes de Pierre' et leur
remaniement," *ANRW* II 25/6:4363–83; see esp. 4365–66).

[8] Theodor Zahn, *Geschichte des neutestamentlichen Kanons* (2 vols.; Erlangen:
Deichert, 1888–92), 2:841 n. 3.

[9] *AAA* 1:62.30–63.4. References are to page and line number in this edition. All
English translations are mine.

[10] I have replicated the reading of the manuscript here, rather than the editors'
emendations. The asterisks in the English translation indicate words which make no
grammatical sense in the actual text. Both Lipsius and Vouaux, *Actes de Pierre*, emend
to *quandam mulierem Eubolam*.

> When it had become light, he recounted to the brothers that the Lord had appeared to him and what he had commanded. "Believe me, then, my brothers, I drove Simon out of Judaea after he had wrought many evils with his magical incantations, while he was staying in Judaea with a certain *woman (named) *Eubula, a quite *respectable woman in this world, who possessed much gold and pearls of no little value."

The switch into direct speech is not explicitly signalled with as much as a *Petrus autem dixit*.[11] "Judaea" is spelled in two different ways in the same sentence. Most telling is the sudden appearance of Eubula in the nominative. She appears in exactly the case and manner that one would expect her to be introduced, not in direct or indirect speech, but rather in an independent narrative.[12] The grammatical anacoluthon strongly suggests that the person who inserted this passage in chapter 17 drew it from a Latin source document; if the individual were simultaneously redacting and translating from Greek, this type of grammatical slip would be far less likely. In the very act of translating, the author would have composed the sentence in the proper case.

The responsible party is probably the scribe of the Vercelli codex, who was otherwise interested in Peter's activities in Jerusalem and elsewhere. In the sixth- to seventh-century codex, the *Actus Vercellenses* follows the Clementine *Recognitions* without any intervening title, and the text of the *Actus Vercellenses* itself contains an interpolation from that source (book 4, chapter 5 to chapter 10).[13] Schmidt first suggested that the motivation for the truncation of the first third of the *Actus Vercellenses* may have been to harmonize it with the *Recognitions*.[14] The redactor of the *Actus Vercellenses* would have purposely suppressed all parts of the narrative taking place in Judaea, with the exception of

---

[11] Vouaux also notes the rough transition in this chapter, which he considers an interpolation (*Actes de Pierre*, 33–35).

[12] The end of chapter 17, which mentions the death of Eubula, also seems more appropriate to an independent narrative.

[13] Noted by Vouaux, *Actes de Pierre*, 17. The interpolation comprises two pages of the codex, 363–64, just before chapter 29 in the text, and follows four pages written in a different seventh-century hand, 359–62. The copyist's mistake here was recognized already in the eighth century by a corrector.

[14] Schmidt, "Studien II," 510–13.

this "flashback." This would harmonize well with the *Recognitions*, which treat Peter's activities in the east. The Vercelli redactor would then have been attempting to chronicle Peter's deeds, using one source for his activities in Syria and Palestine (the *Recognitions*) and another for those in Rome (the *Acts of Peter*). One of the Greek codices (Athos, Vatopedi 79) of the martyrdom has a superscript denoting its source as . . .ἐκ τῶν ἱστορικῶν Κλήμεντος Ῥώμης ἐπισκόπου. . . (". . .from the histories of Clement, bishop of Rome. . ."). The manuscript source copied by the Vatopedi codex, then, contained the martyrdom as part of the *Recognitions*, just as the Vercelli codex does.

The *Actus Vercellenses* represents, in turn, a Latin translation of a Greek narrative. As noted above (n. 4), C. H. Turner has dated the translation to the third or fourth century C.E. on the basis of its style. If the interpolation of chapter 17 was from a source document in Latin, the translation must have covered the entire scope of the narrative of the *Actus Vercellenses*, including the portion of it set in Jerusalem. That the *Actus Vercellenses* is a translation of a Greek text is demonstrated by the earliest Greek witness, *Papyrus Oxyrhynchus 849*, which is a vellum fragment dating to the third or fourth century C.E., with twenty-eight lines of text that fall at the end of chapter 25 and the beginning of chapter 26 of Lipsius's edition of the Latin text.[15]

Gérard Poupon has most recently argued, basing his hypotheses in part on observations put forward by Adolf von Harnack and Léon Vouaux, that the continuous narrative, as presented in the *Actus Vercellenses*, underwent a thoroughgoing redaction in the early third century.[16] The purpose of the redaction was chiefly to introduce into the story the figure of the apostle Paul, who had not been present in

---

[15] *AAA* 1:73. Incorrectly identified by Wilhelm Schneemelcher and Maurice Geerard as papyrus (*NTApoc*[5] 2:278; also *NTApoc*[3] 2:269; Geerard, *Clavis Apocryphorum*, no. 190). It is because the fragment is vellum and not papyrus that Grenfell and Hunt date it to the early fourth century rather than the later third. The script is of a type commonly used from the reigns of Diocletian to Constantine, but vellum is uncommon in Egypt before the fourth century. The stratigraphy is no help here, since the immediate context contained finds from the third to the fifth century (*The Oxyrhynchus Papyri*, ed. Bernard P. Grenfell and Arthur S. Hunt [London: Egypt Exploration Fund, 1908], 6:6–12; see esp. 7).

[16] Poupon, "Remaniement."

earlier versions of the narrative. Paul is presented as the founder of the Christian community at Rome (*AVer* 1–3); shortly after his departure for Spain, the appearance of Simon Magus in the city results in the apostasy of the entire nascent Christian community (*AVer* 4). Poupon demonstrates that the previous version of the story presented the crisis in Rome as the unparalleled success of Simon Magus at winning over converts from polytheism; Peter then arrives to show the truth and power of the Christian god and to correct the error of Simon's converts. As presented in the *Actus Vercellenses*, however, Peter's assignment is to reconvert *Christians* who have lapsed because of Simon's demonstrations. Based on redactional seams within the narrative, Poupon shows that this stage of redaction is largely confined to chapters 1–3, a wholesale interpolation that details Paul's work in Rome; to chapter 4, telling of Simon's appearance and initial success in Rome; to chapter 6, which narrates Peter's voyage to Rome; to chapter 10, in which Marcellus makes a speech confessing his apostasy; and to chapter 41, which again mentions the figure of Paul.[17]

All of these passages were either interpolated into or redacted in the continuous narrative. Even the three chapters that stand initially in the *Actus Vercellenses*, those that tell of Paul's activities in Rome, must likewise have been an interpolation into the continuous narrative, rather than a brace of chapters appended at the beginning of an already-excerpted text. These chapters date to the third century on the basis of their theological concerns, and the Latin translation dates to the fourth century c.e. The narrative of the *Acts of Peter*, however, was probably first truncated in the seventh century, as argued above; since the interpolation of chapter 17 points to a *Latin* text, this excision took place, at the very earliest, subsequent to the translation of the Greek text into Latin. The insertion of entire chapters, such as chapters 1–3, at various points into the stream of the continuous Greek narrative is not an impossibility. Chapter 10, for example, if not an interpolation, is extraordinarily heavily redacted.

---

[17] Poupon also argues that *AVer* 29–30, containing the tale of the promiscuous Chryse and her gift to the Christian community, is interpolated, but this is here rejected as having no compelling textual or theological basis ("Remaniement," 4377–78).

A further level of redaction can be detected, prior to the editorial activity postulated by Poupon and others.[18] This earliest written activity is best described as the composition of the *Acts of Peter* out of various sources, some of them written. Especially in the chapters recounting miracle stories (8–15), redactional seams suggest that a written source containing miracle stories was manipulated to introduce a series of narrative units elaborating the figure of Marcellus, who was, indeed, already present in the narrative at a level even prior to the redaction postulated by Poupon. Other seams, such as the repetition of words introducing speech, illustrate that brief oracular utterances were introduced into the written text to connect the various segments of the continuous narrative: the miracles, the contest with Simon, and Peter's martyrdom.[19] To give a single example, in chapter 12, after an initial encounter with Simon in chapter 9, a talking dog runs out to Peter to report on his activities (*AAA* 1:60.14–20):

> et canis renuntians quid gessisset cum Simone. haec autem locutus est canis: angel‹e› et apostol‹e›[20] dei uer‹i›[21] Petre, agonem magnum habebis contra Simonem inimicum Christi. . .multos autem conuertes in fidem seductos ab eo. propter quod accipies mercedem a deo operis tui. haec cum dixisset canis, caecidit ante pedes apostoli Petri et deposuit spiritum.

> And the dog reported what he had done with Simon. Moreover, the dog also said: "Messenger and apostle of the true God, Peter, you shall have a great contest against Simon, the enemy of Christ. . .and you shall convert many to the faith that were deceived by him. For this you will receive from God the wages for your labor." When the dog had said this, he fell before the feet of the apostle Peter and laid aside his spirit.

---

[18] Christine M. Thomas, "Word and Deed: The *Acts of Peter* and Orality," *Apocrypha* 3 (1992): 125–64.

[19] Thomas, "Word and Deed," 138–44.

[20] The manuscript reads *angelo et apostolo*; Turner suggests this emendation ("Latin Acts," 126).

[21] The manuscript reads *uere*. If one does not follow Turner's emendation (see n. 20), this reading still results in a meaningful sentence ("the dog said to the messenger and apostle of God, 'Truly, Peter. . .' "). Without Turner's emendation, Lipsius's emendation to *ueri* here makes grammatical sense but does not seem particularly apt.

The account places two messages in the dog's mouth, one in indirect speech, and one in direct speech. They are linked by a redactional formula, "moreover. . .also said:. . ." (*haec autem locutus est*. . .). The two statements are unrelated: when the dog switches to direct speech, he does not mention any of the foregoing dealings with Simon Magus. Instead, this prophecy is connected to the entire scope of the *Actus Vercellenses*: not only does it mention the later contest between him and Simon, it alludes to the martyrdom of Peter in speaking of his "wages."

There are two other instances of this technique in chapters 8–15 alone;[22] outside of this brace of miracle stories, the oracle in chapter 16 may serve a similar function, although it is difficult to demonstrate the existence of a redactional seam here on a textual level.

Thoroughgoing stylistic analysis needs to be undertaken in the various sections of the narrative of the *Acts of Peter*. The Greek text is available for chapters 30–41 and shows a consistent mix of parataxis with hypotaxis throughout, with two exceptions: the discourse from the cross in chapters 37 and 38 becomes much more paratactic in style, and the final chapters 40 and 41 have a much higher ratio of participles to finite verbs than elsewhere in the narrative.[23] These are parts of the narrative that look suspiciously like submerged sources for other reasons: chapters 37 and 38 for their otherwise unattested philosophical and theological interests (see below), and chapters 40 and 41 for the sudden appearance of Nero and Paul, which suggests later reworking. A glance at the Latin

---

[22] The demoniac in chapter 11 prophesies about the conclusion of the dog story that frames the entire sequence of miracles, and the talking infant in chapter 15 recounts the dog episode and foretells the contest between Simon and Peter in the forum.

[23] Taking inspiration from David H. Warren, "The Greek Language of the Apocryphal Acts of the Apostles," in this volume, I calculated the percentage of circumstantial participles from the total number of finite verbs and circumstantial participles in each chapter. The ratio for most of chapters 30–41 runs at about 35 to 40 percent. Chapters 37 and 38 dip suddenly to 20 and 21 percent, and chapters 40 and 41 soar to 46 and 45 percent, respectively. Clearly, the style is at times influenced by the type of discourse: chapters 37 and 38 are a reproduction of an oral address containing many apophthegms, though chapters 40 and 41 represent the same type of narrative as elsewhere in chapters 30–41. This evidence is of interest because there are reasons independent of stylistic analysis for considering these passages to reflect earlier sources.

translation of the martyrdom, however, suggests an even Latin style in the martyrdom, and largely the same Latin style present in the rest of the *Actus Vercellenses*, and thus illustrates how difficult would be stylistic analysis for the rest of the narrative, those parts preserved only in Latin. The idiom of the third- or fourth-century Latin translator may have overlaid the idiosyncrasies of the various Greek sources almost completely.

Although less compelling evidence, the theological and philosophical peculiarities of the martyrdom also suggest that it may well come from a separate source. Nothing in the rest of the narrative parallels the discourse from the cross in chapter 38, in which Peter claims to be the type of the first man, who was born into the world upside down, and thus mistook the order of creation because he saw all things reversed. This sort of philosophical meditation on the nature of evil and error has more resonance with parts of the *Acts of Andrew*, or the *Acts of Thomas*,[24] than it does with any elements in the rest of the narrative of the *Acts of Peter*.

The *Acts of Peter*, Fast Forward

The earliest isolable level of composition, then, is the working of various sources, some of them written, into a continuous narrative in Greek. This is the methodological limit of source-critical observations, which can only demonstrate editorial activity at the written level of the history of transmission. Other features of the written narrative, however, suggest that the *Acts of Peter* enjoyed a considerable life in the sort of telling and retelling best illustrated in oral transmission. This is not to claim that the *Acts of Peter* existed ever or only on an oral level in the history of its transmission, or to claim that this use of the narratives of the *Acts of Peter* ceased once the first written version appeared. Oral transmission is elusive and can only be demonstrated with difficulty for ancient

---

[24] Cf. *AAn* 5–7, in which Andrew describes himself as Adam and his disciple Maximilla as Eve, both of them correcting the error of the first Fall from grace. See also *ATh* 108–13, the famous "Hymn of the Pearl," in which the same general philosophical horizon emerges: the origin of evil in primal error and forgetfulness.

cultures. The evidence for it will necessarily be written, and, in the case of a society in which writing is already known, it is more judicious to claim that a written text is behaving in the fashion that oral tradition would, that is, with fluidity rather than fixity, rather than to claim the written text as definite evidence of a hypothetical oral tradition.[25] Many recent works have questioned that there was a hard and fast distinction between oral and written modes in later antiquity; consequently, it may not always be true that "the letter kills," that is, that the introduction of writing into a narrative or epic tradition immediately stills oral retelling, or determines that written works will be treated as fixed.[26]

The first stage of the development of the *Acts of Peter* narrative trajectory was an "expansive" phase of repeated performances of the narrative, probably at first on an oral level. The characters in the narrative were elaborated and developed into stock figures, but the tellings and retellings of the story led to considerable variety in the details of the narrative. Written activity is by no means excluded as a possibility during

[25] The first introduction of writing into a society, as in the case of archaic Greece, will, logically, record oral tradition, such as the Homeric epic cycle, since no written traditions exist. Once writing is known, however, the relationship between written and oral composition becomes more complicated; the two realms are permeable, exerting mutual influence on each other. The later work of Albert Lord and the research of John Miles Foley and Ruth Finegan demonstrate that, in cultures with high residual orality, written compositions can be treated as single performances of multiform narratives rather than as fixed and authoritative texts. As Foley remarks, ". . .we are learning from the comparative study of oral traditions worldwide that orality, literacy, and texts form a complex and interactive continuum rather than discrete categories, so it is no longer a contradiction to speak of oral traditional features in a written document," ("*Guslar* and *Aiodos*: What South Slavic Oral Epic Can—and Cannot—Tell Us about Homer," *Abstracts* for the American Philological Association Annual Meeting, San Diego, 28 December 1995). See also Albert B. Lord, "The Merging of Two Worlds: Oral and Written Poetry as Carriers of Ancient Values," in *Oral Tradition in Literature: Interpretation in Context*, ed. John Miles Foley (Columbia: University of Missouri Press, 1986), 19–64.

[26] This field is vast and expanding, encompassing studies not only in Classical Greek and Hellenistic literature but in the texts of early Christianity, including the Coptic Gnostic texts, and in the study of both intertestamental and rabbinic Judaism. Two recent comprehensive works on widely different topics: Gregory Nagy, *Poetry and Performance: Homer and Beyond* (Cambridge: Cambridge University Press, 1996); and Harry Y. Gamble, *Books and Readers in the Early Church: A History of Early Christian Texts* (New Haven: Yale University Press, 1995).

this period; at the very least, this phase ends with the gradual coalescing of the narrative material into short written units of topically related materials. The features of the *Acts of Peter* narrative complex that most resemble oral tradition are the presence of multiforms, chronological telescoping, and the inexact memory of first-century figures in the narrative trajectory.[27]

Multiforms are the relics of multiple performances on an oral level; each separate version of the same story results from a separate retelling for another audience.[28] The literary equivalent is the "doublet," considered to be evidence of the mindless compilation of two separate sources by an author or scribe, which results in the same pericope or saying appearing twice, once because of its presence in one source and a second time because of its presence in another source. The terms are related; from a performance perspective, the doublets are a subset of multiforms. In the case of the *Acts of Peter*, the term "multiform" seems more apt, because it does not assume that the duplication is in every case a result of multiple written sources. The duplicate stories are not exact copies of each other; each shows creative additions and refinements, so their origin is not a case of *literal* transcription from a written source, though written sources may be involved on some level. The *Acts of Peter* contains four complexes of multiforms: both Agrippa and Albinus, as the unhappy husbands of wives recently turned to the Christian teaching of sexual abstinence, are involved in the arrest of Peter (*AVer* 33–34); Simon flies twice over the city of Rome (*AVer* 4 and 32); Peter raises three young men from the dead in his contest with Simon (*AVer* 25–28); and he strikes two virgins with paralysis or death

---

[27] "Narrative trajectory" here denotes what narratologists describe as *fabula*, the basic elements of the narrative, such as situation, location, and characters. In the case of the *Acts of Peter*, the *fabula* would be the sum of individual narratives about Peter. See Mieke Bal for the distinctions between *fabula*, story, and text (Mieke Bal, *Narratology: Introduction to the Theory of Narrative*, trans. Christine van Boheemen [Toronto: University of Toronto Press, 1985], 5–8). She adds the third category of "text" to the two already described by the Russian Formalists, story (*sjuzhet*) and *fabula*.

[28] The term "multiform" is described and employed in Albert Lord, *The Singer of Tales* (Harvard Studies in Comparative Literature 24; Cambridge, Mass.: Harvard University Press, 1960), passim.

to preserve their virginity (Coptic *Papyrus Berolinensis 8502* and the *Epistle* of Pseudo-Titus).[29]

Yet, more relevant to the question of the origin, the "prehistory," of the *Acts of Peter* is its inclusion of first-century characters, and the chronological telescoping this involves. The presence of some first-century characters in a narrative concerning the earliest history of Christianity is obligatory; the appearance of Peter, Nero, and Simon Magus in the *Acts of Peter* is hardly surprising. The secondary characters, however, also seem to be in part dim reflections of first-century personages. As Carl Erbes has suggested, the Agrippa in the *Acts of Peter* seems to be a hybrid of the younger and elder Herod Agrippas, the tales about whom are found in the Acts of the Apostles, Josephus, and Eusebius.[30] The figure of Albinus may similarly be a reminiscence of the Albinus who was the successor of Festus in ruling Judaea.[31] Marcellus, like the Queen Tryphaina of the *Acts of Paul and Thecla* (*AThec* 27–41),[32] does not have a Jerusalem pedigree but has roots in Asia Minor. As Gerhard Ficker pointed out long ago, this character is an echo of the governor of Bithynia, Marcus Granius Marcellus,

---

[29] Schmidt, *Die alten Petrusakten*; James Brashler and Douglas M. Parrott, "The Act of Peter," in *Nag Hammadi Codices V, 2-5 and VI with Papyrus Berolinensis 8502, 1 and 4*, ed. Douglas M. Parrott (NHS 11; Leiden: Brill, 1979), 473–93. Donatien De Bruyne, "Nouveaux fragments des Actes de Pierre, de Paul, de Jean, d'André et de l'Apocalypse d'Élie," *Revue Bénédictine* 25 (1908): 149–60; see esp. 151–53.

[30] Carl Erbes, "Petrus nicht in Rom, sondern in Jerusalem gestorben," *ZKG* 22 (1901): 1–47, 161–224; see esp. 186–88. The relevant passages are Acts 12:1–4; Josephus *Ant.* 18.6.1 §146, 18.6.6 §187–91; Eusebius *Hist. eccl.* 2.9.1–4.

[31] Erbes, "Petrus," 183–86; Josephus *Ant.* 20.9.1 §197–203.

[32] Tryphaina was, as the *Acts of Paul* presents her, local royalty, and a kinswoman of Caesar. A distant relative of the Claudians, she made her home in Kyzikos, not Pisidian Antioch, where the *Acts of Paul* places her. She is known to have been a queen of Pontus; she was also a priestess of Livia, popular for the many benefactions she gave to the city. See William M. Ramsay, *The Church in the Roman Empire before* A.D. *170* (London: Hodder and Stoughton, 1893), 382–89, who provides a useful collection of the historical evidence, though he downplays the divergences between this and the presentation in the *Acts of Paul*. See, more recently, David Magie, *Roman Rule in Asia Minor to the End of the Third Century* (2 vols.; Princeton: Princeton University Press, 1950), 1:513, 2:1368 n. 51; and Dennis R. MacDonald, *The Legend and the Apostle*, 20–21.

described in Tacitus's *Annals* (1.74).[33] Like the figure in Tacitus, Marcellus in the *Acts of Peter* is similarly accused of the desecration of an imperial statue (*AVer* 11) and of embezzlement of funds collected from the provinces (*AVer* 8). The details differ significantly, but the *leitmotiv* is the same. The peculiarity of the *Acts of Peter* is that it imbues both stories with typically Christian concerns. The ruined statue is miraculously restored, in the name of Jesus Christ—although the symbolic connection to the imperial cult cannot have been absent to a second-century reader! And the money diverted from the imperial fisc comes to benefit the Christians, a chronological impossibility for a governor whose term of office was circa 15–16 c.e., according to the chronology of Tacitus—a hallmark example of chronological telescoping.

These secondary characters persist stubbornly throughout the narrative trajectory of the *Acts of Peter*, often altering the roles that they play in the actual plot, but never disappearing completely. Even in the sixth-century *Martyrdom of the Holy Apostles Peter and Paul* (the Pseudo-Marcellus text), the character of Agrippa still appears, if only to suggest the manner of death for the two martyrs (Pseudo-Marcellus 58),[34] and the entire narrative is attributed to Marcellus.[35] Despite the general "expansiveness" of the narrative trajectory in this phase, it shows itself strikingly conservative here; it preserves these characters because of some recognition that the tale of Peter cannot be told without them, even if they no longer have a role in the plot.

In fine, then, the *Acts of Peter* began, in this first, "expansive" phase, as a loose collection of individual narrative units about first-century characters. In the process of telling and retelling, which may have taken place on both written and oral levels, Christian motivations were attributed to the figures and they were integrated into the story of Peter.

---

[33] Ficker, *Die Petrusakten*, 38–39, 43–44.

[34] Agrippa suggests that Paul be beheaded and Peter crucified, rather than allowing them to be tortured in the iron artichokes (κινάρας σιδηρᾶς or *cardis ferreis* [*AAA* 1:168.8, 169.7]) suggested by Nero.

[35] Several Latin manuscripts of the Marcellus text append a *subscriptio* that reads, *ego Marcellus discipulus domini mei Petri quae uidi scripsi* ("I, Marcellus, a disciple of my Lord Peter, wrote what I saw"). See *AAA* 1:177.

The individual units were most probably performed as part of a continuous narrative about Peter, although significant creative license must have existed in terms of the specific units included in any given telling, and in the elaboration of the base narrative units, for example, whether the virgin daughter was the gardener's daughter or Peter's daughter. This creativity led to the existence of numerous multiforms of the most memorable narrative units.

The appearance of shorter written segments belongs to this "expansive" stage of the development of the narrative trajectory. In the seamless continuum of orality and literacy proposed here, these written pieces appear as so many discrete performances of parts of the narrative. The most ancient redactional level explored in the last, source-critical section suggests that the earliest written sources for the *Acts of Peter* began as comprehensive collections of closely similar narrative units. The brace of miracle stories in chapters 8–15, for example, clearly existed as a written unit even before it was placed in the context of the continuous narrative. An author sat down at some point and penned together a collection of the miracles that Peter was known to have performed against Simon Magus to convince Marcellus and his friends of the power of the Christian god.

Isolation of other early written sources, as suggested above, is difficult to justify on a textual level. One redactional slip, in which Agrippa is mistakenly addressed as "Caesar," suggests that the contest in the forum between Simon Magus and Peter may have had a written existence prior to the creation of a continuous narrative about Peter (*AVer* 28).[36] The martyrdom, too, because of its apparent linguistic, theological, and philosophical heterogeneity, is a good candidate for an independent written source, although the linguistic sophistication may well be the result of subsequent work on the text a few centuries later, after it was

---

[36] Vouaux also wonders how it is that the emperor suddenly appears in the forum without any introduction. He rightly notes that this chapter is well integrated with the rest of the narrative and shows no stylistic differences, concluding that the slip of a word does not, in itself, betray the use of a written source (*Actes de Pierre*, 388–89). It is possible, however, that the compiler rewrote or paraphrased a source, while retaining some of its details.

again divorced from the rest of the narrative and used independently as a martyrology. The redactional oracles (*AVer* 12 and 15), which divide the narrative into an account of miracles, the contest, and the martyrdom, may be the redactor's recognition of the three main preexistent sources of the *Acts of Peter*.

When the author of the continuous Greek narrative sat down to work, then, he or she may have had at hand at least three discrete bodies of narrative units, which lent a potential structure to the entire story. At least one of these was in written form, a collection of several miracle stories in which the character Marcellus was already present. Moreover, one would need to postulate, at the least, a cycle of stories about Eubula in Jerusalem. About the other events in Jerusalem, one can, barring new manuscript discoveries, only speculate.

The second phase of the development of the *Acts of Peter* narrative, in which it became a continuous, written narrative, is characterized by a certain "conservatism." At this point in the *Acts of Peter* narrative trajectory, for example, the multiforms are all treated as separate events. Their similarity, however, is recognized in that most of them appear in close proximity to one another: the three resurrection accounts, for example, not only cluster together in the contest section of the *Acts of Peter* narrative (*AVer* 25–28), but are literarily intercalated to heighten the effects of suspense. The resurrection of the first victim only takes place after Peter has performed another complete resuscitation. The narrative tradition, then, is inherently conservative; in the complete version of the *Acts of Peter* such as lies at the foundation of the *Actus Vercellenses*, the author or compiler attempts to preserve every relevant narrative that is known about the events of Peter's career in Rome. At the level of the initial collection of the narrative, very similar narrative units find their place in the train of the story, even if they result in the double motivation of some events, such as the persecution of Peter both by Albinus and Agrippa. The narrative economy of a well-told story, at least at this level, is abdicated in favor of inclusiveness. Oddly, the clustering of similar narrative units together is less a function of written compilation than it is of the mnemonic propensity to group like events together. This may have taken place either on an oral level or a written level: stories heard may have been recounted in groups of similar stories, or stories read from one or more sources may have coalesced into these units in the mind of the author. In both the inclusiveness of the narrative tradition and the tendency to group like stories together, the functions of memory take precedence over literary considerations.

Like the storytellers in the first phase, the author of the continuous narrative had limits to creative license: the basic characters, Peter, Agrippa, Nero, Eubula, and Marcellus, were already part and parcel of the narrative. The basic outline of the story was also given. As suggested above, however, this author was not consciously attempting innovation, but was striving to collect and preserve as much of the story of Peter as possible. Any story relevant to Peter, even if a multiform, was collected, written down if necessary, and inserted at the appropriate point in the narrative. The degree to which the author intervened in the use of the sources is not entirely clear. With the miracle stories, however, the procedure seemed to be to break into the written narrative and interpolate newer materials, whether to emphasize the character of Marcellus as in chapters 10 and 11, or to lend structure to the overall narrative, as in the various oracles and prophecies that foretell the action to come (*AVer* 12 and 15). This same technique is also seen in the intercalation of the three resurrection accounts (*AVer* 25–28). In general, the practice of foretelling and recapitulating action is prevalent throughout the narrative, beyond these miracle chapters, and seems to be the most characteristic contribution of the compiler/author who presented us with a complete written account of the *Acts of Peter*, as we find it in the *Actus Vercellenses*.

Although a date for the continuous narrative is hard to defend, the theological and political concerns bespeak an origin in mid-second-century Asia Minor. The geographic data about Rome range from the vague to the inaccurate.[37] The otherwise inexplicable mention of the only two lay Christians in Rome who live *in hospitio Bytinorum*, elderly women who have not been deceived by Simon (*AVer* 4; *AAA* 1:49.16), could also be explained by Asian provenance. The figure Marcellus is most likely a provincial governor of Bithynia from the reign of

---

[37] On the Roman topography known in this document, see Ficker, *Die Petrusakten*, 34–38.

Tiberius.[38] 1 Peter directs a letter from Peter to Pontus, Galatia, Cappadocia, Asia, and Bithynia, so traditions about him may have existed in these locations. The *Acts of Peter* shares the *quo vadis* story (*APt* 35) with the *Acts of Paul* (PHam 7–8), which Tertullian places in Asia Minor (*De baptismo* 17).[39] The stories of Peter's downfall because of the teaching of sexual abstention to Roman matrons also finds an echo in both *Acts of John* 63 and *Acts of Thecla* 11–16, each of which has ties to different regions in Asia Minor; Justin Martyr tells of a similar story in Rome at the same time, and Tertullian of another in Cappadocia.[40] Justin is also concerned with Simon Magus, but the absolute lack of overlap between his lore about Simon and that in the *Acts of Peter* denies the possibility of a Roman provenance, although granting a general chronological niche.[41]

This text did not remain untouched for long. The redaction postulated by Poupon is dated to the early third century, but may be even earlier. Several considerations suggest that it was not far removed in space or time from the early continuous narrative. In general, there is a pattern of similarity with detectable differences indicating that the historical context was much the same, but that some time had passed. The literary feel of the narrative is similar, and the first three chapters share some

[38] For these arguments, see Ficker, *Die Petrusakten*, 38–46.

[39] The *Acts of Peter* are usually dated to between 180 and 190, because the *Acts of Paul* depend on them for the *quo vadis* story (agreeing with Schmidt, ΠΡΑΞΕΙΣ ΠΑΥΛΟΥ, 128–30, and "Zur Datierung der alten Petrusakten," *ZNW* 29 [1930]: 150–55; arguments against this are presented in Dennis R. MacDonald, "The Acts of Paul and The Acts of Peter: Which Came First?" in *Society of Biblical Literature 1992 Seminar Papers*, ed. Eugene H. Lovering, Jr. [Atlanta: Scholars Press, 1992], 214–24). We have early external attestation for the *Acts of Paul*: Tertullian writes that a presbyter in Asia Minor composed them out of love for Paul. The successive redactions and re-editions that the *Acts of Peter* underwent, however, make such external testimony difficult to evaluate. On which edition of the *Acts of Peter* were the *Acts of Paul* dependent? Once the text is no longer a monolith, this approach to dating becomes complicated.

[40] Justin Martyr *2 Apology* 2; Tertullian *ad Scapulam* 3. See Robert M. Grant, "A Woman of Rome: The Matron in Justin, *2 Apology* 2.1-9," *Church History* 54 (1985): 461–72.

[41] Justin places Simon's appearance at Rome and the erection of a statue in his honor during the reign of Claudius (*1 Apology* 26, 56); both of these show coherence with the *Acts of Peter*. Justin, however, knows nothing of the contest in the forum between Simon and Peter, the centerpiece of the *Actus Vercellenses* narrative.

redactional features.[42] Visions and prophecies, such as the voice from heaven that predicts Paul's martyrdom in chapter 1, are common throughout the rest of the narrative. Paul fasts to determine God's will, as Peter does elsewhere in the *Actus Vercellenses*. Paul offers a eucharist without wine; but here, the eucharist is with water and bread (*AVer* 2), rather than merely with bread, as in both chapter five and the Coptic fragment containing the story of Peter's daughter. The terminology differs as well; the ceremony is called *sacrificium* in chapter 2 (*AAA* 1:46.12), but *eucharistia* in chapter 5 (*AAA* 1:51.8). The *Strafwunder* that paralyzes Rufina in chapter 2 is ostensibly similar to the episode concerning Peter's daughter in the Coptic fragment, but the theological purpose of each differs radically. The paralysis of Peter's daughter is not truly a *Strafwunder*, since it is the beneficent act of God that preserves her virginity. In the case of Rufina, it is, on the other hand, a punishment for past sins. Last, although the narrative technique is similar, the Latin of the first three chapters of the *Actus Vercellenses* differs slightly from the Latin from chapter 5 onward; the sentences are longer, less often paratactic, and the vocabulary is less repetitive than in the main section of the narrative.

In the redaction, the interest in Asia Minor evident elsewhere in the narrative finds its echo in the knights from Asia, Dionysius and Balbus, mentioned in chapter 3 along with a senator named Demetrius (one assumes this is his cognomen). Moreover, the apostasy of entire congregations from catholic Christianity, such as occurs at Rome in chapters 1–3, is hardly uncommon in second-century Asia Minor, the age of Montanism, which erupted in nearby Phrygia; Marcion himself hailed from northern Asia Minor. Even the vague and improbable data concerning Roman geography have apparently been left to stand both in the Greek redaction and the Latin translation. The theological and geographic perspective of the continuous text and of its redaction is thus not tremendously different.

Chronologically, the redaction could also date to late-second-century Asia Minor. The chief concern, that of characterizing Peter and Paul as

---

[42] A point also noted by Vouaux, *Actes de Pierre*, 28, who nevertheless also holds these chapters to be an interpolation.

co-martyrs, is reflected in other sources from the second century,[43] and can account sufficiently for that redactional feature. Moreover, Dionysius of Corinth sent a letter around 170 C.E. to the churches in Amastris and Pontus, encouraging them to receive reconverted Christians from among those who have backslid into bad conduct or heresy (καὶ τοὺς ἐξ οἵας δ' οὖν ἀποπτώσεως εἴτε πλημμελείας εἴτε μὴν αἱρετικῆς πλάνης ἐπιστρέφοντας, "and those who repent from any backsliding, whether from offensive conduct or sectarian error").[44] If it is necessary to claim a specific interest in reclaiming the lapsed to account for the redaction—one assumes that such moral quandaries were widespread in early Christian communities—this witness is much closer geographically and temporally to the text than are Tertullian and Hippolytus of Rome, the authorities cited by Poupon for his third-century dating.[45]

The rather slight differences in theological perspective and narrative technique suggest that the redaction postulated by Poupon was not undertaken so much for polemical reasons as to update the narrative for a slightly different church-political situation. The geographic situation seems not to have changed at all. The main objectives of the redaction, to unite Peter and Paul in ministry in Rome and to provide a textual location for discussion of the problem of apostasy and forgiveness, are not even carried out with complete consistency throughout the narrative. As Poupon has noted, the references to Paul cluster in the chapters introducing the section on Rome (*AVer* 1–3) and at the end of the narrative (*AVer* 41); elsewhere, this text is completely Peter's narrative. Moreover, the constitution of the crowd of Simon's onlookers is not characterized with absolute consistency. The Greek version of the final episode concerning Simon, that is, his last flight over Rome, as preserved in Vatopedi codex *79*, chapters 30 to 32,

---

[43] *1 Clement* alludes to the deaths of both Peter and Paul (5–6); Dionysius of Corinth, writing to Rome around 170, is the first to say that the two apostles were martyred in the same era, and that they taught together in Italy (κατὰ τὸν αὐτὸν. . .καιρόν, in Eusebius *Hist. eccl.* 2.25.8).

[44] In Eusebius *Hist. eccl.* 4.23.6, cited by Ficker, *Die Petrusakten*, 41.

[45] Poupon, "Remaniement," 4381–82.

assumes that Simon and Peter are battling chiefly for the unconverted crowds of Rome. Simon's final salvo is reserved for them (*APt* 31[2]; *AAA* 1:80.20–21, 29–33):

Σίμων δὲ ὁ μάγος τῷ ὄχλῳ ἡμερῶν ὀλίγων διελθουσῶν ὑπισχνεῖτο τὸν Πέτρον ἀπελέγξαι. . . . ταῦτα δὲ πάντα ὁ Πέτρος ἀκολουθῶν διήλεγχεν αὐτὸν πρὸς τοὺς ὁρῶντας. καὶ δὴ ἀεὶ ἀσχημονοῦντος καὶ ἐγγελωμένου ὑπὸ τοῦ 'Ρωμαίων ὄχλου καὶ ἀπιστουμένου ἐφ' οἷς ὑπισχνεῖτο ποιεῖν μὴ ἐπιτυγχάνοντος, ἐν τούτῳ τοῦτον πάντα εἰπεῖν αὐτοῖς· ἄνδρες 'Ρωμαῖοι. . . .

After a few days, Simon Magus promised *the crowd* that he would refute Peter decisively. . . . Through all this, Peter kept following him and unmasking him before the onlookers. Since he [Simon] was constantly disgraced and ridiculed by *the crowd of Romans*, and no one believed him since he did not achieve what he had promised to do, it came to such a point, he said to them, "*Men of Rome.* . . ." (emphases added)

After this, Simon promises to fly up to God over the Sacred Way on the following day. The Greek version later alludes to Simon's earlier attempt to fly through the air over Rome (*APt* 32[3]; *AAA* 1:82.7–10):

ὅτε γὰρ εἰσίει εἰς τὴν 'Ρώμην, ἐξέστησεν τοὺς ὄχλους πετώμενος. ἀλλ' οὔπω Πέτρος ὁ ἐλέγχων αὐτὸν ἦν ἐνδημῶν τῇ 'Ρώμῃ, ἥνπερ οὕτως πλανῶν ἐφάντασεν, ὡς ἐκστῆναί τινας ἐπ' αὐτῷ.

For when he [Simon] made his entrance in Rome, he amazed *the crowds* by flying. But Peter, the one who exposed him, was not yet in *Rome, which* he led astray to such an extent by his ruses, that they went wild about him. (emphases added)

This is very different from the account given in the first three chapters of the *Actus Vercellenses* of the situation in Rome prior to Peter's arrival. No mention is made of Paul. Simon and Peter are battling for the crowds of Rome; those whom Simon leads astray are not the Christians but the people of Rome. The text assumes that, had Peter been there, not even the polytheistic Romans would have been won over by Simon at all. The issues are not apostasy and heresy, intra-Christian concerns, but rather the efficacy of Christianity in the competition of the religious marketplace, where the new religion has not yet achieved pride of place, and where every Roman deceived by a rival miracle-worker is a potential loss to Christianity.

Last, the interest in forgiveness after apostasy ("second penance") in the redaction was grafted onto a narrative already conducive to the exploration of this theological issue. Not only was it an easy matter, in terms of narrative technique, to alter the Roman followers of Simon Magus into apostate Christians, the entire narrative complex about Peter characterizes him as the "apostle of the second chance." In chapter 7 of the *Actus Vercellenses*, Peter begins at the gospel account of his attempt to walk on the water (Matt 14:22–33), in which his initial faith is overcome by doubt; Christ's gracious hand outstretched restores him. He then admits with sorrow that he also denied his Lord three times. From this he draws the theological conclusion that Christ does not lay such disappointments to the account of his followers, but rather has compassion on the weakness of their flesh, and restores them. Addressing his audience, he asks why they should be surprised if Satan attacks them, since the evil one was able to overthrow him, a very apostle, whom the Lord held in great honor. In the same vein, the *quo vadis* story is typically Petrine (*APt* 35). Convinced against his better judgment to flee Rome rather than face certain martyrdom, Peter meets Christ on the road out of Rome and is gently reproved, yet again, for his lack of faith. Restored, Peter again takes the second chance, turns around, and becomes, despite his initial cowardice, a glorious and courageous martyr. By making Simon's converts lapsed Christians, and introducing the subject of apostasy, the redaction emphasizes a theological tendency already present in the base text, in the very story of Peter; the redaction is thus in harmony with the tendency of the narrative itself, rather than in polemical engagement with it.

The later stages in the process of redaction of the *Actus Vercellenses*, outlined in reverse order in the previous section, include the third-century translation into Latin and the sixth- to seventh-century truncation of the first part of the narrative. The *Acts of Peter*, of course, does not stop there, but lives on, in the Western tradition in various later versions such as the fourth-century Latin Pseudo-Linus text (Lipsius's *Martyrium beati Petri apostoli a Lino episcopo conscriptum*), the fifth- or sixth-century Pseudo-Marcellus text (the μαρτύριον τῶν ἁγίων ἀποστόλων

Πέτρου καὶ Παύλου), and the *Acts of Nereus and Achilleus*. These editions form a separate area of inquiry, but do illustrate the liveliness of the narrative tradition and the relative fluidity of the base story of Peter.

This quick overview of the "prehistory" of the *Acts of Peter* in the various stages of the *Actus Vercellenses* provides a general impression of the gestation of an early Christian narrative. For students of other works of early Christian literature, of the gospels, for example, the process of development should sound eerily familiar: various narratives about first-century figures are told and retold, in written and oral form, over a period of time long enough to result in several multiforms of many of the narrative units, in the attribution of Christian motivations to characters who are polytheist in other sources, in the fixed attribution of roles in the plots to various secondary characters, in the gradual erasure of non-essential details, and in the telescoping of chronology. The narrative at this point exists in oral tradition and in a number of small written units; the written units are largely collections of topically or generically related materials, such as a martyrdom (passion) or catenae of miracle stories. At a point in time quite a bit later than this first, "expansive" stage of narrative development, an author/compiler begins to collect the available written and oral sources and to shape them into a coherent, extended narrative. This activity is inherently more conservative than the earlier stage. All available materials are integrated into their proper location; multiforms are treated as separate historical events, and, when the tradition knows of two separate individuals playing the same role in the plot, the event in question is simply described with a double motivation, as when both Albinus and Agrippa move to arrest Peter. The author's intervention in the work, aside from the selection and collection of materials, lies in lending the work an overall theological direction through the use of transitional passages, which either presage or recapitulate the most important aspects of the action. Later redactions begin with this base text and are even more modest, involving largely nonpolemical introductions of new theological issues or the service of providing the text in another language. These later activities also follow the creation of the continuous text in relatively rapid succession; it seems to be more common to alter or improve the text rather than merely to transmit it exactly as found. The parting of the ways between canonical and apocryphal, of course, is that these processes of change and benevolent improvement make less and less intrusion into the canonical text as it becomes more fixed, being relegated to the status of variant readings (even in the case of the radical Western text of the New Testament). For the apocrypha, on the other hand, the light of creativity was extinguished much later.

The *Acts of Mark*: Tradition, Transmission, and Translation of the Arabic Version

Allen Dwight Callahan

Traduttore traditore.
—Old Italian proverb

Introduction

The apocryphal materials saved from literary extinction by the Arabic scribes of the Coptic Orthodox Church have escaped oblivion only by being conveyed by an obscure Christian corpus in an equally obscure Christian tradition.[1] Written in one of the languages of the so-called

Many thanks to my fellow laborers in the Apocryphal Acts Group for their helpful suggestions for improving this essay. Special thanks to Patrick Tiller for his patient and careful reading of several earlier drafts of this paper and to Christopher R. Matthews for his critical review of the penultimate draft: the reader has been spared the infelicities and inaccuracies that they brought to my attention.

[1] For the classic survey of the Arabic New Testament Apocrypha, see Georg Graf, *Geschichte der christlichen arabischen Literatur* (Studi e Testi 118, 133, 146–47, 172; Vatican City: Biblioteca Apostolica Vaticana, 1944–53), 1:224–46. Graf's treatment has been updated by Gérard Troupeau, *Catalogue des manuscrits arabes*, vol. 7, *Manuscrits chrétiens* (Paris: Bibliothèque Nationale, 1972–74). For a helpful *Forschungsbericht*, see Gawdat Gabra, "Christian Arabic Literature: Notes on the State of Research, 1988–92," in *Acts of the Fifth International Congress of Coptic Studies*, vol. 1, *Reports on Recent Research*, ed. Tito Orlandi (Rome: International Association of Coptic Studies, 1993), 51–55. For the relation of the Arabic apocrypha to its Coptic antecedents and Ethiopic versions, see Françoise Morard, "Notes sur le recueil copte des Actes apocryphes des apôtres," *Revue de théologie et de philosophie* 113 (1981): 403–13.

oriental versions of New Testament literature, the corpus has never enjoyed the attention lavished upon materials written in the languages of the Western classics. As a tertiary translation, the witness of the Arabic version of canonical literature is of limited text-critical value. In addition, the Arabic version of the New Testament is an admixture of recensions, informed (or "contaminated," as we say in the infelicitous language of textual criticism) by Greek, Syriac, and not one but two Coptic dialects.[2] If this is so for the New Testament, which was subject to standardizing forces of canonicity, how much more so for the Arabic apocrypha, where the literature continued to develop and fluctuate long after the canon had capped, or at least delimited, alterations of the New Testament literature. In the early Christian apocrypha we encounter not only change in text type but permutation of plot, creation of characters, and restructuring of recensions. Thus, early Christian Arabic apocrypha have come down to us doubly disadvantaged. Because they are of Eastern provenance, Western attention has been less than luxuriant. And because they are noncanonical, the protection and stability of Christian canonicity was not accorded to them. Nevertheless, the Arabic apocrypha of the Coptic Church belong to a tradition of Christian literature more than a millennium old that reaches even farther back in antiquity to draw on ancient apocryphal works.

The early Christian apocrypha in all languages constitute a troublesome corpus of texts often poorly and idiosyncratically preserved. Jean-Daniel Kaestli has observed that even before the historical milieu or the literary character of an apocryphal work can be established, the first order of business in apocrypha research must be the reconstruction of the often-mutilated texts in which apocryphal works come to us.[3] One of the most formidable challenges of apocrypha scholarship is the problem of textual transmission, and this problem promises to be most daunting for the Arabic apocrypha of the Coptic Orthodox Church. But

---

[2] For a summary of the textual complexity of the Arabic version of the New Testament, see Bruce M. Metzger, *The Early Versions of the New Testament* (Oxford: Oxford University Press, 1977), 257–68.

[3] Jean-Daniel Kaestli, "Les principales orientations de la recherche sur les Actes apocryphes des apôtres," in *Actes apocryphes des apôtres*, 49.

it is the faithfulness of the tradition, its tenacity in holding on to its elements across time and texts, that may prove to make its transformations accessible to careful reconstruction. For this Arabic tradition, it is its essential stability over a millennium that renders discernible to modern criticism the changes the tradition underwent in the transfer that took place repeatedly from generation to generation and from language to language. It is precisely because of the stability of its tradition that we may appreciate the betrayals of translation, so to speak. In what follows I shall trace the transmission of one work of the Arabic apocrypha, the *Acts of Mark*, following a path of retroverted and conjecturally emended texts to a reconstruction of the faithful betrayals of a Coptic *Vorlage*. This *Vorlage*, I will argue, ultimately stands behind all the versions, but we may discern this only by a subtle reading of the complexities of the Arabic.

Early Christian Apocrypha in the Coptic Orthodox Tradition

During the Middle Ages the Copts translated and transmitted as many Arabic works as the Nestorians, Melkites, Syrians, and Maronites combined.[4] Though these other Arabic-speaking churches also composed in Greek or Syriac, the Copts wrote in Arabic exclusively: the intensity of Arabization had extinguished the production of native Coptic literature by the end of the ninth century, and few works were being translated into Coptic by that time.[5] Translation of Coptic, Greek, and Syriac texts into Arabic became a necessity for the Coptic Church by the tenth century, after three hundred years of Arabization under Muslim rule.[6] In the twelfth century the Coptic patriarch Gabriel II ordered his bishops to provide Arabic glosses for the Church's Coptic liturgy and

---

[4] Khalil Samir, "Arabic Sources in Early Egyptian Christianity," in *The Roots of Egyptian Christianity*, ed. Birger A. Pearson and James E. Goehring (Studies in Antiquity and Christianity; Philadelphia: Fortress Press, 1986), 84.

[5] Ibid., 83.

[6] Ira Lapidus, "The Conversion of Egypt to Islam," *Israel Oriental Studies* 2 (1972): 261.

teaching.[7] The thirteenth century witnessed a renaissance in all humane letters among the Copts, and the language of this revival of the humanities was Arabic. This century of literary activity occasioned the translation of biblical literature from Coptic into Arabic. The great medieval Coptic scholar Ibn al-'Assal applied an eclectic method of manuscript collation and comparison in his critical edition of the Arabic version of the Gospels, taking into consideration Greek, Syriac, and Coptic witnesses.[8] This eclectic collation and translation of texts thus constitutes both the richness and the complexity of the transmission of Arabic Coptic ecclesiastical works. It is with this linguistic and textual eclecticism that the Coptic Church embraced much of the literature of Christian antiquity, and it is in this way that Arabic became the language in which some otherwise lost or little-known apocryphal works were saved for posterity by the Copts.

The *Acts of Mark*

One of these little-known works, the *Acts of Mark*,[9] is an etiological tale of the founding of the Egyptian church by Mark the Evangelist. Its transmission history illustrates both the narrative stability and the

[7] Simiha Abd El-Shadeed Abd El-Nour, "Epact Numerals," in *Acts of the Fifth International Congress of Coptic Studies*, vol. 2/1, *Papers from the Sections*, ed. D. W. Johnson (Rome: International Association of Coptic Studies, 1993), 14–15.

[8] See Duncan B. MacDonald, "Ibn al-'Assal's Arabic Version of the Gospels," in *Homenaje á D. Francisco Codera en su jubilación del profesorado*, ed. D. E. Saavedra (Saragossa: Escar, 1904), 375–92. On the contribution of the celebrated al-'Assal family of scholars to the medieval revival, see Alexis Mallon, "Ibn 'Assal: Les trois écrivains de ce nom," *Journal asiatique* 6 (1905): 509–29; idem, "Une école de savants égyptiens au moyen âge," *Mélanges de l'université Saint-Joseph* 1 (1906): 109–31, and 2 (1907): 213–64; Georg Graf, "Die koptische Gelehrtenfamilie der Aulad al-'Assal und ihr Schriftum," *Orientalia*, n.s., 1 (1932): 34–56, 129–48, 193–204.

[9] See Aurelio de Santos Otero's introduction to this text in *NTApoc*[5] 2:461–64, under the title *Martyrium Marci*. This account of Mark's ministry and martyrdom is to be distinguished from those stories of the Evangelist's missionary labors that are recounted in the synaxaries, ecclesiastical encomia and histories, and other hagiographical literature. These stories identify the Evangelist with John Mark of the canonical Acts (Acts 12:12, 25; 15:37, 39), the Mark of the Pauline corpus (Col 4:10; Philem 24; 2 Tim 4:11), and the "beloved son" of 1 Pet 5:13. These embellished versions of Mark's

linguistic and textual complexity of the apocrypha that come to us through the Arabic corpus of the Coptic Orthodox Church. The general transmission history of the *Acts of Mark* may be reconstructed with confidence, for its several versions differ little from each other. The Arabic, however, when compared with the other versions of the narrative, parts company with them in matters of detail. A close examination of the peculiarities of the Arabic version of the *Acts of Mark* shows at once the general reliability of the Coptic Arabic tradition as well as the idiosyncrasy of its preservation. It is these qualities taken together that render the Coptic Arabic tradition a resource for reconstructing the transmission history of Christian apocryphal materials.

The narrative of the *Acts of Mark* recounts the call, career, and violent death of Mark the Evangelist, the first to preach the gospel in Egypt. The narrative relates that at the time the apostles were dispatched to preach the gospel to the uttermost parts of the earth, Mark received as his lot the lands of northern Africa, including Egypt. Arriving at Cyrene, he performs many miracles, and multitudes are converted. Directed by a vision, the Evangelist then sets off for Alexandria. There, in a place called Mendion or Bennidion (the versions vary), his sandal strap breaks. Mark takes the sandal to a local cobbler named Anianus, who accidentally injures his own hand with an awl while repairing the sandal. The Evangelist immediately heals the cobbler's hand in the name of Jesus Christ, and the amazed and grateful cobbler invites the stranger into his home. There, Mark preaches the gospel of Jesus Christ, and the cobbler and his family, as well as many others in the neighborhood, are converted and baptized. Meanwhile, the Alexandrian Greeks, who

---

biography and career are treated in *NTApoc*[5] 2:464–65, under the title *Acta Marci*. These ecclesiastical works used some form of the martyrdom tale I am calling the *Acts of Mark*, or at least its constituent traditions. The *Acts of Mark* treated here do not conflate the figures of the New Testament named Mark, nor do they reflect any awareness of patristic traditions about Mark's association with St. Peter or his authorship of the Second Gospel. For more on the ecclesiastical legends of Mark's mission and their significance for the tradition history and dating of the *Acts of Mark*, see Allen Dwight Callahan, "The *Acts of Saint Mark*: An Introduction and Translation," *Coptic Church Review* 14 (1993): 2–10. All the works mentioned above supplement the fulsome but dated introduction of Lipsius, *Die apokryphen Apostelgeschichten* 2/2:321–53.

consider the Evangelist's extraordinary miracle-working to be a threat to local idol worship, plot the Evangelist's murder. Perceiving the evil intentions of his pagan enemies, Mark ordains a number of church leaders, including Anianus as bishop of Alexandria, then departs to Pentapolis. After two years, Mark returns to Alexandria to find a flourishing church there. But pagan resentment has mounted. While celebrating Easter, the Evangelist is seized by an angry mob of idol-worshipers and dragged through the city streets at the end of a rope tied around his neck. Battered and bleeding, he is thrown into prison for the night, where he is encouraged first by an angel and then by a vision of Jesus Christ. In the morning the Evangelist is again dragged through the city streets, and finally expires. The mob attempts to burn his body, but a sudden, violent storm breaks over the pyre and disperses the terrified crowd. The Christians rescue the saint's remains and, after preparing the body "according to custom," they bury Mark in a stone tomb east of the city. Mark the Evangelist thus becomes the first martyr of the Alexandrian church on Pharmouthi 30, that is, April 25 according to the Roman calendar.

The Arabic version of the *Acts of Mark* (*Shahadat Marqos*, literally, "The Martyrdom of Mark") was published in 1904 by Agnes Smith Lewis in a collection of Apocryphal Acts of the Apostles and Evangelists in Arabic and Syriac languages.[10] In the same year she also published English translations of these acts with introductions and prefatory notes on the manuscripts.[11] Lewis edited and translated the *Acts of Mark* from one manuscript, codex *Sinaiticus arabicus 539*. Though she makes passing reference to a Greek version of the narrative,[12] she did not directly consult it or any of the other versions of the *Acts of Mark* then accessible. A closer look at the differences between the Arabic version and the Greek, Latin, and Coptic versions of the *Acts of Mark* promises to give us greater purchase on the text of *Sinaiticus arabicus 539* and the complex transmission history behind it.

---

[10] Agnes Smith Lewis, *Acta Mythologica Apostolorum* (Horae Semiticae 3; London: Cambridge University Press, 1904), 126–29.

[11] Agnes Smith Lewis, *The Mythological Acts of the Apostles* (Horae Semiticae 4; London: Cambridge University Press, 1904), 147–51.

[12] Ibid., x.

Two Greek recensions of the *Acts of Mark* are represented respectively by the eleventh-century *Parisinus graecus 881*, published by Jacques Paul Migne,[13] and *Vaticanus graecus 866*, printed in the great Bollandist hagiographic collection, the *Acta Sanctorum*.[14] *Vaticanus graecus 866* provides an extended title and preamble describing the incarnation of the preexistent Jesus, followed by a rehearsal of the Matthean Great Commission and a physical description of the Evangelist in the penultimate paragraph: all these features are lacking in *Parisinus graecus 881*. On the basis of these observations, Richard Adelbert Lipsius considered the two witnesses to be but different redactions of the same Greek text.[15] Three collections of Coptic fragments bear testimony to the Coptic version of the *Acts of Mark*. One source is Oscar von Lemm's publication of three Sahidic fragments, one of which mentions Mendion and another the island of Pharos, the first two stops on the Evangelist's Alexandrian itinerary.[16] A second source is the eleventh-century Sahidic fragment published by Théodore Lefort,[17] which treats the Evangelist's personal description and interment. The dating of the fragment places it just prior to the relocation of the Coptic Patriarchate to Cairo in the third quarter of the eleventh century, at which time the literature of the Church was translated into the northern, or Bohairic, dialect.[18] The third is the thirteenth-century Bohairic fragment published by William H. P. Hatch,[19] which describes Mark's arrival in Alexandria. A text of the Latin version is found in the *Acta Sanctorum*, which Godefroi Henschenius, the editor of the Greek

---

[13] *PG* 115, 164–69. For an English translation of this text, see Callahan, "Acts of Saint Mark," 3–10.

[14] "Martyrdom of Saint Mark the Evangelist" (Greek), in *ActaSS* 12: April 3, XXXVII–XLVII.

[15] Lipsius, *Die apokryphen Apostelgeschichten*, 2/2:330.

[16] Oscar von Lemm, "Zur Topographie Alexandriens," in idem, *Kleine koptische Studien I–LVIII* (1899–1910; reprint, Leipzig: Zentralantiquariat der DDR, 1972), 253–57.

[17] Théodore Lefort, "Fragment copte-sahidique du Martyre de St.-Marc," *Mélanges d'histoire offerts à Charles Moeller* (Louvain: Bureau du Recueil; Paris: Picard et fils, 1914), 1:226–31.

[18] Shanudah III, *Mark and the Coptic Church* (Cairo: Coptic Orthodox Patriarchate, 1968), 141.

[19] William H. P. Hatch, "Three Leaves from the MS of the *Acta Apostolorum*" (reprint, Boston: Byzantine Institute, 1956), 305–17.

and Latin texts published therein, notes as being derived from twelve unnamed Greek and Latin manuscripts.[20] This means that the Latin text he published may be contaminated with Greek readings. Henschenius's method, however, does not compromise our review of the Latin version. Both Lipsius's descriptions of the Latin manuscripts that he himself had seen and identified in other European libraries and published manuscript catalogues,[21] as well as the published Latin edition of Boninus Mombritius,[22] agree with Henschenius's text. The differences between the text and the variorum readings in Mombritius's apparatus are few and minor. Even without an exhaustive account of the Latin witnesses, we may be certain that we have before us a reliable witness to the Latin tradition of the *Acts of Mark*.

The Arabic Version of the *Acts of Mark* and the Recovery of a Coptic *Vorlage*

The Arabic version of the *Acts of Mark*, though agreeing generally with the other versions, differs significantly from them at several points in the narrative. The Arabic *Acts of Mark* recounts that after some time in Alexandria, Mark ordains the first bishop, elders, and deacons of the Alexandrian church.

> And because of him [i.e., Mark] many people believed in the Lord. And the citizens heard that a Galilean man had come. And they said, "A man has arrived in this city who will destroy the sacrifices of the gods and their worship." And they sought for him that they might kill him. And they laid in ambush for him, and traps. And the Blessed Mark knew of what they had resolved about him. And he made Anianus bishop, and three presbyters with him: the first was called Melian, and Sabinus, and Kerdona. And seven deacons; he appointed eleven for the service of the church. And he took them, and fled with them to Pentapolis, and abode there for two years. And he strengthened the brethren and appointed bishops over them also, and priests throughout Pentapolis.[23]

---

[20] *ActaSS* 12:347. Full Latin text is given on pp. 347–49.
[21] Lipsius, *Die apocryphen Apostelgeschichten*, 2/2:330–31.
[22] Boninus Mombritius, *Sanctuarium seu Vitae Sanctorum* (reprint, Paris: Fontemoing et Socii, 1910), 2:173–75, 688–89.
[23] Lewis, *Mythological Acts*, 128, slightly modified.

Mark selects leaders for the fledgling Alexandrian church in anticipation of his own departure. He must evade the danger of heathen plots against his life and presumably wishes to leave behind duly ordained clerics who will continue to oversee the church in his absence. Yet the Arabic is oblivious to this concern, reading that the newly ordained clergy accompany Mark when he leaves for Pentapolis:

واخذهم وفر معهم الى تلك الخمس مدن, "And he took them and fled with them to Pentapolis"

The other witnesses, however, unanimously indicate that the clergy stayed behind. Unlike the other versions, the Arabic understands the narrative to say that Mark selected leaders for the church in Alexandria on the eve of his departure, only to leave it bereft of all leadership in the wake of his flight to Pentapolis.

This sentence calls for some remedial reading. The verb "he took" (اخذ) is better translated "he appointed," and so "he appointed them" (اخذهم). The Greek and Latin recensions agree with the Arabic that Mark flees to Pentapolis: but whereas the Evangelist departs for Pentapolis according to the Latin and the Arabic, he both flees (ἔφυγε) and returns (ἀπῆλθε πάλιν) to Pentapolis in the Greek recensions. The versions read as follows:

Latin: . . .*et Pentapolim pergit*, "he made his way to Pentapolis"

Parisinus graecus 881: ἔφυγε καὶ ἀπῆλθε πάλιν εἰς τὴν Πεντάπολιν, "he fled and went away again to Pentapolis"

Vaticanus graecus 866: ἔφυγε καὶ πάλιν ἀπῆλθε εἰς τὴν Πεντάπολιν, "he fled and again went away to Pentapolis"

Arabic: وفر معهم الى تلك الخمس مدن, "and he fled with them to Pentapolis"

A common Coptic *Vorlage* explains Arabic, Greek, and Latin versions. The verbs ἀπέρχομαι and φεύγω in Greek and *pergo* in Latin all may render the Coptic ⲡⲱⲧ, which means "run," "depart," and "go away," "go back." Like other verbs of coming and going in Coptic, ⲡⲱⲧ is occasionally used with an ethical dative; therefore the perfect of ⲡⲱⲧ, "he fled," may be rendered ⲁϥⲡⲱⲧ ⲛⲁϥ. If this Coptic verb stands behind the versions, it may have been rendered into Greek and Latin in the following way. The Latin translator either correctly translated ⲁϥⲡⲱⲧ ⲛⲁϥ as *pergit* or translated from a Greek *Vorlage* that had here ἀπῆλθε πάλιν. (Presumably the text before the Latin translator did not have φεύγω, which probably, though not certainly, would have been rendered into Latin by *fugio*.) The translator of the Greek recensions, however, knew that ⲡⲱⲧ covered a semantic field that includes both "depart" and "run away," "go away": he was unsure of which meaning suited the context, and so included both meanings in his translation by rendering ⲡⲱⲧ with not one but two Greek verbs, ἔφυγε and ἀπῆλθε (πάλιν), conjoined with καί. The Arabic translator read the construction of ⲡⲱⲧ with ethical dative but rendered it *ad litteram*. The literal translation of ⲁϥⲡⲱⲧ ⲛⲁϥ, "he fled with him," was nonsensical, and so he translated his Coptic text as though it read ⲁϥⲡⲱⲧ ⲛⲁⲩ, "he fled with them," a difference of only one letter, resulting in our Arabic text.

In sum, the Latin version here represents a translation from the Coptic into Latin, perhaps by way of a Greek intermediary, that understood ⲁϥⲡⲱⲧ ⲛⲁϥ as a perfect verb with an ethical dative. The Greek translator rendered the Coptic verb by translating it with two Greek verbs; this translation is rendered in both Greek recensions, and points to their common origin. The Arabic translator, however, did not recognize ⲛⲁϥ as an ethical dative and so emended the text before him to make sense of it. This reconstruction not only implies the relation of the Arabic to a reconstructed Coptic intermediary, but the relation of the other versions to the Coptic *Vorlage* as well. This part of the text of the *Acts of Mark* suggests a Coptic *Vorlage* at the head of the stream of tradition.

The relation of the versions of the *Acts of Mark* further corroborates the proposal of a Coptic *Vorlage* in another part of the text where a Coptic version is extant. The penultimate section of the *Acts of Mark* provides the following physical description of the Evangelist in *Vaticanus graecus 866*: "And the blessed Mark had a long nose, knitted brows, keen eyes, a bald pate, and a long beard the color of ripe wheat. He was quick, healthy, middle-aged, graying, of ascetical constitution, full of the grace of God." This description is paralleled in the Latin and the Coptic fragment published by Lefort. These features of the Evangelist's aspect and stature are physiognomic; that is, the saint's physical features are an outward sign of his inward grace, as the reference to the Evangelist's plenitude of divine grace at the end of the description attests. The panegyric rhetorical tradition of physiognomy, which held that the nature of the mind and the presence of the divine spirit were evident from the person's physical appearance, continued to be influential in biographical literature from the time of Pliny the Younger through the fourth century.[24] By the fourth century patristic authors are availing themselves of the physiognomic tradition.[25] The awkward resumption of the narrative immediately following this physiognomic description suggests that a redactor early in the transmission history of the martyrdom has interpolated the pericope.

Lewis notes with some qualification the opinion that the personal description in the *Acts of Mark* is "partly borrowed" from that of Paul in the *Acts of Paul and Thecla* 3.[26] But this can hardly be so. The preeminent characteristic of Paul's description is his short stature, and this is in no way paralleled in the description of the Evangelist. J. Rendel Harris has shown that Jesus was reputed to have been of small stature according to patristic and apocryphal literature of the East,[27] and that the report of Paul's diminutive stature in the *Acts of Paul and Thecla* is "an artificial similarity between Jesus and Paul."[28] The author of the Markan description gives no hint of such mimesis. Those characteristics that both descriptions do share—bald forehead, long nose, and long

[24] Elizabeth C. Evans, *Physiognomics in the Ancient World* (Philadelphia: American Philosophical Society, 1969), 44.

[25] See, for example, Gregory Nazianzus's unflattering portrait of the emperor Julian, *Orations* 5.23. For a recent treatment of the influence of physiognomy on the development of early Christian literature and art, see Christopher R. Matthews, "Nicephorus Callistus' Physical Description of Peter: An Original Component of the *Acts of Peter?" Apocrypha* 7 (1996): 135–45, especially his discussion, with important bibliographical notices, of the description of Paul, 137–43.

[26] Lewis, *Mythological Acts*, xxxi. In *AThec* 3, Paul is described as "a man small of stature, with a bald head and crooked legs, in a good state of body with his eyebrows meeting and nose somewhat hooked, full of friendliness; for now he appeared like a man, and now he had the face of an angel." In *NTApoc*[5] 2:239.

[27] J. Rendel Harris, "On the Stature of Our Lord," *Bulletin of the John Rylands Library* 10 (1926; reprint, London: Manchester University Press, 1926): 1–15. Harris adduces among others Origen *Contra Celsum* 7.75, and Ephraim Syrus, *Hymns for the Church and the Virgins*, in which Christ is said to have possessed "a stature of three cubits."

[28] Harris, "Stature," 7.

beard—are common to the iconic stereotype of the Greek philosopher
that so influenced Christian representations of Jesus and especially the
apostles in the third and fourth centuries.[29] H. P. L'Orange has shown
in his comparative study of the portraiture of the apostle Paul and the
philosopher Plotinus that the representation of the former was indelibly
influenced by the stereotyped portraiture of the latter.

> . . .the striking similarity between our Plotinus-type and the Christian
> Paul. . .achieves special significance. Paul, too, has a slender lofty face,
> with a mighty forehead and a bald pate; he has the same long aquiline
> nose with a pendulous tip, the same look, now meditatively introspective,
> now ecstatically visionary, while the face narrows down to the long
> pointed beard.[30]

This suggests that the similarities between the respective descriptions
of Paul the Apostle and Mark the Evangelist may be explained by the
common influence of iconic conventions for the depiction of Greek
philosophers that informed the depiction of Christian heroes. The
differences between the two indicate that they bear no literary relation
to each other. The Markan description must be understood on its own
terms.

There are, altogether, seven elements of the personal description
common to the Greek, Latin, and Coptic versions. The Evangelist is
described as having 1) knit eyebrows or "touching eyebrows," generally
a sign of beauty in the Graeco-Roman physiognomic tradition;[31] 2) keen
or beautiful eyes; 3) a bald (fore)head; 4) long beard; 5) gray hair;
6) ascetical demeanor; and 7) plenitude of divine grace. In addition,
between notices of the long beard and gray hair, there is another element
that is indecipherable in the Coptic description due to the condition of
the fragment. In the Greek and Latin lists, respectively, three characteristics stand between the mention of the long beard and gray hair: the
Evangelist is described as quick (ὀξύς, *velox*), having a hearty constitution
(εὐεκτικός, *habitudinis optimae*), and middle-aged (μεσῆλιξ, *aetatis*

---

[29] See, for example, the apostle John's description of the Lord's appearance in *AJn*
89: he is described as having "a bald head" and "a thick, flowing beard."

[30] H. P. L'Orange, "Plotinus-Paul," *Byzantion* 25-27 (1955–57): 484.

[31] See Evans, *Physiognomics*, 54.

mediae). In the Coptic fragment only the letters ⲉⲩⲙ[. . .](ⲉ)ⲛ[. . .]ⲛⲣⲱⲙⲉ
ⲡⲉ are legible here. On the basis of what remains of the line and a
comparison with the Greek and Latin versions, it is likely that the Coptic
said something about the Evangelist's quickness, fitness, or age. The
reconstruction ⲉⲩⲙ[ⲏⲧ](ⲉ) ⲛ̄ [ϭⲟⲧ] ⲛ̄ ⲣⲱⲙⲉ ⲡⲉ, "being the middle of
the age of a man," that is, "middle-aged," fits well here. If this is accepted
as the proper reconstruction of the damaged line of the Coptic, the
three versions share a total of eight elements of the description.

There is, however, one more parallel in the description. Both Greek
and Latin lists begin by describing Mark's nose as long (*Vaticanus
graecus 866*, μακρόρυγχος; Latin, *longo naso*). In the Graeco-Roman
physiognomic tradition, a prominent nose signifies a noble soul.[32] Lefort
translates the Coptic here, no doubt under the influence of the other
versions, as "au long nez." But for "long nose" in Sahidic we expect
ϣⲁⲛⲧϥ̄ ⲭⲟⲥⲉ; the fragment, however, reads ⲡⲉϥϣⲁ ⲭⲟⲥⲉ. Though
the word ϣⲁ in Sahidic means "nose," it also means "festival," as in the
Coptic gloss for Easter, ⲡϣⲁ ⲛ̄ ⲡⲉⲛⲥⲱⲧⲏⲣ, literally, "the festival of
our Savior."[33] The possessive for "nose" is formed usually with a
pronominal suffix (ϣⲁⲛⲧϥ̄); a possessive infix is used with "festival"
(ⲡⲉϥϣⲁ), as we have in our text.[34] Therefore, the more likely translation
of ⲡⲉϥϣⲁ ⲭⲟⲥⲉ is not "his nose (ϣⲁ) is long," but "his festival (ϣⲁ) is
exalted." And so the Coptic description begins, "His person (ⲡⲣⲱⲥⲟⲡⲟⲛ;
Greek, πρόσωπον) is great, and his festival is exalted." The annual
memorial of the Evangelist, celebrated "gloriously, gravely, and
prayerfully," is mentioned several lines earlier in Lefort's fragment.[35]
The proposed reconstruction suggests that the Greek and Latin witnesses
are posterior to that of the Coptic fragment, indeed derived from it. The

[32] Ibid.

[33] Cited in W. E. Crum, *A Coptic Dictionary* (Oxford: Clarendon Press, 1939),
543a.

[34] Crum, in his entry for "nose" (*Coptic Dictionary*, 544a), cites only Lefort's
fragment for reading ⲡⲉϥϣⲁ ⲭⲟⲥⲉ as μακρόρυγχος. In the same place he cites
J. Pierpont Morgan Library *44*, 39, in which it is said of Christ that he is ϣⲁⲛⲧϥ̄
ⲭⲟⲥⲉ. Presumably Crum understands both Coptic phrases to describe a long, high, or
otherwise "exalted" nose. As I argue here, however, we need not assume that these two
phrases, ⲡⲉϥϣⲁ ⲭⲟⲥⲉ and ϣⲁⲛⲧϥ̄ ⲭⲟⲥⲉ, are equivalent.

[35] Lefort, "Fragment copte-sahidique," 227.

former two witnesses subsequently misconstrued the meaning of ϣⲁ here at the point of translation from the Coptic. Perhaps with physiognomic conventions in mind, the Latin and Greek read πρόσωπον as "face" instead of "personage," and so ϣⲁ as "nose" instead of "festival." The physical description thus offers additional evidence for the priority of the Coptic version.

Though possessing a few elements in common with the personal description found in Greek, Latin, and Coptic, the Arabic differs from the other witnesses and as such is another profile altogether: "And this pure one was of middle height, with dark blue eyes, and large eyebrows, with curly hair, full of divine grace."[36] Here we see that the Arabic phase of transmission was discriminating as well as faithful. This discrimination of the Arabic version is also manifest in its account of the signal event of the *Acts of Mark*—the lynching of the Evangelist by devotees of the Hellenistic Egyptian god Sarapis. The enraged crowd that lynches Mark cries out, "Drag the buffalo to the Boukolou" (σύρομεν τὸν βούβαλον εἰς τὰ Βουκόλου, *trahamus bubalum ad loca Buculi*). This is an alliterative catchphrase in Greek and Latin, apparently a pun that was transparent enough to the story's first audiences.[37] The bucolic wordplay here suggests an allusion to the ancient cult of Apis, which contributed the distinctively Egyptian element of the syncretized Hellenistic Sarapis cult. The Apis bull, a representation of the eternal Osiris, had, since Pharaonic times, been ceremonially interred at Memphis in a special burial ground west of the city. The cult of Sarapis and the cult of Jesus Christ occasionally were engaged in bitter conflict with each other in Alexandria. The persecution of Christians in Egypt at the turn of the third century may have been due to Septimius Severus's championing of the Sarapis cult.[38] As early as the mid-fourth century

[36] Lewis, *Mythological Acts*, 129.

[37] The phrase is repeated in an early medieval Coptic homily on Mark the Evangelist: ⲥⲩⲗⲁ (Greek, σύρειν) ⲡϣⲟϣ ⲉ ⲡⲙⲁ ⲛ̄ ⲛ̄ⲃⲟⲩⲕⲟⲗⲟⲥ. In describing the location of an Egyptian church, a manuscript in the Bibliothèque Nationale provides a gloss for the place-name "Boukolou": ⲧⲁ ⲃⲟⲩⲕⲟⲗⲟⲥ ⲉⲧⲉⲡⲙⲁ ⲛ̄ ⲛ̄ϣⲟⲟϣ ⲡⲉ, "the Boukolou, that is, the place of the buffaloes."

[38] John G. Davies, "Was the Devotion of Septimius Severus to Serapis the Cause of the Persecution of 202–3?" *JTS* 5 (1954): 73–76.

C.E., the Christian poet Paulinus of Nola knows of this tradition of Mark's conflict with Apis in Alexandria (*Carmen* 19, lines 84–85).[39] The patriarch Cyril (412–444) was still suppressing the cults of Sarapis and Isis during his episcopate, more than a quarter century after the destruction of the Alexandrian Serapeum by a Christian mob in 391. The lexical association of the place of Mark's martyrdom and the cultic terms of Sarapis worship suggest that this site of Christian veneration was somehow identified with Sarapis prior to its sacralization as a martyrion; perhaps it was a terrain of contestation for the two popular Alexandrian cults. All these narrative cues indicate that the relation of early Egyptian Christianity to the Sarapis cult was important to the story in its earliest form. Remarkably, however, the Arabic version of the *Acts of Mark* makes no mention of Sarapis. For the Arabic, the conflict between Christ and Sarapis is less than a memory. Perhaps in the tradition of transmission through which our Arabic comes, a scribe (and the readership) no longer understood the Sarapis references and so dropped them. The Arabic translation of the *Acts of Mark* may have been initiated as early as the ninth century in Egypt: by this time the cult of Sarapis had been dead for almost four hundred years, and its memory may have been much too dim to recuperate. The translator of the Arabic, or perhaps one of the predecessors, did not mindlessly hand down the narrative, but removed material that was irrelevant or unclear.

A reconstructed Coptic *Vorlage* may explain other peculiarities of the Arabic. After Mark is abducted by the mob and dragged through the city streets, he is thrown into prison for the night while the Greeks decide his fate. There, behind closed and guarded doors, Jesus Christ appears to the Evangelist in a midnight vision.

> And when he had finished his prayer, the Lord Jesus the Christ appeared to him as He had been seen among his disciples in the light that takes away pains, and said to him, "Peace to you, O Mark the Evangelist!" The Blessed Mark replied and said, "Praise be to you, O Jesus the Christ, my Lord!"[40]

---

[39] "Marcus Alexandria, tibi datus, ut boue pulso / cum Ioue nec pecudes Aegyptus in Apide demens," in *Carmina*, ed. Wilhelm August de Hartel (Leipzig: Freytag, 1894), 121.

[40] Lewis, *Mythological Acts*, 129, slightly modified.

This epiphany is related in all the versions with explicit reference to the physical form of Jesus before his passion. The phrase "light that takes away pains" has no parallel in the other versions, and has no ostensible parallel in ancient Christian literature. Where we find "in the light," we expect, on the basis of the other versions, some mention of the form of the Lord's appearance. The Arabic may be explained as a misreading of a lost Coptic *Vorlage*. If the Coptic text had referred to Jesus' form, the Coptic word lying behind the Greek μορφή, Latin *forma*, would have been ⲁⲅⲉⲓⲛ, thus the prepositional phrase ϩⲛ ⲡⲁⲅⲉⲓⲛ, "in the form." But if our Arabic translator, or the copyist of the Coptic text that was before him, misread ⲡⲁⲅⲉⲓⲛ, "the form," as ⲡⲟⲩⲟⲉⲓⲛ, "the light," the resulting prepositional phrase is ϩⲛ ⲡⲟⲩⲟⲉⲓⲛ, "in the light," the first part of this quizzical clause. The second part of the clause refers to Jesus' passion. Jesus' form in the Evangelist's epiphany is one "that takes away pains," that is, a vision of the suffering Jesus and not the exalted risen Lord: the other versions speak of the pain Jesus suffered, whereas the Arabic speaks of pain he removed. It is possible that the difference is one of theological perspective: the other versions speak of the experience of the Passion, while the Arabic speaks of its benefits. But the problem here is more likely philological than theological, and we may find its solution in a reconstruction of the lost Coptic *Vorlage* at this place in the text as well. The verb "suffer" is rendered in Coptic by the idiom ϣⲱⲡ ⲛ̄ ⲛ̄ϩⲓⲥⲉ. The verb ϣⲱⲡ by itself means "take" or "take away"; ϩⲓⲥⲉ may be glossed as "pain" or "toil." A literal translation of the Coptic idiom for "suffer," ϣⲱⲡ ⲛ̄ ⲛ̄ϩⲓⲥⲉ, is thus "to take (away) pains," and this literal translation is exactly what we read in the Arabic text. The peculiar Arabic clause therefore reflects an attempt to render a Coptic idiom. The original sense of the entire clause, then, was, "the form in which he suffered," foreshadowing Mark's suffering later in the narrative. But corruption of the Coptic intermediary in the first part of the clause and a literal translation of the second part of the clause resulted in the Arabic text, "the light which takes away pains." Though *Sinaiticus arabicus 539* corresponds very closely to the text of *Vaticanus graecus 886*, the peculiarities of this passage suggest that the Arabic was not rendered directly from Greek but from a Coptic text which was similar to *Vaticanus graecus 886* in this part of the narrative.

The Ethiopic Version of the *Acts of Mark* and the Recovery of an Arabic Intermediary

A comparative examination of the Ethiopic version of the *Acts of Mark* shows that Arabic also informs the subsequent transmission history of the narrative. There are two Ethiopic recensions of the *Martyrdom*. One is the text published and translated by E. A. Wallis Budge,[41] based on British Museum, Oriental manuscripts, *678* and *683*. These manuscripts are dated to the fifteenth century and the first half of the seventeenth century, respectively. The other Ethiopic recension is Getatchew Haile's text of the Ethiopic Manuscript Microfilm Library, Pr. no. 1763, ff. 224a–227a, which Haile himself discovered and published in 1981.[42] This manuscript is found in a collection of homilies dated 1336/37 or 1339/40 C.E., and thus is even earlier than either of those used by Budge. Using the nomenclature coined by Haile, I refer to Budge's text as *Gadla Marqos* A, that is, *Acts of Mark* A, and Haile's text as *Gadla Marqos* B. The manuscript evidence does not reach farther back than the first half of the fourteenth century. But as has been noted in another connection with respect to the Ethiopic manuscript witnesses for the Pauline epistles and their remarkable agreement with the third-century P[46] (Dublin, *Papyrus Chester Beatty II*, and Ann Arbor, *6238*), the date of an Ethiopic manuscript per se tells us little about its overall text-critical value.[43] A comparison of the two Ethiopic witnesses discloses that they represent two independently transmitted recensions of the narrative. Though the two share many readings identical in meaning, they respectively employ different though synonymous lexical items and grammatical constructions. *Gadla Marqos* A has several readings, however, that not only go against *Gadla Marqos* B but against the other witnesses as well. Upon closer examination, these readings can be explained by retroversion to an Arabic intermediary that was not thoroughly understood by the translator, as Haile has suggested.[44]

---

[41] Budge, *Contendings of the Apostles*, 1:257–64 (text); 2:309–18 (translation).
[42] Getatchew Haile, "A New Version of the *Acts of Mark*," *AnBoll* 99 (1981): 117–34.
[43] Metzger, *Early Versions of the New Testament*, 232.
[44] Haile, "New Version," 117.

Gadla Marqos B follows *Parisinus graecus 881* very closely, and Haile suggests that *Gadla Marqos* B was translated directly from the Greek.[45] But, as we shall see, the transmission history may be more complicated. Neither of the two Ethiopic recensions follow *Vaticanus graecus 866* closely, as our Arabic version does, and both make mention of Sarapis, as our Arabic does not. Therefore it is evident that, if any Arabic intermediary stands behind either or both of these recensions, it is not represented by our Arabic text but by another as yet unknown to us.

At the beginning of the narrative, Mark receives as his missionary lot the lands of Egypt, Libya, Marmarike, Ammaniake, and Pentapolis, contiguous regions of northern Africa. These regions were politically united under the Ptolemies, and this unification was augmented by the settlement of Jews throughout these areas in Ptolemaic through Roman times.[46] Under later Christian ecclesiastical administration, the Sixth Canon of Nicea recognized the "ancient custom" of jurisdiction of the Alexandrian See over all Egypt, "including Libya and Pentapolis."[47] For the name "Libya," here the *Gadla Marqos* A reads *Lonya*. This reading may be explained by positing an Arabic intermediary for *Gadla Marqos* A, as Haile has suggested.[48] The Arabic intermediary would have read, as does our Arabic version, *lubyati*. The translator had a text before him that, like most non-Quranic Arabic texts, was pointed either inconsistently or not at all. In this way the Arabic script posed special difficulties for Ethiopic translators of the Arabic texts of the Coptic Church.[49]

[45] Ibid., 118.

[46] Shim'on Applebaum, *Jews and Greeks in Ancient Cyrene* (Leiden: Brill, 1979), 131–44.

[47] William Telfer, "Episcopal Succession in Egypt," *Journal of Ecclesiastical History* 3 (1952): 12.

[48] Haile, "New Version," 118, n. 5.

[49] See the account of Murad Kamil, "Translations from Arabic in Ethiopic Literature," *Bulletin de la Société d'Archéologie Copte* 7 (1941): 69–70. Lewis also calls attention to the ambiguity of the Arabic of her manuscript for Ethiopian translators (*Mythological Acts*, xxxii). In a short article on the place-name *Hierakion* (von Lemm, "Hierakion," in *Kleine koptische Studien*, 10–12), Oscar von Lemm shows that the alternate form of the name *Hierakon* (ϩⲓⲉⲣⲁⲕⲟⲛ) was rendered in a corrupt form in Arabic due to the misconstrual of pointed Arabic consonants. This misconstrual underwent further corruption due to subsequent misconstrual by Ethiopic translators.

Ethiopic translators were constrained to render a consonantal Arabic text into a syllabary script that does not permit consonants to stand alone and allows for little ambiguity among consonantal signifiers. It is this occasional ambiguity of Arabic consonants that has garbled the transmission of *Gadla Marqos* A here. The consonants of the place-name *lubyati* without distinguishing diacritics is identical to *lunyati*, which was then rendered into Ethiopic as *lonya*. The Arabic text before the Ethiopian translator also accounts for the transliterations of "Marmarike" in *Gadla Marqos* A. The *Gadla Marqos* A scribe had before him an Arabic text reading *marmarqiya*: the translator then had to make a choice between reading the last two Arabic letters as -*qiya* or -*qī*. The former reading was chosen in *Gadla Marqos* A, thus rendered as -*qeyā*. The transliteration of *Gadla Marqos* B, *marmarqe*, could have been derived directly from the Greek *Marmarike*, and thus *Gadla Marqos* B has been translated directly from the Greek as Haile has suggested.[50] But the transliteration of the place-name may also be explained as having been transliterated from an Arabic intermediary in which the *qaf* and final *ya* were read as one syllable, -*qī*. This syllable was rendered into Ethiopic as *qē*: *Gadla Marqos* B would have been translated from an Arabic version that closely followed *Parisinus graecus 881*. This latter possibility is at least as likely as direct translation from the Greek.

The ambiguous script of an Arabic intermediary gave rise to at least one other variant in *Gadla Marqos* A. Later in the narrative, Mark is attacked and abducted by a pagan mob. The date of the attack is given first according to Egyptian and then Roman reckoning, "Pharmouthi 29, that is, April 24." *Gadla Marqos* A, however, has here not the twenty-ninth day of *Miyazya* (Pharmouthi in the Egyptian calendar), but the seventeenth. Presuming an Arabic intermediary, *Gadla Marqos* A either misread or read the misreading of the Arabic number *tis 'ati wa ishrina* ("29") as *sab 'ati 'ashrata* ("17"). The numbers 17 and 29 are almost identical orthographically, and here the former was read as the latter in the transmission of the Arabic version.

---

[50] Haile, "New Version," 118.

The Ethiopic Recensions and the Recovery of a Coptic *Vorlage*

The two Ethiopic witnesses also may indirectly testify to the Coptic version of the tradition as it has been mediated through Arabic. At the point in the narrative where Mark arrives in Alexandria, the saint is described in all the versions as having the bearing of "a noble athlete." The term "athlete" is an appellation for the martyr in Hellenistic Jewish literature,[51] and the "terminology of the games, reminiscent of the Maccabees, was long to remain the terminology of the *Acta Martyrum*."[52] Clement of Alexandria calls those who rush to martyrdom "athletes of death,"[53] and Eusebius refers to Christians who endured the violence of the third-century Severan persecution as "athletes."[54] Clearly, the description of Mark is a narrative cue that anticipates his martyrdom. But instead of the phrase "a noble athlete," *Gadla Marqos* A reads, against all the other versions, *wareza za-delewa lataqatlo*, which Budge has translated, "a young man fit to be slain." Here Hatch's Coptic fragment offers an indirect witness to the origin of this idiosyncratic reading in *Gadla Marqos* A. Where the other witnesses read the sentence, "The blessed Evangelist Mark eagerly stepped up to the arena like a noble athlete," Hatch's Bohairic fragment reads, ⲡⲓⲉⲩⲁⲅⲅⲉⲗⲓⲥⲧⲏⲥ ⲛⲁϥⲙⲟϣⲓ ⲡⲉ ⲙ̄ ⲫⲣⲏⲧ ⲛ̄ ⲟⲩⲅⲉⲛⲛⲉⲟⲥ ⲛ̄ ⲁⲑⲗⲓⲧⲏⲥ ⲉ ⲡⲓⲙⲁ ⲛ̄ †, "The Evangelist stepped up like a noble athlete to the arena." This text is related to the variant in *Gadla Marqos* A, but several steps remove it from the variant. The text of *Gadla Marqos* A is the result of a corruption that crept into the Coptic tradition at an early stage. The existence of the fragment published by Lefort is proof that the narrative had an earlier, Sahidic recension in Coptic. The earliest Coptic version of the *Acts of Mark*

---

[51] E.g., 4 Macc 17:16. D. F. Winslow ("The Maccabean Martyrs: Early Christian Attitudes," *Judaism* 23 [1974]: 81) has observed that Origen, in his *Exhortation to Martyrdom*, insinuates in his quotations from 2 Maccabees the language of the Greek games: "the martyrs are 'athletes', their struggle a 'contest', their accomplishments a 'victory.'"

[52] W. H. C. Frend, *Martyrdom and Persecution in the Early Church* (Oxford: Blackwell, 1965), 40.

[53] *Strom.* 4.17–18.

[54] Eusebius *Hist. eccl.* 6.1.

was therefore in the Sahidic dialect. Retroverted from Bohairic into the Sahidic dialect, the text reads, ⲡⲓⲉⲩⲁⲅⲅⲉⲗⲓⲥⲧⲏⲥ ⲛⲉϥⲙⲟⲟϣⲉ ⲡⲉ ⲛ̄ ⲑⲉ ⲛ̄ ⲟⲩⲅⲉⲛ ⲛⲉⲟⲥ ⲛ̄ ϣⲟⲉⲓⲝ ⲉ ⲡⲙⲁ ⲛ̄ ϣⲱⲝⲉ. If ⲅⲉⲛ were dropped from ⲟⲩⲅⲉⲛ in the first line, the following text is the result: ⲡⲓⲉⲩⲁⲅⲅⲉⲗⲓⲥⲧⲏⲥ ⲛⲉϥⲙⲟⲟϣⲉ ⲡⲉ ⲛ̄ ⲑⲉ ⲛ̄ⲟⲩⲛⲉⲟⲥ ⲛ̄ ϣⲟⲉⲓⲝ ⲉ ⲡⲙⲁ ⲛ̄ ϣⲱⲝⲉ. Instead of the adjective "noble" (ⲅⲉⲛⲛⲉⲟⲥ; Greek, γενναῖος), the fragment ⲛⲉⲟⲥ survives the parablepsis to be translated as the adjective "young" (Greek, νέος), thus, ⲟⲩⲛⲉⲟⲥ ⲛ̄ ϣⲟⲉⲓⲝ, "a young athlete." The ⲛ̄ ϣⲟⲉⲓⲝ, "(an) athlete," fell out at some point in the Sahidic transmission of the *Acts of Mark*. In the resultant reading, ⲟⲩⲛⲉⲟⲥ ⲉ ⲡⲙⲁ ⲛ̄ ϣⲱⲝⲉ, the word ⲟⲩⲛⲉⲟⲥ is read not as the adjective "young" but as the substantive "a young man," thus the phrase "a young man to the place of battle." The second part of this phrase in *Gadla Marqos* A, "worthy of death," may be explained as a misreading of the last line in the retroverted passage, ⲉ ⲡⲙⲁ ⲛ̄ ϣⲱⲝⲉ, "to the place of battle." In the continuous script of the Sahidic text, the single letter ⲡ was read as the two letters ⲧⲓ. This resultant reading was ⲉ ⲧⲓⲙⲁ (Greek, τιμᾶ) ⲛ̄ ϣⲱⲝⲉ, "to be worthy to fight." ⲛ̄ ϣⲱⲝⲉ is read not as the noun ϣⲱⲝⲉ, "battle," with the genitive particle ⲛ̄, but as the verb ϣⲱⲝⲉ, "to fight," a complementary infinitive introduced by the particle ⲛ̄. This reading was then translated into Arabic, the missing Arabic intermediary between the Sahidic Coptic version and the Ethiopic version of *Gadla Marqos* A. This chain of transmission is obscured by Budge's translation. Budge has translated *la-taqatlo* here as "to be slain," the passive of *qatala*, "to kill." But this passive form of the verb is also used idiomatically, meaning "to fight, to engage in battle."[55] If we so translate *Gadla Marqos* A here, *za-delewa la-taqatlo*, "worthy to fight," is a perfect verbatim translation of the proposed misreading ⲉ ⲧⲓⲙⲁ ⲛ̄ ϣⲱⲝⲉ. These conjectures suggest that the chain of variants begins with the Sahidic. The Sahidic variants are linked by an Arabic intermediary to the Ethiopic tradition as represented by *Gadla Marqos* A. The conjectures also indicate an independent transmission history for the two Ethiopic versions, for *Gadla Marqos* B agrees with the other versions here against *Gadla Marqos* A.

---

[55] See August Dillmann, *Lexicon Linguae Ethiopicae* (New York: Ungar, 1955), 440, § III.2.

We may discern the residual effects of a Coptic *Vorlage* in *Gadla Marqos* B as well. The trace, however, is at first puzzling. At the end of the narrative, the text of *Gadla Marqos* B reads that Mark was martyred "in Greece, in Alexandria," *ba-ṣer' ba-'eleskenderya*. None of the other versions say anything about Greece here or anywhere else in the *Acts of Mark*. This bizarre reading may be explained by reading *ṣer'* not as the place-name "Greece" but, with the preposition *ba* ("in"), as the noun "the Greek (language)," that is, "in the Greek language." The phrase *ba-ṣer'* is so rendered in the Ethiopic version of Luke 23:38 as one of the three languages on the titulus of Jesus' cross. Thus we must read here, "in the Greek language, in Alexandria." This remark in the text indicates that, in its *Vorlage*, the name "Alexandria," the Greek name of the city, was not used. It is only at this point in the text that, out of consideration for a readership more familiar with the Greek place-name, the redactor or translator provides it. Throughout the *Vorlage* of the *Gadla Marqos* B, another name was used to refer to Alexandria. That other name could only be the autochthonous Sahidic name for the city, "Rhakote" (Bohairic, "Rhakoti"). Only in a Coptic text would Alexandria be referred to consistently as Rakote. The language of the *Vorlage*, therefore, must have been Coptic. The fragmentary Coptic witnesses refer to the city only by its Egyptian name in the Coptic language. The *Vorlage* of the *Gadla Marqos* B used "Rhakote" wherever we now read "Alexandria" except here at the very end of the text, where the *Vorlage* glossed "Rhakote" as "Alexandria" for the benefit of readers who knew the city by its Greek name. The vestigial note of the Coptic *Vorlage* was retained in the chain of transmission and translated as it stood in *Gadla Marqos* B.

Conclusion

The purpose of translating the Holy Gospel into the Arabic language was originally only because of its coming to predominate in a community, such as happened among us; or because of the proficiency of the person who produced the book in two languages; or for some purpose other than these two. And because of the certainty that [the Gospel] must not be read in the churches except in their own languages, apart from which they know no other, they went to the limit of their capacity in its translation, and the demands of effective composition did not stop them from the translation of what they had begun. Therefore, a certain degree of disparity is found between [the Gospel] and. . .[its translations].[56]

The foregoing comparison of the Arabic with the Greek, Latin, Coptic, and Ethiopic versions of the *Acts of Mark* suggests that a Coptic *Vorlage* ultimately stands behind them. The Arabic thus serves as a linguistic pivot on which we may turn in the transmission history to both the translation of the Greek, Latin, and Ethiopic versions and to the early Coptic stage of transmission. We have seen in our investigation of one work of the Arabic apocrypha that it is only because of the faithfulness of the Arabic tradents that we can discern and reconstruct the discontinuities in a continuous tradition of a thousand years. The medieval Arabic translators insisted on being faithful to the texts they betrayed: their faithfulness forced them "to the limit of their capacity" and, apparently, beyond. They were compelled to undertake the collation of disparate manuscripts in several languages, practicing a textual science that, through evaluation and emendation, corrected into existence yet more texts, new texts beside the old, producing new texts by reproducing old ones. The Arabic tradition, straddled between versions and recensions, is thus poised to tell us about the whole transmission history of the text from the sum of its parts. Without the fidelity of the tradents, the complexity of their labors would leave no residuum of correction, emendation, and error. Perhaps here, taking exception to the old adage, we may say that in a profound sense the translators did not betray what was before them. They rose to the challenge of rendering in the tongue of the infidel and oppressor, a tongue now their own, the polyglot heritage of the Christian East. The Arabic version of the *Acts of Mark* bears cryptic testimony to both the fidelity and complexity, the continuity and discontinuity, of Coptic Christendom's transmission and translation of the New Testament apocrypha as part of its precious, ancient heritage.

---

[56] From the preface of a mid-thirteenth-century diglot Coptic-Arabic manuscript of the four gospels, in Abd El-Nour, "Epact Numerals," 15.

Byzantine Witnesses for the Apocryphal Acts of the Apostles

François Bovon

In the ninth century, Photius, patriarch of Constantinople, gave a double witness: first, that he still had direct access to several Apocryphal Acts of the Apostles; second, that he believed that this literature was pernicious to the Christian faith.[1] Photius's attitude toward the apocryphal acts was not the only one represented in the Byzantine period. At that time there was strong interest in the lives of the apostles—as well as that of the Virgin Mary—for hagiographic, liturgical, homiletic, historiographic, and artistic purposes. With this interest in mind, priests, monks, historians, and hierarchs were eager to find, preserve, and transmit narrative material about the first Christian generation. However, much of the so-called apocryphal material had been either eliminated by the official church or domesticated in one way or another by the end of the patristic period. In the latter case, it was no longer perceived as apocryphal at all, but, instead, was viewed as historical documentation[2]

My thanks to Steven J. Larson, a former M.T.S. student at the Harvard Divinity School, now a doctoral student at Brown University, who helped with the editing of this paper. I appreciate his willingness to help and his interest in Byzantine literature.

[1] *Bibliotheca*, Codex 114, *PG* 103, 389; Photius *Bibliothèque* 2, ed. and trans. René Henry (Paris: Les Belles Lettres, 1960), 84–86; see also Éric Junod, "Actes apocryphes et hérésie. Le jugement de Photius," in *Actes apocryphes des apôtres*, 11–24.

[2] For example, the *Protevangelium of James*, which had never been condemned in the eastern part of the Christian world. See Émile Amann, *Le Protévangile de Jacques et ses remaniements latins* (Paris: Letouzey et Ané, 1910), 119–21, on its reception in the Byzantine Church. See also François Bovon, "The Suspension of Time in Chapter 18 of *Protevangelium Jacobi*," in *The Future of Early Christianity: Essays in Honor of Helmut Koester*, ed. Birger A. Pearson (Minneapolis: Fortress Press, 1991), 393–405.

or hagiographic material.[3] Let me provide several examples of this survival of the apocryphal Christian literature.

The church leaders responsible for the liturgical lives of their congregations used apocryphal legends. At the feasts of each apostle they sang hymns in their honor and gave a summary or larger report of each of their lives.[4] The source from which such material was drawn was often apocryphal stock, as can be seen particularly well in the case of the apostle Peter. The earliest form of the *Acts of Peter* has been transformed and adapted to the extent that, as early as Pseudo-Hegesippus,[5] for example, Paul and Peter are martyred in Rome simultaneously. It is not by chance that most of the lost apocryphal material has been recovered from hagiographic sources.[6]

What was true for liturgical needs was equally true for homiletic purposes. There is, for instance, a Byzantine homily which explicitly mentions the book of the *Acts of Philip*.[7] As a preacher, then, the eighth- or ninth-century priest who consulted it did not hesitate to look to the original *Acts of Philip*, which others despised as an unorthodox text. The same can be said several centuries later for Pseudo-Anastasius the Sinaite who quotes the same book, in order to establish the validity of

---

[3] For example, the *Metastasis of John*, which is *AJn* 106–15 (Junod and Kaestli, *Acta Iohannis*, 1:317–43); see also Junod and Kaestli, *L'histoire des Actes apocryphes des apôtres*.

[4] Hymns and odes are collected in the *Menaia* or the *Akolouthia* of the saint. Biographical summaries are given in the *Synaxarion*, while expanded narratives are given in the *Menologion*. On these terms, see pp. 9–10 of this volume.

[5] This is a late-fourth-century text. *Hegesippi Qui Dicitur Historiae Libri V*, ed. Vincent Ussani (CSEL 66; Vienna: Hoelder-Pichler-Tempski; Leipzig: Akademische Verlagsgesellschaft, 1932), 1.183–87; see also Gérard Poupon in *Actes apocryphes des apôtres*, 299–301; and Thomas, "Acts of Peter."

[6] *Menologia*, particularly premetaphrastic *Menologia*, have been the most productive of the liturgical sources. See above, pp. 9–10. See, for example, the *Acts of Thomas* in *AAA* 2/2:99–291; Yves Tissot in *Actes apocryphes des apôtres*, 304–5; idem, "L'encratisme des Actes de Thomas," *ANRW* II 25/6:4415–30; André-Jean Festugière, *Les Actes apocryphes de Jean et de Thomas* (Geneva: Cramer, 1983); and Caroline Johnson, "Ritual Epicleses in the Greek *Acts of Thomas*," included in this volume.

[7] *BHG* 1530b; published by Albert Frey, "L'*Éloge de Philippe, saint apôtre et évangéliste du Christ (BHG* 1530b)," *Apocrypha* 3 (1992): 165–209.

the fasting period before Christmas.[8] Such interest in this literature is explained by the desire to know more about the life of the apostles and the origins of the church. At the same time, however, many were convinced that the apocryphal acts contained speeches that were at odds with the established orthodoxy. Furthermore, the fact that these writings had been respected as authoritative documents by heretical communities, like the Manichaeans, confirmed the suspicions of orthodox readers.

During the Byzantine period there were several cultural renaissances, each of which involved an interest in historical research. Interest in the history of the church never diminished from the time of Eusebius to that of the Byzantine historian Nicephorus Callistus Xanthopulus.[9] Each Byzantine church historian had to write a chapter—and often more than one chapter—on the early church, particularly the lives and responsibilities of the apostles. It is not surprising that these historians, in spite of Photius's reluctance, used the Apocryphal Acts of the Apostles abundantly to fill these first chapters of their works.

This historical perspective was sometimes connected with exhortation, edification, or even entertainment. Note what Gregory of Tours did with the *Acts of Andrew*: he prepared a complete orthodox rewriting, the so-called *Epitome*, omitting the suspect sermons.[10] The same was done in the East with the *Acts of Thomas* by Nicetas of Thessaloniki,[11] with the *Acts of Philip* by an anonymous author,[12] and with the *Acts of John* in Ireland.[13] This Byzantine or medieval material

---

[8] *PG* 89, 1396–97. The forty days of fasting started on the fourteenth of November, the date of the feast of St. Philip. On Pseudo-Anastasius the Sinaite, see François Bovon, "Les Actes de Philippe," *ANRW* II 25/6:4452–53.

[9] This is particularly clear in Nicephorus *Historia ecclesiastica* 2.39 (*PG* 145, 860–61). Nicephorus lived between approximately 1256 and 1335.

[10] In *Gregorii episcopi Turonensis liber de miraculis beati Andreae apostoli*, ed. Maximilien Bonnet, Monumenta Germaniae Historica, Scriptores Rerum Merouingicarum 1 (Hannover: Hahn, 1885), 821–46; reprinted with a French translation and an introduction in Prieur, *Acta Andreae* 1:8–12, 2:551–651.

[11] *BHG* 1832; see Geerard, *Clavis Apocryphorum*, no. 247.

[12] *Parisinus graecus 1551* in *AAA* 2/2:91–98; see also François Bovon, "Les Actes de Philippe" *ANRW* II 25/6:4445.

[13] See Martin McNamara, *Apocrypha in the Irish Church* (Dublin: Dublin Institute for Advanced Studies, 1975), 95–98; see also Junod and Kaestli, *Acta Iohannis* 1:11–12, 109–16.

in all its forms is useful not only for understanding the ongoing influence of apocryphal literature in Christian culture but also occasionally to recover the plot of the narrative sequence of lost acts.

The iconographic material is no less interesting. In Monreale (Sicily) one finds apocryphal scenes alongside biblical motifs, such as Peter crucified upside down or Simon Magus falling from the sky.[14] The monastery of Dionysiou on Mount Athos contains frescoes with portrayals of the martyrdom of several apostles, particularly that of Philip.[15] The handbook for Byzantine painters by Dionysos of Fourna is full of advice derived from apocryphal material.[16] Even earlier Christian art witnesses to the interest in apocryphal literature. The apocryphal story of the conversion and baptism of Peter's jailers in the Mamertine prison is known through fourth-century representations on sarcophagi that predate any literary evidence.[17]

It is important, therefore, to search not only in the patristic quotations but also in the ocean of Byzantine, so-called oriental, and Latin literature of the Middle Ages. Byzantine scholars, from Karl Krumbacher to Hans-Georg Beck, agree that authors and preachers of the Byzantine period read and used apocryphal traditions.[18] Surely much more can be found

---

[14] The latter scene was chosen as a logo for the Series Apocryphorum.

[15] This last image served as the front page of the first catalogue of the Series Apocryphorum.

[16] For example, for the prophetess Anna, whose praise of God has now been formulated: "This child is the creator of the world" (compare Luke 2:36–38), *The "Painter's Manual" of Dionysius of Fourna*, trans. Paul Hetherington (London: Sagitarius, 1974), 32.

[17] See Erich Dinkler, *Die ersten Petrusdarstellungen. Ein archäologischer Beitrag zur Geschichte des Petrusprimates* (Marburger Jahrbuch für Kunstwissenschaft 11 [1938], published with vol. 12 [1939]; Marburg: n.p., 1941), 1–79; see also François Bovon, *De Vocatione Gentium. Histoire de l'interprétation d'Act. 10, 1–11, 18 dans les six premiers siècles* (BGBE 8; Tübingen: Mohr [Siebeck], 1967), 292–95.

[18] See Karl Krumbacher, *Geschichte der byzantinischen Literatur von Justinian bis zum Ende des oströmischen Reiches (527–1453)*, zweite Auflage bearbeitet unter der Mitwirkung von A. Ehrhard und H. Gelzer (Handbuch der klassischen Altertums-wissenschaft 9.1; Munich: Beck, 1897), 167–68; Hans-Georg Beck, *Kirche und theologische Literatur im byzantinischen Reich* (Byzantinisches Handbuch im Rahmen des Handbuches der Altertumswissenschaft 2.1; Munich: Beck, 1977), 402–13; and Éveline Patlagean, "Remarques sur la diffusion et la production des apocryphes dans le monde byzantin," *Apocrypha* 2 (1991): 155–63.

to improve our knowledge of early apocryphal texts. One example from the field of homiletics will not only illustrate this statement but, at the same time, call for further research in this field.

Nicetas David, or Nicetas of Paphlagonia, was born around 885. He was initially a professor, but after opposing, with Arethas, Emperor Leo VI on the question of his "four marriages," he withdrew for several years to a monastery, living as a monk under the name of David. Around 910, he left the monastery, wrote a series of documents against the patriarch Photius, and eventually became a very famous and active preacher. We know of more than fifty sermons written by him for saints' days or for various other feast days.[19] Jacques Paul Migne's *Patrologia Graeca* contains a collection of twenty of his homilies, mainly on the apostles.[20]

Of these homilies, I shall consider the *Oratio octava* on James, son of Alphaeus, because no ancient acts from this apostle have survived[21] and the only known *Passio* on him has not been published.[22] Reading through it and the entire collection, I understand the main reason for the Byzantine interest in and remembrance of the apostles' lives. This insight may already have occurred to Eastern Orthodox or Roman Catholic theologians, but it was only recently that I, a Protestant scholar, gained it through the reading and analysis of this homily. A review of the text, with attention given to its structure and composition, will help you to understand what I learned.[23]

The beginning brings us into a liturgical framework, particularly into the liturgical calendar: it is a feast day, "to the holy and most famous

---

[19] See *The Oxford Dictionary of Byzantium*, ed. Alexander Kazhdan (New York/ Oxford: Oxford University Press, 1991), 1480; Krumbacher, *Geschichte der byzantinischen Literatur*, 167–68; Beck, *Kirche und theologische Literatur*, 548, 565–66.

[20] *PG* 105, 15–488.

[21] On James, son of Alphaeus, see Lipsius, *Die apokryphen Apostelgeschichten* 2/2:229–38. For a criticism of Lipsius's position, see pp. 96–97.

[22] *BHG* 762z.

[23] *Oratio VIII. Laudatio sancti ac celebratissimi Jacobi Alphaei* [I correct the misprint "Alphœi"] *apostoli*, *PG* 105, 145–64. This is *BHG* 763. The Greek text, which is not divided into numbered paragraphs, is accompanied by a Latin translation and several footnotes.

apostle James son of Alphaeus."[24] On such a day the preacher has the task of reminding his audience—reminding "us"—of the pains, struggles, and martyrdom of that particular saint. The apostle himself, who is believed to be alive in heaven, calls both "us" and the choir of holy angels to join in communion and festival. This means that for this day the apostle in heaven and the preacher on earth bring together the heavenly company and the earthly congregation. During this mystical meeting, the Christians in the church will both give and receive. They will bring as spiritual fruits their prayers, their good disposition, and their faith, and they will simultaneously receive spiritual fruits from the homiletic evocation of both the spiritual and bodily life of James. The holy apostle, as a disciple of Christ, will contribute to our spiritual education and help us to receive the knowledge of the great mystery of piety. Nicetas contends that it is necessary to start from this spiritual gathering and not just from a historical recollection. Such is the summary of this theoretical and practical introduction. The memory of the apostle and of his life is therefore not just interesting, it is vital. To know the apostle James is not just a cultural accessory; for the Byzantine audience it corresponds to a theological necessity.[25]

What, though, is to be remembered about the apostle? Reading through this and several other homilies by Nicetas, for example on the apostles John, Philip, Bartholomew, and Andrew, I was initially disappointed by the bombastic style and lack of concrete information on the apostles' lives. Only later, when I understood the strategy of the preacher in his liturgical setting, was I able to follow and appreciate his homiletic construction. First, after the introduction, there is a spiritual description of the apostle.[26] What the preacher wants his congregation to know and to remember about James, son of Alphaeus, is not what a modern specialist of the Apocryphal Acts of the Apostles wishes to hear. It is the disclosure of the apostle's spiritual life: what James received from God's grace, through the Son of God, with the pouring

---

[24] εἰς τὸν ἅγιον καὶ πανεύφημον ἀπόστολον Ἰάκωβον τὸν τοῦ Ἀλφαίου, *PG* 105, 145. Such is the title of the text (see the Latin translation in the previous note). It is not certain that this title comes from Nicetas himself.

[25] What is summarized in this paragraph is found in *PG* 105, 149.

[26] Ibid., 152–53.

out of the Holy Spirit, that is, the spiritual ascension of the apostle through virtue and asceticism, which gave him merit to be one member of the most venerable "dodecade."

Nicetas thus gives his audience a detailed description of James's spiritual identity, religious itinerary, and interior life. He describes the holy man as a genuine child of divine grace, a noble branch of the true grapevine, which was pruned by God, the heavenly farmer, rooted in the Son, and enriched by the Holy Spirit.[27] Reading this long description makes one aware that it was not only—nor primarily—the absence of historical information that led to the overblown language of this section of the sermon. There was instead a theological reason: to know someone correctly is to know her or him through the eyes of faith and piety, an internal knowledge superior to that which is external or historical.

The preacher, however, progressively makes it clear that Christianity is not only a form of spirituality; it is a historical religion. This aspect receives emphasis in the second part of his homily. The soul and the body cannot be separated. James attached himself to Christ not only in his spirit, but also in his own flesh.[28] He learned that one cannot serve two masters, so he chose to obey Christ's law. Nicetas gives a description of James's conversion to Christ. In his admiration, the preacher starts to address James himself. He declares blessed "your body, sacred tent" (σου τὸ σῶμα, τὸ ἱερὸν σκήνωμα) of the Trinity and "the soul in which the Father was pleased to dwell, which the Only Begotten chose and on which the Holy Spirit came to repose marvelously" (τὴν ψυχὴν ἐν ᾗ εὐδόκησεν ὁ πατήρ, ἣν ᾑρέτισεν ὁ μονογενής, ἐφ᾽ ᾗ τὸ πνεῦμα τὸ ἅγιον θαυμαστῶς ἐπανεπαύσατο).[29]

James is historically relevant on several accounts: as an eyewitness to Christ's miracles, as an adherent to Christ's words, as a participant in Christ's passion,[30] and, after Christ's ascension, as an active apostle and a martyr. Nicetas mentions all sorts of travels, agonies, and humiliations, including persecution by the Jews and heathen uprisings against him. Finally, James is crucified, wherein Nicetas emphasizes

[27] Ibid., 152A.
[28] Ibid., 153CD.
[29] Ibid., 153D.
[30] Ibid., 156B.

that he left his body behind him as a sanctuary for us and joined God to enjoy in spirit the divine company.[31]

Nicetas suddenly stops and indicates that his speech mentioning James's laurel wreaths, which Nicetas had given before enumerating James's struggles, had, like an ardent horse, escaped Nicetas's attention. At this point he returns to James's historical life.[32] The following sentence, which the reader then meets, needs an explanation: "Therefore, the roads of Wisdom's children, namely Christ's fortunate disciples, are difficult to detect and their actions impossible to know with precision" (οὕτω καὶ τῶν τῆς σοφίας τέκνων, τῶν πανολβίων, λέγω, Χριστοῦ μαθητῶν, δυσθεώρητοι μὲν αἱ ὁδοί, ἀνεπίγνωστοι δὲ πρὸς ἀκρίβειαν αἱ πράξεις).[33] At first glance one could understand the sentence as saying that Nicetas had at his disposal little historical material on James. Upon reflection, however, one could say that Nicetas, as a modest preacher, could not properly understand the high quality of James's life. The next sentence supports this second reading: "The great works of these men exceed any human intelligence or human speech."[34] Still, the first interpretation may also possess an element of truth, namely, that Nicetas did not have at his disposal very much information on James. As we shall see, though, what he did have was not an insignificant amount.

In the concluding paragraphs of his *Oratio*,[35] Nicetas writes in a very flowery style of the depth of James's miracles, the wisdom of his speeches, the extent of his travels, and the dangers and persecutions he had to face, particularly from the "Hellenists."[36] With increasingly precise detail—and probably building upon a legend derived from the lost *Acts of James, son of Alphaeus*—Nicetas describes the suffering

---

[31] Ibid., 156BC.

[32] Ibid., 157AB.

[33] Ibid., 157B.

[34] Ibid.

[35] Ibid., 157B–164C.

[36] Ibid., 157C. The term "Hellenists" is interesting and means precisely, as in Acts 6–9, Jewish people speaking Greek and living in Palestine. The first two cities mentioned as places of James's activity, Eleutheropolis and Gaza, are both in Palestine and inhabited by Jews, most of whom spoke Greek. On the Hellenists, see Martin Hengel, "Between Jesus and Paul," in idem, *Between Jesus and Paul: The Earliest Christian Response to Jesus* (Philadelphia: Fortress Press, 1983), 1–29.

James endured in Eleutheropolis. The subsequent section is an itinerary moving through Gaza, Tyre, and the surrounding villages. The numerous conversions and baptisms there, as well as the installation of priests and archpriests—in a word, the establishment of new churches—are also worth mentioning. As Nicetas says: One full day would not be sufficient to mention with precision all the apostolic theology and activity (πρᾶξις).[37]

Finally, Nicetas comes to the story of James's crucifixion,[38] which inspires him to recite a hymn to the cross: "Then you added it [the cross] as a most beautiful last stroke to your great pains and struggles. I sing to the cross to which you extended your venerable and sacred arms, through which you gave glory to your God and Lord. I sing to the cross because it was planted for you as a ladder leading straight from earth to heaven. . . ."[39] Following this, Nicetas gives a summary of James's passion narrative in Egypt, where he had established his camp at Cedar[40] as the true Israelite.[41] The name of the city of James's martyrdom was Ostrakine.[42] Paradoxically, this martyrdom brought Christ's favor to these regions and cities, undoubtedly because of the expiatory power that the martyrdom possessed.[43] Like the apostle Andrew in the *Acts of Andrew*,[44] James here is said to have spoken at length to his persecutors and to the crowd from the cross. Judging from the narrative, his agony was not difficult to bear. The apostle smiled from the cross,[45] while urging the heathens to know Christ,[46] and

[37] *PG* 105, 157D

[38] Ibid., 160.

[39] Ibid., 160A.

[40] Ibid. This biblical expression (compare Ps 119:1) probably has a metaphorical meaning here, namely, the country of the adversary.

[41] *PG* 105, 160A (ὁ ἀληθινὸς Ἰσραηλίτης). See *PG* 105, 152B (ὁ ἀληθῶς Ἰσραηλίτης). James is identified in this way, as Nathanael is identified by Jesus in John 1:48.

[42] *PG* 105, 160B.

[43] Ibid.

[44] *AAn* 53(3). See Prieur, *Acta Andreae*, 2:510–15 and 2:735–45.

[45] *PG* 105, 160B.

[46] There is a lay lyric passage giving many epithets to Christ and describing what it means to know God (ibid., 160C–161A). As the italics in Migne's edition suggests, these lines may well be a quotation, but from which text?

admonishing them to stop idolatrous behavior.[47] He then died quietly at the end of his last sermon.[48] Nicetas's *Oratio* ends with an ornate series of salutations and congratulations to James.[49]

Nicetas is certainly not inventing the story of James's travel, mission, and martyrdom. He probably used a traditional martyrdom narrative. We know that such hagiographical texts were composed during the early Byzantine period, either by excising the last part of ancient Apocryphal Acts of the Apostles or by imitating one of them. Two pieces of information are important about James, son of Alphaeus.[50] First, about three centuries after Nicetas, the Byzantine historian Nicephorus Callistus Xanthopulus mentions the same story about the same apostle in his *Historia ecclesiastica*.[51] There is one discrepancy between the two accounts. Nicetas's itinerary seems to move from Eleutheropolis to Gaza, while Nicephorus's moves in the opposite direction. Both accounts, however, have borrowed from the same older story concerning James, son of Alphaeus. Second, there is a different—although very similar—narrative, which some have attributed to Simon-Judas[52] and others to Thaddaeus-Lebbaeus.[53] According to Richard Adelbert Lipsius, this other story is older and Nicetas used it to write James's life and martyrdom. As we know, however, the whole matter concerning the so-called *Lives of the Apostles* has to be studied again.

---

[47] Ibid., 161A.

[48] Ibid., 161BC.

[49] Ibid., 161C–164C, with the anaphor, χαῖρε ("hail").

[50] If the Eastern churches distinguished between the three Jameses (Zebedee's son, the Lord's brother, and Alphaeus's son), the Western world—with some exception, influenced by Jerome, who was not always consistent—merged into one person the Lord's brother and Alphaeus's son, recognizing, therefore, only two Jameses in their liturgical calendar; see Lipsius, *Die apokryphen Apostelgeschichten* 2/2:229–31, 235–38.

[51] Nicephorus *Historia ecclesiastica* 2.40 (*PG* 145, 864).

[52] Found in Dorotheos's text B and, in a shorter version, in text A of the *Lives of the Apostles*; see Theodor Schermann, *Propheten- und Apostellegenden nebst Jüngerkatalogen des Dorotheus und verwandter Texte* (TU 31/3; Leipzig: Hinrichs, 1907), 281–82.

[53] Located in the Dorotheos-Hippolytus text of the *Lives of the Apostles*; see Lipsius, *Die apokryphen Apostelgeschichten*, 2/2:233, and Schermann, *Propheten- und Apostellegenden*, 283.

It may well be that the story of one apostle has been used to tell the life of another. I am inclined, though, to believe that the mission to Eleutheropolis and the martyrdom in Ostrakine belongs to James, son of Alphaeus, and not originally to Simon-Judas or Thaddaeus-Lebbaeus. Study of the still unpublished *Passio* of James, son of Alphaeus,[54] may help us in the future. Even if Lipsius were right, Nicetas's homily would still be an important source of information, not for the rediscovery of the *Acts of James, son of Alphaeus*, but of another apostolic figure (Simon-Judas or Thaddaeus-Lebbaeus).

In any case, the itinerary of our text is important. Starting in Jerusalem, the apostle moves south to Eleutheropolis (a city located in Palestina prima, today Beit Jibrin) and Gaza, then to Tyre in the north, and finally south again—probably by sea—to Egypt. For Nicetas, the itinerary has two parts: the first takes place in Palestine in a Jewish background; the second in Egypt among the heathen. We should, however, be cautious about the sequence of the three cities of Palestine. Although they are mentioned along this itinerary (Eleutheropolis, Gaza, Tyre), the text does not explicitly say that James's travels followed this order. Nicetas, though, probably believed that they did.

Conclusion

Traces of the Apocryphal Acts of the Apostles are accessible in Byzantine writings—hagiographic, liturgical, historical, or homiletic— as well as in iconographic monuments of that period, though these documents have been neglected in favor of direct witnesses and patristic quotations. Scholars in the field of apocryphal literature should enter into what for many may be a terra incognita.

The reading of parts of this Byzantine literature helps us to understand the real interest of this period for the study of the apostles. The apostles were of vital importance inasmuch as they served as spiritual intermediaries between the church and the heavenly Christ. According to the Christian doctrine of incarnation, however, both their spiritual

---

[54] *BHG* 762z; see above, p. 91.

presence and their historical past belong to this function of mediation. Here, more than in human curiosity or local devotion, lies the main reason why Christians through the centuries remembered the destiny, not only of Christ, but also of his disciples, the apostles.

Language

The Greek Language of the Apocryphal Acts of the Apostles: A Study in Style

David H. Warren

Seventy years after it was first begun in 1906, James Hope Moulton's monumental work, *A Grammar of New Testament Greek*, was finally completed with the addition of a fourth volume entitled *Style*.[1] While a few reviewers have criticized this final contribution for some of its positions,[2] all should applaud Nigel Turner's effort in attempting to expand the scope of traditional grammar. Before Turner, style had been a neglected area in most Greek grammars on the New Testament.

---

[1] James Hope Moulton began the grammar with his famous *Prolegomena* (Edinburgh: Clark, 1906) and had written most of the second volume, *Accidence and Word Formation* (Edinburgh: Clark, 1929), when he died in 1917. Wilbert Francis Howard completed that volume, adding an important excursus on Semitisms in the New Testament (pp. 411–85). But he himself died before he could complete the volume on syntax (1952), as did his assistant, Henry George Meecham (1955). Finally Meecham's assistant, Nigel Turner, completed the volume entitled *Syntax* (Edinburgh: Clark, 1963) and concluded the grammar with the volume *Style* (Edinburgh: Clark, 1976).

[2] See especially the scathing review by G. H. R. Horsley (*New Documents Illustrating Early Christianity*, vol. 5, *Linguistic Essays* [Macquarie, New South Wales: Macquarie University, 1989], 49–65), who characterizes Turner's contribution as "markedly inferior" (p. 49) to the rest of the grammar and concludes that it is "so misguided" that it should never have been published at all (p. 61). Other reviewers, such as George Dunbar Kilpatrick (*Theologische Literaturzeitung* 104 [1979]: 109–11) and Francis T. Gignac (*Catholic Biblical Quarterly* 39 [1977]: 165–67), have been much more favorable (and charitable) in their assessments. One disappointment in the fourth volume is the use of transliteration for Greek words, an odd practice for a Greek grammar.

Friedrich Blass and Albert Debrunner[3] never specifically addressed the matter,[4] while Archibald Thomas Robertson[5] spent nearly as much time detailing the various uses of negative particles as he did analyzing the various styles of writing. Others like Turner have attempted to fill this void,[6] but the lack of agreement on methodology and even on the nature of the Greek language itself has hindered their progress.[7]

As might be expected, research on the apocryphal writings has lagged behind that of their canonical cousins. While many have written on the Greek of the New Testament, there is as yet no grammar devoted

---

[3] Friedrich Blass and Albert Debrunner, *A Greek Grammar of the New Testament and Other Early Christian Literature* (trans. and rev. Robert W. Funk; Chicago: University of Chicago Press, 1961), hereafter cited as BDF.

[4] They do incorporate some observations on style under such headings as "The Place of the New Testament within Hellenistic Greek" (§ 3), "Conjunctive Participles Combined" (§ 421, under "Mood" in the section on the syntax of the verb), and "Sentence Structure" (§ 458).

[5] Archibald Thomas Robertson, *A Grammar of the Greek New Testament in the Light of Historical Research*, 4th ed. (1923; reprint, Nashville: Broadman, 1934). The various uses of negative particles are treated on pp. 1155–75; styles of writing are discussed on pp. 116–37 (see also pp. 1194–97).

[6] Noteworthy is the monograph by Lars Rydbeck (*Fachprosa, vermeintliche Volkssprache und Neues Testament. Zur Beurteilung der sprachlichen Niveauunterschiede im nachklassischen Griechisch* [Studia Graeca Upsaliensia 5; Uppsala: University of Uppsala, 1967]), who argues that the language of the New Testament occupies a middle ground between the non-literary Koine of the papyri and inscriptions and the literary style of authors like Diodorus Siculus, Plutarch, Polybius, Strabo, and the Jewish writers Josephus and Philo. More recently, others have focused their attention on the style of individual New Testament authors, like the studies of Cuthbert Hamilton Turner on Mark's gospel, which have now been collectively published by James K. Elliott in *The Language and Style of the Gospel of Mark* (Novum Testamentum, Supplements 71; Leiden: Brill, 1993).

[7] Consider, for example, the recent debate on the existence of a "Jewish Greek" dialect. Turner claims that the language of the New Testament constitutes "a separate dialect of Greek" rather than merely a form of the Koine, and he insists that it should be assigned a separate category along with that of Classical, Hellenistic, Koine, and Imperial Greek (*Grammatical Insights into the New Testament* [Edinburgh: Clark, 1965], 183). Others, like Lars Rydbeck ("What happened to New Testament Greek Grammar after Albert Debrunner?" *NTS* 21 [1975]: 425), and G. H. R. Horsley ("The Fiction of 'Jewish Greek'," in his *Linguistic Essays*, 5), categorically denounce such a classification as "a modern fabrication, anachronistically imposed upon the New Testament and certain other writings."

specifically to the early Christian Apocrypha.[8] In my research, I could find only three scholars who have specifically grappled with the language of the Greek apocryphal texts: Heinrich Reinhold,[9] Friedrich Rostalski,[10] and Herman Ljungvik.[11] Reinhold's study is rather broad, embracing the whole of the early Christian Apocrypha as well as the Apostolic Fathers. His work mainly details matters pertaining to orthography, accidence, and morphology, but one wonders what conclusions can be drawn from such information. For example, he notes that the spelling τέσσαρσιν is found in *AAn* 12 (Lipsius and Bonnet's numeration, *AAA* 2/1:28, line 26) rather than the more vulgar (Ionic) form τέσσερσιν.[12] Now certain locales did prefer one form over the other,[13] and perhaps one could make a case for the provenance of a work based on such information. But Reinhold was unaware of the textual variants found by Jean-Marc Prieur (in Prieur's numeration, *AAn* 59.18),[14] which

---

[8] Blass and Debrunner do contain a handful of references to the New Testament Apocrypha in their *Greek Grammar*, but these hardly begin to illuminate the language of the Apocrypha. Fortunately, Maximilien Bonnet has provided an invaluable aid in his "Index graecus" (*AAA* 2/2:308–82), which includes an important section on syntax (pp. 359–82).

[9] Heinrich Reinhold, *De graecitate Patrum Apostolicorum Librorumque Apocryphorum Novi Testamenti Quaestiones Grammaticae* (Dissertationes Philologicae Halenses 14.1; Halle: Karras, 1897).

[10] Friedrich Rostalski, *Sprachliches zu den apocryphen Apostelgeschichten* (2 vols.; Myslowitz: Rölle, 1910–11). See also his later work, *Die Sprache der griechischen Paulusakten mit Berücksichtigung ihrer lateinischen Übersetzungen* (Myslowitz: Rölle, 1913).

[11] Herman Ljungvik, *Studien zur Sprache der apokryphen Apostelgeschichten* (Uppsala Universitets Årsskrift 1926; Filosofi, Språkvetenskap Och Historiska Vetenskaper 8; Uppsala: Lundequistska, 1926).

[12] Reinhold, *Quaestiones Grammaticae*, 38.

[13] Vit Bubenik has observed how certain cities in Asia Minor preferred one form over another (Vit Bubenik, *Hellenistic and Roman Greece as a Sociolinguistic Area* [Amsterdam Studies in the Theory and History of Linguistic Science 4, Current Issues in Linguistic History 57; Amsterdam: Benjamins, 1989], 250–52).

[14] The reading τέσσαρσιν is supported by two fourteenth-century manuscripts, codex *Parisinus graecus 770* and codex of Ann Arbor, *36*, along with an excerpt found in one version of the *Epistle of the Presbyters and Deacons of Achaea*. But the two earliest manuscripts, codex *Sinaiticus graecus 526* (tenth century) and codex of Jerusalem, St. Sabas, *103* (twelfth century), have τέτρασιν. See the apparatus in Prieur, *Acta Andreae*, 2:531, line 18.

now render any conclusions uncertain.[15] In contrast, Rostalski focuses his research on the apocryphal acts and advanced beyond Reinhold by expanding his purview to include some discussion on syntax. Further work on syntax in the apocryphal acts is provided by Ljungvik, who also addresses lexical issues. Yet nowhere in their works do these three ever attempt to tackle the specific question of the style of the various apocryphal writings.

In this study of the Greek language of the apocryphal acts, I do not intend to retrace the investigations of Reinhold, Rostalski, and Ljungvik in an examination of the grammatical details of orthography, morphology, accidence, or even of syntax per se. Rather, I am attempting to follow Turner's trail in exploring beyond these traditional boundaries in order to delineate the distinctive modes of expression found among the various apocryphal writings. I seek to exhibit more clearly their stylistic differences with one another in order to highlight their similarities, for one cannot fully appreciate the similarities without first understanding clearly the differences. While the analysis of style involves the study of both traditional grammar (accidence and syntax) and lexicography, it has an entirely different end in view. Stylistic inquiry seeks to highlight the habitual choices which an author makes in the act of writing and to identify the genre of the writing. The stylologist hopes to uncover the background of the writer and to reveal his or her implied audience.

The most important task for a study of this kind is the selection of criteria. One approach to investigating a Greek writer's style might focus on word selection and vocabulary. It is true that Atticist stylists like Moeris[16] and Phrynichus[17] listed many spellings, words, phrases, and expressions which were to be avoided if one wanted to write in a good literary style. But one problem with this methodology is the

---

[15] Bubenik, *Hellenistic and Roman Greece*, based his work on inscriptions, not manuscripts, which often suffer corruption at the hands of scribes.

[16] Moeris, *Moeridis Atticistae Lexicon Atticum*, ed. Johannes Pierson and Georg Aenotheus Koch (Leipzig: Laufferi, 1830; reprint, Hildesheim: Olms, 1969).

[17] Phrynichus, *The New Phrynichus, Being a Revised Text of the Ecloga of the Grammarian Phrynichus with Introductions and Commentary*, ed. William Gunion Rutherford (London: Macmillan, 1881).

uncertainty whether the Atticism in a given text is original or a substitution by a later scribe.[18] In a similar approach, stylometry restricts such analysis to function words like particles, conjunctions, and prepositions.[19] But this approach yields little information about the author and suffers the same inherent weakness with regard to the integrity of the text. Perhaps the clearest indications of style are those most readily noticed by the reader, namely, those relating to Greek sentence structure. In addition, these criteria also have the advantage of being those features of a writer's style which are the least likely to have been altered in transmission.

My methodology in this investigation employs some of the techniques developed by Turner in his finishing stroke to Moulton's grammar[20] as well as by Loveday Alexander in her recent monograph on the preface to Luke's gospel.[21] I have chosen the following four criteria for analyzing literary style: 1) the level of complexity in sentence structure; 2) the style of the preface; 3) the position of the verb in the

---

[18] Again, the same problem noted earlier (pp. 103–4 above) in regard to Reinhold's work. This is also the fundamental problem with the eclectic policy formulated by George Dunbar Kilpatrick and James Keith Elliott for handling textual variants in the New Testament. See the critique by Gordon D. Fee, "Rigorous or Reasoned Eclecticism– Which?" in *Studies in New Testament Language and Text: Essays in Honour of George D. Kilpatrick on the Occasion of His Sixty-Fifth Birthday*, ed. James Keith Elliott (Novum Testamentum, Supplements 44; Leiden: Brill, 1976), 185; now in Eldon Jay Epp and Gordon D. Fee, *Studies in the Theory and Method of New Testament Textual Criticism* (Studies and Documents 45; Grand Rapids: Eerdmans, 1993), 131.

[19] For a concise explanation of stylometry and the stylometric principles to be used in the study of Greek prose, see David S. Williams, *Stylometric Authorship Studies in Flavius Josephus and Related Literature* (Jewish Studies 12; Lewiston, N.Y.: Mellen, 1992), 8–22, where it is claimed that the frequency of words like καί and δέ can determine with a "95% confidence level" whether two writings come from the same author or not (p. 12).

[20] Vol. 5, *Style*. In particular, I have used the statistical test Turner developed for determining the level of parataxis in Luke-Acts (pp. 50–51) and in Paul (p. 99), and the characteristic position of the verb in the sentence (p. 94). See also his article, "The Quality of the Greek of Luke-Acts," in Elliott, *Studies in New Testament Language and Text*, 387–400.

[21] Loveday Alexander, *The Preface to Luke's Gospel: Literary Convention and Social Context in Luke 1.1–4 and Acts 1.1* (Society for New Testament Studies Monograph Series 78; Cambridge: Cambridge University Press, 1993).

sentence; and 4) peculiarities of expression involving syntactical features like Semitic expressions, the use of the optative mood, and superlative forms.

For considerations of space, I have limited this study to the five apocryphal acts of Andrew, John, Paul, Peter, and Thomas. I have sought to follow the best critical text available for each of these writings: For the *Acts of Andrew* I have followed the textual reconstruction (and numeration) of Prieur,[22] and for the *Acts of Andrew and Matthias* I have used the text of Dennis MacDonald.[23] For the *Acts of John* I have employed the critical edition by Éric Junod and Jean-Daniel Kaestli,[24] and for the *Acts of Paul* and the *Acts of Peter* I have used the critical editions by Léon Vouaux.[25] For the *Acts of Thomas* I have had to rely on the old edition by Bonnet.[26]

The Level of Complexity in Sentence Structure

In his *Art of Rhetoric*, Aristotle recognizes two distinct styles of written expression in the Greek language:

> The style must be either continuous (εἰρομένην) and united by connecting particles, like the dithyrambic preludes, or periodic (κατεστραμμένην), like the antistrophes of the ancient poets. The continuous style is the ancient one; . . . It was formerly used by all, but now is used only by a few. By a continuous style (εἰρομένην) I mean that which has no end in itself and only stops when the sense is complete. It is unpleasant, because it is endless, for all wish to have the end in sight. . . . The other style consists of periods (κατεσραμμένη δὲ ἡ ἐν

---

[22] Prieur, *Acta Andreae*, 2:441–549. Space forbids any discussion of the complicated textual history of the *Martyrdom*. For Prieur's own defense of his reconstruction, see ibid., 5–8.

[23] MacDonald, *Acts of Andrew*, 70–169.

[24] Junod and Kaestli, *Acta Iohannis*, 1:159–315.

[25] Vouaux, *Actes de Paul*, 146–229 (*Acts of Paul and Thecla*) and 278–314 (*Martyrdom of Paul*). And idem, *Actes de Pierre*, 398–467 (*Martyrdom of Peter*). The few fragmentary lines of *Papyrus Oxyrhynchus 849* (*The Oxyrhynchus Papyri*, ed. Bernard P. Grenfell and Arthur S. Hunt [London: Egypt Exploration Fund, 1908], 6:10) were not helpful for my analysis of the *Acts of Peter*.

[26] *AAA* 2/2:99–291.

περιόδοις), and by period I mean a sentence that has a beginning and end in itself and a magnitude that can be easily grasped. What is written in this style is pleasant and easy to learn.[27]

Aristotle's first type of style, the "continuous" (εἰρομένη, from the verb εἴρω, "to string together"), exhibits what grammarians call parataxis (παράταξις, "an arranging side by side") since the author arranges two independent sentences side by side, even though one is subordinate in thought to the other.[28] He explains that it was the common form of expression in older writers like Homer and in the earliest Attic writers of both prose and poetry. But throughout all periods of the Greek language it also remained the characteristic style of simple, unsophisticated writers who monotonously strung together their sentences with connectives like καί without any indication of their logical relationship to each other. His other type of style, the "periodic" (κατεστραμμένη, from the verb καταστρέφω, "to turn over," "to bring to an end"), exhibits what is called hypotaxis (ὑπόταξις, "an arranging underneath") since the writer subordinates his thoughts by using the elaborate system of syntax found in the Greek language. Characteristic of this style is the Greek period (περίοδος, "a going around"), a stylistic device in which the various clauses and phrases of a sentence are organized into "a well-rounded unity"[29] where the completion of the main clause is left until the end, creating suspense in the reader. Authors attempting to achieve a most elegant style, including scientific and other technical writers, had a particular fondness for employing the periodic construction, especially at the beginning of their works.[30]

The distinction between paratactic and hypotactic style is the most readily noticed feature of any Greek writing and is the clearest indication of its literary quality. The level of parataxis (or conversely, of hypotaxis) can be determined by simply counting the number of main verbs as opposed to the number of subordinate verbs and other verbals like

[27] Aristotle *Rhet.* 3.9.1–3. The translation is that of John Henry Freese (LCL, 1926).
[28] Herbert Weir Smyth, *Greek Grammar*, rev. Gordon M. Messing (Cambridge, Mass.: Harvard University Press, 1956), § 2168.
[29] BDF § 464.
[30] Alexander, *Preface to Luke's Gospel*, 91.

circumstantial/adverbial participles (in contrast to attributive/adjectival participles)[31] and genitive absolutes used in subordinate clauses.[32] Passages from the five apocryphal acts were selected for analysis upon the basis of their being narrative prose rather than discourse, where a skilled author might employ a simpler style to represent vernacular speech. The findings are displayed in table 1.

TABLE 1

Text	Main Verb	Subordinated Verb	Circumstantial Participle	Genitive Absolute
AAn 1–10	98 (41%)	49 (21%)	89 (38%)	14 (16% of all participles)
AAnMt 1–7	148 (59%)	56 (22%)	49 (19%)	4 (4% of all participles)
AJn 18–25	131 (59%)	25 (11%)	67 (30%)	6 (9% of all participles)
AJn 106–15	72 (51%)	22 (15%)	49 (34%)	5 (10% of all participles)
AThec 1–21	155 (54%)	69 (24%)	62 (21%)	9 (15% of all participles)
MartPl 1–7	116 (54%)	36 (17%)	55 (25%)	9 (16% of all participles)
MartPt 1–12	186 (46%)	91 (22%)	132 (32%)	32 (24% of all participles)
ATh 1–29	486 (57%)	210 (24%)	162 (19%)	30 (16% of all participles)
ATh 107–9	94 (55%)	35 (21%)	41 (24%)	7 (15% of all participles)
ATh 159–71*	147 (55%)	58 (22%)	60 (23%)	13 (18% of all participles)

*Statistics limited to codex *Vallicellianus B 35*.

Immediately apparent from table 1 is the striking contrast between the literary style of the *Acts of Andrew* and that of the *Acts of Andrew*

---

[31] For a simple, concise explanation of the important differences between these two types of the Greek participle, see the appendix in Sakae Kubo, *A Reader's Greek-English Lexicon of the New Testament*, 3d impression with new appendix (Andrews University Monographs 4; Grand Rapids: Zondervan, 1975), 303–6. For a more detailed discussion, see Smyth, *Grammar*, §§ 2039–87, and BDF §§ 411–25. The occurrence of the supplementary participle in completing the thought of the main verb was not included in the count.

[32] The main difference between Turner's methodology (as explained in *Style*, 50) and my own adaptation of it concerns the choice of the nonvariable, or the constant, used in determining a ratio: Turner counted the number of lines of printed text on a given page (which differs from edition to edition), whereas I have counted the number of clauses (i.e., the total number of independent/main clauses and of dependent/subordinate clauses) found in each text.

and Matthias. The author of the *Acts of Andrew* wanted to achieve a very elegant style. He artistically developed his prose by employing the elaborate system of grammatical subordination found in the more skillful writers of literary Greek. For example, note carefully the complexity and the intricate weaving of finite verbs with circumstantial participles and genitive absolutes in the following passage, in which Stratocles is left spellbound by the divine wisdom of Andrew:

οὐκέτι γὰρ ἐπί τινος ὅλως ἐξήταζε τὸν μακάριον, ἀλλ᾽ ἢ τῶν λοιπῶν ἀδελφῶν ἄλλο τι πρασσόντων αὐτὸς ἰδιάζων ἐπυνθάνετο αὐτοῦ, εἰς ὕπνον τρεπομένων αὐτὸς διαγρυπνῶν καὶ μηδὲ τὸν Ἀνδρέαν ἐῶν καθεύδειν διανεπαύετο ἀγαλλιῶν. (*AAn* 8.9–13)

> For no longer around anyone at all did he question the blessed one, but while the rest of the brethren were doing something else, he himself privately inquired of him; while they turned to sleep, he stayed awake and could not even stop rejoicing to allow Andrew to sleep.[33]

Or observe the balance and the rhythmic cadences in this transitional scene immediately following the conversion of Stratocles, when the serenity of the Christian assembly is suddenly interrupted by the arrival of Aegeates the proconsul:

ἀγαλλιάσεως οὖν μεγάλης οὔσης ἐν τοῖς ἀδελφοῖς, νυκτὸς καὶ ἡμέρας συνερχομένων αὐτῶν ἐν τῷ πραιτωρίῳ πρὸς τὴν Μαξιμίλλαν, κυριακῆς οὔσης παραγίνεται ὁ ἀνθύπατος, τῶν ἀδελφῶν συνηγμένων ἐν τῷ κοιτῶνι αὐτοῦ καὶ ἀκρωμένων τοῦ Ἀνδρέα. (*AAn* 13.1–4)

> Now there was great joy among the brethren as night and day they came together in the praetorium with Maximilla; and when it was the Lord's day, the proconsul arrived, while the brethren were assembled together in his bedroom listening to Andrew.

Such a complex interlocking of participles, genitive absolutes, and finite verbs serves to increase the reader's involvement in the action of the story and in the lives of its characters. Now contrast this artistic style

---

[33] All translations are my own, although I have compared them with Elliott, *Apocryphal New Testament*.

with the simple, monotonous prose of the following passage taken from the *Acts of Andrew and Matthias*:

τοῦ οὖν Ματθεία εἰσελθόντος ἐν τῇ πύλῃ τῆς πόλεως [Μυρμιδονίας],[34] ἐκράτησαν αὐτὸν οἱ ἄνθρωποι τῆς πόλεως ἐκείνης, καὶ ἐξέβαλον αὐτοῦ τοὺς ὀφθαλμούς, ἐπότισαν αὐτὸν τὸ φάρμακον τῆς μαγικῆς αὐτῶν πλάνης, καὶ ἀπήγαγον αὐτὸν ἐν τῇ φυλακῇ, καὶ παρέθηκαν αὐτὸν χόρτον ἐσθίειν. (*AAnMt* 2)

Therefore when Matthias entered the gate of the city [of Myrmidonia], the people of that city seized him, and they put out his eyes, they made him drink the drug of their magical deception, and they led him off to prison, and they set before him grass to eat.

While the author begins with a genitive absolute (one of only two found in the first seven sections, the other occurring at the beginning of *AAnMt* 3), he quickly abandons the use of the participle, which would have given brevity to his expression, and resorts simply to stringing together clauses with καί.[35] As table 1 shows, the language of the *Acts of Andrew and Matthias* is the language of the people. Its affinity with vernacular expression and everyday idiom can be seen in the author's preference for parataxis over subordination, as with the infinitive of

---

[34] The place name Μυρμιδονία does not occur in any Greek manuscript and is probably not original, but I include it here because MacDonald insists on having it in his text (*Acts of Andrew*, 7–15).

[35] Contrast this passage with the following examples taken from the *Acts of Andrew*, where the author adds brevity and power to his or her expression through the use of participles rather than diluting it with a long series of finite verbs or relative clauses: καὶ ἐν τούτῳ ὄντος αὐτοῦ παῖς τις τῶν πρὸς χεῖρα τοῦ Στρατοκλέους ὑπὸ δαίμονος πληγεὶς ἐν κοπρῶνι ἔκειτο παραπλήξ (*AAn* 2; "While he was busy in this, a certain slave of the household of Stratocles was smitten by a demon and lay paralyzed in an outhouse"); or, καὶ μηδὲ πυθόμενός τινος εἴσεισιν εὐθέως δρομαίως ἔνθα ὁ παῖς τοῦ Στρατοκλέους ἤφριζεν διάστροφος ὅλος γενόμενος· ὃν ἰδόντες πάντες ἄφνω οἱ διὰ τὰς βοὰς τοῦ Στρατοκλέους συνδραμόντες μειδιῶντα καὶ διιστῶντα τοὺς παρόντας καὶ αὐτῷ τόπον ποιοῦντα μέχρις ἂν ἔλθῃ πρὸς τὸν κείμενον ἐπὶ γῆς παῖδα, διηπόρουν ὅστις εἴη (*AAn* 3; "Without asking questions, he [i.e., Andrew] burst into the room where the servant of Stratocles was foaming at the mouth, writhing in a seizure; all those who came running at the cries of Stratocles watched him [again, Andrew] as he, with a smile, separated those present and made room for himself until he came to the servant lying on the ground, and they were quite at a loss as to who he was").

purpose or ἵνα with the subjunctive.[36] Thus, in *AAnMt* 3 we read μετὰ ταῦτα ἐξαποστελῶ σοι ᾿Ανδρέαν καὶ ἐξάξει σε ἐκ τῆς φυλακῆς ταύτης ("After these things I will send to you Andrew, and he will lead you out of this prison"), where the action of the second verb is clearly subordinate to the first: "I will send Andrew *to lead* you out of this prison."

Next in literary quality after the *Acts of Andrew* stands the *Martyrdom of Peter*. Like the composer of the *Acts of Andrew*, this author shows a predilection for participles and a particular fondness for genitive absolutes, which account for nearly one-fourth of all his participial expressions. The author of the *Acts of John* is also partial to participles but maintains a high level of parataxis, since he or she is reluctant to use subordinating conjunctions. Also exhibiting a high level of parataxis is the *Acts of Thomas*, which we will return to later in our discussion on the priority of the verb.

The Style of the Preface

Much can be learned about the literary character and nature of a work by simply noticing how it begins. For example, in the New Testament there is a clear difference in the way each gospel begins. Luke differs from both Matthew and Mark by prefixing a prologue or preface to his gospel narrative, and such literary pretensions earmark his gospel as a work directed toward a different audience than that of his synoptic siblings. As Martin Dibelius has explained:

> Luke wrote two books. He composed them for a reading public which was not the public of Mark and Matthew. When an author writes a dedication like Luke 1.1–4—a dedication whose style and choice of words are closely akin to the opening of many literary, secular writings—he has in mind readers who will understand and appreciate such a prologue.[37]

---

[36] "Especially in those cases which go together with the preference for direct speech," BDF § 471.1.

[37] Martin Dibelius, "The Text of Acts: An Urgent Critical Task," *JR* 21 (1941): 426, reprinted in idem, *Studies in the Acts of the Apostle*, ed. Heinrich Greeven, trans. Mary Ling (London: SCM, 1956), 88.

But the literary form of the preface not only reveals the intellectual level of the implied audience; it also discloses the author's own perception of his work. Aristotle insisted on the importance of the preface (not πρόλογος but προοίμιον, "the prelude") in providing the audience with the keynote (τὸ ἐνδόσιμον) for everything that followed.[38] In antiquity, the reader could tell whether the author intended to write a common novel, a formal history, a scientific treatise, or some other kind of technical writing simply by noting the style of the first sentence. Technical writers and those well-schooled in rhetoric often began their works with a sonorous tone by employing a periodic construction, usually with a subordinate clause with ἐπεί or ἐπειδή, with a genitive absolute, or with a circumstantial participle in the first line.[39] Those less educated began their works more abruptly without any introduction or formal opening.

It is unfortunate that we are missing the beginning for most of the apocryphal acts, for their opening lines could have told us something about each author and his or her target audience. MacDonald's proposal that the *Acts of Andrew and Matthias* represents the original beginning for the *Acts of Andrew*[40] does not square with the contrast in their literary styles. As seen in the previous section, the *Acts of Andrew* evinces a more literary style than that of the *Acts of Andrew and Matthias*. One would expect the *Acts of Andrew* to begin with a preface, whereas the *Acts of Andrew and Matthias* begins abruptly with the story itself. While the author of the *Acts of Andrew and Matthias* does employ some degree of subordination in the first sentence, one would expect that the *Acts of Andrew* had to have commenced with a periodic construction or some elaborate opening due to its author's concern for literary style.

---

[38] Aristotle *Rhet.* 3.14.1. Though primarily concerned with formal speeches, Aristotle's rules may be applied to writing, since Greek literary theory was merely a by-product of rhetoric. See Alexander, *Preface to Luke's Gospel*, 16–22.

[39] Alexander, *Preface to Luke's Gospel*, 91–92. Note especially Alexander's analysis of five such typical prefaces in her appendix A (pp. 213–16).

[40] "The beginning of the *AA*. . .appears in its original form in the *AAMt*" (MacDonald, *Acts of Andrew*, 32). See the exchange between MacDonald and Prieur, "The *Acts of Andrew and Matthias* and the *Acts of Andrew*," in MacDonald, *Apocryphal Acts of the Apostles*, 9–39.

One does find such an opening in the *Martyrdom of Peter*. It begins with a very long, complex sentence which starts with a series of five genitive absolutes (the main clause is highlighted below in italics):

κυριακῆς οὔσης, ὁμιλοῦντος τοῦ Πέτρου τοῖς ἀδελφοῖς, καὶ προτρέποντος εἰς τὴν τοῦ Χριστοῦ πίστιν, παρόντων πολλῶν συγκλητικῶν καὶ ἱππικῶν πλειόνων καὶ γυναικῶν πλουσίων [καὶ] ματρωνῶν καὶ στηριζομένων τῇ πίστει, *μία τις ἔνθα οὖσα γυνὴ πάνυ πλουσία*, ἥτις τὴν ἐπίκλησιν Χρυσῆ εἶχεν, διὰ τὸ πᾶν αὐτῆς σκεῦος χρύσεον ὑπάρχειν—ἥτις γεννηθεῖσα οὔτε ἀργυρέῳ ποτὲ σκεύει ἐχρήσατο οὔτε ὑελῷ, εἰ μὴ μόνοις χρυσέοις—*εἶπεν τῷ Πέτρῳ·* Πέτρε, θεοῦ δοῦλε· εἰς ὄναρ ἐμοὶ παραστὰς ὃν λέγεις θεὸν εἶπεν· "Χρυσή, Πέτρῳ τῷ διακόνῳ μου ἀποκόμισον μυρίους χρυσίνους· ὀφείλεις γὰρ αὐτῷ." (*MartPt* 1 = *APt* 30)

Now it being the Lord's day, while Peter was preaching to the brethren and exhorting them to faith in Christ, as many senators were present, and many more knights, and wealthy women, [and] matrons, and while they were being strengthened in the faith, *a certain woman* there, being very wealthy, who had the nickname Chryse [= "golden one"] on account of all her vessels being gold, who from her birth had never used a vessel of silver or glass, only those of gold, *said to Peter*, "Peter, servant of God, the one whom you say is God came to me in a dream and said, 'Chryse, bring to my servant Peter ten thousand gold (staters), For you are in debt to him.'"

While such excessive use of participles, especially in close proximity, might signal "a careless style,"[41] it does show that the author was educated and sought a literary style in imitation of the ancients, even though the result sounds somewhat pretentious. He or she lacked the rhetorical skill of the author of the *Acts of Andrew*, and this expresses itself through the lack of balance and cadence in his or her expression.

Such an elaborate period as that quoted above would have made an appropriate beginning for the *Acts of Peter*. But the existence of other texts containing earlier events shows that the *Martyrdom* formed only

---

[41] Smyth, *Grammar*, § 2147.

the latter part of the original *Acts of Peter. Papyrus Oxyrhynchus 849*,[42] codex *Vercellensis 158*,[43] and quotations in the *Vita Abercii* (fourth century C.E.) contain portions of the original *Acts of Peter* that occur much earlier than the account of the *Martyrdom*. The *Stichometry* of Nicephorus[44] (Patriarch of Constantinople, 806–15) states that the entire work consisted of some 2,750 lines (stichoi), which means that we are still missing over a third of the text. While such a long period at the beginning of the *Martyrdom* may simply be a transitional marker signaling a new episode, the final episode in Peter's life, it is also quite possible that it is not original and represents a later redactional stage when the *Martyrdom* had been separated from the rest of the *Acts*.[45]

Of the five apocryphal acts considered in this study, the beginning of only one, the *Acts of Thomas*, has survived. The story begins with a scene in Jerusalem where the apostles are casting lots to determine their respective fields of mission work.[46] Similar in style to the *Acts of Andrew and Matthias*, the *Acts of Thomas* begins with simple prose without any literary pretensions. It is written in the everyday language of the common people, for whom it was intended.

Fortunately, we do possess the endings for all five of these acts, and Aristotle mentions (*Rhet.* 3.19.1) that a careful style requires an epilogue. He later adds that the most appropriate style is one in which there are

---

[42] Grenfell and Hunt, *Oxyrhynchus Papyri*, 6:6–12.

[43] Cuthbert Hamilton Turner ("The Latin Acts of Peter," *JTS* 32 [1931]: 119) points out that the correct nomenclature is 158, not 108 as in *AAA* 1:xxxiii.

[44] The Greek text is found in Theodor Zahn, *Geschichte des neutestamentlichen Kanons* (2 vols. in 4; Erlangen: Deichert, 1888–92), 2/1:300 (English trans. in *NTApoc*[5] 1:42).

[45] Gérard Poupon ("Les 'Actes de Pierre' et leur remaniement," *ANRW* II 25/6:4378) has argued that chapter 30 is an interpolation which interrupts the chronological sequence from chapter 29 to chapter 31. Also, the Latin text of codex *Vercellensis 158* breaks up the long Greek period in chapter 30 with several finite clauses, which Vouaux (*Actes de Pierre*, 398 n. e) assigned to the editorial activity of the Latin translator. But the simpler grammar of the Latin may be evidence of an earlier Greek text with a simpler grammatical structure.

[46] Jean-Daniel Kaestli has argued that the *Acts of John*, the *Acts of Paul*, and the *Acts of Peter* could not have begun with this scene ("Les scènes d'attribution des champs de mission et de départ de l'apôtre dans les Actes apocryphes," in *Actes apocryphes des apôtres*, 261–63).

no connecting particles (τελευτῇ δὲ τῆς λέξεως ἁρμόττει ἡ ἀσύνδετος,
3.19.6). Only the *Acts of Andrew* attempts such an epilogue,[47] and this
observation reinforces the earlier judgment that the author was
attempting to achieve a more elegant style. The other four acts merely
end with the final scene in the story. There is no attempt to provide a
proper conclusion or epilogue. They end abruptly, without any editorial
comment from their authors.

The Position of the Verb in the Sentence

One can also learn something about the linguistic background of each
author by observing where he customarily positioned finite verbs. In
Greek there is a strong tendency among literary writers to place a finite
verb in the middle of a clause rather than at the beginning or the end.[48]
In Herodotus (fifth century B.C.E.), for example, one finds the verb in
the middle of a clause in 59 percent of the instances, whereas the initial
position accounts for 16 percent and the final position for 25 percent of
all occurrences.[49] The exceptions to the middle position usually occur
when the author desires to effect a different word order for the sake of
emphasis.[50]

---

[47] For a good discussion on the conclusion to the *Acts of Andrew*, see Laura S.
Nasrallah, "She Became What the Words Signified: The Greek *Acts of Andrew*'s
Construction of the Reader-Disciple," in this volume.

[48] Blass and Debrunner comment that the predicate usually occurs first, before the
subject (BDF § 472; see also Robertson, *Grammar*, 417). But an actual count of the
frequency in good prose of the fifth and fourth centuries B.C.E. reveals just the opposite.
Normally, "the subject tends to precede its verb" (Turner, *Style*, 18). And thus, "In
contemporary non-Biblical, as in the modern language, the predominant order is the
middle position for the verb" (*Style*, 94).

[49] These figures are taken from Ernst Kieckers as they are tabulated by Howard
(*Accidence and Word Formation*, 418), where one finds similar numbers for Polybius,
Thucydides, and other literary writers. See further Ernst Kieckers, *Stellung des Verbs
im Griechischen und in den verwandten Sprachen* (Untersuchungen zur indo-
germanischen Sprach- und Kulturwissenschaft 2; Strasbourg: Trübner, 1911), 5.

[50] Actually, there are no "rules" for word order. The Greeks' love of liberty and
freedom extends even to their language, where response to the spontaneity of the mind
and the sensibilities of the ear override all other considerations. See Robertson,
Grammar, 417.

In stark contrast stands the language of the New Testament, where the finite verb usually begins the sentence. For example, in Matthew the priority of the verb reaches a frequency of 34 percent, in Mark 31 percent, and in Luke it is even higher (42 percent, but only 30 percent in the "We" sections of Acts), whereas in some literary writers like Polybius the frequency is much lower than that usually found in the classics (11 percent, compared with the 17 percent average of the best Attic writers).[51] This tendency for the verb to take precedence over other words in a clause is significant for recognizing the true nature of the New Testament idiom. Eduard Norden has labeled this striking phenomenon as the surest Semitism of the New Testament, especially in those instances involving a series of clauses.[52] Even Paul cannot escape its influence.[53] Higher frequencies like that found in the *Testament of Abraham* (45 percent in Recension B) may point to a Semitic original (the 36 percent in Recension A probably represents a revision of the Greek text).[54]

The contrast in the position of the verb is no less striking among the five apocryphal acts, as can be seen from table 2, where the frequencies for the position of the verb (first, middle, and last) are given for each book.

[51] These figures are taken from Turner, "Quality of the Greek of Luke-Acts," 391–92.

[52] Eduard Norden, *Agnostos Theos. Untersuchungen zur Formengeschichte religiöser Rede*, 4th ed. (Leipzig: Teubner, 1923; reprint, Darmstadt: Wissenschaftliche Buchgesellschaft, 1956), 365.

[53] See Turner's examination of the primacy of the verb in Romans, 1 Corinthians, and Galatians, where he concludes that "Paul is not a whit behind the gospels in preferring this position" (*Style*, 94).

[54] Again, these figures are taken from Turner, "Quality of the Greek of Luke-Acts," 391–92. On the origin of the *Testament of Abraham*, see the survey by E. P. Sanders ("Testament of Abraham," in *The Old Testament Pseudepigrapha*, ed. James H. Charlesworth [2 vols.; Garden City, N.Y.: Doubleday, 1983–85], 1:873–74), where he mentions the conclusion by Turner (in his unpublished 1951 dissertation) that Recension B, the shorter version, was originally written in Hebrew (a judgment later shared by Francis Schmidt in his 1971 dissertation at the University of Strasbourg, later published as *Le Testament grec d'Abraham. Introduction, édition critique des deux recensions grecques, traduction* [Texte und Studien zum antiken Judentum 11; Tübingen: Mohr-Siebeck, 1986]). Sanders rejects a Hebrew *Vorlage* for either recension.

TABLE 2

Text	First Position	Middle Position	Last Position
AAn 1–10	31 (23%)	57 (43%)	45 (34%)
AAnMt 1–7	91 (49%)	73 (40%)	21 (11%)
AJn 18–25	50 (34%)	67 (45%)	31 (21%)
AJn 106 15	38 (44%)	28 (33%)	20 (23%)
AThec 1–21	70 (34%)	81 (39%)	56 (27%)
MartPl 1–7	54 (38%)	48 (34%)	39 (28%)
MartPt 1–12	69 (26%)	108 (41%)	88 (33%)
ATh 1–29	237 (36%)	245 (38%)	170 (26%)
ATh 107–9	54 (45%)	40 (34%)	25 (21%)
ATh 159–71*	73 (39%)	61 (33%)	52 (28%)

*Statistics limited to codex *Vallicellianus B 35.*

Like the contrast in sentence complexity (table 1), the position of the finite verb in the *Acts of Andrew* and the *Acts of Andrew and Matthias* indicates that the two works are from two different authors whose styles are quite different. In the *Acts of Andrew*, the verb normally occurs somewhere in the middle of the clause (43 percent), while other elements like the subject or the object are in the initial position or last, depending upon the desired emphasis. This tendency is the same as that found among the better literary writers and accords with our earlier judgment that the author of the *Acts of Andrew* was an individual schooled in rhetoric and the best Attic literature. In contrast, the priority of the verb is most prominent in the *Acts of Andrew and Matthias*, where the frequency (49 percent to the *Acts of Andrew*'s 23 percent)[55] rivals that of the *Testament of Abraham* (45 percent), in which the Greek translation mostly retains the Semitic priority of the verb. (The Semitic character

---

[55] Actually the priority count for the *Acts of Andrew* (23 percent) is artificially high due to the extended passage in *AAn* 7.7–18 (Prieur, *Acta Andreae*, 2:451), where Andrew is pleading with Stratocles to become "born again," and the priority of the verb is preferred for rhetorical effect (note the asyndeton). See two similar passages in *AJn* 106.15–107.10 (Junod and Kaestli, *Acta Iohannis*, 1:295–97) and 114.1–9 (Junod and Kaestli, *Acta Iohannis*, 1:313–15), where the verb suddenly reverses from being first to last for rhetorical effect and balance.

of *Andrew and Matthias* will be noticed again in the final section on syntactical peculiarities.)

Next in the frequency of verbal priority stands the *Acts of Thomas*, where Semitic influence is most keenly felt in the "Hymn of the Pearl" (*ATh* 107–9, 45 percent).[56] The question whether our present Greek text is a translation from Syriac is difficult to answer. The Greek text extant for the *Acts of Thomas* appears to go back to a stage prior to our present Syriac version, since the Syriac manifests a catholicizing tendency not found in the Greek. Albertus Frederik Johannes Klijn holds that quotations of the New Testament in the *Acts of Thomas* demonstrate a Syriac *Vorlage*, since they betray the influence of Tatian's *Diatessaron*.[57]

The *Acts of John* also bears a high frequency for the primacy of the verb in the final section, the so-called *Metastasis* (*AJn* 106–15, 44 percent). As in the previous case with the *Acts of Thomas*, such a high frequency might indicate a Semitic original underlying this section, and Knut Schäferdiek has argued for one based on other grounds.[58] But the predominance of direct speech in *AJn* 106–15 may have actually skewed the numbers. The many exhortations and imperatives in this section would naturally prefer the initial position for the verb, so that a

---

[56] Interestingly, Paul-Hubert Poirier (*L'hymne de la perle des Actes de Thomas. Introduction, texte, traduction, commentaire* [Homo religiosus 8; Louvain-la-Neuve: Pierier, 1981], 182) feels that, based on vocabulary, the hymn was originally written in Syriac and actually predates the *Acts of Thomas* itself.

[57] Klijn, *Acts of Thomas*, 17. According to Richard Adelbert Lipsius (*Die apokryphen Apostelgeschichten*, 2/2:423), Theodor Nöldeke was the first to suggest that the original language of the *Acts of Thomas* was Syriac. Francis Crawford Burkitt ("The Original Language of the Acts of Judas Thomas," *JTS* 1 [1900]: 280–90) finds examples where the Greek text clearly mistranslates a known Syriac idiom. Since the Greek text rests on a confusion possible only in Syriac, Burkitt concludes that such phenomena prove a Syriac origin. Initially, Lipsius himself thought that the *Acts of Thomas* was originally written in Greek (*Die apokryphen Apostelgeschichten*, 1:300), but later he changed his mind to agree with Nöldeke (2/2:425).

[58] Knut Schäferdiek, "Herkunft und Interesse der alten Johannesakten," *ZNW* 74 (1983): 251–53, where he bases his conclusion on a quotation of *AJn* 101 in Gregory Bar Hebraeus (*Adv. haer.* 22), which he claims preserves a more primitive form of the text than that found in our extant Greek manuscripts of the *Acts of John* or even in the known Syriac versions.

high frequency in the primacy of the verb for this section is quite misleading and hence does not necessarily signal Semitic thought.

But the numbers for the *Acts of Paul* match those for the New Testament and are what we would expect for a document imitating biblical Greek. The *Acts of Peter*, on the other hand, prefers the middle position for the verb, and this reinforces our earlier judgment concerning its literary quality. However, the position of the verb is not the only syntactical feature providing clues as to the nature of the Greek language in these works. There are other peculiarities that deserve notice.

Peculiarities of Expression Involving Syntax

The strong Semitic flavor of the *Acts of Andrew and Matthias* is quickly detected in certain syntactical features. Its repeated use of the periphrastic participle, though common in Hellenistic Greek, betrays a Semitic influence when it is frequently employed for the imperfect:[59] οὔτε ἄρτον ἤσθιον οὔτε ὕδωρ ἔπινον, ἀλλ' ἦσαν ἐσθίοντες σάρκας ἀνθρώπων καὶ πίνοντες αὐτῶν τὸ αἷμα ("they ate no bread and drank no water, but were eating human flesh and drinking their blood" [*AAnMt* 1]); also ἦν εὐχόμενος τῷ θεῷ ("he was praying to God" [*AAnMt* 2]), ἦν ψάλλων ("he was singing" [*AAnMt* 3]), ἦν ὁ Ματθείας κλείων αὐτοῦ τοὺς ὀφθαλμούς ("Matthias was closing his eyes" [*AAnMt* 3], notice the Semitic priority of the verb), ἦν διδάσκων ὁ Ἀνδρέας ("Andrew was teaching" [*AAnMt* 4]), and so on. Other Semitisms include the frequent use of καὶ ἐγένετο ὅτε with a finite verb ("And it came to pass when. . ." [*AAnMt* 4]) and especially the temporal use of ἐν τῷ with the infinitive: καὶ ἐγένετο ἐν τῷ εἰσέρχεσθαι ("And it came to pass when he entered. . ." [*AAnMt* 3]). The use of ἀποκριθεὶς εἶπεν

---

[59] "In the New Testament circumlocution [i.e., the periphrastic participle with εἰμί] is so frequent for the imperfect that it can scarcely be explained otherwise than as due to Aramaic influence" (Maximilian Zerwick, *Biblical Greek*, trans. Joseph Smith [Rome: Pontifical Biblical Institute, 1963], § 361). For a good list of the chief points of Semitic influence, see ibid., § 494. This idiom occurs several times in Luke, where it is based on the author's imitation of the "biblical language" of the LXX (Alain Verboomen, *L'imparfait périphrastique dans l'Évangile de Luc et dans la Septante. Contribution à l'étude du système verbal du grec néotestamentaire* [Académie Royale de Belgique, Classe des Lettres, Fonds René Draguet 10; Louvain: Peeters, 1992], esp. 71).

("And answering he said. . . ," three times in *AAnMt* 4 and 5, several times in *AAnMt* 7) is clearly a Semitism, as is the use of such phrases as ἀναστὰς δὲ ᾽Ανδρέας τῷ πρωὶ ἐπορεύετο ("Arising early in the morning Andrew went. . ." [*AAnMt* 5]), ἀναστὰς κάτελθε ("Arising, go below!" [*AAnMt* 7]), and ἀναστὰς κατῆλθεν ("Arising, he went below" [*AAnMt* 7]). Then there is the use of the cognate accusative (e.g., ἐχάρη χαρὰν μεγάλην σφόδρα, "he rejoiced an exceedingly great joy" [*AAnMt* 5]). Though not entirely foreign even to classical Greek, nevertheless, here it surely reflects a Semitic base. These syntactical features do not prove that the Greek *Acts of Andrew and Matthias* is a translation of a Semitic *Vorlage*, no more than their presence in the New Testament does for the gospels. Yet they do show that the writer was either heavily influenced by Semitic thought or, at least, that he intentionally imitated Semitic idiom.[60]

Similar syntactical features in the *Acts of Thomas* also show a Semitic influence: ἔτυχεν δὲ ἐκεῖ εἶναι λέοντα ("And it happened that there was a lion there" [*ATh* 8, *AAA* 2/2:112.2]); the temporal use of ἐν τῷ plus the infinitive (*ATh* 23, *AAA* 2/2:136.8–9); ἀποκριθεὶς εἶπεν (*ATh* 23, *AAA* 2/2:137.8; cf. *ATh* 21, *AAA* 2/2:132.6); the preference for coordination over subordination, ἀπέβλεπον δὲ καὶ τὸ εἶδος αὐτοῦ ἐναλλαγέν ("and they saw also *that* his appearance changed" [*ATh* 8, *AAA* 2/2:111.2–3]); the Semitic manner of expressing possession, καὶ τί αὐτῷ ὄνομα; ("What is his name?" *ATh* 163 in codex *Vallicellianus B 35*, *AAA* 2/2:276.2–3);[61] as well as the frequent use of chiasmus (*ATh* 13, *AAA* 2/2:119.5–7; *ATh* 17, *AAA* 2/2:125.8–9; *ATh* 19, *AAA* 2/2:128.7–9; *ATh* 24, *AAA* 2/2:139.5–6; etc.).

Some anomalies are present, however, that clearly show Greek influence. For example, sometimes the genitive is separated from the

---

[60] While MacDonald recognizes the Semitic influences and allows the author to be a Syrian bilingual, he argues that lexical parallels with the *Acts of Thomas*, which he also assumes to have been composed originally in Greek, "weigh in favor of a Greek original" (*Acts of Andrew*, 32). But as we shall see, the *Acts of Thomas* also bears a Semitic imprint.

[61] Cf. Mark 5:9, where the emphasis is on the possessor, proving that the expression is Semitic and not Greek; see BDF § 189. Note how the Semitic construction has been removed in codex *Parisinus graecus 1510*, καὶ τί τὸ ὄνομα αὐτοῦ; (*AAA* 2/2:276.11).

noun it modifies, where the Semitic construct form would have to precede the absolute of the modifying noun. Thus, even in the "Hymn of the Pearl," the most Semitic-sounding section in the *Acts of Thomas*, one still finds βασιλέων εἰμὶ υἱός ("I am a son of kings" [*ATh* 111, *AAA* 2/2:222.10–11]), which surely reflects Greek emphasis.[62] Also, the occasional great distance between the verb and its subject (as in σὺ δὲ αὐτῷ. . .δύνασαι οἰκοδομῆσαι καὶ κτίσαι παλάτιον, *ATh* 18, *AAA* 2/2:127.3) and the use of some classical terms (e.g., ἐπειδήπερ[63] in *ATh* 165, *AAA* 2/2:279.5, 6, 8, and 10) clearly represent Greek influence. These elements do not preclude the possibility of a Semitic original, but they do show areas where Greek syntax has overridden Semitic thought.

In stark contrast to the Semitic-sounding syntax of the *Acts of Andrew and Matthias* and the *Acts of Thomas* is the literary Greek of the *Acts of Andrew*. The author frequently employs the optative, which had already dropped out of vogue by the time of the New Testament:[64] καταλάβοι (*AAn* 2, Prieur, *Acta Andreae*, 2:445.12), μὴ τολμήσειεν (lines 15–16). The text also uses the superlative form of the adjective for the elative sense, where popular Hellenistic practice preferred the comparative:[65] ἀνὴρ θεοσεβέστατος ("a very god-fearing man" [*AAn* 2, Prieur, *Acta Andreae*, 2:445.11]), βλασφημότατος and ταλαιπωρότατος ("very blasphemous" and "despicable" [*AAn* 6, Prieur, *Acta Andreae*, 2:449.7–8]), and μαντικώτατε ἄνθρωπε ("most prophetic human" [*AAn* 8, Prieur, *Acta Andreae*, 2:453.2]). The author's concern for classical standards is shown in the careful use of the genitive absolute, which remains "absolute" by not having its subject reused in any way in the main clause (13 out of the first 14 occurrences).[66] Such carefulness stands in

---

[62] The order is for the sake of emphasis as in 1 Cor 1:19; see BDF § 475.2 n. The order θεοῦ υἱός only appears three other times (Matt 14:33; 27:43, 54) out of the fifty possibilities available in the New Testament.

[63] A hapax legomenon in the New Testament (Luke 1:1); see BDF § 107.

[64] BDF § 65.2.

[65] Zerwick, *Biblical Greek*, §§ 147–48.

[66] Ibid., § 48. It is a mark of elegance to refrain from using the genitive absolute when the subject of the subordinate phrase reoccurs in the principal sentence and to employ the circumstantial participle instead (cf. Matt 9:18 and 9:27). But see Smyth (*Grammar*, § 2073) for exceptions due to emphasis.

stark contrast to the other acts. Only two genitive absolutes occur in the first seven paragraphs of the *Acts of Andrew and Matthias*. In the first instance the author fails to maintain the absoluteness of the genitive clause by reusing its subject in the main clause (*AAnMt* 1, MacDonald, *Acts of Andrew*, 72.8; cf. *AAnMt* 3, MacDonald, *Acts of Andrew*, 74.12). The author of the *Acts of John* is more careful, maintaining the absoluteness of the genitive participle in over two-thirds of the 11 instances. This same ratio is found in both the *Acts of Paul* (12 out of 18) and the *Acts of Thomas* (36 out of 50). But, surprisingly, the author of the *Acts of Peter* maintains this distinction only about half the time (17 out of 32 instances). The less careful use of the genitive absolute (e.g., *APt* 31 [= *MartPt* 2, *AAA* 1:80.30–32] and *APt* 33 [= *MartPt* 4, *AAA* 1:84.19–22)[67] shows that the author does not possess the literary skill of the author of the *Acts of Andrew*. In fact, the language of the *Acts of Peter* often sounds pretentious and even artificial when compared to that of the *Acts of Andrew*.

The language of both the *Acts of John* and the *Acts of Paul* is Hellenistic and lacks the elegance and the concern for classical standards found in the *Acts of Andrew*. For example, the author of the *Acts of Paul* uses ὥστε with the infinitive to indicate both purpose and result,[68] so that only the context can determine which is intended. In classical Greek the distinction was maintained by restricting the use of ὥστε with an infinitive or a finite verb to result clauses.[69]

Conclusions to Be Drawn?

What can we conclude about the authors of the various apocryphal acts from this analysis of their different styles? The style of the *Acts of Andrew* shows that the author was a skillful writer, well acquainted

---

[67] Note how in this passage the author begins with two genitive absolutes, whose subject then becomes the subject of the principal clause, which is then followed by a nominative participle!

[68] Nine times in the *Martyrdom of Paul* alone, e.g. *MartPl* 1 (Vouaux, *Actes de Paul*, 278.3 and 282.5), 3 (290.6), 5 (294.5), etc. Cf. *AThec* 1 and 8 (Vouaux, *Actes de Paul*, 146.6 and 162.7). I did not find it so used in any of the other acts.

[69] Smyth, *Grammar*, §§ 2206, 2249–55, 2267; BDF §§ 390.3 and 391.3.

with the best literary works of Attic Greek. He or she was well educated in rhetoric and philosophy,[70] and the style reflects a concern to reach others of a similar educational level.[71] It is markedly different from the style of the *Acts of Andrew and Matthias*, whose simplicity betrays the author's lack of schooling. In the *Acts of Andrew and Matthias*, the author's Semitic background constantly interferes with the Greek (though possibly the style reflects a Greek translation of a Semitic original). It is difficult to imagine that such divergent styles ever belonged to the same work, as it has been argued.

The author of the *Acts of John* appears to write in the language of the people, as seen in his or her preference for parataxis and the general avoidance of subordinating conjunctions. The style is simple and unsophisticated, far removed from the complexities of the *Acts of Andrew*.[72] Yet it can still reach a level of rhetorical beauty reminiscent of the *Acts of Andrew* (see *AJn* 106.15–107.10 and 144.1–9).

Concerning the *Acts of Paul*, we know from Tertullian (*De bapt.* 17) that the author lived in Asia Minor, and the style of both the *Martyrdom* and the *Acts of Paul and Thecla* bears nothing to refute this. The language is Hellenistic and resembles the more common diction of the New Testament.

The author of the *Acts of Peter* sought a more literary style, as shown by the presence of hypotaxis throughout. He or she resorts to the genitive absolute more than any other writer, 24 percent of all participial expressions. And while the use of the long periodic sentence at the beginning of the *Martyrdom* probably reflects later redaction, other features, like the author's predilection for the participle, demonstrate a desire to imitate the language of the ancients. Yet the author is lacking

---

[70] For indications of the author's acquaintance with Platonic, neo-Pythagorean, and Stoic thought, see Prieur, *Acta Andreae*, 1:372–79.

[71] His literary skills "assurent aux discours. . .une certaine élégance. . .leur confèrent surtout un caractère incantatoire, destiné à renforcer leur capacité de persuasion" (ibid., 1:174).

[72] *Pace* Montague Rhodes James (*Apocrypha anecdota* [2 vols.; Texts and Studies 2.3 and 5.1; Cambridge: Cambridge University Press, 1893–97], 2:xxxi), who accepts the ancient tradition that the *Acts of Andrew*, the *Acts of Peter*, and the *Acts of John* were all works from "one and the same author who may be called, for the sake of convenience, Leucius."

in rhetorical skill and shows an ignorance of the classical standards in the details of syntax. These inadequacies make the language sound artificial and prevent it from reaching the levels of cadence and elegance found in the *Acts of Andrew*.

Like the *Acts of Andrew and Matthias*, the language of the *Acts of Thomas* is also popular and very Semitic in sound. The author was probably a Syrian, and the high level of parataxis (55 percent) along with the strong primacy of the verb (45 percent in the "Hymn of the Pearl") may suggest a Syriac *Vorlage* underlying at least some of the Greek text (our present Syriac text reflects a later, orthodox-expurgated edition).

The immensity of this subject matter is overwhelming, but I hope that this attempt to go beyond the traditional boundaries of grammar and language study will help us to understand better the writings, and perhaps even the writers themselves, of the Apocryphal Acts of the Apostles. May this study encourage others to do for the apocryphal acts what Turner attempted to do for the New Testament: to increase our understanding of these works, of the Christians who wrote them, and of those who might have read them, in order to deepen our appreciation of these important writings and their influence on early Christianity.

Philological Aspects of the Apocryphal Acts of the Apostles

Evie Zachariades-Holmberg

Problems Pertaining to the Greek Language of the Apocryphal Acts

Eleven centuries ago Patriarch Photius of Constantinople said of the apocryphal acts: ". . .the style is completely uneven and strange. At times, indeed, there are devices and terms which are not well turned. And most of the time they are common and overly used. There is no trace of the homogeneous and unpretentious style with an innate grace in which the evangelic and apostolic language is molded."[1] Today, we might reach a similar conclusion concerning the language in which the majority of these texts were written.[2]

The "uneven" and "strange" style that Patriarch Photius mentions is mainly due to the variety of forms of diction the language employs. Apocryphal literature is often written in a style that ranges from imitations of ancient prototypes—from archaic to Attic Greek, mixed with

---

[1] Photius *Bibliotheca*, Codex 114, my translation.

[2] A very useful work, in which one can find information on the development of the language from Attic Greek to that of the early Christian literature, is James Hope Moulton and Wilbert Francis Howard, *A Grammar of New Testament Greek Accidence and Word-Formation*, with an appendix on "Semitisms in the New Testament" (Edinburgh: Clark, 1921). Also helpful is Friedrich Blass and Albert Debrunner, *A Greek Grammar of the New Testament and Other Early Christian Literature*, trans. Robert Walter Funk (Chicago: University of Chicago Press, 1961). There are few works that deal with the development of the language of the New Testament into Modern Greek. The most important is George Hatzidakis, *Μεσαιωνικὰ καὶ Νέα Ἑλληνικά* (2 vols.; Athens: Sakellariou, 1905–1907); see also the work by Stylianos Kapsomenos mentioned in n. 5, below.

elements betraying influences from the rhetorical schools of the classical through the Hellenistic periods—to compositions written in a language bordering on the vernacular. In view of such a variety of forms of diction, a study of this literature presupposes taking into consideration a diachronic overview of points of reference within the development of the Greek language, from archaic through classical, Hellenistic, and Byzantine Greek to Modern Greek, since many new elements found in the early Christian writings are the result of the development of the language during the Hellenistic period into Modern Greek. Many of the so-called Semitisms that occur in these writings can be explained in this light.

Numerous indications of this development are found in the language of the New Testament. We see changes in phonetics, in syntax and grammar, and in the meaning of words. The main characteristics of these changes are: the simplification of complex phonetic and syntactical combinations; the expression of the tenses of the verb in a periphrasis; the gradual elimination of the optative mood and the dative case; the analysis of the participles and infinitives into clauses introduced by ἵνα and the subjunctive and ὅτι and the indicative; the gradual elimination of certain prepositions; and changes in the declensions of nouns, pronouns, and adjectives, and the conjugations of verbs. Through this gradual simplification, the language develops into what will become Modern Greek.

Additional signs of the further development into simpler and more analytical forms of diction, as well as characteristics indicative of artificial constructions in syntax and grammar, although present in other early Christian texts, become more apparent in texts from the apocryphal literature. Because most of the apocryphal texts were not accepted by the official Church, they exhibit fewer indications of having been edited. In the various texts which constitute the apocryphal acts, and occasionally within the same text, we can observe the following:

1. Elements indicative of a stage of development in the language beyond that already observed in the New Testament. These elements exhibit a further proximity to and occasionally coincidence with Modern Greek forms of diction and usually occur in the texts as: gradual change of nouns, pronouns, and adjectives from the third declension to the second or first, in part or in whole; addition of -ν in the accusative singular ending -α of the third declension; changing of the genitive singular masculine ending -ου of the first declension into -α or -η; using the ending -ες in the nominative and accusative plural of feminine nouns and adjectives of the first declension instead of -αι and -ας, respectively; elimination of the second aorist endings in favor of those of the first; use of -σαι ending in the second person singular of primary tenses of the middle and passive voice; and elimination of the proper use of the middle voice, which eventually becomes restricted to reflexive verbs. Most importantly, however, what indicates the further development of the language into its future mode of modern diction is the even greater periphrastic expression in the syntax (that is, the virtual elimination of the infinitive and participle of indirect speech in favor of the use of ὅτι and the indicative), the progressively more frequent use of relative clauses, of prepositions instead of the dative or genitive case, and changes in the position of words in a sentence, especially in the position of the verb. These changes often create problems in determining the correct use of grammar and syntax, especially when there is some effort to "edit" the text for a "better" appearance.

2. Tendency to return to earlier prototypes. Many of these texts also exhibit a common tendency found in Hellenistic and Byzantine literature, namely, the return to antique/Attic forms of diction. For this reason, study of the texts presupposes that the language in which they are written be considered in its entirety, perhaps excluding orthography, which suffered the most during their transmission. Although Atticisms may only have been superimposed on a text in a later attempt to create a sophisticated effect, they still must be taken into account, as Attic forms figure prominently in many of these compositions.

Some of the basic characteristics of the Atticizing movement are found in many of the texts from the apocryphal acts. The degree to which Attic elements are present should be considered in order to compare variations in Atticisms not only in texts of different origin but in texts determined to be of the same provenance, as such variation indicates several hands at work or different dates of composition. This matter may be profitably explored in the martyrdoms, for example, where one is presented with several versions of the same story.

3. Preference for complicated, often awkward, sentence construction.
The conscious effort toward "sophistication" in expression often results
in extremely complicated and contorted compositions. Some of the texts
of the apocryphal acts occasionally contain incorrect use of the language
as well as a certain awkwardness in the excessive use of antique/Attic
forms. The antique style appears at times to be a superficial veneer
applied at a later date in an attempt to improve the original version.
This is probably one of the reasons why variety in style often exists
within the same text.

Style alone is thus not a decisive criterion for the classification of
these documents in place and time. A careful study indicates that, in
most cases, all one can do is pinpoint the stylistic characteristics of
each text—and sometimes differences in style within the same text—
and compare the various texts to each other. Such a comparison usually
determines the degree of awkwardness in expression or the effort to
create a sophisticated antique or Atticizing effect. The use of a more
ancient syntax and vocabulary rather than a simpler, more analytical
one characteristic of a later stage in the development of the language is
not necessarily sufficient to place a text at an earlier or later date.[3] In
most cases all one can say is that the writer who uses the more ancient
syntax and vocabulary is striving to create a sophisticated effect and is
addressing a group of readers with similar expectations. In general, it
would be safer to say that the tendency to use progressively more

---

[3] This difficulty of ascribing place and time to a particular style becomes evident
when one studies the writings of the early apologists and the Greek Fathers. We could
say that as we move on from the time of the composition of canonical apostolic writings,
the style of the composition of Christian writings becomes progressively more
sophisticated in its effort to imitate antique prototypes. If we wished to prove this
hypothesis, we could use as examples for the first, second, third, and fourth centuries
excerpts from the writings of Clement of Rome, Justin Martyr, Origen, and the
Cappadocian Fathers, respectively. An examination of their work could support our
thesis for the progressive use of a more antique and sophisticated style. But then, Clement
of Alexandria would easily disprove this thesis, writing as he did, at the end of the
second century, using an affluent Attic vocabulary, the dual number in adjectives, nouns,
and pronouns, and the optative mood in indirect speech—i.e., a more antique style. We
would need to formulate another thesis ascribing these characteristics to an "Alexandrian
School," since Cyril of Alexandria also writes in an ancient, sophisticated style two
centuries later, without, however, using a similar vocabulary or the dual number.

sophisticated language after the second century C.E. is not alone sufficient to date texts.[4]

4. Abundance of mistakes in grammar and syntax. Grammatical and syntactical mistakes are scattered throughout texts of various origin, varying degrees of sophistication, and different dates of composition, and they can be attributed to such factors as copying errors, difficulty in imitating an older mode of diction, or lack of editing. An abundance of such mistakes, however—especially those which betray confusion with Modern Greek grammar and syntax—can be an indication of a very late date of composition.

As a point of clarification, it should be mentioned that the designation Modern Greek instead of medieval or Byzantine Greek is used here in those instances where the language of the texts under discussion borders on the vernacular. Medieval or Byzantine Greek refers mainly to texts written in a style seeking its prototypes in times past; therefore, most written sources of medieval or Byzantine times do not help us trace the evolution of the language. For this, we usually have to turn our attention to epigraphic material and the unofficial correspondence. These writings are closer to the oral tradition and local dialects, most of which exhibit coincidence with certain Modern Greek modes of diction. An important work on the development of the Greek language from Hellenistic into modern times, containing extensive bibliography on the subject, is that of Stylianos Kapsomenos.[5]

The Apocryphal Acts of the Apostles

This study of the language of the apocryphal acts will concentrate on the *Acts of Andrew*, the *Acts of Peter*, and the *Acts of Paul*. Selections

---

[4] The language, for example, of Theodoretus of Cyrrhus, writing in the fifth century, is simpler and more analytical than the language of the Cappadocian Fathers. In fact, it is closer to the language of the New Testament than to the language used by Clement of Rome, who was writing three centuries earlier and whose writing exhibits a richer vocabulary and a more complicated syntax than that used in the canonical Gospels.

[5] Stylianos Kapsomenos, Ἀπὸ τὴν ἱστορία τῆς Ἑλληνικῆς γλώσσας: ἡ Ἑλληνικὴ γλῶσσα ἀπὸ τὰ Ἑλληνιστικὰ ὡς τὰ νεώτερα χρόνια (Thessalonike: Aristoteleio Panepistemio Thessalonikes, Institouto Neoellenikon Spoudon, 1985).

from these works will be used to illustrate some of the characteristics discussed above. The variety of the linguistic expression observed in these texts does not conform to any particular chronological order, and in many cases it creates problems of homogeneity within texts that have come down to us as excerpts of a single work.

Acts of Andrew

The collection of Greek texts related to the apostle Andrew exemplifies most of the points already discussed. There is a consistent use of antique Atticizing style in what remains from the oldest *Acts of Andrew*,[6] which contrasts with instances where the text exhibits numerous indications of later stages in the development of the language. There are even examples where expressions border on Modern Greek.[7] There are obvious differences in style in the two later rewritings of the Martyrdom, the *Martyrium prius* and the *Laudatio*,[8] both between themselves and between these two later texts and the older *Acts of Andrew*. The language of the *Acts of Andrew and Matthias* (which has been connected with the older *Acts of Andrew*) bears no similarity to the texts mentioned above.

The language of the older *Acts of Andrew*, with pretensions of a sophisticated, Atticizing style, is close to the Greek Koine of the New Testament. However, there is, in general, a preference for a more complex and archaic vocabulary than that of the Greek of the New Testament. For example, the verb εἶμι is constantly used in place of ἔρχομαι, more commonly found in the New Testament; οἶδα is used instead of γι(γ)νώσκω-γνωρίζω; and οἴομαι replaces νομίζω.

---

[6] Prieur, *Acta Andreae*.

[7] These are not only indications that bear characteristics representative of the gradual development of the Attic Koine into the Koine of the New Testament. Dispersed within the text there are also instances where the language is clearly indicative of its development into modes of Modern Greek diction: the oversimplification in the syntactical combinations becomes extremely frequent, and Modern Greek endings are occasionally found in the vocabulary. Certain words also acquire meanings similar to those used in Modern Greek. *Martyrium prius*, a later text published in Prieur, *Acta Andreae*, 2:684–703, is a good example of such a tendency.

[8] On the *Martyrium Prius*, see the previous note. On the *Laudatio*, see Maximilien Bonnet, "Acta Andreae Apostoli cum Laudatione contexta," *AnBoll* 13 (1894): 311–52.

The syntax is also often more complex than that of the New Testament, to the point of being occasionally awkward and sometimes even incomprehensible. The optative is sometimes, but not consistently, found in indirect speech, according to classical Attic standards, and it often occurs in sentences which reveal later stages in the development of the language.

There is a frequent—occasionally too frequent—use of the genitive absolute, disclosing at times pretensions of sophistication in style, at times simple difficulty in using the proper, classical Attic form in the syntax. *Acts of Andrew* 13 is a good example of the latter case, unless the writer is trying to produce some kind of a rhetorical effect here with the repetitive use of the genitive absolute. The extensive use of the genitive absolute within the same syntactical period is a tendency characteristic of many texts from the apocryphal acts. Apparently, the author, in his attempt to create a sophisticated style, transforms the verbs of a paratactic syntax into participles in the genitive absolute because he lacks the skill of classical sentence construction, which would have required a combination of infinitives and participles. The result of his effort, thus, is awkward. A paratactic syntax would have been a better choice.[9]

Some passages exhibit obvious attempts at creating rhetorical effects: repeated use of the exhortative subjunctive (33.1–5; 50.18–24), the imperative (39; 41; 48; 57.16–22), numerous short rhetorical questions (42), repetitive use of an abundance of adjectives (38.9–12; 40.6–10; 57.5–11; 59.7–11; 62.16–19), repeated use of sentences made up of a single verb in the indicative (58.12–19). Many of these characteristics are reminiscent of the language used by Clement of Rome. They are also common in most of the apocryphal acts in exhortative speeches and prayers. Among all these devices, however, are numerous indications of a later stage in the development of the language, with syntactical forms that border on Modern Greek forms of diction. *Acts of Andrew* 44 is a good example, with an abundance of relative clauses where the proper style would have required the use of infinitives and participles.

---

[9] Further discussion of *AAn* 13.1–5 is found in the section on modes of diction (see below, pp. 138–40).

Yet, a few lines later in the same paragraph, there is a proper use of the optative for indirect speech (44.12–14).

The general appearance of this text indicates an effort to create a style that is more scholarly than that of the New Testament. In spite of this conscious effort to achieve a sophisticated style of composition, there are many instances where even the use of the vernacular of the time becomes obvious in the text.

At times, the attempt at sophistication results in complicated, occasionally cumbersome, compositions, as if someone were trying to write in a style far removed from the spoken language of his time. In these instances, the syntax becomes very artificial and hard to follow. For example, in 4.9–11 we read: τὸ μάλιστα δυσωποῦν, τέκνον μου, τοὺς ἐκ πολλῆς ζάλης καὶ πλάνης ἐπὶ τὴν τοῦ θεοῦ πίστιν ἐπιστρέφοντας τοῦτό ἐστιν τὰ ἀπεγνωσμένα τοῖς πολλοῖς πάθη ταῦτα ὁρᾶν θεραπευόμενα ("what troubles the most those who return to the faith of God from great dizziness and delusion is to find that those passions which seem hopeless to most people are healed"). A less distorted syntax, according to classical standards, would have been: τὸ μάλιστα δυσωποῦν, τέκνον μου, τοῦτό ἐστιν, τοὺς ἐκ πολλῆς ζάλης καὶ πλάνης ἐπὶ τὴν τοῦ θεοῦ πίστιν ἐπιστρέφοντας τὰ ἀπεγνωσμένα τοῖς πολλοῖς πάθη ὁρᾶν θεραπευόμενα.

In spite of these several variations, the text of the oldest *Acts of Andrew* makes up a relatively continuous and somewhat homogeneous unit. There are, however, some differences among the various parts of the work. The text of chapters 1–32 abounds with the use of the participle in the genitive absolute in order to express time in the narrative; there is the occasional use of the optative in indirect speech; and there is the frequent use of εἶμι instead of ἔρχομαι. The effort to create a sophisticated, antique effect is obvious, but only as a superficial veneer to the text.

The text of chapters 33–50 more often contains vocabulary, expressions, and syntax that betray a later period in the development of the language. Of course, this may just mean that the text is written in a style closer to the vernacular or that it has not been "edited" sufficiently to appear as antique as chapters 1–32. There are numerous rhetorical devices, the use of εἶμι instead of ἔρχομαι, and the occasional use of the optative in indirect speech. Some passages in the text are awkward and obscure. The language in this excerpt ranges from an effort to achieve an "educated" look to examples that must be close to the vernacular and border on Modern Greek.

The text of chapters 51–65 begins with three participles in the genitive absolute, indicating time, and continues in a simple language very similar to that of the canonical Gospels, with, however, occasional use of older forms (the use of the verb εἶμι, for example), and, in only one instance (60.5), the use of the optative in indirect speech. The syntax becomes awkward on occasion[10] and in the speeches the text generally abounds with rhetorical devices. These rhetorical devices are used here more extensively than anywhere else in the *Acts of Andrew*. Again, in spite of the veneer of older forms in an effort to create an educated effect, there are expressions throughout the text bordering on Modern Greek forms of diction. *Acts of Andrew* 33–50 and 51–65 are very similar in style.

The two later rewritings of the Martyrdom also exemplify many of the characteristics typical of such texts. Both have indications of later stages of editing; both use a mixed language (from Atticizing[11] to near coincidence with Modern Greek forms of diction[12]); both exhibit a certain awkwardness in expression as well as mistakes in syntax and grammar;[13] and one of the texts appears to be either a rewritten version of the other or a later edition of a source common to both texts.[14]

Although it is difficult to determine accurately the time of composition of the *Acts of Andrew and Matthias*, its language is very different

---

[10] See, e.g., 53.4–5 and 18–19, which will be discussed in more detail below, pp. 139–40.

[11] Extreme differences in style are often found in texts of late composition. *Martyrium prius* probably dates from the eighth century and the *Laudatio* from the ninth or the tenth. See *NTApoc*[5] 2:105.

[12] This is especially so in the *Laudatio*.

[13] This may also be an indication of late composition.

[14] *Martyrium prius*: This text is written in a simple New Testament Koine. There is no obvious attempt to render it more "antique," there is no use of the optative mood for indirect speech, and the verb εἶμι is used only once (14.2). Chapters 1–13 of this text appear to be slightly different in style from chapters 14–19. The text of the first thirteen chapters is in the familiar New Testament Koine, with occasional use of the genitive absolute, betraying a later stage of development. Chapters 14–19 seem to summarize

from that in the *Acts of Andrew*. There is no conscious effort to create a sophisticated mode of diction through either syntax or choice of vocabulary. The language of the *Acts of Andrew and Matthias* is simple and uses a limited vocabulary.[15]

---

excerpts from *AAn* 54–64 occasionally retaining certain, almost intact, phrases as well as adding to the narrative. The additions as well as the differences in the similar phrases exhibit a later stage in the development of the language.

There are many instances where the expressions and the syntax exhibit coincidence with Modern Greek forms of diction, suggesting the late composition of the text. The genitive singular of the name of Andrew takes the Modern Greek ending -α instead of -ου in 7.2. It is characteristic that in 15.2 there is an incorrect use of the article (feminine instead of masculine: τὰς πόδας instead of τοὺς πόδας), a mistake probably due to the fact that the original *Acts of Andrew* which the text of *Martyrium prius* is following had at that place a noun requiring the feminine article (*AAn* 54.15: τὰς μασχάλας).

The *Laudatio*: This text differs from the ones examined so far. It is the latest one, and it offers numerous indications of its late composition. Next to constructions with pretensions of a higher style (occasional use of older vocabulary and syntax such as εἶμι instead of ἔρχομαι, very rarely optative for indirect speech, and even one instance of the dual number—in 17.11, τὼ χεῖρε), there are errors of syntax and grammar. What is very different from the other texts is the fact that this text is written in two distinctly different styles. Chapters 1–6 and chapter 23 are in a complicated, Attic style using older vocabulary and complicated syntax. The syntax sometimes becomes very cumbersome, with extremely long sentences reminiscent of similar syntactical constructions of Justin Martyr, Origen, and the Cappadocian Fathers. The difference is that here the syntax is occasionally wrong.

In the passages where the narrative is similar to that of the text of *Martyrium prius*, a comparison between the two indicates the following: The text of *Martyrium prius* is written in a more vivid and free style, close to the language of the New Testament but also containing expressions which betray a later stage in the development of the language. The language of the *Laudatio* is a carefully crafted narrative style, reminiscent of the language of the New Testament but with a tendency toward the more ancient and "educated" form of expression.

[15] See Dennis R. MacDonald, "The *Acts of Andrew and Matthias*, and the *Acts of Andrew*," in MacDonald, *Apocryphal Acts of Apostles*, 9–26. For the discussion of the language of the *Acts of Andrew and Matthias*, I have used MacDonald, *Acts of Andrew*. This language aims at sensationalism in the description of Andrew's torture, bearing much resemblance in that respect to the text of the *Acts of Thecla*. It abounds with paratactic syntax and relative clauses. There are a few scattered grammatical errors, perhaps because of the proximity to Modern Greek forms of diction. For example, there is the occasional use of the imperative mood of the simple past tense of the verb ἔρχομαι, with an α as part of the ending, because there is no strong aorist in Modern Greek: ἔλθατε instead of ἔλθετε. There are also mistakes in the syntax, such as ἐθεασάμεθα Δαυὶδ ᾄδων instead of ᾄδοντα.

Acts of Peter

Composed in Greek probably toward the end of the second century,[16] manuscripts of the *Acts of Peter* in Greek have been lost, save for the Martyrdom and a short fragment on papyrus. I will examine the Martyrdom here.

The language of the Martyrdom exhibits many similarities to that of the *Acts of Andrew*, in that it uses complex vocabulary, ancient forms, and, at times, complicated syntax. There is the same tendency to attempt to use a sophisticated, Atticizing style, with occasional mistakes in syntax and grammar. One obvious similarity between the two texts is the frequent use of the genitive absolute, which sometimes creates extremely long and awkward constructions in syntax. A characteristic example of this is found at the beginning of the narrative in the construction of the first lines, which constitute a single sentence.[17] The syntax of these lines resembles that of the *Acts of Andrew* 13.1–5.

Dispersed throughout the overabundant use of the genitive absolute participle are numerous indications of a more simplistic mode of diction, with less sophisticated or antiquated vocabulary and sentence construction—reminiscent, again, of the *Acts of Andrew*. Among these indications are changes in the endings of nouns into those found in Modern Greek,[18] vocabulary used in later stages of the development of the language,[19] and sentence constructions and expressions similar to those encountered in Modern Greek.[20] And all these forms of diction—indicative of the vernacular—are found beneath a veneer of vocabulary and syntax with pretenses of sophistication, but which in essence consists of a limited number of Attic constructions and an overabundance of the genitive absolute participle.[21]

In spite of the occasional attempt at a sophisticated style, there is no

---

[16] See *Actes apocryphes des apôtres*, 299; edition used: *AAA* 1:78–102.

[17] See below, p. 139, in the discussion of modes of diction in the Apocryphal Acts of the Apostles.

[18] Ἀγρίππα instead of Ἀγρίππου in the genitive singular in 4.18–19.

[19] περιμένεις instead of ἀναμένεις in 5.16.

[20] μέχρις με θέλει ὁ κύριος in 7.20.

[21] In 5.11–16 alone there are four such constructions: θορύβου οὖν μεγίστου ὄντος. . .τοῦ Ἀλβίνου δηλώσαντος. . .λέγοντος αὐτῷ. . .χωρίσαντός μου. . . .

use of the optative of indirect speech in the Martyrdom from the *Acts of Peter*—in contrast to the optative occasionally used in the *Acts of Andrew*—although indirect questions are properly introduced with the relative pronoun. There is occasional proximity and often coincidence to Modern Greek forms of diction.[22]

Acts of Paul

Although the Coptic papyrus discovered in Heidelberg (1904) suggests that the several fragments that had circulated independently and/or as part of the *Acts of Paul*—the *Acts of Thecla*, the *Martyrdom of Paul*, and the Corinthian correspondence—were originally part of a single work,[23] some minor variations in style can be observed throughout these texts. There are definite differences in style between the first two texts and the Corinthian correspondence. The following discussion will include the *Acts of Thecla*,[24] the *Martyrdom of Paul*,[25] the Hamburg Papyrus,[26] and the *Letter to the Corinthians*, the so-called *Third Corinthians*.[27] The order in which these texts are presented here is intended to facilitate the discussion of the peculiarities observed in the language they employ.

The language in both the *Acts of Thecla* and the *Martyrdom of Paul* is simple in construction and vocabulary, and in many places it reads almost as an archaic form of Modern Greek. In most instances the narrative is filled with vocabulary, expressions, and syntactical constructions bordering on Modern Greek. For example, the dative of the indirect object dissolves into prepositional phrases, and there is a constant use of the interrogative pronoun to introduce indirect questions as well as the frequent occurrence of simplistic arrangement of sentences

---

[22] With regard to the proximity—and often coincidence—to Modern Greek, the text of the *Acts of Peter* exhibits some similarities to the text of the *Martyrium prius* of Andrew. See the discussion of this and similar coincidences in other texts from the apocryphal acts in the section on common modes of diction.

[23] See *NTApoc*⁵ 2:213–33.

[24] *AAA* 1:235–72.

[25] Ibid., 1:104–17.

[26] Schmidt, *ΠΡΑΞΕΙΣ ΠΑΥΛΟΥ*.

[27] *Papyrus Bodmer X–XII. Correspondance apocryphe des Corinthiens et de l'apôtre Paul*, ed. Michel Testuz (Geneva: Bibliotheca Bodmeriana, 1959).

in parataxis in the narrative, of awkward constructions in the syntax, and of ὡς or ὡστε and the infinitive. In the *Martyrdom of Paul* there is also an excessive use of the genitive absolute and many simplistic, often awkward, syntactical constructions, without any effort to apply an antique or sophisticated façade, as is the case in the *Acts of Andrew*.

Stylistically, these texts stand apart from the old *Acts of Andrew* but have certain similarities to the *Acts of Andrew and Matthias*. The use of ὡστε and the infinitive is a common characteristic of the *Acts of Thecla* and the *Martyrdom of Paul*, though it is used less extensively in the latter. It is interesting to note that in the *Acts of Thecla* the use of ὡστε and the infinitive abounds in the portions of the text dealing primarily with Thecla, whereas both texts are very similar in style and use of vocabulary and syntax when the primary focus is Paul. We could assume, then, that the incidents referring to Thecla and the incidents referring to Paul may have been two different stages in the creation of the story brought together at some later point in time.

Pages 1–5 of the Hamburg Papyrus exhibit many similarities to the *Acts of Thecla*. The same simplistic syntax, abundant use of the genitive absolute and of ὡστε with the infinitive, the occasional substitution of the accusative for the dative case all indicate a style suggesting the development toward Modern Greek. One would have expected this, since the Hamburg Papyrus represents a different witness of several portions of the same text. The last five pages (6–11), however, are written in a slightly more sophisticated style, with care being taken to avoid the excessive use of the genitive absolute as well as ὡστε and the infinitive, and the syntax is closer to that used in the writing of the Gospels. On page 7, line 2, there is even an instance of the optative of indirect speech, unique in the texts examined here under the general title of the *Acts of Paul*. Pages 9–11 are another witness of the *Martyrdom of Paul*.[28] The *Martyrdom of Paul* and pages 9–11 of the Hamburg Papyrus are almost identical. Pages 9–11 of the Hamburg Papyrus present slight variations in syntax and/or additions and subtractions which betray a slightly less sophisticated style.

---

[28] The *Martyrdom of Paul* was edited by Richard Adelbert Lipsius, *AAA* 1:104–17, before the discovery of the Hamburg Papyrus.

Third Corinthians differs from the previous texts included under the rubric the *Acts of Paul*. At first glance, the style seems so similar to that used in the canonical Pauline letters that this work might also pass as a Pauline letter, which was the author's intent. Pauline expressions and vocabulary occur frequently throughout the text.

In spite of the obvious similarities to Pauline language, however, there are some critical differences: 1) There are expressions and vocabulary not used in the canonical Pauline correspondence, italicized in the following phrases: μὴ βουλόμενος *ἀκυρῶσαι* τὸ *ἴδιον* πλάσμα (*3 Cor* 12), *τέκνα ὀργῆς* οἵτινες τὴν θεοῦ *πρόνοιαν ἀνακόπτουσιν* (*3 Cor* 19), *κατηραμένην* γὰρ τοῦ *ὄφεως* πίστιν ἔχουσι (*3 Cor* 20), τοῦ *πυροῦ σπόρον* (*3 Cor* 26), *ἠμφιεσμένα* (*3 Cor* 27), and *τεκνήματα ἐχιδνῶν* (*3 Cor* 39). 2) Twice (*3 Cor* 5, 15) there are references to Mary by name, the second time as *Μαρίαν τὴν Γαλιλαίαν* (which is the exact expression used in Hamburg Papyrus 8.26), although in Gal 4:5 the reference is γενόμενον *ἐκ γυναικός*. 3) There is a subtle difference in style. The Pauline letters have, in general, a more elaborate way of introducing and ending the text, but, most importantly, a more analytical mode of expression. *Third Corinthians*, in spite of mistakes in orthography and the occasional use of later forms, maintains a more concise style, which is more evident in passages dealing with subject matter similar to that of the canonical letters (that is, *3 Cor* 26–27 and 1 Cor 15:36–43).

Examples of Modes of Diction Common in the Apocryphal Acts

Proximity and/or Coincidence to Modern Greek

Martyrdom of the *Acts of Peter*   ὅλῃ τῇ Ῥώμῃ (1, p. 80, line 7) instead of τῇ Ῥώμῃ πάσῃ, and again εἰς ὅλην τὴν Ῥώμην (3.18); λόγια (4.17) instead of λόγους; περιμένεις (5.16) instead of ἀναμένεις.

Hamburg Papyrus of the *Acts of Paul*   ἤκουσεν ὑπὸ Διοφάντου (3.1), in which the preposition ὑπό is reminiscent of the later Modern Greek diction: ἄκουσε ἀπὸ τὸν Διοφάντη; τὸν κόσμον ὅλον (3.7) instead of τὸν κόσμον ἅπαντα; ἐκυνηγήθης (5.3) instead of ἐθηράθης.

Acts of Paul and Thecla εἰ ἐγὼ σήμερον ἀνακρίνομαι τί διδάσκω, ἄκουσον, ἀνθύπατε (17.9–10) (use of simplistic/awkward syntax and vocabulary bordering on Modern Greek forms of diction). Similarly, καὶ τὰ μεγαλεῖα τοῦ θεοῦ, πῶς ἀπεκαλύφθη αὐτῷ (1.4), and οἱ τρέμοντες τὰ λόγια τοῦ θεοῦ (6.3).

Tendency to Return to Earlier Prototypes

Acts of Andrew 13.1–5

> ἀγαλλιάσεως οὖν μεγάλης οὔσης ἐν τοῖς ἀδελφοῖς, νυκτὸς καὶ ἡμέρας συνερχομένων αὐτῶν ἐν τῷ πραιτωρίῳ πρὸς τὴν Μαξιμίλλαν, κυριακῆς οὔσης παραγίνεται ὁ ἀνθύπατος, τῶν ἀδελφῶν συνηγμένων ἐν τῷ κοιτῶνι αὐτοῦ καὶ ἀκροουμένων τοῦ Ἀνδρέα.

Martyrdom of the *Acts of Peter* 1.1–9

> κυριακῆς οὔσης, ὁμιλοῦντος τοῦ Πέτρου τοῖς ἀδελφοῖς καὶ προτρέποντος εἰς τὴν τοῦ Χριστοῦ πίστιν, παρόντων πολλῶν συγκλητικῶν καὶ ἱππικῶν πλειόνων καὶ γυναικῶν πλουσίων καὶ ματρώνων καὶ στηριζομένων τῇ πίστει μία τις ἔνθα οὖσα γυνὴ πάνυ πλουσία, ἥτις τὴν ἐπίκλησιν τοὔνομα Χρυσῆ εἶχεν, διὰ τὸ πᾶν αὐτῆς σκεῦος χρύσεον ὑπάρχειν—ἥτις γεννηθεῖσα οὔτε ἀργυρέῳ ποτὲ σκεύει ἐχρήσατο οὔτε ὑέλῳ, εἰ μὴ μόνοις χρυσέοις—εἶπεν τῷ Πέτρῳ·

There is an obvious similarity in style between these two passages from the *Acts of Andrew* and the *Acts of Peter*. The constant use of the genitive absolute participle within the same sentence creates the impression of an artificial construction in order to alter a simplistic parataxis in the syntax to create an antique effect.

Preference for Complicated Sentence Constructions

The effort to create a sophisticated, antique style often results in unnecessarily complex syntax. For example, in *Acts of Andrew* 53.4–5, the text reads: ὁπότε τῷ καταδικασθέντι φίλων τὴν ἀφ᾽ ὑμῶν ἀπαλλαγὴν ποιήσασθε.... It would have been simpler to write ὁπότε τῶν τῷ καταδικασθέντι φίλων ἀπηλλάγητε....

A few lines later, in 53.18–19, the text reads: ἐρῶ δέ τι πρὸς σὲ ἕτερον καὶ τοὺς σὺν ἐμοὶ βαδίζοντας ἀδελφοὺς περὶ τῶν ἀλλοτρίων ἡμῖν ἀνθρώπων. A simpler way to say the same thing would be: ἐρῶ δέ τι ἕτερον πρὸς σὲ καὶ τοὺς σὺν ἐμοὶ βαδίζοντας ἀδελφοὺς περὶ τῶν ἀλλοτρίων ἡμῖν ἀνθρώπων.

Confusion between Earlier and Later Modes of Diction

There are grammatical errors that are due either to an attempt to add more sophistication to the form used or to confusion between older and modern forms of the language (the genitive singular Ἀγρίππα [4.18], according to the Modern Greek ending, the use of the first aorist thematic vowel instead of the second, as in the Modern Greek: γενάμενος [7.10] instead of γενόμενος, and other expressions found in Modern Greek forms of diction, such as μέχρις μὲ θέλει ὁ κύριος [7.20]).

In the *Acts of Andrew and Matthias* we read ἵνα ἐξάξει instead of ἵνα ἐξαγάγῃ (4.2–3); καὶ ἀνέλθῃς, where the aorist conjunctive assumes the function of the future indicative (4.10); ἀνέλθατε instead of ἀνέλθετε (5, p. 71, line 3); ηὕραμεν (use of first aorist ending) instead of ηὕρομεν (7.8); ἀποκριθῆναι. . .λόγον (7.11) instead of ἀποκριθῆναι λόγῳ; and καὶ ἐπιλάθωνται τὸν φόβον (8.12) instead of καὶ ἐπιλάθωνται τοῦ φόβου.

Conclusions

When we compare the texts of the apocryphal acts examined above, we can make the following observations:

The *Acts of Andrew* ranks highest in the effort to achieve a degree of sophistication in the choice of vocabulary and syntax. Although there are occasional differences of style in the various parts which constitute the work, this effort is more or less consistent and there are no mistakes in grammar or syntax. Only rarely do expressions bordering on Modern Greek forms of diction occur, probably a result of the vernacular creeping in. The *Acts of Andrew and Matthias* is a work written in a very different style; its syntax is very simplistic and the language more generally exhibits characteristics common in Modern Greek forms of diction. The Martyrdom of the *Acts of Peter* is written in a language which exhibits most similarity to that of the *Acts of Andrew*.

The language of the *Acts of Thecla* is very similar in its choice of vocabulary and its grammatical and syntactical composition to the language found in the *Martyrdom of Paul*. In both, expression is very simplistic and there is no effort to create an antique façade, as is the case in most of the other texts. The persistant use of ὥστε and the infinitive is characteristic of the simplistic device used to lend a sense of urgency to the narrative. The language of *Third Corinthians* resembles that of the canonical Pauline letters, but this may merely be the result of an artificial compilation of Pauline expressions dispersed within a composition of a later date. The language of the *Acts of Paul* and the *Acts of Andrew and Matthias* exhibit the most simplistic syntax of all the texts examined here.

The differences observed in the various texts published together under the name of an apostle (*Acts of Andrew*, *Acts of Paul*) may be due to the various hands that have written or edited these texts in part or in their entirety. This may also be the reason for the unevenness of attempts to superimpose a sophisticated façade on many of these texts. It may also be that some texts were "edited" by the author so that the style is made more antique than the one he would comfortably use—the author abiding by the literary demands of his time—and some portions were not as carefully edited as others, a common enough pitfall, even when revisions are made by the author himself. Wherever an attempt to create such an antique style has been made, one can detect its traces, for the language appears in most of these instances artificial.

Some texts which have been published as part of one work under the name of a single apostle are written in a style readily distinguishable from the rest of the composition. *Third Corinthians*, which is very close to the canonical Pauline letters, is quite distinct from the rest of the *Acts of Paul*. Such examples are an indication that different works were assembled at some point to constitute one work. Similarly, the *Acts of Andrew and Matthias*, which is written in a very simplistic language, stands out from the *Acts of Andrew*.

The reason why most of the martyrdoms are, in general, written in an even and well-defined style is probably due to the fact that, as they are used more often than the rest of the apocryphal acts for the respective feasts of the apostles, they have been more carefully edited.

Given all the problems presented at the beginning of this article and throughout the analysis of the various texts, it becomes obvious why it is so difficult to reach definite conclusions about place of origin, time of composition, and authorship when one examines the language of the apocryphal acts. A definite conclusion that can be reached is that there is an unevenness of composition that indicates various hands at work and/or various revisions or emendations in different parts of each work. Some of the similarities that occur may indicate a later attempt at editing these texts. The artificial style, with numerous indications of awkward constructions in grammar and syntax, may have resulted from the improper use of older forms with which the authors or editors were not completely at ease. Finally, these problems are more pronounced in the noncanonical writings probably because they were neither edited as carefully nor copied as many times as the texts officially used by the Church.

Literary and Religious Studies

Political Authority and Cultural Accommodation: Social Diversity in the *Acts of Paul* and the *Acts of Peter*

Ann Graham Brock

For a number of reasons the *Acts of Paul* and the *Acts of Peter* rank among the most outstanding apocryphal accounts of the early Christian missionary movement. One particularly intriguing element concerning these two accounts is the way in which they share characteristics, such as themes, narrative details, and a parallel ordering of events. Further similarities between the two accounts include journeys by both apostles, their respective dialogues with sea captains, conversions of Nero's servants, and the ensuing martyrdoms for both Peter and Paul. While some of these likenesses, such as sea captains and martyrdoms, could simply be attributable to the similarity of elements that are typical of the oral legends behind the apocryphal acts,[1] other elements in the two acts are so close in detail as to make an interrelationship between the two texts practically a foregone conclusion. Especially prominent among these commonalities is the well-known *quo vadis* scene in which Jesus personally appears to Peter and to Paul, respectively, and has a strikingly similar encounter with each of them.

My thanks go especially to François Bovon, Dennis R. MacDonald, and Christopher R. Matthews for reading and responding to my paper, in addition to the contributions and lively discussion of the Apocryphal Acts Group as a whole.

[1] Richard Valantasis, "Narrative Strategies and Synoptic Quandaries: A Response to Dennis MacDonald's Reading of *Acts of Paul* and *Acts of Peter*," in *Society of Biblical Literature 1992 Seminar Papers*, ed. Eugene H. Lovering, Jr. (Atlanta: Scholars Press, 1992), 238.

The similarities between these two apocryphal Christian documents from the second century are thus generally undeniable, especially with respect to narrative details and parallel events.[2] The presence of so many commonalities in the narrative could lead one to surmise that these texts are the products of authors or redactors who share similar worldviews. In this examination, however, I will argue that, although similarities clearly exist between the two texts, the differences between them seem to bear even more significance. Furthermore, these differences may, in fact, indicate early Christian perspectives that stand in tension with one another.

Despite the fact that the manuscripts for both the *Acts of Peter* and the *Acts of Paul* are fragmentary at points, scholars have nevertheless reconstructed major portions of each text.[3] From these reconstructed texts an interesting dynamic emerges when one examines specifically the way in which the apostles Paul and Peter interact with secondary figures in each of the two texts. Since most of the similarities existing between these two works have already been thoroughly examined elsewhere, this essay will focus primarily upon the critical differences between the two texts. By comparing how the figures of Peter and Paul interact with their followers in each text, I will demonstrate the way in which these two accounts portray different social worlds. The

---

[2] For a detailed examination see the paper by Dennis R. MacDonald, "*The Acts of Paul* and *The Acts of Peter*: Which Came First?" in *Society of Biblical Literature 1992 Seminar Papers*, ed. Eugene H. Lovering, Jr. (Atlanta: Scholars Press, 1992), 214–24, and the two responses by Robert F. Stoops, "Peter, Paul and Priority in the Apocryphal Acts," 225–33, and Valantasis, "Narrative Strategies and Synoptic Quandaries," 234–39.

[3] An analysis of both of these texts is complicated by the lack of an "original" manuscript for either act as a whole. Comments on the *Acts of Peter* will primarily draw from observations on the *Actus Vercellenses* (*AVer*), the Latin version of the *Acts of Peter*, which preserves the bulk of the *Acts of Peter*. Latin and Greek quotations from the *Acts of Peter* are drawn from Vouaux, *Actes de Pierre*. Although the text that Richard Lipsius published closely parallels the manuscript from which he worked, even including errors, Vouaux improved upon the text whenever he saw the need. Greek quotations from the *Acts of Paul* are taken from Vouaux, *Actes de Paul*, or from Schmidt, *ΠΡΑΞΕΙΣ ΠΑΥΛΟΥ*. The Coptic quotations from the *Acts of Paul* are taken from Schmidt, *Acta Pauli*. English quotations from these two apocryphal acts are either my own translation or are taken from the "Acts of Peter," and the "Acts of Paul," *NTApoc*[5] 2:276–322, 352–87. Critical editions of the *Acts of Paul* by Willy Rordorf and of the *Acts of Peter* by Gérard Poupon are forthcoming in CChrSA.

methodology for this study will include a literary analysis of the portrayals of both the apostles and their secondary characters in the narrative. The specific areas of focus will be the descriptions of political authorities in power, the indications of women's positions in leadership roles, and the portrayal of accountability to familial, social, and ecclesiastical responsibilities.

Attitudes toward Political Authority

Among the primary differences between the *Acts of Paul* and the *Acts of Peter* is a discernible contrast in the underlying attitude toward the authorities in power. The following section describes numerous encounters in the *Acts of Paul* in which Paul comes into conflict with the reigning political powers. Since such conflict is frequently portrayed in the Apocryphal Acts, it fits well within the realm of normal expectations. Yet, a conflictual relationship with the authorities is not the only type of interaction portrayed. There are basically two attitudes toward political powers recognizable in these two acts: a somewhat adversarial position in the *Acts of Paul* and an accommodating position evident to some degree in the *Martyrdom of Peter* and to a greater degree in the rest of the text preserved in the Latin version of the *Acts of Peter*, which precedes the martyrdom and portrays a more congenial perspective toward political authorities, especially Roman rulers.

Political Authorities in the Acts of Paul

The *Acts of Paul* is consistent with many apocryphal acts of the apostles in that it portrays numerous instances in which the primary characters and their followers come into conflict with figures holding political power, such as governors, emperors, and other officials. For instance, already early in the text of the *Acts of Paul*, Demas and Hermogenes request that Paul be brought before the governor Castellius on the grounds that "he is seducing the crowds to the new doctrine of the Christians" (14). Subsequently, both rulers (ἄρχοντες) and officers (δημόσιοι) are depicted as accompanying Thamyris, Thecla's fiancé, along with a great crowd bearing cudgels in order to bring Paul before the proconsul to defend himself (15). At this point in the text, the governor responds by ordering Paul to be bound and led off to prison (17). These encounters with gubernatorial figures thus tend to be rather negative in tone. In this case, the governor not only orders Paul scourged and driven out of the city, but he also commands Thecla to be burned to death. When Thecla is saved by miraculous intervention, the governor tries again by sending in more beasts and then even extends his consent for her to be tied to bulls (35).[4] Only after Thecla's third divine reprieve does the governor finally release her. The adversarial nature of such encounters with political figures extends to Thecla's prayer in which she praises God, who is "my helper in prison, my helper before governors, my helper in the fire, my helper among the beasts" (42). Thus, governors are not depicted as benevolent powers but are instead part of the oppressive force from whom early Christians such as Thecla pray for rescue.

Similarly, Paul does not fare very well with respect to the political authorities, as in Ephesus when he is again brought before a governor who subsequently puts the decision before the people to decide whether Paul should be burned or thrown to the beasts. Since the people are not able to agree upon Paul's punishment, this governor condemns Paul to the beasts, but only after having him scourged first (PHam 1). When Artemilla, the wife of the governor, asks to be baptized by Paul, the governor is described as "not a little irate" (οὐ μικρῶς ὀργίζετο) that she and Eubula sat night and day with Paul (PHam 2–3). The text states that the governor Hieronymus then withdraws early that he may quickly plan the beast hunt. Moreover, the governor is depicted as so upset that he orders a very fierce lion, only recently captured, to be set loose against Paul (PHam 4). When this tactic does not work, he is portrayed as subsequently sending even more beasts against Paul.

The most anti-imperial sentiment appears in the depiction of Roman authority in the *Martyrdom of Paul*. When Nero finds out that some of his people have converted to Christianity, he is portrayed as "torturing dreadfully men whom he greatly loved" (*MartPl* 2). Moreover, he issued

---

[4] Although the governor "weeps that such beauty should be devoured by seals" and "frowns" when Alexander requests the bulls, in neither case does this prevent him from trying a total of three times to execute her.

a decree that "all who were found to be Christians and soldiers of Christ should be put to death" (*MartPl* 3). The text goes on to elaborate that many Christians were subsequently put to death without trial. When Paul returns after his death to make an appearance, he accuses the emperor of having unjustly shed the blood of the righteous, with the result that Paul predicts many evils and great punishment for him (*MartPl* 6). The cultural imagery and language in the *Martyrdom of Paul* clearly displays the antipathy between Christians and the empire and emperor.

Political Authorities in the Acts of Peter

A certain amount of contrast between the *Acts of Peter* and the *Acts of Paul* is visible in the description of the martyrdoms of the two apostles. In the *Martyrdom of Paul* the anti-imperial sentiment is especially strong as the Roman political structure is portrayed in its total culpability for the act, whereas in the *Acts of Peter* the causes for Peter's martyrdom are more complexly portrayed. In the latter case, for instance, one of the most significant grievances to which one can ultimately trace the cause of the martyrdom is the anger of the husbands who are rejected by their converted wives (*AVer* 35). Thus, the striking lack of strong political overtones in the *Martyrdom of Peter* distinguishes it from the *Martyrdom of Paul*. Some of the most common elements of the martyrdom genre are not present in the *Martyrdom of Peter*: no direct confrontation with political authority, no trial, and no apologetic speech.[5] According to Robert F. Stoops, the author effectively makes the martyrdom a less pressing issue in the *Acts of Peter* than in the other apocryphal acts.[6] Indeed, "Simon, rather than Nero, is the great persecutor in the text."[7]

When one compares the *Acts of Paul* with the *Acts of Peter*, one of the most intriguing aspects is the extent to which the tensions between political figures and the apostles are mitigated in the *Acts of Peter*. In

---

[5] Stoops, "Peter, Paul, and Priority in the Apocryphal Acts," 231.

[6] Ibid. He states that if one leaves aside chapter 41, persecution takes the form of religious competition.

[7] Ibid.

this text, interestingly, both the apostles Paul and Peter exhibit a rather harmonious relationship with political figures and other authorities in power.[8] The negativity and confrontation between the apostles and authority figures, which are evident in the *Acts of Paul*, rarely appear in the rest of the *Acts of Peter*. Instead, the authority figures are frequently portrayed as possessing a sympathetic attitude toward the two apostles.

Already in the first paragraph of the extant *Actus Vercellenses*, for example, Quartus, a prison officer, is portrayed as open to the cause of Christianity. He not only converts to Christianity but subsequently releases Paul from prison, and thus he "permits Paul to leave the city (and go) where he wished" (*permansit Paulo ut ubi uellet iret ab urbe* [*AVer* 1]). The conversion of Quartus and his easy release of Paul are in strong contrast to the behavior described in the *Acts of Paul*, in which the governor makes a threefold attempt to overcome miraculous intervention in the hopes of finally punishing Thecla.

The most omnipresent character in Paul's section of the *Acts of Peter* is a political figure—a senator. This sympathetically portrayed senator, named Demetrius, is described as a magistrate and as one who keeps "close to Paul on his right hand" (*adherens Paulo ad dexteram eius*), even escorting Paul to the harbor when he departs (*AVer* 3). Demetrius is not, however, a lone convert among the authority figures, as other characters, such as Dionysius and Balub, who are "Roman knights and illustrious men" (*equites Romani, splendidi uiri*), also accompany Paul to the harbor, along with some "from Caesar's household" (*de domo Caesaris* [*AVer* 3]).

Not surprisingly, except for Peter and his opponent Simon, the most prominent character in Peter's section of the *Acts of Peter* also happens to be a senator. Not only is he called "a senator of noble birth" (*senator sum generis magni* [*AVer* 22]), but he is also praised that "no one was so wise among men as this Marcellus" (*nemo fuit tam sapientior inter homines quam hic Marcellus* [*AVer* 8]). Senator Marcellus is so impressed

---

[8] Numerous scholars now believe that the first three chapters featuring the apostle Paul may be an addition to an earlier version of the *Acts of Peter*; this possibility will be explored later in the essay. For a thorough summary of the versions, editions, and recensions of this text, see Gérard Poupon, "Les '*Actes de Pierre*' et leur remaniement," *ANRW* II 25/6:4363–83.

with Peter that he becomes a committed Christian and, after ousting Simon from his house, even becomes Peter's patron. This senator plays a strong role throughout the narrative as he invites widows and the aged to meet with Peter in his house (*AVer* 19) and is even one of the few recipients of a vision.[9] The text explicitly states that Peter was especially encouraged because the senator received such a vision (*AVer* 22).

Marcellus and Peter also go together to the forum, where the brethren have assembled and where the text again specifically points out the involvement of political figures as it states that "senators, prefects, and officers also collected together" (*concurrerunt autem et senatores et praefecti et officia* [*AVer* 23]). After Marcellus, the next major political figure to be mentioned in the *Acts of Peter* is Agrippa who, holding the office of prefect, offers a kind of confession of faith in the forum, declaring to Peter, "I trust in you, and in your Lord whom you preach" (*confidens in te et in dominum tuum quem praedicas* [*AVer* 26]). This prefect even takes the right hand of his young servant lying in front of him and at Peter's encouragement brings him back to life. This positive relationship with political figures further manifests itself in the detail that this was not just any boy brought back to life but one "of whom even the emperor thinks kindly" (*AVer* 26).

The campaign to portray political figures positively and inclusively in the *Acts of Peter* continues with the next figure who, not co-incidentally, is the mother of a senator (*AVer* 28). After approaching Peter, she throws herself at his feet and asks him to restore her son to life. She confesses her faith with the words, "I believe, Peter, I believe" (*credo, Petre, credo*). Among the mourners who bring the body of her son to the assembly, the author specifically mentions that senators and ladies followed her; indeed, the text states that a "throng of senators

---

[9] Variation in the portrayal of the figure of Marcellus is one of the indications of redactional activity in the *Actus Vercellenses*. Originally, in chapter 8, Marcellus appears as a polytheist who becomes known as a patron for Christians; in chapter 10, however, he is described as a lapsed Christian. The redactional activity appears to heighten the status of Peter, who is so impressive in his actions that Marcellus confesses his apostasy, thus providing the opportunity for Peter to make a speech to bring him back into the fold. For further details on the redactional activity with respect to the figures of Marcellus and the apostle Paul, see Poupon, "Remaniement," 4374–77, and Thomas, "Acts of Peter," 43–44.

and ladies" (*turba senatorum et matronarum*) came to "see the wonderful works of God" (*uidentes Dei mirabilia* [AVer 28]). This positive dynamic with respect to political figures is continually reinforced with small details in the narrative, such as the description of the person whom Peter brings back to life as one who is "moreover noble and most respected among the senate" (*liberalis autem magis carissimus erat in senato* [AVer 28]).

Finally, one other event that appears to undergird the positive attitude toward political authority portrayed in the *Acts of Peter* is the most intriguing of miracles in this text—the restoration of a marble statue of Caesar. When a demon from a possessed young man kicks a great marble statue of Caesar to pieces, Marcellus receives empowerment through Peter to sprinkle the stones with water to restore the statue to its original state (*AVer* 11). The act of restoring an imperial statue to wholeness coheres well with what appears to be the overarching positive political portrayal at work in the *Acts of Peter*. Such a miracle would be incongruent in the *Acts of Paul*, where political figures do not become patrons, perform miracles, or receive visions, but instead frequently lead the opposition and the persecution.

Portrayals of Characters in the Narrative

Both the *Acts of Peter* and the *Acts of Paul* are Christian religious works which, in addition to providing instruction and entertainment,[10] also function as a source for early Christian propaganda.[11] Part of the agenda of the authors of these texts is to fortify the authority of each apostle and, in doing so, the authors frequently attempt to increase the status of the apostolic leader in numerous ways.[12] For example, in Tertullian's treatise on baptism, he relates that the Asian presbyter who wrote the

---

[10] For more information on this thesis see Richard Pervo, *Profit with Delight: The Literary Genre of the Acts of the Apostles* (Philadelphia: Fortress Press, 1987).

[11] Ann Graham Brock, "Genre of the *Acts of Paul*: One Tradition Enhancing Another," *Apocrypha* 5 (1994): 119–36.

[12] To fortify the authority of an apostle in such texts is not an argument for an episcopal type of authority in the *Acts of Paul* but can be interpreted as an effort to give greater depth and weight to the early Christian message of the apostle.

Acts of Paul did so because he wished to enhance the prominence of Paul as an apostle. In Tertullian's words, he was "adding something of his own to the prestige of Paul" (*titulo Pauli de suo cumulans*).[13] I find that the dynamic of adding to the prestige of the apostle is operating not only within the *Acts of Paul* but is also the underlying strategy within the *Acts of Peter*.

Despite the high degree of similarity between the *Acts of Peter* and the *Acts of Paul*, the following literary analysis of the secondary characters that appear in the two narratives will demonstrate that the interactions of the apostles with their followers portray significantly different dynamics in the two texts. Not only is there a difference between the interactions that the apostles Peter and Paul have with political figures, as has just been shown, but the types of interactions they have with their male and female followers are highly illuminating and play an integral part in the underlying agenda of the text.

Interactions with Characters in the Acts of Paul

In numerous ways the *Acts of Paul* incorporates images of strong female leadership. Most prominent among the female figures is Thecla, who experiences an abundance of miraculous events and thus serves as a witness to many nonbelievers. Similarly, two other characters, Eubula and Artemilla, also desire to be baptized and subsequently renounce familial and societal pressure in order to follow Paul. In addition to these figures, significant roles are also played by such other female figures as Queen Tryphaena, Myrta, and Theocleia.

Since speeches composed by the authors are one of the primary means by which they convey their messages, this section carefully examines the speeches and dialogues that the authors place upon the lips of the apostles and their accompanying characters. Interestingly, when the apostle Paul is portrayed as speaking to women, his messages differ in the *Acts of Paul* and in the *Acts of Peter*. The *Acts of Paul* does not, for

---

[13] Tertullian *De baptismo* 17.5, in *Q. Septimii Florentis Tertulliani De Baptismo Liber*, ed. Ernest Evans (London: SPCK, 1964), 37. For further interpretation of this text, see Gérard Poupon, "Encore une fois: Tertullien, De baptismo 17, 5," in *Nomen Latinum. Mélanges André Schneider* (Neuchâtel: Faculté de lettres; Geneva: Droz, 1997), 199–203.

example, transmit any speeches by Paul in which he chastises women or refuses them the eucharist, as in the *Acts of Peter*, but rather depicts him strengthening and commissioning them. He tells Thecla, for example, "Go and teach the word of God!" (ὕπαγε καὶ δίδασκε τὸν λόγον τοῦ θεοῦ [41]).

Whereas the *Acts of Peter* contains three variations of instances in which women either die or become paralyzed because of sexual temptations,[14] the *Acts of Paul* engenders a different attitude toward women. For example, when a Syrian named Alexander falls in love with Thecla and forces his embrace upon her, Thecla takes hold of him, rips his cloak, takes the crown from his head, and "makes him a laughing-stock" (καὶ ἔστησεν αὐτὸν θρίαμβον [26]). Such active resistance is a far cry from becoming passively paralyzed.

Although an examination of the dialogue shows that almost all of the speaking parts for women in the *Acts of Paul* lie in the *Acts of Paul and Thecla*, the speaking parts are not strictly limited to Thecla. Additionally, other figures, such as Tryphaena, Theocleia, Nympha, Eubula, and Artemilla, are depicted with small amounts of dialogue, as well as Myrta, whose speech provides a good case study.[15] Myrta in the *Acts of Paul* is depicted with the Spirit coming down upon her in order that she may prophecy and encourage the brethren. She comforts them with the words,

Παῦλος ὁ τοῦ κυρίου δοῦλος πολλ[ο]ὑ[ς] εἰς τὴν ['Ρώμην σώσει κ]αὶ πολλοὺς θρέψει τῷ λόγῳ, ὡς μὴ εἶναι ἀριθμὸν κα[ὶ φα][νερὸν γεν]έσθαι ὑπὲρ πάντας τοὺς πιστούς, καὶ μεγάλως ἡ δόξ[α τοῦ] [κυρίου Χριστοῦ Ιησοῦ] ἐπ᾽ αὐτὸν ὡς μεγάλην χάριν ἔσεσθε ἐν 'Ρώμῃ. (PHam 7)

Paul the servant of the Lord will save many in Rome, and will nourish many with the word, so that there is no number (to count them), and he will become manifest above all the faithful, and greatly will the glory [of the Lord Jesus Christ] <...come> upon him, so that there will be great grace in Rome.

---

[14] I.e., Peter's daughter, the gardener's daughter, and Rufina.

[15] For a more detailed examination of the dialogue, see Brock, "Genre of the *Acts of Paul*," 129–30.

Although one must grant that in the *Acts of Paul* as a whole the women's actions are frequently portrayed as uplifting the prestige of the apostle Paul and not their own positions, nevertheless, the women at least play a part in the narrative. Thus, Myrta's contribution of encouragement to her brethren carries with it a significantly different dynamic than the complete lack of leadership contributions by female figures in the *Acts of Peter*, where no women give speeches of encouragement to anyone.

Peter's Interactions with Characters in the Acts of Peter

In contrast to the *Acts of Paul*, the *Acts of Peter* exhibits a significant lack of autonomous actions on the part of women. Whereas strong female characters such as Thecla and the other women leave their households, husbands, or fiancés to follow Paul in the *Acts of Paul*, in the *Acts of Peter* not until the last section, the martyrdom, do women leave everything behind to follow Peter.[16]

The leading roles in the *Acts of Peter* are instead dominated by male figures, such as Peter, Marcellus, and Simon Magus, while roles elucidating women's leadership and contributions are scarce. One of the female roles portrayed in the Coptic fragment of the *Acts of Peter* is Peter's daughter, whose side is paralyzed and wasted. Because of her state, the crowd questions why Peter, who is so successful in healing others, does not heal his own daughter. He explains that her paralyzed physical condition "is profitable" (ⲣ̄ ⲛⲟϥⲣⲉ) both for her and for himself in that it prevented her from being married at an early age to Ptolemaeus. The text even portrays the Lord himself as claiming that the girl had been a temptation to many already at the age of ten years old. Peter and his wife therefore praise the Lord for preserving their daughter from uncleanness and shame (Coptic *Papyrus Berolinensis 8502*, 135). In this text, apparently, the preferred response to suitors is not actively to fight them off but to become paralyzed. Predictably, in the *Acts of Peter* the blame for the attraction is placed directly upon the young girl. In fact, Peter even quotes the Lord as having said, "for this (daughter) will do harm to many souls if her body remains healthy" (ⲧⲁⲓ ⲅⲁⲣ

---

[16] In this last section Xanthippe, wife of Albinus, and the concubines of Agrippa, Nicaria, Agrippina, Euphemia, and Doris, all convert to the doctrine of purity.

ⲥⲛⲁϣⲱⲱⲃⲉ ⲛ̄ⲣⲁϩ ⲛ̄ ϯⲯⲨⲬⲎ ⲉϣⲱⲡⲉ ⲡⲉⲥⲥⲱⲙⲁ ⲛⲁϣⲱⲡⲉ ⲉϥⲙⲟⲧⲛ̄ ⲉⲣⲟⲥ [Coptic *Papyrus Berolinensis 8502*, 132]). On the other hand, in the *Acts of Paul*, it is Alexander who seems to be more at fault for inappropriate attraction, since he is described as a "powerful man" who "embraced her [Thecla] on the open street" (αὐτὸς αὐτῇ περιεπλάκη εἰς ἄμφοδον [26]). In fact, the Syriac version of this text implicates Alexander further by specifically identifying him as "one who wished to do uncleanness with her" (ܪܐܗܘܪܐܠ ܡܢܚ ܟܐܘܗ ܟܒ̈ܕܐ ܘܗ).[17] Curiously, in all the versions of the *Acts of Paul*, it is nevertheless Alexander who brings Thecla up on charges before the governor. Alexander's actions make Thecla's being brought before the governor seem all the more unjust, except that an important explanatory detail not in the Greek has either been preserved or added in three of the four Syriac manuscripts, namely, when Thecla fights off Alexander, the crown she knocks from his head is the "crown of Caesar." The accusation brought against her is the following:

$$ܕܐܗܠܐ ܥܠ ܒܕ ܩܪܐܗܘܗ ܕܒܠܝ̈ܘܬܐ ܒܠ ܐ̈ܗܠܐ .ܕܐܗܘ ܐܦܣܠܝܘܡܗܝܢ.$$

Thecla they have called a violator of the temples because she cast down the crown of Caesar from the head of Alexander.[18]

In another episode stemming from the *Acts of Peter*, a peasant has a virgin daughter for whom he asks Peter to pray.[19] Ironically, after Peter prays that the daughter be bestowed with what is expedient, "the girl

---

[17] Wright, *Apocryphal Acts of the Apostles*, vol. 1, *Syriac Texts*, p. ܩܠܒ; vol. 2, *English Translation*, 133. MacDonald discovered a similar dynamic in the Armenian version of the Thecla text, where the accusation against Thecla is not assault but sacrilege: her actions are interpreted as an affront against the imperial cult because of her defilement of the headgear associated with imperial power (MacDonald, *Legend and the Apostle*, 41).

[18] Wright, *Apocryphal Acts of the Apostles*, vol. 1, *Syriac Texts*, p. ܩܠܒ; vol. 2, *English Translation*, 132–33.

[19] This narrative is preserved in the Pseudo-Titus Epistle (*De dispositione sanctimonii*, lines 83–93), on page 50 of the text edited by Donatien De Bruyne, "*Epistula Titi, discipuli Pauli, De dispositione sanctimonii*," *Revue Bénédictine* 37 (1925): 47–72. As a storehouse of quotations from apocryphal works, it frequently provides supplementary

immediately fell down dead" (*statim puella iacuit mortua*). The text explains that this happened so that she would be able to "escape the shamelessness of the flesh and to break the pride of the blood" (*effugire carnis audatiam ac mortificare sanguinis gloriam*). After the old man begs Peter to raise her from the dead, she then falls prey to someone who passes himself off as a believer and seduces her, and, according to the narrative, neither ever appears to anyone again. Although this episode may represent a multiform (called a doublet in written texts), it nevertheless reinforces the same message as the previously mentioned episode: that it is preferable for women to be paralyzed or even dead rather than undergo struggles with the physical body.

The next major female character in the *Acts of Peter* is Eubula (*AVer* 17) whose interaction with Peter's primary antagonist places her in a negative light. The character named Simon, whose confrontation with Peter in Rome provides the climax of the narrative, is the same antagonist whom Peter had previously driven out of Judaea. When Simon had been in Judaea, "where he did much harm" (*multa mala facientem*), he had stayed with Eubula, "a woman of some distinction in this world" (*honestam nimis in saeculo hoc*), whom Simon repaid with theft before fleeing the city. Following the theft, Eubula, in a state of dishevelment, receives instructions from Peter to rise from bed, put up her hair, and pray to the Lord Jesus Christ who judges every soul. He tells her, "In him you must be saved, if indeed you repent with all your heart of your former sins" (*in quem te necesse est saluari, si tamen ex toto corde penitueris a prioribus tuis peccatis* [*AVer* 17]). It is interesting that Eubula, guilty of being the victim of both deception and robbery, nevertheless receives the charge from Peter to repent with all her heart. The narrative continues with Peter advising Eubula to place some of her people by the gate that leads toward Neapolis to keep watch for Simon. In her response to Peter, Eubula throws herself at his feet, acquiesces to his instructions, and because she is greatly

---

material to the apocryphal acts. Augustine's reference to the gardener's daughter side by side with Peter's daughter (in *Contra Adimantum Manichaei discipulum* 17) indicates that this narrative from Pseudo-Titus most likely stemmed from the *Acts of Peter*; see *NTApoc*[5] 2:57, 276, 279.

distressed even goes to the magistrate, although "she had never (before) come out in public" (*quae numquam in publicum processerat*). As a result, Eubula recovers her property and, after renouncing the world, she gives alms both to the widows and the orphans as well as clothing to the poor.[20] This woman who had never before been out in public thus receives the most significant female role in the *Acts of Peter*, a role circumscribed to include repentance and almsgiving.

The next major female figure in the narrative is a blind widow whom Peter heals at Marcellus's house (*AVer* 20). Subsequently, the other old blind widows say, "We beg you, Peter, sir, share also with us his compassion and kindness" (*praecamur, domine Petre, misericordiam et pietatem illius tribuas et nobis* [*AVer* 21]). They ask for mercy and as a result see the Lord in a variety of forms: as an old man, as a growing youth, and as a boy who gently touched their eyes (*AVer* 21). This incident is closely followed by another story about a widow who cries out to Peter that her only son is dead (*AVer* 25). After Peter raises him from the dead, the mother of a senator throws herself at Peter's feet and begs him to bring her son back to life. Peter asks that she distribute to the widows the money that she would have laid out for her son's funeral. After the revival of her son, the senator's mother offers her house to Peter, but when she is refused, she brings two thousand pieces of silver.[21]

Although the *Acts of Peter* portrays women involved in a number of situations, the number of speaking parts for women in the *Acts of Peter* are few. The woman suckling the seven-month-old child at her breast, for example, carries out Peter's instructions, but it is her child and not she who delivers Peter's message to Simon. The young child's speech contains approximately fifteen lines of dialogue, which is more than the dialogue of all the women characters combined (*AVer* 15). The speaking parts for women occur in only five chapters and consist mainly

[20] In a sense this story foreshadows that of Marcellus, who similarly housed Simon and who is also portrayed as asking for Peter's forgiveness. Marcellus, however, becomes more of the model of proper repentance in the narrative, with his transformed status being affirmed positively both by his reception of a vision and his ability to perform a miracle.

[21] For more information on patronage, see Robert F. Stoops, Jr., "Patronage in the *Acts of Peter*," in MacDonald, *Apocryphal Acts of Apostles*, 91–100.

of entreaties for help. In the *Acts of Peter* the women who speak are generally only widows and the mother of a senator (possibly also a widow). One widow, for example, begs Peter to revive her dead son because she is concerned that no one will take care of her. She asks, "Now he is dead, who will offer me a hand?" (*Hoc mortuo, qui mihi manum porriget?* [*AVer* 25]). In this way the actions and dialogue of the women serve primarily as opportunities for Peter to demonstrate his abilities to perform miracles. Only two instances occur in which women receive speaking parts outside of requests for Peter's miracles. The mother of the senator receives one line of dialogue when she brings the two thousand pieces of silver and says, "Divide these among the virgins of Christ who serve him" (*Haec diuide uirginibus Christi qui ei deseruiunt* [*AVer* 29]). The other instance is Chryse, the woman "notorious all over Rome for fornication" (διαβέβληται γὰρ ἐν ὅλῃ τῇ Ῥώμῃ ἐπὶ πορνείᾳ), who receives a few lines of dialogue when she brings ten thousand pieces of gold (*AVer* 30).

In summary, in both texts women serve as facilitators to showcase the authority and power of Peter and Paul. They do so, however, in significantly different ways. In the *Acts of Peter* women's participation or interactions with Peter are acceptable whenever they donate from their wealth or ask for help, but opportunities for women's leadership are almost nonexistent. Not only are there no primary female roles, but even merely positive examples are scarce. The unmarried women in the *Acts of Peter* clearly do not fare well in the narrative, as they are in turn either paralyzed, seduced, deceived, notorious, speechless, or dead.[22] The widows who receive various visions are the best models the text has to offer, but in the Latin version of the *Acts of Peter* they are not named and are generally grouped together.

Paul's Interactions with Characters in the Acts of Peter

Not only do the actions of Peter, the primary character, in the *Acts of Peter* make an interesting study in the interrelationships between characters, but the portrayal of the secondary apostle Paul, based on

---

[22] Virgins are mentioned as the intended recipients of some financial support (*AVer* 29), but as characters they never make it into the narrative.

his interactions with characters in the narrative of the *Acts of Peter*, especially in Rome, is also informative. Among those who respond to Paul is a woman named Candida, the wife of the prison officer Quartus. Because of Paul's words, she instructs her husband and he, too, believes. If this event were to follow the pattern of the conversion of women typical for the *Acts of Paul*, one would expect that when Candida heard Paul's preaching and converted, she, too, would have left or rejected her husband. In this text, however, she is depicted as converting her spouse. Unfortunately, however, if she is to be included in the description several paragraphs later that "they all fell away" (*omnes dissoluti sunt* [*AVer* 4]), then neither her conversion nor her husband's was long-lasting. Moreover, this character seems less the example of a convert than a contrived figure through which the apostle Paul is released from house arrest in Rome in order to heighten the need for Peter's arrival.

The most detailed description of interaction between Paul and a female character occurs in the scene with Rufina, who is introduced specifically as a woman who wished that "even she should receive the eucharist at Paul's hands" (*uolens itaque et ipsa eucharistiam de manibus Pauli percipere* [*AVer* 2]). When she approaches Paul, his response to her is not to grant her request but instead immediately to chastise her. Paul, "filled with the Spirit of God" (*spiritu Dei repletus* [*AVer* 2]), declares that she is not coming to the altar like a true worshipper. Instead he accuses her of rising from beside one who is not her husband but an adulterer, and he declares to her harshly, "behold Satan shall break your body and cast you down in the sight of all who believe in the Lord" (*Ecce. . .Satanas contribulato corde tuo proiiciet te ante oculos omnium credentium in domino* [*AVer* 2]). Interestingly, in a manner similar to the women in the interactions with Peter, Rufina subsequently falls down, becoming paralyzed on her left side from head to toe and with no power to speak.

Only a few other female characters interact with Paul in the text. These women pay homage to Paul in this way: "And a great crowd of women knelt down and fervently entreated the blessed Paul, and they kissed his feet and escorted him to the harbor" (*AVer* 3). Two women are specifically named, Berenice and Philostrate, the two matrons who conducted Paul to the harbor (*AVer* 3). Although this kind of adulation toward Paul, especially from a crowd of women kissing Paul's feet, portrays an initially adoring position toward him, the significant dynamic with respect to Paul follows shortly thereafter, where it is pivotal for the narrative that almost all of the disciples of Paul subsequently fall away. The unfolding of the plot next describes Simon Magus arriving and making such an impact that "out of so great a number that were established in the faith, they all fell away except for the presbyter Narcissus and two women in the lodging-house of the Bithynians and four who could no longer go out of their house" (*AVer* 4). Therefore, even though Paul made "so great a number" (*tam magnae multitudinis* [*AVer* 4]) of converts, including the explicit reference in the text to a "great crowd of women" (*plurima turba mulierum* [*AVer* 3]), nevertheless, only seven Christians continued steadfast as a result of his efforts, with as few as two of them being women. Thus, with Paul's departure the narrative stage is set for Peter to become the primary focus and to save the Christian community in Rome.

The summary of these cases with respect to Paul and the individual women characters shows little uplifting of women in Christian leadership roles in the *Acts of Peter*. Two matrons are mentioned in passing, however, in the sections concerning the apostle Paul, the "brethren" (*fratres* [*AVer* 1–2]) speak three times and Demetrius, at Paul's right hand, speaks once (*AVer* 3), but none of the women with whom Paul has any contact has a speaking part in the *Acts of Peter*. In fact, Rufina, to whom Paul refuses to offer the eucharist, becomes speechless. Paul's interactions with women in the *Acts of Peter* thus mirror Peter's interactions with women in this text. The resulting portrayal is therefore quite distinct from Paul's treatment of women in the *Acts of Paul*. In fact, interactions with both apostles in the *Acts of Peter* portray women as visible, as useful for the narrative, but definitely not affirmed in leadership roles. When compared to the types of interactions between Paul and women in the *Acts of Paul*, the contrast is critical.

Conformity to Familial and Social Responsibilities

A third major difference between the *Acts of Paul* and the *Acts of Peter* lies in their respective portrayals of familial and societal accountability, a factor closely connected with the depiction of women's leadership. For example, since the *Acts of Paul* tends to portray women positively, Thecla's resistance to social and familial pressures ultimately makes her the heroine of the story and wins Paul's confirmation of her right to teach. In the *Acts of Paul*, therefore, the usual biological family ties are replaced by the kinship of the Christian family. Only one female figure, Theocleia, Thecla's mother, is characterized in less than positive terms in all of the *Acts of Paul*. This unaffirming portrayal is not the result of Theocleia's failings because of sexuality, adultery, or fornication, as in the typical female failings in the *Acts of Peter*; rather, this sole dissenting female is a proponent of women fulfilling their familial obligations. When Thecla does not go through with her betrothal to Thamyris, the narrative portrays Thecla's mother as condemning her own daughter to death with the words, "Burn the lawless one!" (κατάκαιε τὴν ἄνομον [*AThec* 20]). In the Syriac version of this text, Theocleia goes even further in her denouncement of her daughter, saying,

ܐܘܩܕܘܗܝ ܠܗܕܐ ܫܛܝܬܐ ܒܓܘ ܬܐܛܪܘܢ ܕܟܠܗܝܢ ܢܫܐ ܕܚܙܝܢ ܠܗ ܢܕܚܠܢ ܘܐܦ ܗܢܝܢ ܕܗܢܐ ܝܘܠܦܢܗܝܢ.

Burn the fool in the midst of the theater, that all the women who see her, those whose doctrine this is, may be afraid.[23]

Thecla's mother, whose own status is at risk because of Thecla's actions, is thus the strongest proponent of culture-conforming behavior in the *Acts of Paul*, resulting in her position being directly antithetical to the heroine of the story.[24]

Among the other more prominent female figures in the *Acts of Paul* is Tryphaena. She is described as significantly more concerned for Thecla's welfare than Thecla's biological mother, with the result that she ultimately becomes Thecla's surrogate Christian mother. In the narrative she embraces Thecla, advocates on her behalf, and even invites her into her home both before and after Thecla's fight with the beasts.

---

[23] See Wright, *Apocryphal Acts of the Apostles*, vol. 1, *Syriac Texts*, p. ܩܣܒ; vol. 2, *English Translation*, 127.

[24] The text portrays Thecla as returning to her mother at the end of her narrative (43) in order to attempt to reassure her or reconcile with her, but no outcome is recorded.

She appears to have some stature as a kinswoman of Caesar but perhaps not much political power, as she has less influence with the governor concerning Thecla than Alexander has with him.[25] Nevertheless, as Tryphaena steadfastly accompanies Thecla to the battle with the beasts, her character represents the way in which newly adopted Christian families supported one another in times of persecution and functioned in place of the original family ties.

The last section of the *Acts of Peter*, the martyrdom, is the only section which includes the chastity/persecution motif for women.[26] In this respect, therefore, this section seems to resonate more with the *Acts of Paul* than with the rest of the *Acts of Peter*. However, the chastity/persecution motif in this case has a slightly different tenor to it, in that it is the primary means by which the culpability of the authorities is somewhat mitigated and shifted away from the political arena.

Contrasted with the *Acts of Paul*, in which the conversions are frequently those of women (including members of the upper-class, whose husbands then become upset), the Latin version of the *Acts of Peter* portrays significantly more positive responses from upper-class male figures, including the senators Marcellus and Demetrius and even a statement of faith from the prefect Agrippa. Thus, in the bulk of the *Acts of Peter* the threat to familial unity is lessened by the depiction of greater responses and conversions by primary male characters. In numerous ways, therefore, the *Acts of Peter* demonstrates a commitment to social and familial ties. Peter himself sets the example in the portrayal of his own married status and his concern for his daughter, with the result that this is one of the few apocryphal narratives that makes mention of any of the children of the apostles. Peter's advocacy for a primary accountability to familial ties is especially clear in his command to the widow's son whom he brings back to life: "Young man, arise and walk with your mother, so long as you are useful to her" (*iuuenis, surge et*

---

[25] Both Alexander and the governor take it seriously, however, when Tryphaena faints and is thought to be dead (35).

[26] For more information on the chastity/persecution motif, see François Bovon, "The Life of the Apostles: Biblical Traditions and Apocryphal Narratives," in idem, *New Testament Traditions and Apocryphal Narratives* (Allison Park, Pa.: Pickwick, 1995), 161; and Burrus, *Chastity as Autonomy*.

ambula cum matre tua usque dum ei prode es [*AVer* 27]). Peter then
makes a point to instruct the young man that only later, after he has
fulfilled his obligations to his mother, should he then come forward to
serve (*AVer* 27).

In a similar manner, the senator Demetrius is portrayed as bowing to
previous societal responsibilities as he regretfully informs Paul that he
cannot join him on his missionary journey. Demetrius tells him, "Paul,
I could wish to leave the city, if I were not a magistrate, so as not to
leave you" (*Paulo, uellem fugere ab urbe, si non essem magistratus, ut
a te non discederem* [*AVer* 3]). Also depicted as honoring a previous
commitment is Candida who, when she converts, remains in her
marriage and instructs her husband, with the result that he, too, converts.
Another widow and her daughter are described thus: "So Peter went in
and saw one of the old people, a widow that was blind, and her daughter
giving her a hand and leading her to Marcellus's house" (*AVer* 20).
Even the inclusion of such a small detail as the daughter giving her
mother a hand indicates the presence of familial support. Thus, while
in the *Acts of Peter* loyalty to family ties undergirds the Christian life,
in the *Acts of Paul* the familial bond can be replaced with an adopted
Christian family. In terms of conformity or resistance to familial
obligations, therefore, the *Acts of Paul* and the *Acts of Peter* stand on
opposite sides of the fence.

Ecclesiastical Organization

One last significant characteristic of the *Acts of Peter* and the *Acts of
Paul* that bears investigation is the difference in the portrayal of
ecclesiastical organization present in each of the acts. With respect to
church offices, the *Acts of Peter*, for instance, contains a significant
number of references to ecclesiastical designations and titles. First
among the numerous indications of ecclesiastical organization are three
references to an "elder" (*praesbyter*) named Narcissus, who escorts
Paul to the harbor (*AVer* 3). This presbyter is also one of the few Pauline
converts who does not fall away (*AVer* 4) and is thus mentioned once
again when Ariston brings Peter and Theon to his house (*AVer* 6). Later
in the narrative, the healing of the widow's son includes two more

significant ecclesiastical terms: "deacon" (*diaconus*) and "bishop" (*episcopus*). Peter tells the widow's son to stay with his mother as long as he can be useful to her and then explicitly explains to the young man, "Afterwards, however, you will be free to offer yourself to me in a higher service, in the office of deacon and bishop" (*Postea autem mihi uacabis altius ministrans, diaconi ac episcopi <sor>te* [*AVer* 27]).

The *Acts of Paul* contains so few ecclesiastical designations that even references to the term "apostle" are rare or nonexistent.[27] In contrast, the *Acts of Peter* frequently employs the designation "apostle" (*apostolus*), as well as two uses of the title "co-apostle" (*coapostolus* [*AVer* 10]). Moreover, Peter receives numerous additional titles, including "apostle of Christ" (*apostolus Christi* [*AVer* 22]) and "apostle of the Lord" (*domini apostolus* [*AVer* 7]), as well as the special description that God had chosen Peter among all the apostles (*AVer* 5). By contrast, the extant *Acts of Paul* mirrors the canonical letters of Paul in its scarcity or lack of references to bishops,[28] as well as its absence of references to presbyters or any hierarchical church titles.[29] Thus, in dissimilarity to the *Acts of Peter*, the *Acts of Paul* exhibits a noticeable lack of references to ecclesiastical positions or designations.

[27] The only exception occurs in the Corinthian correspondence which may be an accretion to the *Acts of Paul*. The use of the term in the colophon is probably also secondary. Thomas MacKay presents reasons why "we cannot be certain that the epistle was originally or typically associated with the API" in his article, "Response," in MacDonald, *Apocryphal Acts of Apostles*, 148. He also refers to his earlier detailed examination in "Observations on P. Bodmer X (Apocryphal Correspondence between Paul and the Corinthian Saints)," in vol. 3 of *Papyrologica Bruxellensia 18. Actes du XVᵉ Congrès International de Papyrologie* (Brussels: Fondation Égyptologique Reine Élisabeth, 1979), 119–28.

[28] Phil 1:1 is the only site in the authentically Pauline letters where the word ἐπίσκοπος appears, and even then it not only appears in the plural but exhibits more of the word's original meaning of "one who oversees," rather than the more technical meaning of "bishop" that appears later (Hermann Beyer, "ἐπίσκοπος," *TDNT* 2:610). Moreover, MacDonald points out that the placement of ἐπίσκοποι in 1:1 may be the work of an assembler, since it is the introductory verse situated at the beginning of what appears to be three Pauline fragments. For further discussion, see MacDonald, *Legend and the Apostle*, 99.

[29] Again, the exception in the *API* lies in the contested "Letter of the Corinthians to Paul." In this epistle the terms "deacon" and "presbyter" are each used once.

While the absence of ecclesiastical titles could indicate an earlier time frame for the legends of the *Acts of Paul*, it is safer to say that differences concerning the use of such titles at least suggest a more democratic and decentralized perspective toward leadership and hierarchy underlying the *Acts of Paul*. One cannot help but wonder if the presence of a significantly greater number of ecclesiastical titles in the *Acts of Peter* bears any correspondence to the portrayal of women's leadership roles as restricted or nonexistent.

The differences described here between the *Acts of Paul* and the *Acts of Peter* bear a striking resemblance to a similar contrast between the *Acts of Paul* and the Pastoral Epistles. With respect to the portrayal of women's early Christian leadership, Dennis R. MacDonald, in *The Legend and the Apostle*, has cogently described the battle for the claim to Paul's authority as evidenced by the competing portrayals of Paul in the Pastoral Epistles and in the legends of the *Acts of Paul*.[30] He points out that in the legends of the *Acts of Paul*, Paul commissions a woman to teach, while in 1 Tim 2:11–15, he is portrayed as forbidding it. In a similar contrast, in the legends behind the *Acts of Paul*, Paul encourages women to be continent in order to be saved, while in the Pastoral Epistles he is portrayed as telling women they shall be saved by bearing children. MacDonald points out that, "instead of luring Thecla away from her lover and encouraging her to teach the word of God, the author of the Pastorals indicates that Paul would have her marry, be submissive to her husband, raise lots of children, and live happily—in silent domestication—ever after."[31] Thus, the role of women's leadership is one of the primary areas of contention between the Pastoral Epistles and the legends of the *Acts of Paul*.

Second, not only do the Pastoral Epistles depict the restriction of women's leadership in the church, they also tend to discourage critical

---

[30] Compare the article by Peter Dunn, "Women's Liberation: The *Acts of Paul*, and Other Apocryphal Acts of the Apostles," *Apocrypha* 4 (1993): 245–61. Dunn argues that the *Acts of Paul* and the Pastoral Epistles are not to be polarized so strongly. He is right to observe that both are heirs to the Pauline tradition; however, attempts to harmonize these two groups are unsuccessful. While the similarities cannot be denied, the differences between the two branches are perhaps even more significant.

[31] MacDonald, *Legend and the Apostle*, 59.

political sentiments. To demonstrate this tendency toward social conformity and respectability, MacDonald provides a number of citations, including Titus 3:1, "Remind them to be submissive to rulers and authorities, to be obedient," as well as 2 Timothy with its overall lack of political hostility toward Rome.[32]

Third, the Pastoral Epistles are rife with the presence of ecclesiastical titles, as well as support for familial and household traditions. In fact, the Pastoral Epistles contain descriptions of the qualifications necessary for the offices of bishop, presbyter, and deacon, which include the status of being married and a position at the head of the household. MacDonald rightly points out that, "whereas the legends pit the household and the church against each other as competing social institutions, the Pastorals identify the strength of the church with that of the household."[33] His historical examination convincingly describes the claim for Paul's authority by both the Pastoral Epistles and the *Acts of Paul*.

I would contend that in terms of a number of categories in the political, social, familial, and ecclesiastical realms, the *Acts of Paul* and the *Acts of Peter* also portray two divergent perspectives in much the same manner as do the *Acts of Paul* and the Pastoral Epistles. Furthermore, in a number of significant ways the *Acts of Peter* resonates rather closely with the agenda of the Pastoral Epistles and exhibits a similar kind of claim not only on Peter's but also on Paul's apostolic support for its version of Christianity. Gérard Poupon argues that the apostle Paul appears to have been grafted onto the text of the *Acts of Peter*, as his appearances are concentrated in the first three chapters of the acts where Peter is completely absent.[34] Thus, it seems that Paul's name has been appropriated in the text and used thirty times with the result that the portrayal of the apostle Paul in the *Acts of Peter* is generally more socially conforming and positive toward political authorities and more negative toward women than is his portrayal in the *Acts of Paul*.

---

[32] Ibid., 66–67.

[33] Ibid., 72.

[34] Poupon, "Remaniement," 4372–74. Vouaux also speaks of interpolations in *Les Actes de Pierre*, 26–35. For a summary of the arguments, see Christine Thomas, "The 'Prehistory' of the *Acts of Peter*," in this volume, and for more details, see eadem, "Acts of Peter," 23–71.

In the *Acts of Paul*, for example, when Thecla finds Paul again and tells him everything, the text states that "Paul marveled greatly" (ἐπὶ πολὺ θαυμάσαι τὸν Παῦλον [41]). In the *Acts of Peter*, however, Paul's most prominent encounter with a female follower—that with Rufina—is a threatening, moralistic one, as he tells her, "behold Satan shall break your body and cast you down in the sight of all who believe in the Lord" (*AVer* 2). Thus, when one compares how women ultimately fare, the resulting contrast between the *Acts of Paul* and the *Acts of Peter* seems significant.

In summary, in much the same way that the Pastoral Epistles claim the authority of Paul for the amelioration of conflict with political authorities, for the restriction of women's leadership in the church, and for the hierarchical claims to authority, the *Acts of Peter* portrays both Peter and Paul as demonstrating these attitudes in word and deed. These portrayals indicate ways in which the authors advocate significantly different social roles for their constituents.

Conclusion

Despite numerous similarities between the two apocryphal accounts of the *Acts of Peter* and the *Acts of Paul*, the analysis above indicates ways in which the two texts differ in several critical, meaningful ways. In fact, in a number of places the *Acts of Paul* and the *Acts of Peter* seem ideologically incompatible. The two texts are to some extent disparate both with respect to the portrayal of relationships with figures wielding political authority and with respect to the exercise of female leadership in the early Christian communities. Whereas in the *Acts of Paul* there exists a significant linkage of Pauline apostleship with strong female leadership, in the *Acts of Peter*, no such apostolic link is forged.

Tertullian records that the presbyter who compiled the *Acts of Paul* stepped down from his office because his writing and Thecla's example were being used to claim the right for women to teach and to baptize.[35] From the analysis presented in this chapter, one can clearly surmise that the final author/redactor of the *Acts of Peter* would have faced no

---

[35] Tertullian *De baptismo* 17.5.

such job threat. Thus, the differences in the portrayals of the apostles, their interactions with the other characters, and the attitudes toward accountability to political leadership, conformity to familial and social obligations, and ecclesiastical offices indicate that these two texts arise out of perspectives that diverge significantly from one another.

Ritual Epicleses in the Greek *Acts of Thomas*

Caroline Johnson

The *Acts of Thomas*, thought to have been compiled in Syria in the first half of the third century, chronicles the mission work of the apostle Thomas in the land of India.[1] As he travels from town to town, he exhorts his listeners to abandon their lives of earthly appetites and ignorance and to join him in the life of the spirit, pure and asexual. His message of self-control wreaks havoc in numerous households, for he convinces wives and husbands to forsake their conjugal relationships. In addition, Thomas heals the sick, brings the dead back to life, and exorcises demons from afflicted people.

The narrative of the *Acts of Thomas* is roughly structured around the conversions that result from the apostle's teaching and healing. Integral to these accounts of conversion are detailed descriptions of the initiation rituals which inaugurate the change in status of the new believer. These rituals include baptism, sealing, and the eucharist, all performed by the

I would like to thank Stan Stowers, Susan Harvey, Anke Finger, and especially François Bovon for their help with this project.

[1] Greek edition: *AAA* 2/2:99–288. I am working primarily with the Greek text, as it is thought to preserve an older version of the text (even though the Syriac is most likely the original language). See Han J. W. Drijvers, "The Acts of Thomas," in *NTApoc*[5] 2:323; Klijn, *Acts of Thomas*, 1–13. Klijn translates the Syriac version and provides extensive commentary. He also comments on the Greek version, especially where it differs from the Syriac. For the Syriac edition see Wright, *Apocryphal Acts of the Apostles*, vol. 1. English translations of the Greek *Acts of Thomas* are for the most part adapted from *NTApoc*[5] 2:339–405. I provide my own translation of the epiclesis prayers themselves.

apostle. Further, the text recites prayers uttered by Thomas, both within and without ritual contexts. Thus, the *Acts of Thomas* serves as a rich resource for liturgical traditions in the early Syriac church.[2]

Some of the liturgical material in the *Acts of Thomas* is, however, more mystifying than enlightening. Two such passages are the spirit-epicleses[3] contained in chapters 27 and 50. These two prayers stand out as strikingly parallel to each other; yet, they are unique among the many prayers in the *Acts of Thomas*, and possibly among all the extant prayers of the early centuries of Christianity. Where do these prayers come from and how do they function in the rituals of the *Acts of Thomas*? The goal of this study is to answer these two questions. To search for possible precedents and models for these epicleses, I first look to Christian liturgical traditions of the first three centuries. Finding few answers there, I then turn to a tradition of prayer and petition widely known in the ancient Mediterranean world: magic spells. I propose that the best model for these epiclesis prayers—and in particular for the way they function in ritual—resides in this genre.

---

[2] Two major studies of Syriac liturgy are Sebastian Brock, *Holy Spirit in the Syrian Baptismal Tradition* (The Syrian Churches Series 9; Bronx, N.Y.: Available at John XIII Centre, Fordham University, 1979); and Robert Murray, *Symbols of Church and Kingdom: A Study in Early Syriac Tradition* (Cambridge: Cambridge University Press, 1975). For specific studies of Syrian baptism and anointing see Gabriele Winkler, "The History of the Syriac Prebaptismal Anointing in the Light of the Earliest Armenian Sources," in *Symposium Syriacum 1976* (Orientalia Christiana Analecta 205; Rome: Pontificium Institutum Orientalium Studiorum, 1978), 317–24; and idem, "The Original Meaning of the Prebaptismal Anointing and Its Implications," *Worship* 52 (1978): 24–45.

[3] These prayers are commonly referred to as epicleses, which is correct in the fundamental meaning of invocation (epiclesis is transliterated from the Greek verb ἐπικαλέω, which means "to call upon"). As a liturgical term, however, epiclesis acquires a more technical meaning: an invocation (usually addressed to God the Father) which asks that the Holy Spirit be sent down specifically to consecrate the elements of the eucharist. In this technical sense these prayers are not epicleses. In the eucharist prayer, for example, the apostle asks the Holy Spirit to join the participants in the feast, not to sanctify the elements. In the baptism, the request is to cleanse and seal. In this essay, I will use the term epiclesis in its broader sense, that of invocation. See J. Laager, "Epiklesis," *Reallexikon für Antike und Christentum*, vol. 5 (Stuttgart: Anton Hiersemann, 1962), 578–99.

The Texts of the Epicleses

To begin this investigation, I will discuss the prayers themselves and explain the contexts in which they appear. I present the two prayers below, placed side by side in order to illustrate their parallels:

Chapter 27	Chapter 50
1. Come, holy name of the Christ, the name above every name,	1. Come, perfect compassion,
2. Come, power of the Most High and perfect goodness of heart,	2. Come, fellowship of the male,
3. Come, most high gift,	3. Come, one who knows the mysteries of the chosen one,
4. Come, compassionate mother,	4. Come, partaker in all the contests of the noble combatant,
5. Come, fellowship of the male,	5. Come, silence, one who reveals the splendid things of every height
6. Come, one who reveals the hidden and enigmatic mysteries,	6. Come, one who makes known the enigmatic things and who restores the secret things as manifest, holy dove which gave birth to twin nestlings,
7. Come, mother of the seven houses, so that your rest may be in the eighth house,	7. Come, hidden mother,
8. Come, elder[4] of the five members—mind, thought, wisdom, esteem, reason—share with these newer ones,	8. Come, one who is manifest in her actions and one who grants joy and rest to those who join together in her,

---

[4] Here the Holy Spirit is addressed with a grammatically masculine term: πρεσβύτερος. This could be a reference to Christ, but it could just as easily refer to the Holy Spirit, who was conceived of in both genders in Syriac literature. See n. 91 below.

9. Come, Holy Spirit, cleanse their kidneys[5] and their heart, and put a seal upon them in the name of the Father and the Son and the Holy Spirit.

9. Come and share with us in this eucharist which we perform in your name, and share with us in the *agape*[6] for which we are gathered together at your call.

1. ἐλθέ, τὸ ἅγιον ὄνομα τοῦ Χριστοῦ τὸ ὑπὲρ πᾶν ὄνομα·

1. ἐλθέ, τὰ σπλάγχνα τὰ τέλεια,

2. ἐλθέ, ἡ δύναμις τοῦ ὑψίστου καὶ ἡ εὐσπλαγχνία ἡ τελεία·

2. ἐλθέ, ἡ κοινωνία τοῦ ἄρρενος,

3. ἐλθέ, τὸ χάρισμα τὸ ὕψιστον·

3. ἐλθέ, ἡ ἐπισταμένη τὰ μυστήρια τοῦ ἐπιλέκτου,

4. ἐλθέ, ἡ μήτηρ ἡ εὔσπλαγχνος·

4. ἐλθέ, ἡ κοινωνοῦσα ἐν πᾶσι τοῖς ἄθλοις τοῦ γενναίου ἀθλητοῦ,

5. ἐλθέ, ἡ κοινωνία τοῦ ἄρρενος·

5. ἐλθέ, ἡ ἡσυχία ἡ ἀποκαλύπτουσα τὰ μεγαλεῖα τοῦ παντὸς μεγέθους,

6. ἐλθέ, ἡ τὰ μυστήρια ἀποκαλύπτουσα τὰ ἀπόκρυφα·

6. ἐλθέ, ἡ τὰ ἀπόκρυφα ἐκφαίνουσα καὶ τὰ ἀπόρρητα φανερὰ καθιστῶσα, ἡ ἱερὰ περιστερὰ ἡ τοὺς διδύμους νεοσσοὺς γεννῶσα,

7. ἐλθέ, ἡ μήτηρ τῶν ἑπτὰ οἴκων, ἵνα ἡ ἀνάπαυσίς σου εἰς τὸν ὄγδοον οἶκον γένηται.

7. ἐλθέ, ἡ ἀπόκρυφος μήτηρ,

8. ἐλθέ, ὁ πρεσβύτερος τῶν πέντε μελῶν, νοὸς ἐννοίας φρονήσεως ἐνθυμήσεως λογισμοῦ, κοινώνησον μετὰ τούτων τῶν νεωτέρων·

8. ἐλθέ, ἡ φανερὰ ἐν ταῖς πράξεσιν αὐτῆς καὶ παρέχουσα χαρὰν καὶ ἀνάπαυσιν τοῖς συνημμένοις αὐτῇ·

---

[5] The word νεφρός literally means "kidneys" and it is often used figuratively to mean "inner parts" of human beings, much as we would use "heart" in modern English (H. Preisker, "νεφρός," *TDNT* 4:911).

[6] Often translated "love feast" to describe the specialized Christian use of ἀγάπη (a Greek word for "love") as a meal.

9. ἐλθέ, τὸ ἅγιον πνεῦμα καὶ
   καθάρισον τοὺς νεφροὺς
   αὐτῶν καὶ τὴν καρδίαν, καὶ
   ἐπισφράγισον αὐτοὺς εἰς
   ὄνομα πατρὸς καὶ υἱοῦ καὶ
   ἁγίου πνεύματος.

9. ἐλθέ, καὶ κοινώνησον ἡμῖν ἐν
   ταύτῃ τῇ εὐχαριστίᾳ ἣν
   ποιοῦμεν ἐπὶ τῷ ὀνόματί σου,
   καὶ τῇ ἀγάπῃ ᾗ συνήγμεθα ἐπὶ
   τῇ κλήσει σου.

Both prayers occur in the context of sacramental rituals which mark the initiation of new believers into Christ's fold. Chapters 26 and 27 recount the conversion and initiation of King Gundaphor and his brother, Gad. First the brothers request the seal: "Since our souls are at leisure and we are zealous for God, give us the seal! For we have heard you say that the God whom you preach knows his own sheep by this seal" (26). The apostle commands the oil to be brought and he seals the brothers. Immediately they hear a voice from the Lord saying, "Peace be with you." Then the apostle delivers the additional sealing of the seal,[7] pouring oil on their heads and reciting the epiclesis. Following this seal, they see a vision of the Lord as a young man carrying a blazing torch. Finally, they break the bread of the eucharist, rejoicing among themselves and with the others who had joined the faithful.

Chapter 50 recounts a similar sequence, although here the epiclesis occurs at the eucharist instead of the anointing. Just prior to this scene, Thomas exorcises a demon from a woman who had come to him for help. After she is healed, she requests the seal: "Apostle of the Most High, give me the seal, that that enemy may not return to me again!" (49). Thomas seals her by laying his hands upon her (no oil is mentioned). The text explains that many others were sealed as well. Then Thomas commands that the table be prepared for the eucharist. Once

[7] This awkward double sealing most likely reflects some emendation from the original version. The Syriac version recounts a nocturnal water baptism prior to the sealing with the oil, which may in fact represent an earlier version (even though in general the Greek is thought to be closer to the original). Notice that the Greek version refers ahead to water baptism in a prayer which leads up to this scene; Thomas asks that the new converts be "cleansed with thy washing and anointed with thy oil" (25). This may indicate that a water baptism was originally there. Scholars disagree on this point, however. See Yves Tissot, "Les Actes de Thomas, exemple de recueil composite," in *Actes apocryphes des apôtres*, 223–27; Heinz Kruse, "Zwei Geist-Epikleses der syrischen Thomasakten," *Oriens Christianus* 69 (1985): 44; and Klijn, *Acts of Thomas*, 15, 57.

this is done, he stands beside the table and gives a short prayer to Jesus and then recites the epiclesis. At the end of the epiclesis, Thomas marks the bread with the cross and gives it to the woman who had been healed, saying, "Let this be for the forgiveness of sins and eternal transgressions!" (50). He then distributes the bread to others who had been sealed.

Similar sequences of events can be found in three other conversion scenes in the *Acts of Thomas* (120–21, 132, 157). The following elements are usually included: a request for the seal by the convert, the epiclesis, the sealing with oil or laying on of hands, baptism with water, and the celebration of the eucharist with bread, water, and wine (notice that baptism with water is excluded from the two scenes under consideration in chapters 27 and 50).[8]

While some form of epiclesis occurs regularly in these scenes,[9] only in chapters 27 and 50 are they addressed to the Holy Spirit. Further, the epicleses of chapters 27 and 50 stand out in that they follow the same formal structure made up of a series of imperative commands beginning with "come" (ἐλθέ). After each command the apostle recites a different epithet for the Holy Spirit, several of which have historically puzzled scholars. Finally, each prayer ends with the request for the Holy Spirit to cleanse and seal the new believers (27) or to partake in the eucharist (50).

Early Liturgical Literature: The Search for Parallels

The obvious place to look for parallels for these epiclesis prayers is in other liturgical texts from the first several centuries of Christianity.[10]

---

[8] But see previous footnote. Another common motif (occurring in 27, 121, 157) is a voice or a vision from heaven which confirms that the divine power has responded.

[9] Chapter 121 (invocation of the power of the oil), chapter 157 (invocation of victorious power of Jesus). Chapter 132 does not contain an invocation but a series of exclamations of praise to the hidden power.

[10] I have also surveyed Jewish prayer and liturgy for possible parallels and found none. See A. Z. Idelsohn, *Jewish Liturgy and Its Development* (New York: Henry Holt, 1932); David Flusser, "Psalms, Hymns and Prayers," in *Jewish Writings of the Second Temple Period: Apocrypha, Pseudepigrapha, Qumran Sectarian Writings, Philo, Josephus*, ed. Michael E. Stone (Philadelphia: Fortress Press, 1984), 551–77; and David A. Fiensy, *Prayers Alleged To Be Jewish: An Examination of the Constitutiones Apostolorum* (Brown Judaic Studies 65; Chico, Calif.: Scholars Press, 1985).

So few texts survive that it is nearly impossible to trace an overall development of the liturgy in these early centuries. Instead, we must work with the snippets we have from different locations and periods. In these examples we find epicleses used in similar ritual contexts, but their form is quite different. In what follows, I review a sampling of extant liturgical texts, first baptismal then eucharistic, in order to demonstrate how the epicleses in chapters 27 and 50 of the *Acts of Thomas* fit into (and stand out from) other early liturgical traditions.

Baptismal epicleses are more difficult to find, especially in the earlier liturgies, than eucharistic epicleses. Neither the *Didache* (probably late first century C.E., Syria)[11] nor *The First Apology* of Justin Martyr (ca. 160, Rome) contains an epiclesis in its description of baptism.[12] The longer description of the baptismal rite in Hippolytus's *Apostolic Tradition* (ca. 215, Rome) records the following epiclesis: "And the bishop shall lay his hand upon them invoking and saying, 'O Lord God, who didst count these worthy of deserving the forgiveness of sins by the laver of regeneration, make them worthy to be filled with thy Holy Spirit and send upon them thy grace, that they may serve thee according to thy will."[13]

In *De baptismo* (ca. 200, North Africa) Tertullian describes what happens in the post-baptismal anointing: "In the next place the hand is laid on in blessing, invoking and inviting the Holy Spirit."[14] He does

[11] The date and the provenance of this text are uncertain. A common suggestion is Syria at the end of the first century C.E. (Helmut Koester, *Introduction to the New Testament*, vol. 2, *History and Literature of Early Christianity* [New York: de Gruyter, 1980], 158); on the *Didache* in general, see Willy Rordorf and André Tuilier, *La Doctrine des Douze Apôtres: Didachè* (Sources Chrétiennes 248; Paris: Éditions du Cerf, 1978); and Arthur Vööbus, *Liturgical Traditions in the Didache* (Stockholm: Etse, 1968).

[12] *Didache* 7 and Justin Martyr *The First Apology* 61.

[13] *Apostolic Tradition* 22; *The Apostolic Tradition of St. Hippolytus*, ed. and trans. Gregory Dix (London: SPCK, 1937), 38. Note that the original Greek of this text does not survive and scholars have had to reconstruct it based on various fragments in other languages. The original was written ca. 215 C.E. in Rome. See E. C. Whitaker, *Documents of the Baptismal Liturgy* (London: SPCK, 1960), 2–3; and Dix, *St. Hippolytus*, lii–lxxxi.

[14] *De baptismo* 8; English translation: Alexander Roberts and James Donaldson, *The Ante-Nicene Fathers: Translations of the Fathers down to A.D. 325*, vol. 3 (American reprint of Edinburgh edition; Edinburgh: Clark, 1993), 672–73.

not provide us with a text of the invocation, but at least we know that it was a part of the rite he knew.

The *Didascalia apostolorum*, the document closest to the *Acts of Thomas* in time and place (first half of the third century, Syria), does not contain a reference to an epiclesis. The descriptions of baptism in this text, however, correspond closely to those described in the *Acts of Thomas*.[15]

Near the end of the fourth century in Antioch, John Chrysostom describes what happens when the initiate goes down into the waters: "Through the words of the priest and his hand the visitation of the Holy Spirit comes upon you and another man arises."[16]

In this group of baptismal texts from the early centuries of Christianity we find no true parallel with the epiclesis in chapter 27 of the *Acts of Thomas*.[17] These texts are certainly witnesses to a tradition of baptismal invocation, but they provide no example which mimics the length and formal structure of the *Acts of Thomas* epicleses. A survey of later Syrian liturgy (which Sebastian Brock has treated at length) yields the same results.[18]

---

[15] *Didascalia apostolorum* 16 describes a baptism with an anointing with oil preceding the water immersion (see *ATh* 121, 132). Also in this chapter are instructions for deaconesses to anoint women initiates (supposedly because the initiates were immersed naked) (see *ATh* 157). For an edition of the *Didascalia apostolorum*, see *Didascalia Apostolorum: The Syriac Version Translated and Accompanied by the Verona Latin Fragments*, trans. R. Hugh Connolly (Oxford: Clarendon Press, 1929).

[16] *Baptismal Homilies* 2.25; published by Antoine Wenger, *Jean Chrysostome: Huit catéchèses baptismales inédites* (Sources Chrétiennes 50; Paris: Éditions du Cerf, 1957), 147; English translation: Leonel L. Mitchell, *Baptismal Anointing* (London: SPCK, 1966), 38.

[17] While the group of texts I list here is by no means comprehensive, it presents a good sampling of what survives from the first three to four centuries of Christianity. I have consulted many more texts than I name here and have still found no parallel. See Whitaker, *Documents of the Baptismal Liturgy*; Brock, *Holy Spirit*; Gregory Dix, *The Shape of the Liturgy* (London: Black, 1945; rev. ed., New York: Seabury, 1982); G. W. H. Lampe, *The Seal of the Spirit. A Study in the Doctrine of Baptism and Confirmation in the New Testament and the Fathers*, 2d ed. (London: SPCK, 1967); Thomas M. Finn, *Early Christian Baptism and the Catechumenate: West and East Syria* (Message of the Fathers of the Church 5; Collegeville, Minn.: Liturgical Press, 1992).

[18] Brock, *Holy Spirit*, 70–115. One invocation of the Holy Spirit cited by Brock comes closer to the *Acts of Thomas* epicleses in that it recites multiple epithets of the

Epicleses are easier to find in eucharistic liturgies than in baptismal liturgies; most texts from the early period record an invocation of some sort. They often take varying forms, are addressed to different aspects of the divine (Father, Son, Holy Spirit, *Logos*), and request different actions. Gregory Dix argues that the epiclesis as a specific request to the Holy Spirit for the consecration of the elements is a later development; the earlier epicleses merely ask the divine to act in the sacrament.[19] The eucharistic epicleses in the *Acts of Thomas* support this theory; the apostle simply asks the Holy Spirit to join the celebrants in the eucharist ("Come and share with us in this eucharist which we perform in your name, and share with us in the *agape* for which we are gathered together at your call"; 50).

Contrary to most liturgical descriptions of the eucharist, however, the *Didache* (perhaps end of the first century C.E., Syria) records no true epiclesis.[20] Arthur Vööbus disputes those who try to read one into the text and rejects the suggestion that the "name of the Lord" or the "*maranatha*" could serve as invocations.[21] The occurrence of *maranatha* is interesting for this discussion. *Maranatha* is a Greek transliteration of an Aramaic sentence which could mean any one of three things: "Our Lord has come"; "Our Lord is coming/will come"; or "Our Lord, come!"[22] Scholars debate this issue largely based on context (the word also appears in 1 Cor 16:22; a possible Greek translation occurs in Rev 22:20: ἔρχου κύριε Ἰησοῦ, "Come, Lord Jesus"). As I mentioned above, some think that *maranatha* serves the function of an epiclesis,

---

Holy Spirit. As Brock points out, however, this is the result of later additions to the prayer (*Holy Spirit*, 72). This development over time can be traced through the different liturgies which record this prayer. See the Liturgy of St. Mark published in *Prayers of the Eucharist: Early and Reformed*, ed. and trans. R. C. D. Jasper and G. J. Cuming (London: Collins, 1975), 49, and the earlier fragment of the same prayer on p. 41 (in this earliest version, there is no listing of epithets).

[19] Gregory Dix, "The Origins of the Epiclesis," *Theology* 28 (1934): 202.

[20] See *Didache* 9 and 10.

[21] Vööbus, *Liturgical Traditions*, 96. "Name of the Lord" occurs in *Didache* 9.5; "*Maranatha*" occurs in *Didache* 10.6.

[22] Max Wilcox, "Maranatha," *ABD* 4:514. The correct translation depends on how the word should be divided, *maran atha* ("Our Lord has come" or "Our Lord is coming") or *marana tha* ("Our Lord, come!").

arguing that both the *Didache* and Paul's letter constitute eucharistic contexts.[23] Others disagree, asserting that this Aramaic phrase expresses eschatological expectation,[24] or that it merely reinforces the ban which occurs before it in each case.[25] I am convinced that it served some liturgical function since these ancient authors chose not to translate it, but I am not persuaded that both contexts are eucharistic.[26] In all three cases (if we include Rev 22:20) it occurs at the end of a text or chapter, which may indicate that it served as a stock motif of closure. I would not rule out a connection to the genre of the epiclesis, however, especially to those of the *Acts of Thomas*. If *maranatha* can be translated, "Our Lord, come!" then it provides a closer parallel to the series of imperative "come's" in the *Acts of Thomas* epicleses than do the following eucharistic invocations (none of which address the divine directly with "come" but usually ask, rather, that the Holy Spirit be sent).[27]

The earliest surviving eucharistic prayer can be found in Hippolytus's *Apostolic Tradition*: "And we ask that thou wouldst send your Holy Spirit upon the oblation of Thy holy Church. . . ."[28] The *Didascalia*

[23] See Oscar Cullmann, *Early Christian Worship*, translation of the 2d ed. (Philadelphia: Westminster Press, 1953), 13; A. J. B. Higgins, *The Lord's Supper in the New Testament* (Chicago: Regnery, 1952), 60; see also the sources cited in notes 1–3 in C. F. D. Moule, "A Reconsideration of the Context of *Maranatha*," *NTS* 6 (1959–60): 307.

[24] Edward J. Kilmartin, "The Eucharistic Prayer: Content and Function of Some Early Eucharistic Prayers," in *The Word in the World*, ed. Richard J. Clifford and George W. MacRae (Cambridge, Mass.: Weston College Press, 1973), 119.

[25] Moule, "A Reconsideration," 307–10. See also Palle Dinesen, "Die Epiklese im Rahmen altkirchlicher Liturgien. Eine Studie über die eucharistische Epiklese," *Studia Theologica* 16 (1962): 75–80. Dinesen sees no connection between the *maranatha* and the epiclesis; the *maranatha* can be found in multiple contexts while the epiclesis is totally tied to a eucharistic context (p. 77).

[26] The *Didache* 10.6 may very well be a eucharistic context; it is at least a thanksgiving grace at the end of a meal (and the description of the eucharist occurs in the previous chapter). It is implausible, however, to argue a eucharistic context for 1 Cor 16:22.

[27] Another possible biblical parallel occurs in a variant reading of Luke 11:2 (the Lord's Prayer). The variant reads "Your holy spirit come upon us and cleanse us" (ἐλθέτω τὸ πνεῦμα σου τὸ ἅγιον ἐφ᾽ ἡμᾶς καὶ καθαρίσατο ἡμᾶς), instead of "Your kingdom come" (ἐλθέτω ἡ βασιλεία σου). Gregory of Nyssa and Marcion witness the variant.

[28] The *Apostolic Tradition* 4.12; English translation: Dix, *St. Hippolytus*, 9. Dix argues that this epiclesis is a fourth-century interpolation, in *Shape of the Liturgy*, 158

apostolorum, although it contains no text of the ritual, nevertheless alludes to the sanctification of the bread: "the Eucharist through the Spirit is accepted and sanctified";[29] and "offer an acceptable Eucharist. . .pure bread made with fire and sanctified with invocations."[30] Dix considers this text to be the first "serious evidence" for a consecratory epiclesis of the Spirit.[31]

The *Anaphora* of Basil of Caesarea (Cappadocia, first half of the fourth century)[32] records the following prayer: ". . .your Holy Spirit may come upon us and upon these gifts that are set before you, and may sanctify them and make them holy of holies."[33]

I conclude this survey with another Syrian example, the *Apostolic Constitutions* (ca. 375, Syria):[34] "and we beseech you. . .to send down your Holy Spirit upon this sacrifice, the witness of the sufferings of the Lord Jesus, that he may make this bread body of your Christ, and this cup blood of your Christ. . . ."[35] This text represents the first complete eucharistic liturgy to have survived, and it is the first one which indicates that the elements become the body and blood of Christ.[36] Further

---

n. 1. Also see his argument in his article "Origins," 127–33. Cyril C. Richardson argues against Dix, "The So-Called Epiclesis in Hippolytus," *HTR* 40 (1947): 106, 108.

[29] *Didascalia apostolorum* 6.21.2; Connolly, 244 (chap. 26).

[30] *Didascalia apostolorum* 6.22.2; Connolly, 252 (chap. 36).

[31] Dix, "Origins," 133.

[32] The constituent parts of the eucharistic liturgy attributed to Basil are difficult to date precisely. While the *Anaphora* as a whole dates back to the fourth century, portions of it were added or changed in later periods. We do not know whether the following prayer was a part of the liturgy from its fourth-century beginning, or whether it is a part of a later development.

[33] The *Anaphora* of Basil; Eusèbe Renaudot, *Liturgiarum Orientalium Collectio*, vol. 1 (Paris: Coignard, 1716), 13–18; English translation: Jasper and Cuming, *Prayers of the Eucharist*, 31.

[34] This text, a collection of liturgical traditions which dates to ca. 375, draws heavily on the anaphora of Hippolytus's *Apostolic Tradition* and probably incorporates Antiochene litanies (Jasper and Cuming, *Prayers of the Eucharist*, 65).

[35] *Apostolic Constitutions* 8.2.12; translation by Jasper and Cuming, *Prayers of the Eucharist*, 72.

[36] R. D. Richardson, "Eastern and Western Liturgies: The Primitive Basis of Their Later Differences," in *Worship in Early Christianity*, ed. Everett Ferguson (Studies in Early Christianity 15; New York: Garland, 1993), 56.

examples I list only in the notes, for they offer no new illumination.[37] Most eucharistic epicleses (like most baptismal epicleses) are no longer than one sentence and they are embedded within longer descriptions of the sacrament and instructions for its performance. The epicleses of the *Acts of Thomas* remain unique among these early church traditions.

Two other areas merit a brief look for parallels. One is the rest of the Apocryphal Acts of the Apostles. Prayers are common in these texts, especially at moments of healing and exorcism.[38] Often, the apostle offers a prayer when performing liturgical functions as well, but these do not resemble the epicleses in language or structure (and often the text simply mentions that a prayer was given without quoting it).[39] Another area is Manichaean literature, which was significantly in-

---

[37] Another Syrian example of a eucharistic epiclesis can be found in the *Anaphora* of Addai and Mari: "May your Holy Spirit, Lord, come and rest on this offering of your servants, and bless and sanctify it, that it may be to us, Lord, for remission of debts. . . ." Although the extant version of this liturgy dates to the eleventh or twelfth century, some parts of it are thought to go back to the third century. The authenticity of this particular prayer, however, is debated by scholars (Jasper and Cuming, *Prayers of the Eucharist*, 26).

Serapion writes in *The Euchologion* (Egypt, 340–60), "O God of truth, let your holy Word come on this bread, that the bread may become body of the Word; and on this cup, that the cup may become blood of the Truth. . ." (translated by Jasper and Cuming, *Prayers of the Eucharist*, 35). Note that this prayer invokes the *Logos* instead of the Son or the Holy Spirit.

Again, as with the baptismal texts, I have included not an exhaustive list, but a sampling of early eucharistic texts. My wider search yielded no parallels to the *Acts of Thomas* epicleses. See E. G. Cuthbert Atchley, *On the Epiclesis of the Eucharistic Liturgy and the Consecration of the Font* (London: Oxford University Press, 1935); Dix, *Shape of the Liturgy*; and Jasper and Cuming, *Prayers of the Eucharist*.

[38] *Acts of John* 22: John prays for help in healing the crowd; 77–85: the apostle raises Drusiana; Drusiana raises Fortunatus (Junod and Kaestli, *Acta Iohannis*, 1:166–69, 278–92). *Acts of Andrew* 15–16: Andrew lays his hand on Maximilla and commits her to the Lord (Prieur, *Acta Andreae*, 2:462).

[39] E.g., *Acts of Peter* 5: Peter prays as he performs the eucharist for a newly baptized person (*AAA* 1:51); *Acts of John* 85–86: John recites a prayer while administering the eucharist); 109–10: again John recites a prayer while breaking the bread; this prayer has in common with the epicleses the recitation of numerous epithets for the divine, in this case Jesus; and 112–15: John speaks a long prayer before sealing himself and lying in his burial trench to die.

fluenced by the *Acts of Thomas*.⁴⁰ Because the Manichaean tradition developed approximately one hundred years after the *Acts of Thomas*, its literature can be ruled out as a possible precedent for the epicleses. Nevertheless, one text is worth mentioning here. There is a Manichaean hymn to Christ which provides a close structural parallel to the *Acts of Thomas* epicleses. The second of the four sections of this hymn consists of a series of twelve invocations, each starting with "Come with Grace!" and followed by an epithet of Jesus.⁴¹ Unfortunately, we have no idea to which liturgical context this text may have belonged, if any. Since it is clear that the *Acts of Thomas* made significant contributions to Manichaeism (at least in its Christian form), it is not inconceivable that the epicleses serve as the model for this hymn to Christ.⁴²

---

⁴⁰ Drijvers describes both the commonalities and differences between the *Acts of Thomas* and Manichaean literature ("The Acts of Thomas," 337–38).

⁴¹ For example, "Come with Grace, Redeemer of the subjected, Healer of the wounded!" "Come with Grace, Awakener of the sleeping and Arouser of the sleepy," "Come with Grace, true Word, great Luminary, and flooding Light." This text (ms. M 28.2), written in Middle Iranian, was found during this century in Turfan. It is published in F. C. Andreas and W. Henning, *Mitteliranische Manichaica aus Chinesisch-Turkestan*, vol. 2 (Berlin: Akademie der Wissenschaften, 1933), 312–16. English translation: Geo Widengren and Charles Kessler, *Mani and Manichaeism* (London: Weidenfeld and Nicolson, 1965), 87. For a thorough description of the finds at Turfan, see Mary Boyce, *A Catalogue of the Iranian Manuscripts in Manichean Script in the German Turfan Collection* (Berlin: Akademie-Verlag, 1960). None of these sources date this hymn.

⁴² It is also possible that the reverse is true: the Manichaean hymn to Christ is the paradigm for the epicleses. To advance this theory, one would have to argue that the epicleses were added into the *Acts of Thomas* by the Manichaeans after they had appropriated the text. And then one would have to account for the fact that the epicleses made their way into all the traditions of transmission, even those that come down to us through orthodox sources (as far as I know, we have no manuscripts without them. See Klijn, *Acts of Thomas*, 1–17). The conglomerate nature of the *Acts of Thomas* makes this possible, but it also renders such a thesis difficult to prove. I agree with Kruse, who considers these epiclesis prayers at least in part as separate (and older) liturgical material which the author incorporated into the narrative at these moments of ritual (Kruse, "Zwei Geist-Epikleses," 34). See also Gerard Rouwhorst, "La célébration de l'eucharistie selon les Actes de Thomas," in *Omnes Circumstandtes: Contributions Towards a History of the Role of the People in Liturgy* (Kampen: Uitgeversmaatschappij J. H. Kok, 1990), 63–64. For an argument that the epicleses are Manichaean additions, see W. Bousset, "Manichäisches in den Thomasakten," *ZNW* 18 (1918): 34–39. For a refutation of Bousset's argument, see Tissot, "Actes de Thomas," 227–28.

Our two epicleses clearly belong to the category of liturgical prayers which invoke the divine into the sacraments. But no extant example of this type explains the reasons for their distinct structure or the significance of the recitation of epithets. Nothing appears to have survived in the Christian tradition that can illuminate the ways in which these unique features contribute to the efficacy of the prayers in their respective sacramental rituals. Outside of Christianity, however, there survives an abundance of texts which offer insight into these enigmatic prayers: magic spells. Although they are not Christian, they nevertheless come from a broadly similar ritual context as these Christian epicleses; in each case their role is to invoke the divine to act in the human realm. Magic spells provide an excellent model for understanding how these prayers function in the *Acts of Thomas*.

Magic

The practice of magic in the ancient world seems to have been simultaneously popular and highly polemicized.[43] The relationship between Christianity and magic was itself ambiguous: Jesus often played the role of the powerful *magos* in the gospel tradition, yet Christianity from its beginnings often distanced itself from magic.[44]

---

[43] The suppression of the practice of magic is attested in Suetonius *Augustus* 31.1, which recounts Augustus's order to burn over two thousand magic texts. Despite this sort of persistent suppression, people still collected and passed on magical handbooks. Hans Dieter Betz explains that these texts survived (barely) because they went underground (*The Greek Magical Papyri in Translation, Including the Demotic Spells*, vol. 1, *Texts* [Chicago: University of Chicago Press, 1986], xli; see also John Gager, *Curse Tablets and Binding Spells from the Ancient World* [New York: Oxford University Press, 1992]).

[44] See Susan R. Garrett, *The Demise of the Devil: Magic and the Demonic in Luke's Writings* (Minneapolis: Fortress Press, 1989), and Morton Smith, *Jesus the Magician* (San Francisco: Harper and Row, 1978). For polemic against magic in the New Testament, see Acts 8:9–24 and 13:8–9. See also John M. Hull's study, *Hellenistic Magic and the Synoptic Tradition* (Studies in Biblical Theology, Second Series, 28; Naperville, Ill.: Allensen, 1974); and Florent Heintz, *Simon «le Magicien». Actes 8, 5–25 et l'accusation de magie contre les prophètes thaumaturges dans l'Antiquité* (Cahiers de la Revue Biblique, 39; Paris: Gabalda, 1997).

The *Acts of Thomas* itself is aware of this tension.[45] Early in the story, the people react to the missionizing activity of Thomas: ". . .he goes about the towns and villages, and if he has anything he gives it all to the poor, and he teaches a new God and heals the sick and drives out demons and does many other wonderful things; and we think he is a *magos*" (20).[46] The name *magos* is clearly associated with admirable actions, not a surprising association given that *magos* was the term used for wise men and healers. In the next sentence, however, the speaker qualifies this description of Thomas:

> But (ἀλλά) his works of compassion, and the healings which are wrought
> by him without reward, and moreover his simplicity and kindness and
> the quality of his faith, show that he is righteous or an apostle of the new
> God whom he preaches. For he continually fasts and prays, and eats
> only bread and salt, and his drink is water, and he wears one garment
> whether in fine weather or in foul, and takes nothing from anyone, and
> what he has he gives to others. (20)

The contrastive ἀλλά which begins this sentence indicates that the ensuing description of Thomas contradicts that of a *magos*, who, for example, would take money for his services as a professional.

Later in the narrative, the label of *magos* becomes a hostile accusation. Tension mounts in the story because Thomas convinces women to reject conjugal relations with their husbands. Mygdonia's husband complains:

> And on this point I have the greater suspicion, for I have heard that that
> *magos* and deceiver teaches that a man should not live with his own
> wife, and what nature requires and the deity has ordained he
> overthrows. . . . My lady and consort Mygdonia, be not led astray by
> deceitful and vain words, nor by the works of magic which I have heard
> this man performs in the name of the Father, Son and Holy Spirit. (96)

---

[45] Accusations of magic are prevalent in the Apocryphal Acts of the Apostles. For a detailed discussion of this phenomenon, see Gérard Poupon, "L'accusation de magie dans les Actes Apocryphes," in *Actes apocryphes des apôtres*, 71–85.

[46] I leave this Greek term (μάγος) untranslated in order to allow for the ambiguity of its meaning. As I will discuss, a *magos* had both positive (as a wise man) and negative (as a sorcerer) reputations in antiquity. English lacks a term that encompasses both meanings.

Notice that the names Thomas invokes in his prayers are highlighted here as part of his magical influence. In another accusation, the instruments of the sacramental rituals are implicated as well. King Misdaeus, a husband made suspicious by Thomas's effect on Mygdonia, says to his wife, "Not yet has that sorcerer prevailed over thee, for as I hear he bewitches men with oil and water and bread, and thee he has not yet bewitched. For I know that so long as he has not given thee oil and water and bread he has not gained power to prevail over thee" (152).

The effect of the comparison of Thomas with a *magos* is twofold. On the one hand, it connects the apostle to this image and carries positive connotations, calling attention to the power of Thomas's rituals and prayers, including the names and instruments he uses. On the other hand, the comparison distances the apostle from a *magos*, for it surfaces as an accusation against Thomas by his enemies, who attempt to discredit him and deflate his popularity. Thus, the label of *magos* serves as a foil to his true identity and power. The author handles this comparison carefully, highlighting Thomas's extraordinary power yet simultaneously erecting a clear boundary between the apostle and a *magos*.

Given this tension in the text, it is ironic (and perhaps not coincidental) that the prayers of the apostle so closely resemble magic incantations. They parallel each other in three significant ways: the overall purpose, the structure of the prayer, and the use of symbols. In what follows I will illustrate this correlation by comparing the two epicleses and their ritual contexts to several magic spells.

Magic incantations and the *Acts of Thomas* epicleses serve the same purpose: to incite the deity to participate in the ritual and effect some sort of change in the human realm. People went to practitioners of magic with various requests: to ask for help or protection from a god, to control other people (both for attracting lovers and cursing enemies), to exorcise demons or to be cured of other ailments, or simply to attain success in business or athletic contests.[47] Although Thomas works not as a professional but as a missionary for his "new God,"[48] he responds to

[47] Betz, *Greek Magical Papyri*, xlvii.
[48] Thomas is described several times in the *Acts of Thomas* as preaching the message of the "new God" (see 20, 123).

some of the same petitions. Thomas seals King Gundaphor and his brother in response to their request to be marked as God's own, so that they become like God's sheep, protected from the wolves.[49] Similarly, in chapters 49–50, after Thomas exorcises the demon from the woman, he seals her in response to her plea for further protection. The apostle, like the *magos*, is seen as a resourceful person, with access to divine power.

Technique is crucial in magic rituals. Every word and action had to be performed correctly for the spell to be effective. Much of the evidence we have for magic spells has survived in the form of handbooks which were used by practitioners. These handbooks contain collections of spells for various purposes, complete with careful instructions regarding which instruments to use, how to use them, the exact words to recite and the order in which to recite them. The complex and lengthy incantations recorded in these handbooks thus follow a formal structure. While this structure is not absolutely fixed, most magical spells follow the same tripartite scheme: invocation, series of epithets, request.[50]

The spell begins with the invocation to the divine power, often with an imperative verb and a name: "Come to me, O beloved mistress, three-faced Selene / kindly hear my sacred chants" (*PGM* 4.2785).[51] A love spell to Hermes begins: "Come to me (ἐλθέ μοι), lord Hermes as fetuses do to the wombs of women. Come to me, lord Hermes, [you] who collect the sustenance of gods and men; Come to me. . .lord Hermes, and give me favor. . ." (*PGM* 8.1–5).[52] The function of the invocation is

---

[49] Thomas prays regarding the brothers, "Preserve them also from the wolves, leading them in thy pastures" (25).

[50] Hull, *Hellenistic Magic*, 42–44. Fritz Graf, "Prayer in Magic and Religious Ritual," in *Magika Hiera: Ancient Greek Magic and Religion*, ed. Christopher A. Faraone and Dirk Obbink (New York: Oxford University Press, 1991), 189.

[51] Translation of all spells from Betz, *Greek Magical Papyri*. The identifying letters and numbers follow the Greek texts of *Papyri Graecae Magicae. Die griechischen Zauberpapyri*, ed. K. Preisendanz (2 vols., Stuttgart: Teubner, 1973–74). Selene is a Greek moon goddess (Roman Luna) who drives a chariot drawn by horses or oxen, or she herself rides horses or oxen. She is often identified with Artemis (Robert C. T. Parker, "Selene," *OCD*, 1379–80).

[52] As I learned near the completion of this article, Hans Lietzmann noted this parallel in passing, *Messe und Herrenmahl. Eine Studie zur Geschichte der Liturgie* (Bonn: Marcus und Weber's Verlag, 1926), 244 and n. 2 on same page.

to catch the attention of the deity so that he or she will listen to the petition and respond.

The middle portion consists of a series of epithets and descriptions of the deity. This section constitutes most of the spell and often goes into lengthy detail on the diverse titles and activities associated with the god. The epithets and descriptions of Selene in the spell mentioned above continue for about eighty lines, of which the following are some examples: "Night's ornament, young, bringing light to mortals, / O child of morn [you] who ride upon fierce bulls. . .Night-Crier, bull-faced, loving solitude, bull-headed, you have eyes of bulls, / the voice of dogs; you hide your forms in shanks of lions. . .you who protect the spacious world at night, before whom daimons quake in fear. . .you of many names, who bear fair offspring, bull-eyed, horned, mother of gods and men, and nature, Mother of all things. . ." (*PGM* 4.2785–890). This detailed and meticulous listing of the epithets and descriptions of the activities of the deities insures that the deity is addressed in all of its relevant aspects, thus increasing the chances that the deity will respond.[53]

The third and final section of a spell articulates the request. As I mentioned above, the ancients employed spells for a variety of reasons, but all spells have in common the request for help. The following example expresses a supplication for general health and well-being: "Keep me healthy, unharmed, not plagued by ghosts, free from calamity and without terror" (*PGM* 4.1063–64). Another request addresses the demon the spell aims to exorcise: "Come out, daimon, whoever you are, and stay away from him. . .now, now; immediately, immediately. Come out, daimon, since I bind you with unbreakable adamantine fetters, and I deliver you into the black chaos in perdition" (*PGM* 4.1241–49). The spell to Selene illustrates a more generic request, which could be applied to various situations.[54] The final line reads, "Come to my sacrifices, and now for me do you fulfill this matter" (*PGM* 4.2869–70). The details of the request would be inserted for each specific situation.

---

[53] Graf, "Prayer in Magic and Religious Ritual," 189.
[54] Ibid., 190.

The components of the *Acts of Thomas* epicleses—the repetition of imperative "come's," the series of epithets and descriptions of the deity, and the final request for the deity to act—follow this pattern exactly.

The power of a *magos*, as the ancients understood it, stems from the ability to manipulate symbols. Each of the instruments used in the ritual, as well as every word spoken in incantation, represents a force in the universe. These forces could be manipulated if one understood the system of symbols and their effects, knowledge which normally belongs to the gods. The exception was the *magos*, on whom the gods bestowed this secret knowledge.[55] Ritual magic consisted of a process by which the practitioner employed both actions and words to manipulate symbols to spur the universe—and specifically a divine power—into action.

A wide variety of instruments are used in magic ritual; herbs, stones, fruit, oil, and animal body parts are common. Eusebius describes this system of symbols: "For there are many kinds of roots, and herbs, and plants, and fruits, and stones, and other powers, both solid and liquid of every kind of matter in the natural world; some of them drive off and expel certain diseases; others are of a nature to attract and superinduce them; some again with power to secrete and disperse, or to harden and to bind. . . ."[56] A clue to the power of herbs is found in a text which describes the words to be recited while the herbalist picks the plants. At the moment of picking, he or she says, "You were sown by Kronos, you were conceived by Hera, you were maintained by Ammon, you were conceived by Isis. . .your roots come from the depths, but your powers are in the heart of Hermes. . . . I am washing you in the resin as I also wash the gods. . . . You also be cleaned by prayer and give us power as Ares and Athena do" (*PGM* 4.2979–98). Conceived by the gods and thus representing the gods and their attributes, the herbs themselves are sacred and contain divine power.[57]

---

[55] Hull, *Hellenistic Magic*, 41, and Betz, *Greek Magical Papyri*, xlvii.

[56] *Praeparatio euangelica* 4.1, 131c–d; Odile Zink, *Eusèbe de Césarée, La Préparation évangélique* (Paris: Éditions du Cerf, 1979), 78; English translation: Hull, *Hellenistic Magic*, 42.

[57] John Scarborough, "The Pharmacology of Sacred Plants, Herbs and Roots," in *Magika Hiera: Ancient Greek Magic and Religion*, ed. Christopher A. Faraone and Dirk Obbink (New York: Oxford University Press, 1991), 157.

For every spell the magical handbooks describe what to do with the instruments. Often some sort of mixing is required or the practitioner or the client (the person who employs the services of the *magos*) must ingest the plants. Another commonly prescribed action is that of marking the instrument. For example, the text of a spell to Selene instructs the *magos* to "take a lodestone and on it have carved / a three-faced Hekate" (*PGM* 4.2880–81).[58]

Like the *magos*, the apostle Thomas performs his rituals well equipped with powerful symbolic instruments. Recall the charge against him that he bewitches people with oil and bread and water (152). At another celebration of the eucharist in the *Acts of Thomas*, the apostle's blessing over the elements explains the symbolism of the bread and the water: "Thy holy body which was crucified for us we eat, and thy blood which was poured out for us for salvation we drink. Let thy body, then, become for us salvation, and thy blood for remission of sins!" (158). Thus within the ritual of the eucharist, the ingestion of the elements symbolizes salvation and forgiveness for the celebrants.

The oil used in the anointing is especially important in Syriac Christian rituals as a symbol of both the Holy Spirit and of Christ.[59] Thomas addresses two prayers to oil, calling it, ". . .fruit fairer than other fruits. . .thou altogether merciful, power of the tree which if men put on they conquer their adversaries. . .symbol of joy of the weary; who has brought to men glad tidings of their salvation. . ." (157) and "Holy oil given to us for sanctification. . .he who shows the hidden treasures; thou art the shoot of goodness" (121). The fourth-century Syrian theologian Ephrem wrote hymns praising the oil: "Oil is, therefore, the friend of the Holy Spirit and Her minister. As a disciple it accompanies Her, since by it She seals priests and anointed ones, for the Holy Spirit by the Anointed brands her sheep."[60] Ephrem's con-

---

[58] Note that in *ATh* 50, Thomas marks the bread with a cross, much as the magical practitioner is instructed to mark the lodestone in this spell to Selene.

[59] The olive tree is a common symbol for Christ among Syriac authors. As an olive tree, he is the tree of life, and sacramental oil, which carries nourishing and healing power, pours forth from his wounds. See Murray, *Symbols of Church and Kingdom*, 112, 115–16, 126–27, 320–24.

[60] Ephrem, *Hymns on Virginity*, 7.6. Translated by Kathleen McVey, *Ephrem the Syrian: Hymns* (New York: Paulist Press, 1989), 294.

ception, that the Holy Spirit works together with Christ through the oil to seal the faithful, corresponds closely to the theology of the sealing rituals in the *Acts of Thomas*. In particular, the metaphor of the believers as sheep, marked as God's own, stands out (25–26). In the Syriac tradition, the oil, like the bread and the water, serves as a conduit for the divine activity in the lives of humans.

Powerful symbols come not only in the form of physical objects but also in the form of the spoken word. In magic, the structured recitation of symbolic words, the magic incantation, usually constitutes the main focus of the whole ritual.[61] The careful descriptions of the deity's traits and activities and the repeated laudatory epithets work together to invoke *all* the aspects of the deity's power. The incantation to Selene cited above lists her many attributes as the fierce protector of "the spacious world at night," before whom "daimons quake in fear," as well as one who "bears fair offspring" and is the "Mother of all things" (*PGM* 4.2785–890).

A similar strategy is evident in the epicleses of the *Acts of Thomas*. These prayers display an elaborate set of symbols for the Holy Spirit—symbols called upon to aid in the initiation of the new believers. The persistent recitation of epithets places one image on top of another, sometimes echoing earlier ones, sometimes producing new ones. New layers of meaning open with each symbol, adding depth and richness to the role of the Holy Spirit, to the Holy Spirit's participation in the ritual, and to the meaning of the ritual itself.

Commentary on the Epicleses

To conclude, I will comment on the symbols and images presented in these prayers. Because many of these images can be found in other liturgical and theological literature of the early Syriac tradition, it seems plausible that the readers of the *Acts of Thomas* would have recognized

---

[61] Magic spells also often recite untranslatable words, called *uoces magicae*. While their meaning is unknown to us (and may also have been unknown to most ancients), their formulaic recitation probably indicates some symbolic significance (Betz, *Greek Magical Papyri*, xxxii). Note that the *Acts of Thomas* epicleses do not share this characteristic with magic spells.

and understood these symbols.[62] But since so much of the evidence
for early Syriac Christianity is lost to us,[63] it is difficult to trace the
origins of several of these images. For these I will present suggestions
and possible referents, although any conclusive statement remains impossible.[64] Other symbols, however, are easier to trace in the Syriac
tradition (or in the *Acts of Thomas* itself). In these cases I will follow
their lead to a fuller interpretation of the rituals of anointing and the
eucharist.

Two images of the Holy Spirit appear multiple times in these two
epicleses: the Holy Spirit as revealer of hidden things and the Holy
Spirit as mother. I will treat these two categories last, as they provide
valuable clues to the meanings of these rituals. I will briefly discuss the
rest of the symbols in the order in which they appear, first in the sealing
epiclesis (27) and then in the eucharistic epiclesis (50).

The first line of the epiclesis in chapter 27 points to a relationship
that is prevalent throughout the *Acts of Thomas* and throughout Syriac
literature: the close identification between the Holy Spirit and Christ.
Here the Holy Spirit is called the name of Christ,[65] "the holy name of
Christ above every name" (τὸ ἅγιον ὄνομα τοῦ Χριστοῦ τὸ ὑπὲρ πᾶν
ὄνομα). A very similar phrase is found in Paul's letter to the Philippians
2:9, "Therefore God also highly exalted him and gave him the name
that is above every name. . ." (τὸ ὄνομα τὸ ὑπὲρ πᾶν ὄνομα).[66]

The second line of the anointing epiclesis also contains a biblical
reference, "power of the Most High" (ἡ δύναμις τοῦ ὑψίστου). This
phrase occurs in Luke 1:35 in the annunciation scene. Gabriel says to
Mary, "The Holy Spirit will come upon you, and the power of the Most

---

[62] Drijvers explains that a certain biblical exegesis had already formed which used
and shaped these symbols and typologies ("The Acts of Thomas," 327).

[63] Susan Ashbrook Harvey, "Feminine Imagery for the Divine: The Holy Spirit, the
Odes of Solomon, and Early Syriac Tradition," *St. Vladimir's Theological Quarterly*
37 (1993): 112.

[64] For more extensive treatment of possible references, see previously cited studies
by Brock, *Holy Spirit*, and Klijn, *Acts of Thomas*. See also Kruse, "Zwei Geist-
Epikleses," 33–53.

[65] Or perhaps this epiclesis is addressed to both Christ and the Holy Spirit.

[66] Translation from the NRSV.

High will overshadow you. . . ."[67] The phrase "Most High" also occurs in the Odes of Solomon, which is thought to be of the same geographical provenance (although the date is unsure)[68] as the *Acts of Thomas*.[69]

In three instances the apostle uses the root σπλαγχν- in addressing the Holy Spirit. In chapter 27 she is ἡ εὐσπλαγχνία ἡ τελεία (line 2, "perfect goodness of heart") and ἡ μήτηρ ἡ εὔσπλαγχνος (line 4, "compassionate mother"). In chapter 50 she is τὰ σπλάγχνα τὰ τέλεια (line 1, "perfect compassion"). In its original meaning, σπλάγχνον meant inward parts, specifically with reference to the choice portions of a sacrifice (heart, liver, lungs, kidneys).[70] This term took on metaphorical meanings as well: seat of passions, the center of feelings or sensibility.[71] In later Jewish and early Christian writings, σπλάγχνον (and its compounds) came to mean the seat of feelings which leads to compassion or mercy.[72] In this context the term began to be applied to God.[73] Its usage in the *Acts of Thomas* epicleses fits into this understanding of the term.[74]

[67] Translation from the NRSV. See Sebastian Brock's article, "Mary and the Eucharist: an Oriental Perspective," *Sobornost* 2 (1979): 50–59, where he argues for a linguistic link (in the Syriac verb *aggen*, "to overshadow") between the annunciation and the eucharist in the Syriac tradition. He asserts that there is a parallel relationship between Mary and the Holy Spirit at the annunciation and the believer and the Holy Spirit at the eucharist.

[68] Because of the paucity of early Syriac literature we have little by which to judge the date of this collection. While there is no certainty on this matter, most scholars date it to the middle of the second century (Susan Ashbrook Harvey, "The Odes of Solomon," in *Searching the Scriptures*, vol. 2, *A Feminist Commentary*, ed. Elisabeth Schüssler Fiorenza [New York: Crossroad Press, 1995], 86).

[69] Ode 18, lines 1, 14; *The Odes of Solomon*, ed. and trans. James Hamilton Charlesworth (Oxford: Clarendon Press, 1973), 78f.

[70] Helmut Koester, "σπλάγχνον," *TDNT* 7:548. This term almost always appears in the plural.

[71] Ibid., 549.

[72] For a list of examples, see ibid., 550ff.

[73] Ibid., 551–52. The first text in which this occurs is the *Testaments of the Twelve Patriarchs*. For a list of Christian usages of εὐσπλαγχνία, see G. W. H. Lampe, *A Patristic Greek Lexicon*, s.v. εὐσπλαγχνία.

[74] The root σπλαγχν- is used in two other places in the *Acts of Thomas* as well. In *ATh* 10 Thomas addresses Christ: "Son of compassion (ὁ τῆς εὐσπλαγχνίας υἱός)." Again speaking to Jesus, Thomas says, "Jesus. . .voice arising like the sun from the perfect mercy (ἀπὸ τῶν σπλάγχνων τῶν τελείων)" (*ATh* 48).

The third line of the epiclesis in chapter 27 invokes the "most high gift" (τὸ χάρισμα τὸ ὕψιστον). The conception of the Holy Spirit as a gift is another common metaphor in Syriac tradition, and it is often associated with baptism, as it is in Acts 10:45.[75]

The only exact parallel between the two epicleses occurs in line 5 of the sealing epiclesis and line 2 of the eucharistic epiclesis: "Come, fellowship of the male" (ἐλθέ, ἡ κοινωνία τοῦ ἄρρενος).[76] A. F. J. Klijn suggests that this refers to a union of the Holy Spirit with Christ, which is plausible given their many shared qualities in this text.[77] Both Heinz Kruse and Robert Murray concur that the male must be Christ, whom the Holy Spirit joins during baptism.[78] Another option is that the "male" is God, and the Holy Spirit, representing a feminine aspect of the divine, is the "fellowship" or "union" with the male aspect of the divine.[79] It is tempting to forge a connection here with the *Gospel of Thomas*, which presents similar language in logion 114: "Jesus said, 'I myself shall lead her [Mary] in order to make her male, so that she too may become a living spirit resembling you males. For every woman who will make herself male will enter the kingdom of heaven.'"[80] We should be extremely careful about assuming connections among the different texts of Thomas literature, however, especially since we do not know where the *Gospel of Thomas* was written and circulated. Further, there is nothing in the *Acts of Thomas* that resembles this

---

[75] Brock, *Holy Spirit*, 44. See his lengthy study of the Holy Spirit as a gift in this same volume, 37–69.

[76] Note that the Syriac version reads, "Come, fellowship of the blessing." This is thought to be secondary; the image of "the male" was intentionally replaced, but the reason is unclear (Murray, *Symbols of Church and Kingdom*, 317).

[77] Klijn, *Acts of Thomas*, 215.

[78] Murray, *Symbols of Church and Kingdom*, 317; Kruse, "Zwei Geist-Epikleses," 40. Kruse argues that this image refers to the specific situation in the Syriac tradition in which the Holy Spirit is the mother of the church (not the church itself). At baptism, the Holy Spirit joins her daughter (the church) with Christ (the phrase could be translated, "sharer of the male"). See Kruse, "Zwei Geist-Epikleses," 40.

[79] This concept fits well into the Syrian context, where God was conceived of with both male and female imagery. I am grateful to Françoise Morard for this observation.

[80] Translated by Thomas O. Lambdin in *NHLE*, 138.

theology of females becoming males to be saved.[81]

Another enigmatic symbol appears in line 8 of the sealing epiclesis: "Come, elder of the five members—mind, thought, wisdom, esteem, reason—share with these newer ones" (ἐλθέ, ὁ πρεσβύτερος τῶν πέντε μελῶν, νοὸς ἐννοίας φρονήσεως ἐνθυμήσεως λογισμοῦ, κοινώνησον μετὰ τούτων τῶν νεωτέρων). This line is commonly cited as evidence of Manichaean revision, since the concept of the five members is Manichaean.[82] While this cannot be ruled out (the *Acts of Thomas* was eventually a part of the Manichaean canon, along with four other apocryphal acts),[83] it is not necessarily the case. A list of five members either very similar or identical to this one appears in many different early Christian as well as Jewish texts.[84] Unfortunately, we have no precedent for it in early Syriac literature.[85]

---

[81] Although the possibility of conflicting theologies within one tradition is not uncommon. Even within the *Gospel of Thomas* itself, e.g., we find another logion (22) which speaks of erasing gender altogether: "Jesus said to them, 'When you make the two one, and when you make the inside like the outside and the outside like the inside, and the above like the below, and when you make the male and the female one and the same, so that the male not be male nor the female female. . .then you will enter the kingdom.'" Translated by Lambdin in *NHLE*, 129. There are two distinct but related themes represented in these texts, and echoed in many other early Christian texts as well: 1) becoming male to achieve salvation; and 2) erasing gender differences to achieve salvation. Both evolve out of a belief in a pure, pre-Fall state, to which all Christians strive to return (I discuss this theme in the *ATh* shortly). The Holy Spirit as the κοινωνία τοῦ ἄρρενος may refer to this theme; in the Godhead the division between male and female is resolved through a joining or communion of male and female principles. I am grateful to Françoise Morard for her thoughts on this matter.

[82] Drijvers, "The Acts of Thomas," 338; Kruse, "Zwei Geist-Epikleses," 42.

[83] Drijvers, "The Acts of Thomas," 323.

[84] See Klijn, *Acts of Thomas*, 216–17, for an extensive list of examples; see also Drijvers, "The Acts of Thomas," 338.

[85] Regarding lines 5 and 8 (which I have just discussed) and line 7 (which I discuss below), many scholars have attempted to use these images to identify the "gnostic" roots of the *Acts of Thomas* (one example is Günther Bornkamm, *Mythos und Legende in den apokryphen Thomas-Akten* [Göttingen: Vandenhoeck und Ruprecht, 1933]). I intentionally avoid using this category because of the difficulties involved with definitions of gnosticism. The more information we gather, the less clear the definitions become, and the less efficient this term becomes to describe any one group or set of beliefs. I am grateful to the insights of Karen L. King, in her paper, "Is There Such a Thing as Gnosticism?" given at the Society of Biblical Literature Annual Meeting, November 20–23, 1993, Washington, D.C.

In line 4 of the eucharistic epiclesis, we finally encounter an image which we can identify as a consistent theme in the *Acts of Thomas*:[86] "Come, partaker in all the contests of the noble combatant" (ἐλθέ, ἡ κοινωνοῦσα ἐν πᾶσι τοῖς ἄθλοις τοῦ γενναίου ἀθλητοῦ). The "noble combatant" is clearly Christ, who aids the faithful by warding off evil forces. In chapter 39 Thomas addresses Christ in prayer, "O Jesus Christ. . .the defender and helper of thine own servants in the fight, who dost turn aside the enemy and drive him away from us, who in many battles does fight for us, and make us conquer in them all, our true and invincible champion, our holy and victorious commander. . . ."

A common motif in the *Acts of Thomas* is the relationship between Thomas and Jesus as twins.[87] Thus it is not surprising that Thomas plays a parallel role in these stories; he, too, has the power to fight the demons. Recall that the occasion of the eucharistic epiclesis is Thomas's exorcism of a demon from a woman and her subsequent conversion. The woman comes to the apostle explaining that she has heard that he heals bodies and that she has been ". . .no little tormented by the adversary these five years past" (42). Thomas calls the demon out of her with a series of exclamations which, interestingly, resemble the form of the epiclesis: "O evil not to be restrained! O shamelessness of the enemy! O envious one, never at rest. . . . O thou of many forms—he appears as he may wish, but his essence cannot be altered. . . ." His words are strikingly similar to those uttered by the *magos* in the

---

[86] Comparing these epicleses to themes in the *Acts of Thomas* as a whole raises the question of the relationship between these prayers and the rest of the text. Because the extant text is of such a composite nature, and because of the complex history of transmission, it is difficult to establish any relationship with certainty. Along with Kruse (see also n. 42 above), I think the author/compiler of the *Acts of Thomas* used older liturgical material for many of his prayers and rituals; the two epicleses are examples. If this is indeed the case (or if he wrote them himself), it is not unlikely that he made some attempt to connect the themes and images of the prayers with other portions of the *Acts of Thomas*. See Michael LaFargue, *Language and Gnosis: The Opening Scenes of the Acts of Thomas* (Harvard Dissertations in Religion 18; Philadelphia: Fortress Press, 1985). In this study LaFargue examines the relationships among the passages which seem to come from different sources (e.g., between the hymns and the narrative).

[87] Thomas and Jesus often appear in the form of the other. See, for example, chapter 11, where Jesus is seen in the form of the apostle. Jesus explains to the puzzled onlookers, "I am not Judas, who is also Thomas, I am his brother."

exorcistic spell discussed above. Although Thomas never articulates an explicit command, his list of epithets achieves the desired effect: the demon steps out and presents himself to Thomas. After lamenting his fate, he disappears in fire and smoke. Once free of the demon, the woman longs to be sealed so that she will always be safe. Thus the Holy Spirit, by acting to seal the faithful, partakes in the protective activity of Christ (and Thomas) the "noble combatant."

One of the most prominent themes in these epicleses is that of the Holy Spirit as a revealer of hidden or secret things. There is an element of paradox which characterizes this aspect of the Holy Spirit. In the eucharistic epiclesis, she is a silent revealer (line 5: ἡ ἡσυχία ἡ ἀποκαλύπτουσα); she is a hidden mother who makes her actions manifest (line 7: ἡ ἀπόκρυφος μήτηρ; line 8: ἡ φανερὰ ἐν ταῖς πράξεσιν αὐτῆς). Although she reveals secrets, she remains a mysterious figure herself.

Once again, the Holy Spirit shares with Christ the role of revealer. Thomas calls Jesus the "hidden mystery that has been revealed to us" (47) and the "Lord who dost reveal hidden mysteries and make manifest words that are secret" (10). Michael LaFargue compares Christ in the *Acts of Thomas* to the Wisdom figure in the Jewish tradition: "I learned both what is secret and what is manifest, for Wisdom, the fashioner of all things, taught me" (Wisdom of Solomon 7:21).[88] Following a familiar pattern, the apostle Thomas also plays the role of revealer. The talking colt addresses him, "Twin brother of Christ, apostle of the Most High and fellow-initiate into the hidden word of Christ, who dost receive his secret saying, fellow-worker of the Son of God" (39). Like the *magos*, Thomas has been bestowed with special power.

What is the secret? What knowledge does Thomas (and Christ and the Holy Spirit) reveal? The *Acts of Thomas* establishes the message of Thomas's preaching early in the narrative. The apostle teaches a bride and groom about Christ and convinces them to abandon their earthly marriage with its "filthy intercourse" for a true union which will guarantee eternal life. He exhorts them to make their bodies into "holy temples, pure and free from afflictions and pains" (12). This sermon to

---

[88] LaFargue, *Language and Gnosis*, 170. Translation from the NRSV.

the bride and groom, which inspires them to change their lives radically,[89] constitutes the core of the theological message of the *Acts of Thomas*. After listening to Thomas's teaching, the groom prays gratefully to Jesus, "I thank thee, Lord, who through the stranger [Thomas] was proclaimed and found in us; who hast removed me from corruption and sown in me life; who didst free me from this sickness. . .didst plant in me sober health; who didst show thyself to me and reveal to me all my condition in which I am. . .who. . .didst show me to seek myself and to recognize who I was and who and how I now am, that I may become again who I was" (15). In the *Acts of Thomas*, coming to believe in Christ means the restoration of one's self to one's original, pure state. This original state is unknown or hidden until it is revealed by some combination of Christ, Thomas, and the Holy Spirit. When someone commits to this new way of life, he or she gains this precious knowledge of self. The rituals of baptism and the eucharist serve to mark this change in the new believer's life and to secure him or her as a member of Christ's flock.[90]

The most telling symbol of the Holy Spirit in these epicleses is that of mother. This image fits into the context of early Syriac literature (pre-400), where the Holy Spirit is regularly described as feminine.[91] The grammar of Syriac—and Greek, to a lesser extent—makes female imagery for the Holy Spirit readily accessible.[92] The word for spirit in

[89] This is the only conversion in the *Acts of Thomas* without ritual.

[90] Again we find similar themes in the *Gospel of Thomas* (logion 5): "Jesus said, 'Recognize what is in your (sg.) sight, and that which is hidden from you (sg.) will become plain to you (sg.). For there is nothing hidden which will not become manifest." See also logion 6: "For nothing hidden will not become manifest, and nothing covered will remain without being uncovered." Logion 3 emphasizes the importance of self-knowledge: "When you come to know yourselves, then you will become known, and you will realize that it is you who are sons of the living father. But if you do not know yourselves, you dwell in poverty and it is you who are that poverty." Translated by Lambdin in *NHLE*, 126–27.

[91] Susan Ashbrook Harvey points out that the Holy Spirit was by no means exclusively described as feminine; much of the time it was described in masculine terms ("Feminine Imagery," 115). For detailed discussions of this imagery, see Murray, *Symbols of Church and Kingdom*, 131–58. See also Brock's general study of the Holy Spirit, *Holy Spirit in the Syrian Baptismal Tradition* (n. 2 above).

[92] Harvey, "Feminine Imagery," 115–16.

Syriac is feminine (*ruha'*), and thus all the verbs used to describe her activity are feminine as well. This grammatical structure develops into maternal metaphors specifically when early Syriac writers discuss baptism, as in the epicleses of the *Acts of Thomas*. In the fifth century, however, a change occurred whereby the noun for spirit—specifically when it referred to the Holy Spirit—was no longer treated as feminine. This blatant defiance of the grammar of the language signals an intentional shift in the imagery of the Holy Spirit from feminine to masculine.[93] The exact reasons for this are unclear, although some have speculated that it represents an attempt on the part of the Syriac church to distance itself from contemporary pagan cults which, with their divine triad of father, mother, and son, appeared suspiciously similar.[94] It is thought that the Syriac version of the *Acts of Thomas* reflects this change: all the references to the Holy Spirit as mother in the epicleses have been removed. The Greek version, although less gendered linguistically (spirit is neuter and finite verbs are not inflected for gender), nevertheless maintains the identification of the Holy Spirit with the symbol of mother.[95]

Scholars have long puzzled over the imagery of line 7 of the sealing epiclesis, "Come, mother of the seven houses, so that your rest may be in the eighth house" (ἐλθέ, ἡ μήτηρ τῶν ἑπτὰ οἴκων, ἵνα ἡ ἀνάπαυσίς σου εἰς τὸν ὄγδοον οἶκον γένηται). In line with a common comparison of the Syriac Holy Spirit with the figure of Wisdom in the Hebrew Bible, some suggest that this verse refers to Proverbs 9:1, "Wisdom has built her house, she has hewn her seven pillars."[96] In the Wisdom of Ben Sira, Wisdom describes her search for a home, which she eventually finds in Israel. She wanders through the heavens and on earth, looking

---

[93] Ibid., 118.

[94] Sebastian Brock, "The Holy Spirit as Feminine in Early Syriac Literature," in *After Eve*, ed. Janet Martin Soskice (London: Collins Marshall Pickering, 1990), 82.

[95] The *Gospel of the Hebrews* also depicts the Holy Spirit as mother. Christ says, "Even so did my mother, the Holy Spirit, take me by one of my hairs and carry me away to the great mountain of Tabor." Unfortunately the origin and transmission of this fragment is so sketchy that it is impossible to say where it comes from. For translation and background information, see Philipp Vielhauer and Georg Strecker, "The Gospel of the Hebrews," in *NTApoc*[5] 1:172–78.

[96] Drijvers, "The Acts of Thomas," 334. Translation from the NRSV.

for a place to dwell, and finally asks, "Among all these I sought a resting place; in whose territory should I abide? Then the Creator of all things gave me a command. . . . He said, 'Make your dwelling in Jacob, and in Israel receive your inheritance" (24:4–8).[97] Unfortunately, despite similar language (houses, resting place), neither wisdom passage provides a satisfactory parallel to the mother of the seven houses in the *Acts of Thomas*.

The numbers seven and eight most likely stem from the common conception in antiquity of seven heavens, which correspond to the seven spheres of the planets. The eighth realm was thought of as the realm of the gods, which would be an appropriate place for the Holy Spirit to find rest.[98] Thanks to the heresiologists, evidence survives of early Christian groups which conceived of a mother figure who resided in the eighth heaven.[99] Unfortunately, we have no other evidence which links the *Acts of Thomas* with any of these other traditions. The number eight is often associated with perfection, being one more than the perfect

[97] Kruse, "Zwei Geist-Epikleses," draws this comparison between the figure of Wisdom and the Holy Spirit in *ATh* 4. Translation from the NRSV.

[98] Douglas Parrott's introduction to "The Discourse on the Eighth and Ninth," in *NHLE*, 321–22. See also J. L. E. Dreyer's study, *A History of Astronomy from Thales to Kepler*, 2d ed. (New York: Dover, 1953). See Book 10 of Plato's *Republic* (615D–617C) for an ancient source which mentions this conception. Whether or not these heavens were ever called "houses" I have been unable to determine. "House" is a typical word for the positions of the astrological signs of the zodiac, although the number twelve is usually associated with this system (Georg Luck, *Arcana Mundi: Magic and the Occult in the Greek and Roman Worlds* [Baltimore: Johns Hopkins University Press, 1985], 318).

[99] The *Panarion* of Epiphanius, 25.2.2. Regarding the sect of Nicolaus, Epiphanius reports: "For some of them glorify a Barbelo who they claim is on high in an eighth heaven. . ."; English translation: Frank Williams, *The Panarion of Epiphanius of Salamis* (NHS 35; Leiden/New York: Brill, 1987), 78. Another example is found in Epiphanius's comment on the Archontics (*Panarion* 40.2.3): "And certain [archons] belong to the seven heavens, one archon to one heaven, and there are bands (of angels) for each archon, and the shining Mother is at the very top in the eighth heaven—like the other sects." English translation: Williams, *Panarion of Epiphanius*, 263. Notice also the reference to a divine mother. Irenaeus also attests this conception of the divine. Discussing the Ophites he explains, "In this way Hebdomad was completed by them, and the Mother held the eighth place" (*Against the Heresies* 1.30.4); English translation: Dominic J. Unger, *St. Irenaeus of Lyons: Against the Heresies*, vol. 1 (New York: Paulist Press, 1992), 97.

number seven.[100] As Robert Murray points out, many early baptistries reflect this concept in their octagonal shape.[101] Perhaps this reference to the eighth house in a baptismal context in the *Acts of Thomas* refers to a common connection between the number eight, perfection, and baptism in early Christianity.[102] Elsewhere in the *Acts of Thomas* (158), the apostle uses similar language. In a eucharistic prayer (which immediately follows a baptism) Thomas asks, "Let us receive the perfect house!" It is tempting to speculate that this perfect house is also the eighth house, the house of perfection and the Holy Spirit, which the new believer receives at initiation.

Another mother image in the epicleses is that of the "holy dove which gave birth to twin nestlings" (line 6 of the eucharistic epiclesis: ἡ ἱερὰ περιστερὰ ἡ τοὺς διδύμους νεοσσοὺς γεννῶσα). The symbol of the dove for the Holy Spirit finds poignant expression in the Syriac tradition. The Odes of Solomon, one of the earliest non-biblical Christian texts from Syria (second century),[103] describes the relationship between the

---

[100] See Auguste Luneau, *L'histoire du salut chez les Pères de l'Église* (Théologie Historique 9; Paris: Beauchesne, 1964). Luneau cites examples of the symbolism of the number eight in various Christian traditions: eternal life (p. 238), the resurrection which occurred on the first—or eighth—day of the week (pp. 338–39, 264), as representing future life (p. 154), divine perfection (p. 343). See his index for further examples. I am grateful to François Bovon for this reference. For further discussion of the symbolism of the eighth day, see Jean Daniélou, *The Bible and the Liturgy* (Notre Dame, Ind.: University of Notre Dame Press, 1956), 255–61 and 262–86.

[101] Murray, *Symbols of Church and Kingdom*, 134.

[102] The *Apocalypse of Paul* (in *NHLE*, 256–59) is relevant to this connection between baptism and the number eight. In this text Paul travels through the heavens, led by a child (who is called the Holy Spirit). In the seventh heaven he is questioned by an old man who refuses to let him pass into the eighth heaven. With the help of the child/Holy Spirit, Paul answers his questions and reveals his "sign" (the text does not clarify what this sign is) and is then allowed to proceed to the eighth heaven where the twelve apostles await him. Françoise Morard, to whom I am grateful for this reference, argues that this test of knowledge and presentation of the sign is a baptism of knowledge, necessary for Paul to continue on his journey. See Françoise Morard, "Les Apocalypses du Codex V," in *Les textes de Nag Hammadi et le problème de leur classification. Actes du Colloque tenu à Québec du 15 au 19 Septembre 1993*, ed. Louis Painchaud and Anne Pasquier (Québec: Les Presses de l'Université Laval, 1995), 346–48.

[103] The origin of the Odes of Solomon is debated. I am following Charlesworth, *Odes of Solomon*, vii. See also *Les Odes de Salomon*, trans. Marie-Joseph Pierre (Apocryphes 4; Turnhout: Brepols, 1994).

Holy Spirit and the believer: "As the wings of doves over their nestlings, and the mouths of their nestlings towards their mouths, so are the wings of the Spirit over my heart. My heart continually refreshes itself and leaps for joy, like the babe who leaps for joy in his mother's womb" (28:1–2).[104]

Bird imagery for the Holy Spirit has a long history in the Syriac tradition. In the Peshitta version of Genesis 1:2, the spirit "hovers" over the face of the waters at creation. This metaphor of the spirit hovering, which develops into the spirit as a bird, becomes an archetypal symbol of the activity of the Holy Spirit both at baptism and the eucharist.[105] The author of the Gospel of John uses the image of the Spirit as a dove to describe Jesus' baptism. John the Baptist testifies to this event: "I saw the Spirit descending from heaven like a dove, and it remained on him" (John 1:32). These biblical images clearly shape the Syriac rituals of baptism. Aphrahat writes in the fourth century: "For by baptism we receive the Spirit of Christ, and at that moment when the priests invoke the Spirit, She opens the heavens and descends and hovers over the waters, and those who are baptized put Her on. For the Spirit is far from all who are born of the body until they come to the birth from water, and then receive the Holy Spirit."[106]

This passage from Aphrahat is particularly relevant to this discussion because it speaks of a ritual of baptism in which a priest invokes the Spirit, much like the apostle Thomas. Further, Aphrahat's words clarify the implications of the maternal connotations of the Holy Spirit; receiving or "putting on" the Holy Spirit at baptism represents a new birth.[107]

---

[104] Charlesworth, *Odes of Solomon*, 107 (Syriac), 108 (translation).

[105] Harvey, "Feminine Imagery," 116; Brock, *Holy Spirit*, 6.

[106] *Demonstration* 6.14. English translation: Harvey, "Feminine Imagery," 117.

[107] Notice the mention of water in Aphrahat's passage. Neither the sealing in chapter 27 nor that in chapter 49 mentions water (see n. 7 above). Most of the conversions in the *Acts of Thomas*, however, involve a sealing with oil (which is sometimes called baptism, in chapter 131, for example) *and* a baptism with water (121, 132, 157). As Klijn points out, it is impossible to extract from this text a certain and uniform ritual of initiation (Klijn, *Acts of Thomas*, 54–59). In the *Acts of Thomas*, it seems that, at the very least, the sealing with oil (although oil is not always used—sometimes the apostle just lays his hands on the believer) was involved with initiation, as was baptism with water.

Thomas himself explains the meaning of baptism: "This baptism is forgiveness of sins. It brings to new birth a light that is shed around. It brings to new birth the new man. . ." (132). Similar themes define the meaning of the eucharist, as Thomas exclaims before breaking the bread: ". . .let us receive renewal of soul and body! Because thou didst rise and come to life again, let us come to life again and live and stand before thee in righteous judgment" (158). In the *Acts of Thomas* this rebirth describes the process of returning to one's pure and original state. Both rituals bring about and celebrate this change.

The twin motif, so prominent throughout the *Acts of Thomas*, appears again in the mother imagery of the Holy Spirit, mother of "twin nestlings." The most straightforward explanation of the identity of these two nestlings is that they represent Thomas and Christ, who have been mirroring each other throughout these stories. Another interpretation offered by Drijvers includes the new believer in the symbolism of the "twin nestlings." One of the nestlings represents the convert who should strive to mimic Christ (as Thomas does) until he or she becomes identical with him.[108] Drijvers traces this theology to Tatian (a Syrian philosopher and theologian writing in Greek in the second half of the second century C.E.) who writes of his own rebirth, "and so I too am reborn in imitation of the *Logos* and have acquired knowledge of the truth."[109] In the *Acts of Thomas* this rebirth is described in terms of being united with Christ,[110] so that returning to one's pure self means becoming more Christlike.

The words of the apostle in the *Acts of Thomas* carry tremendous power and agency in these stories.[111] They are as crucial to the sacramen-

---

[108] Drijvers, "The Acts of Thomas," 335. I think his interpretation is compelling, especially with the theme of imitation of Christ throughout the *Acts of Thomas*.

[109] *Oratio ad Graecos* 5.1–3. Translated by Drijvers, "The Acts of Thomas," 334. Clearly Tatian is drawing on the prologue of the Gospel of John.

[110] In chapter 15 the groom praises Christ for setting aside his greatness so that Christ might "unite" with himself. In chapter 132 Thomas prays to the "hidden power," which is united with the initiates at baptism.

[111] François Bovon has also treated this theme of the power of the words of the apostle in the *Acts of Andrew*: "The Words of Life in the *Acts of the Apostle Andrew*," *HTR* 87 (1994): 139–54. In common with the *Acts of Thomas*, in the *Acts of Andrew* the apostle's words link believers to the divine and perhaps point to ecclesiastical practices (Bovon, "Words of Life," 148ff.).

tal rituals as the utterances of the *magos* are to the efficacy of the spells. In both contexts, a special person, endowed with gifts from a deity, conducts rituals which are designed to create potentially profound and dramatic changes in people's lives. Through these rituals people are healed and demons are exorcised. Both the *magos* and the apostle manipulate powerful symbols, through actions and through words, which cause the divine to respond. To this extent, the magic spells serve as a useful model which helps us understand the mechanics of the rituals in the *Acts of Thomas*.

It is not surprising that the *Acts of Thomas*, coming out of Syria, uses symbols so effectively. Syriac theological writing is known for this method of using networks of symbols to create multifaceted meanings. The metaphors and images which govern this literature create "verbal icons" for the reader.[112] Each of these images in the *Acts of Thomas* epicleses—dove, mother, nestlings, fellowship of the male, noble combatant—contains its own set of associations, stories, and meanings for the ancient Syriac audience. What is striking about these prayers—and what is made clear by a comparison to magic spells—is the way in which the structure of the prayers works together with the use of symbols. As we have seen, the prayers themselves are structured in layers; at each line a new symbol or set of images is released by Thomas's voice. Every release triggers new associations with themes found elsewhere in the *Acts of Thomas*, or elsewhere in contemporary Syriac literature. This rich language of symbol and metaphor allows Thomas to invoke the full power of the Holy Spirit, with all of her diverse attributes and activities, into these rituals of initiation and eucharist.

---

[112] Harvey, "Feminine Imagery," 113–14.

Articulate Animals: A Multivalent Motif in the Apocryphal Acts of the Apostles

Christopher R. Matthews

> For the fate of humans and the fate of animals is the same; as one dies, so dies the other. They all have the same breath, and humans have no advantage over the animals.
> —Qoh 3:19

A large dog addresses Peter with a human voice and performs a commission for the "messenger and apostle of the true God." Thomas encounters a variety of speaking beasts, both favorable and inimical to the apostle's mission. As Paul faces death in the arena at Ephesus, the fierce lion designated as his executioner turns out providentially to be the very beast that had previously requested baptism by the apostle's hands. A talking leopard and kid are converted and follow in the missionary train of the apostle Philip. The episodes of the speaking animals in the Apocryphal Acts of the Apostles are among the more delightful features of these proletarian Christian documents. More than fanciful embellishments, these animals are the heirs of a larger cultural legacy. Embodying the collective genius of diverse streams of literary, philosophical, and religious imagination and speculation, they function within early Christian narrative on a popular theological level to dramatize the uniqueness, strangeness, and comprehensiveness of the young religion. If the Preacher's pessimism found animals engulfed in human mortality, certain strains of early Christian optimism saw them awash in human salvation.

A Lion Baptized

It is fitting to initiate our considerations of the speaking apocryphal animals with the king of beasts. According to the Hamburg Papyrus,[1] while in Ephesus addressing an audience that includes the governor, Hieronymus, Paul is detained and condemned to the beasts at the instigation of certain goldsmiths. While in his cell awaiting the execution of his sentence, the apostle "breaks off his prayer in terror" at the fierce roar of the lion appointed for him. After various intervening events, Paul is brought to the stadium and the lion is released. But a scene of martyrdom is forestalled by one of recognition:

> The lion looked at Paul and Paul at the lion. Then Paul recognized that this was the lion which had come and been baptized. And borne along by faith Paul said: "Lion, was it thou whom I baptized?" And the lion in answer said to Paul: "Yes." Paul spoke to it again and said: "And how wast thou captured?" The lion said with one voice: "Even as thou, Paul." (PHam 4–5)[2]

Frustrated by this prodigious outcome, Hieronymus releases other beasts against Paul and dispatches archers to do away with the lion. But the governor's will is again thwarted, this time by a violent hailstorm. In the confusion, Paul takes leave of his animal convert and departs by ship for Macedonia; the lion returns to the mountains.

In this introductory vignette we encounter two motifs that will be the focus of this paper: the rational speech of animals, and their natural affinity for or conversion to Christianity. Wilhelm Schneemelcher's superb analysis of the witnesses to Paul's dealings with the lion and his interpretation of the ultimate significance of these episodes will set the stage for my own considerations.[3] It will be instructive to attend to Schneemelcher's unfolding of the evidence, which proceeds in the

---

[1] See Schmidt, *ΠΡΑΞΕΙΣ ΠΑΥΛΟΥ*.

[2] Unless noted otherwise, translations of the Apocryphal Acts of the Apostles are taken from *NTApoc*[5], although the angle brackets and parentheses of the latter have not been reproduced.

[3] Wilhelm Schneemelcher, "Der getaufte Löwe in den Acta Pauli," in *Mullus. Festschrift Theodor Klauser*, ed. Alfred Stuiber and Alfred Hermann (JAC Ergänzungsband 1; Münster: Aschendorff, 1964), 316–26.

manner of a protagonist's summary of events at the conclusion of a good mystery novel. He first presents the situation prior to the discovery of the Hamburg Papyrus, when the clues concerning the nature of the incident about Paul and the lion were incomplete. He lays the groundwork for unraveling the puzzle surrounding the story by highlighting Jerome's statement in *De uiris illustribus* 7, which alone among the ancient witnesses to the scene of Paul's encounter with the lion at Ephesus contains an explicit reference to the animal's baptism: "Igitur περιόδους Pauli et Theclae et totam baptizati leonis fabulam inter scripturas apocryphas computemus" ("And so we reckon the journeys of Paul and Thecla and the whole tale of the baptized lion among the apocryphal writings").[4] The other ancient witnesses omit any reference to baptism but do report on the dramatic encounter between Paul and the lion in the arena, in some instances noting their conversation.[5]

Schneemelcher next integrates the evidence of the Greek text of the Ephesus episode found in the Hamburg Papyrus. As is clear in the translated extract cited above, although the baptism of the lion is alluded to, the precise circumstances are not relayed. At this point Schneemelcher introduces the *Letter of Pelagia*, which appears to present a somewhat muted version of this baptismal event. This text informs us that after his release from a judicial proceeding against him in Caesarea, Paul departed "toward the mountain."

---

[4] My translation. For the text, see *Gerolamo. Gli uomini illustri. De viris illustribus*, ed. Aldo Ceresa-Gastaldo (Biblioteca Patristica 12; Florence: Nardini, 1988), 88. Tamás Adamik ("The Influence of the Apocryphal Acts on Jerome's Lives of Saints," in Bremmer, *Apocryphal Acts of John*, 175–76) notes that although Jerome considers the account of the baptized lion to be a "tale" (*fabula*), episodes in his *Lives of the Saints* include speaking wild animals. See Adamik's enumeration of examples from Jerome's accounts and the similar roles played by animals in the Apocryphal Acts of the Apostles (pp. 176–77). Patricia Cox Miller's study of Jerome's *Life of Saint Paul* ("Jerome's Centaur: A Hyper-Icon of the Desert," *Journal of Early Christian Studies* 4 [1996]: 209–33) demonstrates how in Jerome's account "animal wildness and authentic religious understanding are brought together in the hybrid images of the centaur and the satyr" (p. 225).

[5] The pertinent texts, each briefly discussed by Schneemelcher, are Hippolytus *Commentary on Daniel* 3.29; Commodian *Carmen apologeticum* 627–28 (the talking dog of the *Acts of Peter* is mentioned in line 626; Commodian's writings were judged "apocryphal" by the Decretum Gelasianum); *Acts of Titus* 6; *Letter of Pelagia*; and Nicephorus Callistus *Historia ecclesiastica* 2.25 (*PG* 145, 822).

And as he walked there, Paul found a lion, and his height was twelve cubits, and his size as that of a horse. And he met Paul, and they saluted each other as though they knew each other. And the lion said unto Paul, "Well met, Paul, servant of God, and Apostle of the Lord Jesus Christ! I have one thing which I ask thee to do unto me." And Paul said unto him, "Speak; I will hear." And the lion said, "Make me to enter into the great things of the Christians." And Paul took him and made him to enter into the great things of the Christians. And when he had finished the law of the seventh day, then they bade each other farewell.[6]

Although the author of *Letter of Pelagia* apparently seeks to disguise Paul's baptism of an animal here ("Paul took him and made him to enter into the great things of the Christians"),[7] it nevertheless remains obvious.[8] Schneemelcher finds corroboration in a Coptic version of the Ephesus episode in which the baptism is narrated in a speech of Paul which seems to overlap with the beginning of the Hamburg Papyrus.[9] In his speech, Paul is recounting a journey on which he is accompanied by "the widow Lemma and her daughter Ammia." Paul and his companions are in prayer when "a great and terrible lion" comes upon them.

"But when I finished praying, the beast had cast himself at my feet. I was filled with the Spirit and looked upon him, and said to him: 'Lion, what wilt thou?' But he said: 'I wish to be baptized.' I glorified God, who had given speech to the beast and salvation to his servants."

---

[6] The translation is taken from Edgar J. Goodspeed, "The Epistle of Pelagia," *American Journal of Semitic Languages and Literatures* 20 (1903–4): 105–6, quotation marks added.

[7] Goodspeed ("Epistle of Pelagia," 105 n. 2) wonders whether "an error in translation lies back of this: e.g., confusion of the Coptic words for 'baptism' and for 'great, much.'" Schneemelcher ("Der getaufte Löwe," 321 n. 36) comments: "Aber das ist unwahrscheinlich."

[8] Schmidt, *ΠΡΑΞΕΙΣ ΠΑΥΛΟΥ*, 96; Schneemelcher, "Der getaufte Löwe," 321; Bruce M. Metzger, "St. Paul and the Baptized Lion: Apocryphal vs. Canonical Books of the New Testament," *Princeton Seminary Bulletin* 39 (1945): 16 n. 13.

[9] This still unpublished fourth-century Coptic text, which contains an almost complete version of the Ephesus narrative, is described by Rodolphe Kasser, "Acta Pauli 1959," *Revue d'histoire et de philosophie religieuses* 40 (1960): 45–57. A provisional translation is available in *NTApoc*[5] 2:263–65 and is utilized below.

As the narrative continues, Paul leads the lion down to a river bank and prays, with reference to the prophet Daniel and the accomplishment of God's plan.

> "When I had prayed thus, I took the lion by his mane and in the name of Jesus Christ immersed him three times. But when he came up out of the water he shook out his mane and said to me: 'Grace be with thee!' And I said to him: 'And likewise with thee.' The lion ran off to the country rejoicing (for this was revealed to me in my heart). A lioness met him, and he did not yield himself to her but. . .ran off."

Schneemelcher's analysis aims to explain the significance of this singular baptism of a beast and seizes on the concept of the οἰκονομία of God as the key. Prior to proposing his own explanation, Schneemelcher succinctly notes the contributions of others on this issue. He credits Carl Schmidt with clarifying the literary question and confirming Jerome's information with the evidence of the Hamburg Papyrus.[10] Rosa Söder connected the lion with other speaking beasts in the Apocryphal Acts of the Apostles and, justifiably, identified this motif as a teratological element.[11] Bruce Metzger emphasized the contacts with the story of Androcles found in Aulus Gellius's *Noctes Atticae* 5.14 and credited to Apion's *Aegyptiaca*.[12] In Schneemelcher's opinion, however, only Alfons Kurfess put the crucial question, "How is the 'baptized lion' to be explained?" Kurfess supposed that the author of the *Acts of Paul* inserted the story on the authority of Paul's vision of the creature's share in redemption from sin and death in Rom 8:19–23.[13] Schneemelcher judges this to be correct to a point but in need of some modification and limitation. Although in his view Romans 8 plays no role, nevertheless, the story of the baptized lion functions as an example of how God's οἰκονομία reaches its goal. Thus the story allows the author to describe the comprehensive nature of the redemption of

[10] Schmidt, *ΠΡΑΞΕΙΣ ΠΑΥΛΟΥ*, 85–98.

[11] Söder, *Die apokryphen Apostelgeschichten*, 110–12.

[12] Metzger, "Baptized Lion," 11–21. Metzger also presents a survey of the various ancient witnesses to the Ephesus incident.

[13] Alfons Kurfess, "Zu dem Hamburger Papyrus der *Πράξεις Παύλου*," *ZNW* 38 (1939): 170.

the world: Even the creature is brought to faith by Paul's preaching.

Schneemelcher's review of the witnesses to and significance of the "baptized lion" episode is judicious and remains illuminating. Nevertheless, there is room to improve upon his analysis in several respects. First of all, Schneemelcher's consideration of the background and significance of the story of the baptized lion may be enhanced from the perspective of its membership in the class of stories that feature talking animals. Simply to identify the story as an example of how God's οἰκονομία reaches its goal neglects a host of literary, social, philosophical, and theological intertexts that explain why this tactic is so effective. Second, when Schneemelcher wrote, he could indeed say that the "baptized lion" was singular among the animal tales in the Apocryphal Acts of the Apostles. This has now changed with the discovery of Athos, *Xenophontos 32* of the *Acts of Philip* and its text of act 12, which features an impassioned plea for the reception of the eucharist by the speaking animals in the missionary band of the apostle Philip.[14] The animal speech in *Acts of Philip* 12 sheds further light on the significance of the presence of talking animals in the various Apocryphal Acts of the Apostles.

Consequently, in what follows I will consider the talking animals of the Apocryphal Acts of the Apostles as a genus, adding the example of the "eucharistic animals" from the *Acts of Philip*, and so sketch the broader cultural background that is exploited in the telling of these tales as part and parcel of the genre of the apocryphal acts. Thus, I will sketch the literary and cultural antecedents and concomitants to the episodes of speaking animals in this early Christian literature. In the first instance this will involve attention to the obvious biblical precursors (Eden's serpent and Balaam's ass), as well as the general place of

---

[14] See "Les Actes de Philippe," in *Actes apocryphes des apôtres*, 301–4; and Bovon, "Actes de Philippe," 4431–527. The latter article, in addition to providing comprehensive information on the history of research on the *Acts of Philip*, the Greek manuscripts, and versions in other languages, gives an extensive summary of the content of the Greek text with special attention to the new or additional material of *Xenophontos 32*. A new introduction to the *Acts of Philip* and a French translation, which includes the previously unedited material from *Xenophontos 32*, is available in Amsler, Bovon, and Bouvier, *Actes de l'apôtre Philippe*.

animals within the compass of scriptural writings. Next, attention to the presence of speaking animals in Graeco-Roman literature will be pursued against the background of philosophical discussions concerning the rationality of beasts and the widespread appearance of animals in fables and proverbs. The topos of the articulate animal also figures in rabbinic literature, and in some instances insight from this domain clarifies hermeneutical issues presented by scenes from the apocryphal acts. Against this wide sweep of literary and cultural currents, the phenomenon of apostles and speaking animals in the apocryphal acts will be taken up. The ultimate focus will be on the remarkable scene in the *Acts of Philip* where animals make a tearful request to share the eucharist and are appointed associates of the evangelists.

Biblical Zoology

As a rule animals appear in the Hebrew Bible only as part of the backdrop of the biblical world. The inherent superiority of human over animal is established in the dominion granted human beings over the natural world (Gen 1:28–30; 9:2–3), which is symbolized in Adam's naming of the animals (Gen 2:19–20). While animals function as food and useful property in everyday life, and as sacrifices in cultic life, there is little focus on animals per se or animal images in the Hebrew Bible. This secondary role is clearly connected with the demythologization of the animal kingdom in Israelite religion vis-à-vis the perceived excesses of surrounding cultures, notably the Egyptian and Canaanite.[15] The incident of the golden calf (Exodus 32) is fundamental for the Hebrew view of animal images and guarantees modest participation by animals in biblical literature. Accordingly, concern for animals in the Hebrew Bible is more practical than ethical; animals are fundamentally viewed as tools and, with one or two exceptions, play only minor and unremarkable roles. It is precisely these exceptions, however, that are appropriated by certain early Christian storytellers for their own

[15] Elijah Judah Schochet, *Animal Life in Jewish Tradition: Attitudes and Relationships* (New York: Ktav, 1984), 22. On animals as representatives of gods in the Hebrew Bible, see Othmar Keel, "Das Tier in der Bibel," in *Mensch und Tier*, ed. Maja Svilar (Kulturhistorische Vorlesungen, 1984/85; Bern: Lang, 1985), 33–41.

narrative worlds. The serpent of Genesis 3, being "more crafty than any other wild animal," is able to tempt Eve with smooth speech.[16] The apostle Thomas encounters this same speaking snake and, after listening to its self-implication in the more heinous crimes of salvation history, presides over its destruction (*ATh* 31–33).[17] It is also Thomas who meets a member of "that race that served Balaam" (*ATh* 39–41). The episode of Balaam's ass in Numbers 22:21–35 is important not only because it portrays a speaking beast but also because it implies an innate ability on the part of animals to perceive the divine. This motif is operative in every narrative that depicts a favorable meeting between an apostle and a speaking animal.

Elsewhere in the biblical canon, the prophetic visions of the messianic period suggest not only a peaceful coexistence between various members of the animal kingdom but also compassionate relationships between humankind and animals.[18] The New Testament writings offer at most only indirect affirmations concerning the presence of animals in the history of salvation. The placement of the newborn Jesus "in a manger" could imply the presence of animals at his birth, but the text does not say this. Pious Christian eyes later discovered a reference to such animals in Isaiah 1:3. The obscure reference to wild beasts in Mark 1:13 perhaps represents a proleptic fulfillment of the eschatological peace announced by the prophets.[19] More generally, apart from any specific notions, both Paul (Rom 8:19–23) and his successors (Col 1:23) envisaged redemption as encompassing the nonhuman realm of creation.

---

[16] Gen 3:1–5; cf. *Life of Adam and Eve* 37–39. As James L. Kugel (*The Bible As It Was* [Cambridge, Mass.: Harvard University Press, Belknap Press, 1997], 73) notes, various ancient interpreters supposed that snakes (see Philo *De opificio mundi* 156) or all animals (see *Jub.* 3:28; Josephus *Ant.* 1.41) originally knew how to speak.

[17] The serpent in *ATh* 32 identifies itself as "a reptile of reptile nature, the baleful son of a baleful father." *Apocalypse of Moses* 16 records a conversation between the devil and the serpent, indicating that it is the former who will speak through the mouth of the latter.

[18] Isa 11:6–9; 65:25; Hos 2:18; see also *2 Apoc. Bar.* 73:6.

[19] According to Joachim Jeremias ("'Αδάμ," *TDNT* 1:141), "the account of the temptation in Mark (1:13) shows how Jesus as the new man. . .overcame the temptation which overthrew the first man. . . . As Adam was once honoured by the beasts in Paradise according to the Midrash, so Christ is with the wild beasts after overcoming temptation."

Manifold Menageries

Although precedent for speaking apocryphal animals in the Bible is basic, it is but one element in the complex convergence of cultural, literary, and religious factors underlying the phenomenon of talking beasts in early Christian narratives. Attention to the cultural environment of the Graeco-Roman world discloses a number of significant antecedents to the early Christian novelistic employment of speaking animals. Already, apart from any powers of speech, it is obvious that animals played a significant role in mythology and were fully utilized in connection with religious symbolism.[20] Yet, with few exceptions, there is no evidence for an actual cult focused on animals in Greece. Early Christian authors who adduced examples to critique such worship overinterpreted their sources or were influenced by the universally known worship of animals in ancient Egypt.[21] While it is true that the gods were fond of taking on the form of animals and were closely connected with their theriomorphic representations in iconography, the underlying reality is one of animal sacrifice rather than animal worship.[22] If, in the Greek conception, the sacrifice of an animal obviates the need for human sacrifice, nevertheless,

> at that separation of gods and men in the sacrifice, the dying animal belongs to this extent on the side of men, mortals. To the god it stands in a relation of polarity: through the death which it dies, it confirms *e contrario* the superior power of the wholly other, deathless, everlasting god.[23]

A kinship based on mortal nature was not the only alleged similarity between animals and humans in philosophical discussion. Although Stoics maintained that animal sagacity was a manifestation of instinct or nature (φύσις) and not reason (λόγος), dissenters marshaled numerous

[20] See the annotated catalogue compiled by Heinz M. Lins, *Tiere in der Mythologie und ihre religiöse Symbolkraft* (Frankfurt: Fischer, 1990).

[21] Martin P. Nilsson, *Geschichte der griechischen Religion*, vol. 1, *Die Religion Griechenlands bis auf die griechische Weltherrschaft*, 2d ed. (Handbuch der Altertumswissenschaft 5/2/1; Munich: Beck, 1955), 212–14.

[22] Walter Burkert, *Greek Religion*, trans. John Raffan (Cambridge, Mass.: Harvard University Press, 1985), 64–66; Nilsson, *Geschichte*, 1:214–16.

[23] Burkert, *Greek Religion*, 66.

illustrations to demonstrate the presence of "inner reason" among animals.[24] Some of these frequently attested proofs, which detail the activities of the ant, the bee, the spider, and the swallow, already figured in pre-Aristotelian debates on instinct versus reason.[25] The conspicuous champions of the view that animals, like human beings, possessed reason were the Skeptics of the New Academy, most notably Carneades (ca. 213–128 B.C.E.).[26] A battery of arguments deriving from the New Academy in support of the rationality of animals is presented by Philo's nephew Alexander in the former's dialogue *De animalibus*.[27] Such arguments circulated widely in the writings of numerous Hellenistic authors.[28]

[24] See Urs Dierauer, *Tier und Mensch im Denken der Antike. Studien zur Tierpsychologie, Anthropologie und Ethik* (Studien zur antiken Philosophie 6; Amsterdam: Grüner, 1977), 199–293.

[25] See Aristotle *Phys.* 2.8.199a22. Sherwood O. Dickerman, "Some Stock Illustrations of Animal Intelligence in Greek Psychology," *Transactions of the American Philological Association* 42 (1911): 128.

[26] Such arguments were advanced not to defend animal rationality per se but to insist on the necessity of suspending judgment. Thus, the example of the dog in Sextus Empiricus 1.62–77 is extended to all animals to show that "the so-called irrational animals. . .participate in external reason" (1.75). "Consequently we shall not possess a proof which enables us to give our own sense-impressions the preference over those of the so-called irrational animals" (1.61). The only solution to this predicament is suspension of judgment (1.78). Translation by R. G. Bury (LCL, 1933).

[27] The Greek original of this treatise is lost; it is extant only in classical Armenian. See Abraham Terian, *Philonis Alexandrini de animalibus: The Armenian Text with an Introduction, Translation, and Commentary* (Studies in Hellenistic Judaism 1; Chico, Calif.: Scholars Press, 1981). "Although the views on the rationality of animals expressed in Alexander's discourse were anticipated by Plato and Aristotle, they were doubtless taken over by Philo from the arguments used by the opponents of the Stoics in the New Academy" (ibid., 49–50). See especially Aristotle *Historia animalium* 8–9. Note also that "mythological beliefs (such as the primitive belief in metempsychosis, the mantic powers attributed to animals, their congregating, flight, cries, and calls) must have contributed to the early concept of rationality of animals" (Terian, *Philonis Alexandrini de animalibus*, 48–49).

[28] See Terian (*Philonis Alexandrini de animalibus*, 53–56) on Philo's sources. Note especially Plutarch's *De sollertia animalium* (*Mor.* 959A–985C, which appears to employ selectively the same sources utilized by the natural histories of Aelian and Pliny; there are also parallels with Philo's dialogue), *Bruta animalia ratione uti* (*Mor.* 985D–992E), and *De esu carnium* (*Mor.* 993A–999B, which argues in favor of vegetarianism). See also Oppian *Cynegetica*; Celsus in Origen *Contra Celsum* 4; and Porphyry *De abstinentia*.

Alexander's argument in favor of animal rationality (*De animalibus* §§ 10–71) contends that even though the two kinds of reason (speech and thought) "appear to be imperfect in animals, they are none the less fundamental" (§ 12).[29] He argues that the display on the part of animals of both "uttered reason" (§§ 13–15) and "inner reason" (§§ 16–70) makes it "obvious that not only men but also various other animals have inherited the faculty of reason" (§ 71). It is through arrogance and disdain that human beings withhold reason from animals and appropriate it to themselves (§ 11), even though the "faculty of reason is implanted in every creature endowed with a soul" (§ 17). For "animals have wisdom, knowledge, excellent discerning, superior foresight, and all that is related to the intellect—those things which are called 'virtues of the rational soul'" (§ 30). Consequently, "although they are unable to express their mental conceptions because of their inarticulate tongues, they conduct themselves with such abundant wisdom that they exhibit many characteristics of speech. To the keenly perceptive there is something more evident than voice—the truth which their actions reveal" (§ 44).[30]

Philo himself weighs in on the side of the Stoics, employing their counter-arguments, developed from Chrysippus to Posidonius, which asserted that animals exist providentially for the sake of humankind, the irrational for the rational. For Philo, "to elevate animals to the level

---

[29] "Thus nature has placed a sovereign mind in every soul. In some it has a very faint imprint, an inexplicable and ill-defined form of an image; in others it has the likeness of a well-defined, very distinct, and fastidiously clear image; and still in others it is of an indistinct kind. But the deep and distinct impressions are borne upon the image of man" (§ 29). All translations of *De animalibus* are taken from Terian, *Philonis Alexandrini de animalibus*.

[30] Jean-Pierre Mahé ("Preliminary Remarks on the Demotic *Book of Thoth* and the Greek *Hermetica*," *Vigiliae Christianae* 50 [1996]: 353–63) notes that one of the issues raised in the *Book of Thoth* (a ca. second-century C.E. dialogue in question and answer form) concerns "teaching" that comes to "sacred animals and birds" (p. 356). "Whether due to the existence of sacred animals or to other local traditions, Greek-speaking philosophers of Hellenistic and Roman Egypt, just like the BT [*Book of Thoth*], seem to have felt rather concerned with the problem of animal wisdom" (p. 357). He cites Philo's dialogue and refers to its "many allusions to Egypt and Egyptian animals (§§ 13. 14. 22. 28. 50. 52)."

of the human race and to grant equality to unequals is the height of injustice" (§ 100). Philo's position in *De animalibus*, although it contains nothing that suggests a Jewish context, is consistent with his understanding elsewhere of the sovereignty of humankind over the animals.[31] Philo takes up the Stoic view not for its own sake but to defend the "anthropocentric view of the cosmos reflected in Gen 1:26–28; 2:19–20; 9:2—man's dominion over the irrational creation" in the face of Alexander's assault on the "Judaeo-biblical doctrine that only man is endowed with the rational spirit."[32]

While the favorable indications for the rationality of animals emanating from philosophical controversies were routinely mediated to the public at large by numerous authors,[33] there were still more accessible arenas in which animals, articulate or otherwise, intruded on the collective consciousness as companions in life. On the topic of animal wisdom and "resemblances of speech," Alexander attests in *De animalibus* 46 that "nothing has been heard from anyone that is as significant and accurate as Aesop's account in the best part of his works." Aesop was a cultural hero, and his biography, *Life of Aesop*, "is one of

[31] In addition to the discussion in Terian, *Philonis Alexandrini de animalibus*, see Peder Borgen, "Man's Sovereignty over Animals and Nature according to Philo of Alexandria," in *Text and Contexts: Biblical Texts in Their Textual and Situational Contexts. Essays in Honor of Lars Hartman*, ed. Tord Fornberg and David Hellholm (Oslo: Scandinavian University Press, 1995), 369–89.

[32] Terian, *Philonis Alexandrini de animalibus*, 47.

[33] See the texts listed in n. 28. As P. T. Eden observes (*Theobaldi, "Physiologus."* *Edited with Introduction, Critical Apparatus, Translation and Commentary* [Mittellateinische Studien und Texte 6; Leiden: Brill, 1972], 2), the "widespread heterogeneous folklore of the Eastern Mediterranean, on which Aristotle and Pliny the Elder had already drawn, and Aelian was drawing in roughly the same period," issued in the *Physiologus*, a collection of marvelous stories, dating perhaps as early as the second century, that join Christian theological and moral teaching to pagan folklore and work of the paradoxographers on the nature and qualities of animals, birds, plants, and stones. Eden notes that Justin, Tertullian, Origen, and Clement of Alexandria appear to have been familiar with this collection, which was written in Greek and translated into Arabic, Syriac, Armenian, and Ethiopic by the fifth century. A Latin version, attributed to Ambrose, was condemned by Pope Gelasius's decree of 496 C.E. From the fourth century on, for one thousand years the Latin *Physiologus* was a "vital part of Western European culture" (ibid., 3). As early as the ninth century, a new recension attributed to John Chrysostom may be recognized as "the first 'Bestiarium' proper."

the few genuinely popular books that have come down from ancient times."[34] Ben Edwin Perry suggests that Aesop's celebrity was owing to the novelty of his "exploitation of purely fictitious animal stories told orally in prose with comic effect. . .something new in the Greek world of the sixth century B.C."[35] Aesop's fables were regularly employed in the schools in connection with rhetorical exercises, and texts of fables circulated among the public at large.[36] Quintilian advised that the education of young children begin with Aesop's fables prior to their instruction in rhetoric:

> We must however add to their [teachers'] activities instruction in certain rudiments of oratory for the benefit of those who are not yet ripe for the schools of rhetoric. Their pupils should learn to paraphrase Aesop's fables, the natural successors of the fairy stories of the nursery, in simple and restrained language and subsequently to set down this paraphrase in writing with the same simplicity of style: they should begin by analysing each verse, then give its meaning in different language, and finally proceed to a freer paraphrase in which they will be permitted now to abridge and now to embellish the original, so far as this may be done without losing the poet's meaning.[37]

His reference to preserving the "poet's meaning" in this advice likely indicates the employment of Aesopic fables composed in Greek verse

---

[34] Ben Edwin Perry, *Studies in the Text History of the Life and Fables of Aesop* (American Philological Association Monograph Series 7; Lancaster, Pa.: Lancaster, 1936; Chico, Calif.: Scholars Press, 1981), 2.

[35] *Babrius and Phaedrus*, ed. and trans. Ben Edwin Perry (LCL, 1965), xlv. It is possible to demur with respect to Perry's optimism concerning the possibility of saying something about the historical Aesop while noting the early cultural impact of the fable in Greece.

[36] Perry, *Studies*, 157–59.

[37] *Institutio Oratoria* 1.9.1–2; translation by H. E. Butler (LCL, 1920). Terian (*Philonis Alexandrini de animalibus*, 183) finds a reference to Philo's own tutelage under Aesop's fables at *De animalibus* 73: "Now it is not as though I was not taught the things referred to; in fact I was nurtured with such instructions throughout childhood, on account of their certainty, intriguing names, and easy comprehension." Terian (ibid., 183–84) notes that Demetrius of Phalerum replaced the Homeric epics with the Aesopic fables as the preferred educational textbook, and that much of Plutarch's *De sollertia animalium* is presented as a school exercise (e.g., *Mor.* 960B, 963B, 965C–E, 975D).

for such exercises.[38] Phaedrus (born ca. 18 B.C.E.) and Babrius (first century C.E.) both assembled collections of Aesopic fables, in Latin and Greek verse, respectively. Both seem to have drawn on the fourth-century B.C.E. collection of Demetrius of Phalerum,[39] and both had many imitators. Prior to the literary designs of Phaedrus and Babrius, prose collections of Greek fables were utilitarian in orientation and served primarily as "repertoires of rhetorical materials."[40] According to Theon (*Progymnasmata* 3), a fable is "a fictitious story picturing a truth." In short form it is indistinguishable from the metaphorical proverb; both are oblique ways of asserting a general proposition.[41] Concurrent with the metaphorical employment of animal traits in fables and proverbs, one discovers the imputation to animals of "human feelings, appetites, passions, plans of action, reason, insight and other abstract qualities. It is from proverbs of this order that much can be deduced to show the moral significance of the animal according to the ancient Greek."[42] In the collections of Phaedrus and Babrius, however, the fables are no longer set within a specific context and, consequently, concern for the metaphorical meaning of the story gives way to fables "told for their own interest as narratives, whether witty, clever, amusing, dramatic, satirical, sensational, sentimental, or wise. The story itself becomes the main thing, instead of the idea that it is supposed to convey implicitly."[43]

If fictional speaking animals appeared in folklore and literature as a matter of course, in everyday life actual animals played a direct and

[38] Perry, *Babrius and Phaedrus*, li.

[39] Ibid., xiii, lx, lxxxiv. See also idem, "Demetrius of Phalerum and the Aesopic Fables," *Transactions of the American Philological Association* 93 (1962): 287–346.

[40] Perry, *Babrius and Phaedrus*, xi.

[41] Ibid., xxi.

[42] Herbert P. Houghton, *Moral Significance of Animals as Indicated in Greek Proverbs* (Amherst, Mass.: Carpenter and Morehouse, 1915), 8.

[43] Perry, *Babrius and Phaedrus*, xxv. Particularly in Phaedrus one finds "a greater variety of story-types, and more stories told at length for their own sake as fictional entertainment, rather than for their ethical meaning, than is to be found in any ancient collection of prose fables ascribed to Aesop, or even in Babrius. This was bound to happen once fables in quantity came to be exploited as artistic literature in their own right" (ibid., lxxxix–xc). See also J. G. M. van Dijk, "The Function of Fables in Graeco-Roman Romance," *Mnemosyne* 49 (1996): 513–41.

essential role in nearly every human activity.[44] In the Roman period, apart from the transparent importance of animals for food, dress, labor, transport, and so forth, they served as a principal form of public entertainment. Inhabitants of numerous cities in the Roman world had access to frequent exhibitions of familiar and foreign animals. Such occasions ranged from nonviolent showings and performances to displays of arena carnage on a scale almost impossible to comprehend.[45] The contrast between the appreciation of animals in the arts (sculpture, painting, mosaics, etc.), often rendered for their own sakes, and their sadistic extermination in the public theater is close to schizophrenic.[46] The inclusion of Christians among the victims of this blood lust certainly adds a special poignancy to Paul's encounter with the lion in the arena at Ephesus.

In still another telling conjunction, agricultural and pastoral scenes figure in pagan mausoleum paintings and sarcophagus reliefs as symbolic representations of the peace and plenty of the afterlife. Similar scenes are attested for their Christian counterparts.[47] Related funerary

[44] In the conclusion to her study of the relation between the animal and human worlds within the sphere of magical activity, Kathryn C. Smith ("The Role of Animals in Witchcraft and Popular Magic," in *Animals in Folklore*, ed. Joshua R. Porter and William M. S. Russell [Cambridge: Brewer, 1978], 109) draws the obvious connection between the close association of people with animals in earlier times and the prevalence of folk motifs concerning animals, and the isolated and totally fictive nature of such folk themes in modern societies removed from visible dependency on the health and well-being of animals.

[45] See the sources and statistics assembled by Jocelyn M. C. Toynbee, *Animals in Roman Life and Art* (Aspects of Greek and Roman Life; London: Thames and Hudson, 1973), 17–23.

[46] "All this serves to underline what is one of the outstanding paradoxes of the Roman mind—that a people that was so much alive to the interest and beauty of the animal kingdom, that admired the intelligence and skill to be found in so many of its representatives, that never seemed to tire of the sight of rare and unfamiliar specimens, that displayed such devotion to its pets, should yet have taken pleasure in the often hideous sufferings and agonizing deaths of quantities of magnificent and noble creatures. . . . Yet in the written sources the numbers of animals slaughtered on specific occasions are recorded cold-bloodedly and, indeed, as matter for congratulation" (ibid., 21). For a recent analysis of the function of the amphitheater in the Romans' representation of themselves to outsiders and each other, see Paul Plass, *The Game of Death in Ancient Rome: Arena Sport and Political Suicide* (Madison: University of Wisconsin Press, 1995).

[47] Toynbee, *Animals*, 283–84.

or religious artwork accents the abundant animal life of paradise in which animals no longer prey upon each other. Roman eschatological images of the Golden Age are reminiscent of the prophetic forecasts of Isaiah 11:6–9 and 65:25. Thus Virgil weaves a vision in which "the herd will not fear the mighty lion," and "the timid deer will drink beside the hounds" (*Eclogues* 4.2; 8.27–28). Horace concurs that "the trusting herd will not dread the tawny lion" (*Epodes* 16.33). The familiar artistic representations of Orpheus and the beasts in a variety of media vividly express pagan notions of a peaceful future in which wild and tame animals exist in harmony. Early Christian art could not resist reidentifying Orpheus as Christ in the center of the birds and beasts.[48]

In addition to the numerous influences on Christian conceptions of animals in the Graeco-Roman world surveyed above, we must note the latent stimulus of Hellenistic Jewish sources and attend to the instructive developments in rabbinic narratological lore. In general terms, one may reckon with the influence of the allegorical use of animals in the Jewish apocalypses (e.g., Daniel 7; *1 Enoch* 85–90). In the Apocalypse of the New Testament, four living creatures bearing the images of a lion, an ox, a human, and an eagle surround the celestial throne (Rev 4:6–7). These animalistic beings articulate their praise of the Lord God Almighty day and night through song (Rev 4:8).[49] The scene in Revelation 5 of the receipt of the scroll with seven seals by the Lamb (initially introduced as the "Lion of the tribe of Judah," v. 5) eventually leads to a song of praise by "every creature in heaven and on earth and under the earth and in the sea" (5:13).

The availability of articulate apocalyptic creatures, however, was not particularly suited to the conception of the apocryphal acts, which pursue an interest in terrestrial rather than celestial animals. The treatment of animals in various rabbinic writings, which were disinclined to take up apocalyptic antecedents for other reasons, proves to be more

---

[48] For more detailed information on specific artwork, see Toynbee, *Animals*, 288–94. For related artwork featuring Adam, Noah, and the Good Shepherd figure, see ibid., 294–99.

[49] Among their antecedents are the speaking seraphs of Isa 6:1–7 and the four living creatures of Ezekiel 1; cf. *1 Enoch* 40; *2 Enoch* 19–22.

analogous to the elaborations in Christian narratives. In comparison with biblical sources, midrashic literature presents a more adventuresome portrait of animals, a "cautious *re*mythologization."[50] Bypassing some of the more bizarre specimens of rabbinic folklore (leviathan, behemoth, Ziz or Bar Yokni, etc.), rabbinic notions about the special origins and attributes of certain scriptural animals shed light on the narrative thought world of the apocryphal acts. Thus, for example, the demythologized serpent of Genesis here appears with a sharp mind and rules as king over all the animals, Noah's dove converses with God, and an animate golden calf skips and moves about at will.[51] Rabbinic tradition also provides additional information about the fate of Balaam's ass that will prove illuminating in our review below of two key scenes involving talking animals in the apocryphal acts.

While no small part of rabbinic reflections on animals was based on ancient natural science, observations of the physical world were supplemented by proverbs, fables, and legends. In rabbinic folklore animals play a didactic role as the portrayal of their religious nature carries the implicit demand that the hearer at least demonstrate a religious sensitivity equivalent to that of the animals. The influence of the Aesopic fables is evident. The popularity of certain tales is so great that they are only referred to and not repeated. Hillel and Johanan ben Zakkai, among other notables, were reputed masters of animal stories.[52] Numerous tales recount conversations between various biblical personages and representatives of the animal kingdom, including lions, foxes, birds, and ants. Noah's task was made all the easier because of the animals' conscious desire to obey God's commandments.[53] A variety of anecdotes relate the special aid animals rendered to David and Solomon at crucial times. Solomon is particularly well known for his intimate association with the world of animals, including his ability to

---

[50] Schochet, *Animal Life*, 83.

[51] These are among the numerous examples noted by Schochet, *Animal Life*, 87–88. The pertinent primary source references are *Midrash ha-Gadol* 1.87 (serpent), *'Erub.* 18b (dove), *Tanhuma, Ki Tissa* 19:24 (golden calf).

[52] Schochet, *Animal Life*, 115. For Hillel, see *Sop.* 16:7; for Johanan ben Zakkai, see *Sukk.* 23a; *B. Bat.* 134a; *Sop.* 16:6.

[53] See the references in Schochet, *Animal Life*, 325–26, nn. 116–17.

speak with them.[54] Perspicacious lions refuse to harm Daniel but take vengeance upon his enemies.[55] In various ways animals are portrayed as participants in the unfolding of God's designs. A significant subset of these animal tales develops the notion of their prayerful relationship to God. Thus, a frog can claim to surpass even David in the offering of songs and praises.[56] "*Perek Shira* depicts numerous species participating in the chanting of scriptural passages, exhorting one another to greater piety and religious devotion."[57] The efficacy of animal prayers in one instance is judged to account for the deliverance of Jerusalem from the attack of Sennacherib.[58] Other stories illustrate animals adhering to the ethical and ritual obligations of the Law (e.g., with regard to resting on the Sabbath). Tales of animal devotion to God are fittingly exemplified by the story of the bullocks selected to be offered to God and Baal in Elijah's contest on Mount Carmel.

> While Elijah's bullock went willingly to the altar of the Lord, the animal designated for Baal refused to budge from its place in spite of the strenuous efforts of no less than eight hundred and fifty priests of Baal to dislodge it. When Elijah attempted to persuade the reluctant animal to follow the priests, it said to him, "We two, yonder bullock and myself, came forth from the same womb, and we took our food from the same manger. But now he has been destined for God as an instrument for the glorification of the divine name, while I am to be used for Baal, as an instrument to enrage my Creator." Elijah replied, "Bullock, bullock, fear not! Do thou but follow the priest of Baal that they may have no excuse for their failure, and then thou wilt have a share in that glorification of God for which my bullock will be used." The bullock was persuaded by this argument, but insisted that it at least be led to the heathen altar by the prophet Elijah himself.[59]

---

[54] Louis Ginzberg, *The Legends of the Jews* (7 vols.; 1909–38; reprint, Philadelphia: Jewish Publication Society of America, 1968), 4:142, 6:289 n. 38.

[55] Ibid., 4:345–49, 6:432 n. 6, 436 n. 16.

[56] See the references in Schochet, *Animal Life*, 326 n. 127. "Even dumb fishes and frogs and mice chant appropriate verses as their praise to the Lord" (ibid., 134; see Ḥul. 64b).

[57] Schochet, *Animal Life*, 134.

[58] Ibid., 135; see Sanh. 95b.

[59] Schochet, *Animal Life*, 137. See *Tanhuma Masse* 4 and *Num. Rab.* 23:9.

Apostles and Articulate Animals

While a variety of incidents include contact between apostles and nonspeaking animals in the Apocryphal Acts of the Apostles, the focus here will be limited to those talking beasts who lend their aid to the apostolic missions.[60]

In *Acts of Peter* 9, Simon's guard dog acquires a human voice and requests instructions from Peter. When told to fetch Simon, the dog enters Simon's house, evidently stands on its hind legs, and issues Peter's summons. Simon's direction to the dog to tell Peter that he is not in is met with a sharp rebuke from the dog:

> "You most wicked and shameless man, you enemy of all that live and believe in Christ Jesus, here is a dumb animal sent to you and taking a human voice to convict you and prove you a cheat and deceiver." (*APt* 12)

After these and other words, the dog returns to Peter, reports his dealings with Simon, foretells Peter's upcoming contest with Simon in the Roman forum (see *APt* 23–29), and expires at Peter's feet (*APt* 12). In *Acts of Thomas* 39–41, the story is recounted of an ass's colt that implores Thomas to enter the city riding on its back:

> "Twin brother of Christ, apostle of the Most High and fellow-initiate into the hidden word of Christ, who dost receive his secret sayings, fellow-worker of the Son of God, who being free didst become a slave and being sold didst lead many to freedom. . .mount and sit upon me and rest until thou enter the city." (*ATh* 39)

Thomas utters a prayer at this miraculous speech and inquires, in the presence of a crowd, about the colt's origin. The colt replies:

> "I am of that race that served Balaam and thy Lord and teacher also sat upon one that belonged to me by race. And now am I sent to give thee rest as thou dost sit upon me, and that these may receive faith and that to me may be given that portion which I am now to obtain through the service which I render thee, and which if I serve thee not is taken from me." (*ATh* 40)

[60] For scenes of the former class, see the incidents of John and the bugs (*AJn* 60–61) and Peter and the tunny fish (*APt* 13); also note the part played by animals in *AThec*.

Thomas protests: "He who has bestowed on thee this gift of speech is able to cause it to be fulfilled to the end in thee and in those who belong to thee by race." Nevertheless, he relents in the face of the colt's ensuing prayer and entreaty and consents to ride. When Thomas dismounts upon reaching the gates of the city, he tells the colt to return safely from where it came.

> But immediately the colt fell down on the ground at the apostle's feet and died. All those who were present were sorrowful, and said to the apostle: "Bring it to life and raise it up!" But he said in reply: "I could indeed raise it up through the name of Jesus Christ. But this is not expedient at all. For he who gave it speech that it might speak was able also to make it not die." (*ATh* 41)

Although the motive behind the deaths of these speaking animals is not explicit in these apocryphal texts, it appears to be preserved in the traditions concerning the fate of Balaam's ass. According to *Numbers Rabbah* 20:4, "as soon as she [Balaam's talking ass] finished speaking, she died, so that people should not say, 'This is the animal that spoke,' and so make of her an object of reverence."[61]

The motif of the precautionary death of the speaking animal, however, is not uniformly adopted either by rabbinic texts or the apocryphal acts. This is made clear in the *Acts of Thomas* when the apostle comes into contact with a herd of wild asses (*ATh* 68). When the beasts pulling Thomas's wagon become too weary to continue, Thomas has a companion call four wild asses to be yoked in the places of the exhausted animals (*ATh* 69–70). After entering the city and making a short speech (*ATh* 71–72), Thomas directs one of the asses to go and summon the demons of the place before him (*ATh* 73). The ass takes direction well and goes off and makes a small speech (*ATh* 74) summoning the demons. When a woman and her daughter emerge, Thomas exorcises their

---

[61] Schochet, *Animal Life*, 95. A different explanation accounts for the ass's death in terms of preserving Balaam's honor. God created animals without speech, "for had they been able to speak, it would have been impossible to put them to the service of man or to stand one's ground against them. For here was the ass, the most stupid of all beasts, and there was the wisest of all wise men, yet as soon as she opened her mouth he could not stand his ground against her!" (ibid., 127–28; see *Num. Rab.* 20:14–15).

demons, but the women fall down dead (*ATh* 75). After a demonic speech (*ATh* 76) and Thomas's command of banishment to the demons (*ATh* 77), "that wild ass to whom speech was given by the power of the Lord" utters a lengthy speech, full of scriptural allusions (*ATh* 78–79), encouraging Thomas to raise the dead women, which he does after prayer (*ATh* 80–81). The ending of the episode reveals a special apostolic compassion for the animal assistants:

> The apostle said to the wild asses: "Follow me." And they followed him until they were outside the gates. And when they came out he said: "Depart in peace to your pastures." So the wild asses went off readily. But the apostle stood and watched over them, that they might not be harmed by anyone, until they were far off and out of sight. (*ATh* 81)

"Eucharistic" Animals

Acts of Philip 8 through the end recounts the adventures of Philip and his companions on one continuous journey that reaches its goal with the apostle's martyrdom. Philip is joined by his sister Mariamne, Bartholomew, a leopard, a kid, and, near the end, the apostle John; the antagonists include dragons and snakes.[62] Act 8 is interesting for a number of reasons, including its depiction of the division of missionary territory among the various apostles and its portrait of the reluctant Philip. Most of the act, however, is concerned with the "humanization" of animals and their incorporation into an all-encompassing salvation. Accordingly, the title of the act in *Vaticanus graecus 824* and *Xenophontos 32* reads: "When the kid and the leopard believe in the wilderness."

The leopard comes on the scene first as Philip and company are journeying on their way to Ophioryme (Hierapolis):

> When they came to the wilderness of dragons, behold a great leopard came out of a wood on the hill, and ran and cast himself at their feet and

---

[62] There is an obvious division on internal grounds, corroborated by some manuscript evidence, between the first seven acts and those from eight through the martyrdom. In acts 1–7, the apostle Philip is the only constant character, while the supporting cast varies from act to act, with the exception of acts 5–7, which deal with the same ensemble of characters.

spoke with a human voice, "I worship you, servants of the divine greatness and apostles of the only-begotten Son of God; command me to speak perfectly." (*APh* 8.16 [96])[63]

Philip complies with the creature's request and the leopard relates with perfect diction how on the previous night he had seized a kid to eat. But the wounded kid with a human voice exhorted the leopard to shed its fierce nature:

> "O leopard, put off your fierce heart and the beastlike part of your nature, and put on mildness, for the apostles of the divine greatness are about to pass through this desert, to accomplish perfectly the promise of the glory of the only-begotten Son of God." (*APh* 8.17 [97])

As a result of the kid's speech, the leopard's heart is transformed and his ferocity is attenuated. Looking up and seeing Philip and his companions approaching, he runs to them and requests to go with them everywhere and to put off his savage nature. Then, after being led by the leopard to the kid, Philip and Bartholomew glorify the compassion of Jesus and pray on behalf of the animals that their existence be made secure and their tameness confirmed, that they be given human hearts and accompany the apostles everywhere, sharing the same food (i.e., eating no meat) and speaking as human beings. The animals respond by raising their forefeet, mimicking a prayerful stance, and saying:

> "We glorify and bless you who have visited and remembered us in the desert, and changed our beastlike and wild nature into tameness, and granted us the divine word, and put in us a tongue and sense to speak and praise your name, for great is your glory." (*APh* 8.20 [100])

At this point the enlarged missionary company continues on its journey, praising God.

Bonnet's edition of the Greek text of the *Acts of Philip* was based primarily on one manuscript that knew only acts 1–9 and 15 (the beginning was missing) to the end, including the martyrdom. The

---

[63] Translations of act 8 are taken from Elliott, *Apocryphal New Testament*, 515–16. On the female dragons (τὴν ἔρημον τῶν δρακαινῶν), see Amsler, Bovon, and Bouvier, *Actes de l'apôtre Philippe*, 185 n. 381.

"discovery"[64] of *Xenophontos 32* has brought to light the previously unattested acts 11–15.[65] Act 11, which is joined in progress by *Xenophontos 32*,[66] depicts Philip and his human companions sharing the eucharist after a fast of five days. Act 11 is of interest for several reasons, including its speaking dragon, which relates its story in a manner reminiscent of *Acts of Thomas* 32, and especially its adaptation of the well-known hymn of Christ from *Acts of John* 94–96, which now serves as a eucharistic prayer for the "new eucharist" Philip gives to his friends.[67] Our interest is piqued by act 12, entitled: "When the leopard and the kid request the eucharist."

Act 12 opens with Philip, Bartholomew, and Mariamne rejoicing at their reception of the eucharist, while the animal companions look on weeping because they have not been deemed worthy to share it with them. When Philip tells Bartholomew that he wants to know the reason for their tears, the leopard begins to speak and offers an impassioned defense of the grief of the animals to whom God's "name has come, although we are unworthy."[68]

> "For we were unreasoning beasts living in ignorance until the day on which we beheld you. I used to eat flesh and blood and the darkness of night was for me as light as midday. And when day broke, I used to hide myself in the woods. But in the hour in which you were passing through the mountain, fear and distress came upon us; and my bestial nature was

---

[64] Although the manuscript was catalogued, its significance was not immediately exploited. See Bovon, "Actes de Philippe," 4434; Bertrand Bouvier and François Bovon, "Actes de Philippe, I, d'après un manuscrit inédit," in *Œcumenica et Patristica. Festschrift für Wilhelm Schneemelcher zum 75. Geburtstag*, ed. Damaskinos Papandreou, Wolfgang A. Bienert, and Knut Schäferdiek (Stuttgart: Kohlhammer, 1989), 367.

[65] Thus, only act 10, the beginning of 11, and some parts of 14 and 15 remain lost.

[66] Bovon ("Actes de Philippe," 4471) attributes the lost folios of *Xenophontos 32* to an act of censorship. Commenting on *APh* 8, he notes (ibid., 4472) that the text breaks off at folio 71 and "la suite a été manifestement arrachée. L'histoire que contenaient cet Acte et les suivants a dû choquer. . .la lacune correspond à la fin de l'APh VIII, à l'APh IX, à l'APh X et au début de l'APh XI."

[67] Bovon, "Actes de Philippe," 4500–4503.

[68] Translations of act 12 are my own. They are based on the critical edition of the Greek text of the *Acts of Philip* prepared by Bovon, Bouvier, and Amsler and soon to appear in the Series Apocryphorum of the Corpus Christianorum, with thanks to the editors for making the text available to me.

changed and converted to goodness, and I abstained from eating this kid, and the power of God was upon us.

"And now we are weeping because you have not considered us worthy of the eucharist of Christ. We have spoken as human beings and begged God through you that we might follow you; and it happened for us by God. And when in the uproar of the energy of the dragon the only begotten one appeared to you and the beauty of his form killed that dragon and the serpents, he did not make us strangers of his mystery or of the wonder of his face. We heard his voice and we heard the glory of your prayers and blessings.

"Therefore, if God considered us worthy to participate in all these wonders, why now do you consider us unworthy to receive the eucharist? For this reason we are weeping in distress, because we have not been judged worthy. And if this is the case for me because I am a wild beast, why is this kid not worthy of the eucharist? This is why we are weeping, for perhaps we do not have life from God. Grant us mercy, therefore, as was commanded you, without envy, since he himself is in each one, and since he has given us the word without envy. This is a great wonder, that we, a wild beast and a goat's kid, forsook our own nature and became as human beings—and God truly lives in us. Now we beseech you, apostles of the good savior, that you might grant us without hesitation this part which we are in need of, so that our beast-like body might be changed by you and we might forsake the animal form.

"For we believe this will happen for us through you, since the most important thing is the mind which is within all thoughts, even the heart. And behold it lived with us and led us with excellent senses. And it awoke us by its sleepless reason from oppressive savageness and changed us to tameness, bit by bit, until we became completely human in both body and soul. And we will be in harmony with one another, that we might be deemed worthy of the bread of which we have heard, the mystery of glory. This is why we ask you to accept this wonder of glory from God, who watches over every nature, even the wild animals, on account of his great heart." (*APh* 12.2–5)

At the end of the leopard's speech, as both animals continue to weep, Philip acknowledges that God has visited all through Christ—not only human beings but animals of every sort. At this point Philip raises his hands in prayer, and after praising the attributes of Christ in creation, he requests of Christ:

"Just as you changed the form of the soul of these animals, in the same way make them appear to themselves in the form of human bodies." (*APh* 12.7)

Then Philip takes a cup, fills it with water, and sprinkles it over the animals.

And in that hour the form of their face and their body changed little by little after the likeness of human beings. And they stood upon their feet and stretched out their front feet in place of hands and glorified God saying, "We glorify you, Lord, only begotten Son, for the immortal genesis in which we have entered, since we have received a human body in place of a bestial one. In reality you are the true judge of those who come to you, who gave freely the glorious word to us today to the end that we might become partners of your evangelists. For you stripped us of our savage uncleanness and clothed us with the gentleness of the saints. We praise and bless you, because you have brought us from disgrace to glory. We believe that there is life neither in the creature nor in the human being unless God should make a visitation for our salvation." (*APh* 12.8)

It is striking that at the end of this scene with its impassioned plea, which obviously is effective insofar as Philip is concerned, a eucharistic celebration does not ensue. The depiction of the animals in *Acts of Philip* 8 and 12 displays the creaturely sense for the divine that we have become accustomed to elsewhere. The kid, about to be eaten by the leopard, announces in a human voice the approach of the apostolic band. The leopard, already experiencing a distress of divine origin, is tamed by these words and immediately seeks to join Philip's group and be confirmed in gentleness. The immediate source of the animals' transformation fluctuates between the saving action of God or Christ and the intercession of the apostles. While specificity in such matters is not the hallmark of the genre, we may suppose that the apostles confirm and indeed are instructed by what God has accomplished. The situation with the animals is also more complex than the straightforward transformation of wild beasts into tame ones. Both *Acts of Philip* 8 and 12 make it clear that the animal protagonists, the leopard and the kid, represent the classes of wild and domesticated animals, respectively. Thus, the kid already speaks perfectly and its awareness of the divine is clear, whereas that of the leopard is clouded. The words of the kid trigger or coincide with the initial transformation of the leopard. Since the kid already refrains from the eating of meat, it is henceforth delivered from eating ordinary feed. This distinction between the two animals is emphasized by the leopard's speech in *Acts of Philip* 12 when it pleads that even if it could justly be excluded from the eucharist owing to its fierce nature, such a condition never applied to the kid. Above all, the status of the animals as recipients of salvation is communicated by their attributes as enumerated in the leopard's speech. Here the force of the argument is that God's visitation of salvation applies equally to human beings and animals. Consequently, animals are worthy of receiving the eucharist because they have "received God's name," having been transformed "by the power of God." They have looked upon the glorious face of Christ and have been made party to every sort of wonder. They have "the life of God" and have been "given the word without envy." They have become like humans and "God lives in them." The narrative of *Acts of Philip* 12 clearly implies that the animals' argument for receiving the eucharist will be successful. Does a depiction of this event not appear on account of censorship?[69] This is a possibility. But there is perhaps a better explanation. Rather than see the sprinkling with water at the end of *Acts of Philip* 12 as a pale substitute for the eucharist, we should probably recall the five-day fast of Philip and the others in *Acts of Philip* 11 and take the sprinkling as the sign that the animals have now entered into their own fast, which will culminate in the sharing of the eucharist.

Various concerns highlighted by the animal scenes in the *Acts of Philip* coincide with ascetic redactional emphases prominent in the rest of that document and thus may date to the fourth century. This is perhaps true of the stress on conversion from wildness to tameness and certainly seems to be the case with the emphasis on abstention from the eating of meat. One may catalogue these items as elements that change the

[69] This is obvious in the later history of transmission. For example, as Bovon notes ("Actes de Philippe," 4444), the text of Symeon Metaphrastes "représente une parfaite domestication du ou des récits primitifs du Martyre: tout ce qui pouvait choquer— l'encratisme, la colère de l'apôtre, la présence des animaux, la spéculation sur la croix— est éliminé."

emphasis of such stories from the *Acts of Paul* or the *Acts of Thomas*. Nevertheless, the fundamental story line, which connects speaking beasts with the spread of the gospel through the apostles, coincides with its second-century prototypes. Animals possess an innate sense for the divine and a desire to serve God and the servants of God. The apostles for their part either recognize the appropriateness of the animals' inclusion in Christian salvation as a matter of course (as with Paul and the lion or Thomas with the colt and wild asses), or they are persuaded by the rhetorical arguments of the animals and the testimony of heaven on their behalf.

Conclusion

Our survey has uncovered a complex convergence of literary, philosophical, and religious factors underlying the phenomenon of the speaking animals in the Apocryphal Acts of the Apostles. From modest biblical precedents, to Graeco-Roman literature, to philosophical considerations of the rationality of beasts, to the common texts of basic education, talking animals were common elements in the cultural parlance of the ancient world. While their various roles in connection with the apostles to some degree represent the fulfillment of the eschatological visions of Isaiah and Paul, the effectiveness of their employment as characters in the apocryphal acts cannot be appreciated apart from the broader cultural roots identified here. Greek traditions of inborn animal sagacity confirm biblical and extrabiblical testimony of the innate ability of animals to perceive the divine. Basic schooling and even more advanced rhetorical training issued in storytelling and literary productions that employed animals along a continuum from didactic fable to novelistic entertainment. The roles fulfilled by the apocryphal animals are thus not reducible to one dimension. Certainly, in most of the episodes reviewed here, the accent falls on the place of the animal in the fulfillment of God's designs. The various apostolic sanctions signaled by Paul, Thomas, and Philip leave no question concerning the participation of animals in the power of the gospel as it advances throughout the world.

The universe of factors that led to the appearance of talking animals in the apocryphal acts was hardly exhausted with this genre. Talking animals continue to play a role in medieval beast fables and hagiographic traditions, which often portray animals as capable of good works and of responding to the proclamation of the gospel.[70] We may borrow an observation made by Jan M. Ziolkowski in a study of medieval Latin beast poetry and apply it profitably to our consideration of the function of the talking animals in the apocryphal acts. "Apart from being meaningful and approachable to all sorts of people, animals permit authors to take risks that they cannot take in stories explicitly about human beings."[71] While social satire on a level visible in late medieval stories that employ talking animals is clearly beyond the designs of our apocryphal authors, nevertheless, we may assume that the basic underlying message of the speaking animal narratives calls on the hearer to display, at least, the dignity and sensitivity to the divine displayed by these animals. Readers of the apocryphal acts were urged to affirm, along with the leopard and the kid of the *Acts of Philip*, that there is no life, be it human or animal, apart from God.

[70] Jan M. Ziolkowski, *Talking Animals: Medieval Latin Beast Poetry, 750–1150* (Middle Ages Series; Philadelphia: University of Pennsylvania Press, 1993), 33; Witold Witakowski, "The Miracles of Jesus: An Ethiopian Apocryphal Gospel," *Apocrypha* 6 (1995): 295.

[71] Ziolkowski, *Talking Animals*, 7.

"She Became What the Words Signified": The Greek *Acts of Andrew*'s Construction of the Reader-Disciple

Laura S. Nasrallah

The ending of the Greek manuscripts of the *Acts of Andrew* presents a unique complex of concepts and expressions that serve not only to elucidate the work as a whole but also to challenge modern notions of genre, authorship, and reading with regard to the written texts of late antiquity. The author concludes the *Acts of Andrew* in this way:

> Hereabouts I should make an end of the blessed tales, acts, and mysteries difficult—or should I say impossible—to express. Let this stroke of the pen end it. I will pray first for myself, that I heard what was actually said, both the obvious and also the obscure, comprehensible only to the intellect. Then I will pray for all who are convinced by what was said, that they may have fellowship with each other, as God opens the ears of the listeners, in order to make comprehensible all his gifts. . . .

> Ἐνταῦθά που τὸ τέλος τῶν μακαρίων μου διηγημάτων ποιήσαιμι καὶ πράξεων καὶ μυστηρίων δυσφράστων ὄντων, ἵνα μὴ καὶ ἀφράστων εἴπω. ἡ κορωνὶς τελευτάτω. καὶ ἐπεύξομαι πρῶτον μὲν ἐμαυτῷ ἀκοῦσαι τῶν εἰρημένων ὡς εἴρηται, καὶ τούτων εἰς τὸ συμφανές, εἶτα καὶ τῶν ἀφανῶν, διανοίᾳ δὲ ληπτῶν, ἔπειτα καὶ πᾶσι τοῖς διατιθεμένοις ὑπὸ τῶν εἰρημένων, κοινωνίαν ἔχειν ἐπίπαν θεοῦ δὲ ἀνοίγοντος τὰς ἀκόας τῶν ἐντυγχανόντων, ὅπως ᾖ ληπτὰ ἅπαντα αὐτοῦ τὰ χαρίσματα. . . .[1]

---

[1] Unless otherwise noted, all Greek excerpts and quotations in English from the Greek *Acts of Andrew* are taken from MacDonald, *Acts of Andrew*.

Even upon first reading or hearing this passage, one is aware of an expression of concern regarding the reception and transmission of the "blessed tales, acts, and mysteries." This concern and the various ways in which it is expressed form the focus of this study. Thus, the conclusion of the *Acts of Andrew* will serve as an impetus for our exploration and explanation of certain problems within the text; it will also serve to enhance our understanding of the task of reading.

The Story and the Manuscripts

In order to understand *AAn* 65 better, broad and technical questions regarding Andrew legends, manuscripts, dating, and authorship must be addressed. The most extensive witness to the full text of the *Acts of Andrew* is Gregory of Tours's sixth-century *Liber de miraculis*, the so-called *Epitome*. Gregory, in making the text acceptable to contemporary prevailing orthodoxy, largely omitted the speeches, instead focusing on the miracle stories. Other related Andrew traditions include the *Acts of Andrew and Matthias*, which is found at the beginning of Gregory's *Epitome*. While Dennis MacDonald argues that this was originally part of the *Acts of Andrew*,[2] this theory must be questioned, given the stylistic differences between the two works and given that the theory is based in part upon MacDonald's questionable conclusions regarding the authorship of the *Acts of Andrew*.[3]

In comparison with Gregory's story, the extant Greek witnesses represent only a small fragment of some early version of the *Acts of*

---

[2] See MacDonald, *Acts of Andrew*, 1–67; idem, "The *Acts of Andrew and Matthias* and the *Acts of Andrew*," in MacDonald, *Apocryphal Acts of Apostles*, 1–26. For a critique, see Jean-Marc Prieur, "Response," in ibid., 27–33; MacDonald's response to Prieur follows on pp. 35–39.

[3] Dennis MacDonald has recently published an insightful article on the very topics with which I deal here (Dennis Ronald MacDonald, "Is There a Privileged Reader? A Case from the Apocryphal Acts," *Semeia* 71 [1995]: 29–43). Unfortunately, my own work was complete and already in the editorial process when this article appeared. Thus I do not treat it in detail. In his more recent work, which focuses on the reader, MacDonald does not set forth a detailed theory regarding authorship, but his conclusions are derived from and continuous with his earlier theories, which I shall discuss below.

Andrew. I use the Greek edition of the *Acts of Andrew* by Dennis MacDonald, which largely agrees with that of Jean-Marc Prieur.[4] Both editions are based primarily upon the following manuscripts:

TABLE 1

Siglum	Manuscript	Date	Portion of *AAn*
S	*Sinaiticus graecus 526*	13th century	*AAn* 1–65
H	Jerusalem, St. Sabas, *103*	10th century	*AAn* 1–65
V	*Vaticanus graecus 808*	11th century	*AAn* 33–50
C	Ann Arbor, *36*	14th–15th century	*AAn* 51–65
P	*Parisinus graecus 770*	ca. 1315	*AAn* 51–65
O	Jerusalem, St. Sabas, *30*	10th–11th century	*AAn* 51–65
Q	*Parisinus graecus 1539*	10th–11th century	*AAn* 51–65

According to Prieur, two main groups emerge: H, S, and Q, along with the *Narratio* (*N*), a loose recounting of the story available in four tenth- to eleventh-century manuscripts, are probably based on one manuscript tradition, while C, O, P, and Gregory's *Epitome* are probably based on another. In addition to the texts listed above, both MacDonald's and Prieur's editions sometimes make reference to the *Laudatio* (*L*) and the *Martyrium Prius* (*M*), which also depend on a common tradition.[5] This study focuses on portions of the text based on a synthesis of H, S, and V, with reference to the *Narratio*.

For the dating of the early tradition lying behind the versions of the Greek *Acts of Andrew*, Prieur suggests the second half of the second century, since the *Acts of Andrew* may depend on the *Acts of John*.[6] The earliest direct witness to the *Acts of Andrew* is found in Eusebius's

---

[4] MacDonald, *Acts of Andrew*; Prieur, *Acta Andreae*. In Prieur's excellent edition, the first volume provides a commentary and discussion while the second volume presents the edition of the *Acts of Andrew*.

[5] Prieur, *Acta Andreae*, 2:423–39.

[6] This is in contrast to Joseph Flamion (*Les actes apocryphes de l'apôtre André* [Paris: Picard et fils, 1911], 267), who suggests a date in the third century and believes that the philosophical influence of the *Acts of Andrew* is Neoplatonism rather than Middle Platonism.

fourth-century *Historia ecclesiastica*,[7] and MacDonald argues that this witness sets the terminus ad quem of the *Acts of Andrew* to the early third century, since the section in Eusebius is based on a commentary written by Origen before Origen's departure for Caesarea in 231.[8] In any case, the version upon which the Greek *Acts of Andrew* is based was probably written between approximately 150 and 220 C.E. The provenance is also uncertain. Because of the martyrdom in Patras, Flamion suggests that the text was written in Achaia.[9] Prieur casts his net more broadly, suggesting as possibilities not only Achaia but also Syria, because of the encratic nature of the *Acts of Andrew*, and Egypt—particularly Alexandria—because of the philosophical content of the text. MacDonald supports this Alexandrian hypothesis.[10] The themes and vocabulary of the text certainly suggest a connection with the so-called Alexandrian catechetical, or school, tradition.[11]

The authorship of the text is uncertain. MacDonald, Prieur, and François Bovon[12] agree that the *Acts of Andrew* is not only a text informed by Middle Platonic philosophical concepts, but that the author was a "sophisticated Christian Platonist,"[13] and "a cultivated man, a philosopher."[14] The studies of David Warren and Evie Zachariades-Holmberg demonstrate that the *Acts of Andrew* indeed reveals the author's philosophical pretensions: the style is sometimes overly complex and aspires after sophistication.[15]

[7] See Jean-Marc Prieur, "Introduction to the Acts of Andrew," in *NTApoc*[5] 2:101.

[8] MacDonald, *Acts of Andrew*, 56–59. For a discussion of later traditions concerning Andrew, see Francis Dvornik, *The Idea of Apostolicity in Byzantium and the Legend of the Apostle Andrew* (Cambridge, Mass.: Harvard University Press, 1958).

[9] Flamion, *Les actes apocryphes*, 267.

[10] Prieur, *Acta Andreae*, 1:414–16; MacDonald, *Acts of Andrew*, 59.

[11] See Annewies van den Hoek, "The 'Catechetical' School of Early Christian Alexandria and Its Philonic Heritage," *HTR* 90 (1997): 59–87.

[12] Prieur, *Acta Andreae*, 1:372–79; MacDonald, *Acts of Andrew*, 56; François Bovon, "The Words of Life in the Acts of the Apostle Andrew," *HTR* 87 (1994): 12.

[13] MacDonald, *Acts of Andrew*, 50.

[14] Prieur, *Acta Andreae*, 1:375.

[15] See David Warren, "The Greek Language of the Apocryphal Acts of the Apostles: A Study in Style," and Evie Zachariades-Holmberg, "Philological Aspects of the Apocryphal Acts of the Apostles," both in this volume.

Contextualization: The Literary Milieu of the Greek *Acts of Andrew*

How can one explain the sudden shift to first-person authorial voice and the expression of anxiety concerning the reception and transmission of the "tales, acts, and mysteries"? To address this question I shall begin by contextualizing the Greek *Acts of Andrew* within the historical and literary environment of late antiquity. Therefore, this section is devoted to broad questions which will support an investigation of *AAn* 65: What themes arise in the *Acts*? This question leads in turn to the issue of texts that might be similar to the *Acts of Andrew*. To what sorts of materials would one look for parallels?[16]

The various acts of the apostles is the first corpus within which one would look for parallels. The Greek *Acts of Andrew* focuses upon Andrew's relationship with his disciple Maximilla, who is married to the powerful proconsul Aigeates. Although Maximilla and her brother-in-law, the philosopher Stratokles, are convinced by Andrew's words, Aigeates is not. He is dismayed by Maximilla's pursuit of chastity and of Andrew's teachings. He forces her to choose between himself and Andrew; and in a passage that will be discussed later, Andrew insists that Maximilla should continue to be chaste. Her decision to follow Andrew's words results in his crucifixion by Aigeates.

The sort of relationship we see between Maximilla and Andrew is a topos found in many of the apocryphal acts. The same story of a civic leader's wife, converted to the apostle's message and desiring to be continent, thus angering her pagan husband and endangering the life of the apostle, is found in the *Acts of Thomas* with Mygdonia and Thomas, in the *Acts of Peter* with Xanthippe and Peter, and, with slight variation, in the *Acts of John* with Drusiana and John. The speeches in the Greek *Acts of Andrew* are more philosophical in tone and language, however, than those in the other apocryphal acts. Moreover, the relationship between Andrew and his disciple Maximilla is articulated here in a

---

[16] In his section on the historical origins of the *Acts of Andrew*, Bovon suggests that the "words" of the Greek *Acts of Andrew* may be related to Jewish and Christian Wisdom traditions, to gnostic thought, and to Platonic thought. See Bovon, "Words of Life," 152–54.

way that is different from any of the models presented in other texts. There is an intense dependency between Andrew and Maximilla which is not found in the other apocryphal acts.

One may argue that this difference arises from the philosophical nature of the *Acts of Andrew*. Several of its main themes derived from Middle Platonic thought. Unlike the other apocryphal acts, here we find three of the four Stoic passions mentioned: ἐπιθυμία, "desire" or "yearning," ἡδονή, "pleasure," and φόβος, "fear."[17] The theme of ἀπάθεια, the separation from the passions, is found throughout the text. Such interests, although not limited to one region of the empire, may point even more strongly to an Alexandrian milieu, where such ideas were current, as evidenced by Philo's writings[18] and by later Christian works.

Moreover, in the Greek *Acts of Andrew*, Andrew is presented as a sort of divine man. David Tiede explains that, like the "Platonic image of Socrates," the "ideal wise man is divine, not because of his miraculous powers, but because of his moral courage and wisdom."[19] Furthermore, "in the Roman period the sage becomes a pattern of perfection whose goodness and truth is linked to his ability to mediate it to others."[20] I would argue that wisdom and the ability to perform miracles are equally

[17] Prieur, *Acta Andreae*, 1:377–78. For background information on the themes presented here as connected to Middle Platonism, see A. H. Armstrong, *An Introduction to Ancient Philosophy* (1957; reprint, Westminster, Md.: Newman, 1959); John Dillon, *The Middle Platonists: 80 B.C. to A.D. 220* (Ithaca, N.Y.: Cornell University Press, 1977), 3–9; W. K. C. Guthrie, "Pythagoras and Pythagoreanism," and D. A. Rees, "Platonism and the Platonic Tradition," in *Encyclopedia of Philosophy*, ed. Paul Edwards (8 vols.; New York: MacMillan and Free Press, 1967), 7:37–39 and 6:334–38, respectively; J. N. D. Kelly, *Early Christian Doctrines*, rev. ed. (New York: Harper and Row, 1978); Helmut Koester, *Introduction to the New Testament* (2 vols.; New York: de Gruyter, 1982), 1:141–44.

[18] See Peder Borgen, "Philo of Alexandria," in *Jewish Writings of the Second Temple Period*, ed. Michael E. Stone (Philadelphia: Fortress Press, 1984), 233–82.

[19] David Lenz Tiede, *The Charismatic Figure as Miracle Worker* (Society of Biblical Literature Dissertation Series 1; Missoula: University of Montana Printing Department, 1972), 5, 43; see also Moses Hadas and Morton Smith, *Heroes and Gods: Spiritual Biographies in Antiquity* (New York: Harper and Row, 1965); Dieter Georgi, *The Opponents of Paul in Second Corinthians* (Philadelphia: Fortress Press, 1986).

[20] Tiede, *Charismatic Figure*, 54.

important characteristics of the divine man, and in the Greek *Acts of Andrew*, Andrew is both wise and miracle-working.[21]

Patricia Cox Miller further explains that some texts claim actual godhood for the divine human they describe; others merely claim that the person is godlike.[22] Andrew and the other apostles fall into this second category. The teaching of the divine philosophers "changes the lives of their disciples."[23] Miller notes that a devotion to the ascetic lifestyle often characterizes the divine human. Andrew engages in such ascetic practice, which according to Miller is "based on the idea that only by withdrawal from the world of the senses can the soul commune with the spiritual realm."[24]

Do these qualities of the divine human—more clearly articulated in the *Acts of Andrew* than in the other apocryphal acts—explain the unusual relationship between Andrew and Maximilla? Turning to other portrayals of divine men, I searched for parallels. Like Socrates in Plutarch's *De genio Socratis*[25] and like Eleazar in 4 Maccabees,[26] like Porphyry as described by Eunapius,[27] like Proclus as described by

---

[21] For a discussion of Andrew's miracles in the larger Andrew tradition, see David Pao, "Physical and Spiritual Restoration: The Role of Healing Miracles in the *Acts of Andrew*," in this volume.

[22] Patricia Cox, *Biography in Late Antiquity: A Quest for the Holy Man* (Berkeley: University of California Press, 1983), 21.

[23] Ibid., 24. For further discussion on the issue of whether Andrew is here presented as a divine man, see Prieur, *Acta Andreae*, 1:304–7. Following Ludwig Bieler's classic study on the divine man, *ΘΕΙΟΣ ΑΝΗΡ*, Prieur concludes that Andrew is not a divine man, but a new Socrates. See also Richard Goulet, "Les vies de philosophes dans l'antiquité tardive et leur portée mystérique," in *Actes apocryphes des apôtres*, 206. The Greek *Acts of Andrew* does not fit into the genre of the lives of the philosophers, who are often portrayed as divine humans. See also Prieur's speculations (*Acta Andreae*, 1:382–84) regarding the author's choice of genre.

[24] Cox, *Biography*, 27–30, esp. 29–30.

[25] Socrates abstained from "shameful and unlawful pleasures" and his understanding was "pure and free from passion, and commingling with the body but little"; see Plutarch *De gen. Soc.* 588 D–E in *Moralia*, trans. Benedict Einarson and Phillip H. De Lacy (LCL, 1927), 7:451–53.

[26] Eleazar refused Antiochus's command to eat pork and was tortured and killed; see 4 Macc 1:13.

[27] Porphyry's hatred of his body almost led to his death, according to Eunapius (*Lives of the Philosophers and Sophists* 456).

Marinos,[28] and like Pythagoras as described by Diogenes Laertius (8.1.33), Andrew is portrayed as pursuing purification through ascetic practices. Like Origen—whose students, according to Eusebius, came to him for instruction day and night (*Hist. eccl.* 6.8.6)—and like Proclus—who, according to Marinos, participated in all-night hymn sings (*Life of Proclus* 19)—Andrew stayed up at night in order to answer Stratokles' questions. I found no parallel, however, for this teacher-disciple relationship, nor of the puzzle that I believe underlies it: that of words, *logoi*, in the *Acts of Andrew*.

Words in the Greek *Acts of Andrew*

AAn 65 expresses concern with the proper reception and transmission of words, a concern that can be elucidated in part by the rest of the text. Within the *Acts of Andrew* words, or *logoi*, are a complicated matter: they are salvific and transformative, but they are also autonomous and uncontrolled and a source of anxiety for the speaker or writer.

In the Greek *Acts of Andrew*, words are transformative, appealing to and saving the inner person. Both the singular and plural are used to discuss words, but the singular *logos* rarely if ever refers to an abstract or personified Logos. As François Bovon points out, "the author. . . generally prefers 'words'. . . , that is, maxims and discourses which confer life. The author hardly distinguishes the nature of God from the nature of the inner man and thus does not separate the word of God from the apostolic speeches which convey it."[29] In fact, in one of the few mentions of Jesus in the text, he is described as "Jesus Christ, ruler of true words and promises" (29).

Words can transform the hearers. Andrew's four-day speech from the cross, "the sheer abundance of his words," leads the crowd to exclaim: "Although he has eaten nothing, he has glutted us with his

---

[28] According to Marinos (*Life of Proclus*), Proclus neglected his parents' fortune (4), abstained from flesh (12), loved honors, but did not allow this to degenerate into a passion (16), practiced and taught purity (18), and probably only engaged in sexual intercourse in his imagination, and then only barely (20).

[29] Bovon, "Words of Life," 151. See Bovon's article for a complete discussion of the use of "words" in the *AAn* and the possible historical contexts.

words. Bring the man down and we will all become philosophers" (59[6]). The word buoys up Andrew and his disciples at a time of crisis (50[18]), and ultimately the words themselves are salvific. Andrew explains to Stratokles: "Likewise, Stratocles my child, we too must not be passive but bring your embryos [a metaphor meaning "questions"] into the open, in order that many who are kindred may register and bring them forth into the progress of saving words, whose associate I found you to be" (9).[30]

The hearer or reader can be akin (συγγενής) to words, and words can be akin to the hearer. Maximilla and Iphidama rejoice because Stratokles is "at last firmly established upon all the words that were akin to him" (10). This statement reveals that these salvific words appeal to something already within each hearer: Andrew was not called "to teach anyone, but to remind everyone akin to these words" (47[15]; διδάξαι μὲν οὐδένα, ὑπομνῆσαι δὲ πάντα τὸν συγγενῆ τῶν λόγων ἄνθρωπον). Andrew also says to Stratokles: "not in vain have I spoken to you the words which are akin to me" (43). Like a midwife, Andrew brings forth the inner man, who is akin to the salvific words which Andrew proclaims and to which Andrew himself is akin. The *Acts of Andrew* explains that "Stratocles in particular was so elevated in his mind that he forsook all his possessions and devoted himself to the word alone" (13).

Several images used in the *Acts of Andrew* elucidate the concept of the *logoi*. Stratokles says to Andrew: "The words. . .are like flaming javelins impaling me. Each of them strikes me and truly blazes and burns with love for you" (44[12]). Stratokles further comments upon Andrew's words, using a metaphor that can be both sexual and generative: "I received the seeds of the words of salvation while you were my sower; for them to shoot up and reproduce requires no one

---

[30] My translation, following MacDonald. The Greek is obscure: οὕτως δὲ καὶ ἡμᾶς, τέκνον μου Στρατοκλῆ, τὰ σὰ κυήματα εἰς μέσον φέρειν δεῖ καὶ μὴ ἠρεμεῖν, ἵνα ὑπὸ πλειόνων τῶν συγγενῶν ἀναγράφηται καὶ προαγάγηται εἰς ἐπίδοσιν τῶν σωτηρίων λόγων, ὧν κοινωνόν σε εὗρον. MacDonald translates: "Likewise, Stratocles my child, we too must not be passive but bring your embryos into the open, so that they may be registered and be brought to the donative of saving words by many kindred, whose associate I found you to be."

else but you, blessed Andrew" (44[12]).[31] In his closing speech to his disciples, Andrew explains the *logoi* in another way: "Therefore, I consider blessed those who have obeyed the words preached and who through them observe, as in a mirror, the mysteries concerning their proper nature" (47[15]).[32] This simile exposes the complexity of the words which are akin to the inner man and even reflect the mysteries of the "proper nature" of each disciple. They reveal mysteries; they expose that which is true and real.

All of these implications of the *logoi* are also present in the most perplexing aspect of the words: their autonomy. I shall return to the question of how the authorial voice in the conclusion (*AAn* 65) deals with this aspect of *logoi*. Within the body of the text, Andrew says to his disciples: "Words I have handed over to you which I pray were thus received by you as the words themselves wanted" (λόγους ὑμῖν παρέδωκα οὓς εὔχομαι οὕτως καταδέχεσθαι ὑφ᾽ ὑμῶν ὡς αὐτοὶ οἱ λόγοι θέλουσιν).[33] The sentence is structured so that the idea of "words" is primary in the mind of the recipient: λόγους begins the sentence, is the implicit subject of the infinitive in the relative clause, and the word λόγοι is rearticulated and intensified at the end of the sentence. The last phrase is itself a puzzle: Andrew expresses anxiety that he has not correctly transmitted the words as the words desire. Since the text here is clearly not referring to the Logos, this autonomous desire of words is perplexing.

The theme of the autonomy of words surfaces again in Andrew's speech to Maximilla and in her subsequent actions. Andrew encourages Maximilla to resist Aigeates' threats and to remain chaste. In this passage, Andrew importunes Maximilla by appealing to her essence, her inner "man." Aigeates has just begged Maximilla to be "the woman

---

[31] τὰ μὲν σπέρματα τῶν σωτηρίων λόγων δέδεγμαι, σοῦ ὄντος μοι τοῦ σπορέως. τὸ δὲ ἀναβλαστῆσαι ταῦτα καὶ ἐκφῦναι οὐχ ἑτέρου ἀλλ᾽ ἢ σοῦ δεῖται, Ἀνδρέα μακαριώτατε. With regard to this imagery, see Richard Valantasis, *Spiritual Guides of the Third Century: A Semiotic Study of the Guide-Disciple Relationship in Christianity, Neoplatonism, Hermetism, and Gnosticism* (Harvard Dissertations in Religion 27; Minneapolis: Fortress Press, 1991), 28.

[32] μακαρίους οὖν ἐκείνους τίθεμαι τοὺς κατηκόους τῶν κεκηρυγμένων λόγων γεγονότας καὶ δι᾽ αὐτῶν μυστήρια ὀπτριζομένους περὶ τὴν ἰδίαν φύσιν.

[33] *AAn* 48(16). My translation.

you once were" (36[4]), to return to their conjugal bed and married life. Two conflicting and complexly gendered models of identity are held up to Maximilla. Andrew explains: "Inasmuch as I do not keep silent in making the matter visible and actual through you, the most important thing I should say to you now comes to me: I rightly see in you Eve repenting and in me Adam converting" (37[5]).

Andrew has presented an image in which his fate and Maximilla's are bound together. The importance and urgency of this argument become even clearer. Andrew says, "Just as Adam died in Eve through his complicity with her, so also I now live in you through your observing the commandment of the Lord and through your transporting yourself to a state worthy of your essence" (39[7]). He again urges her not to submit to Aigeates' demands:

> Once again my speech (λόγος) is for you, Maximilla. . . . If you do not give yourself up to their opposites, Maximilla, I will rest, even if I am forcibly unloosed from this life for your sake—that is, for my sake. If I am driven from here, perhaps I can help others of my kindred because of you, but if you become won over by the seductions of Aegeates and the flatteries of the serpent, his father, so that you return to your former sexual acts, know this: I will be punished there because of you, until you yourself realize that I despised living this life because of an unworthy soul. Therefore, I beg you, wise man (τοῦ φρονίμου ἀνδρός), that your clearsighted mind stand firm. (40[8]–41[9])

Such radical dependence of an apostle upon his disciple is unparalleled throughout the literature of late antiquity, as far as I have been able to discover. Andrew's speech goes so far as to suggest a confusion or equation of identity: ὑπὲρ σοῦ, τοῦτ᾽ ἔστιν ὑπὲρ ἐμαυτοῦ ("for your sake—that is, for my own sake," 40[8]). Maximilla's correct understanding and performance of Andrew's words are vital to his own spiritual well-being, although the place and form of his possible punishment remain unclear. Indeed, this point is further emphasized in the text. Andrew concludes his speech to Maximilla and then addresses Stratokles. As Andrew finishes, the narrative explains:

> Maximilla was not present when the apostle said this, for when she heard the words that applied to her and in some way was changed by them, she became what the words themselves had signified.

ἡ δὲ Μαξιμίλλα ταῦτα τοῦ ἀποστόλου λέγοντος οὐ παρῆν· ἐκείνη
γὰρ τοὺς λόγους κατακούσασα οὓς πρὸς αὐτὴν ἀπετείνατο, καὶ
τρόπον τινὰ διατεθεῖσα ἀπ᾽ αὐτῶν καὶ γενομένη τοῦτο ὅπερ οἱ λόγοι
ἐδείκνυον. (46[14])

This transformation is radical. In becoming what the words showed,
Maximilla has "bidden farewell to her whole life as well as to wickedness" (46[14]). MacDonald's translation of ἐδείκνυον as "signified"
emphasizes the richness of this passage for theorizing about words and
semiotics. It is not only in this passage, however, that we begin to see
this richness of the words in the *Acts of Andrew*. We know that the
words mirror what is proper to the disciple, that they are akin to Andrew
and to the inner man who awaits discovery in each of the disciples. The
words themselves desire to be transmitted in a certain manner, and even
the apostle cannot guarantee that he has fulfilled their desire.

If the text expresses that the apostle himself cannot guarantee the
correct transmission and reception of the words, how much more
problematic is the transmission and reception of the *Acts of Andrew* as
a whole? The authorial voice in *AAn* 65 is part of the larger theorizing
concerning words that is going on within the entire text of the *Acts of
Andrew*. We now turn to its complex conclusion.

AAn 64: "We Wept"

To understand the meaning of *AAn* 65, one must first look to what
immediately precedes it: *AAn* 64 (in Prieur's edition; *AAn* 63 in
MacDonald's). MacDonald's reconstruction of the text reads, ". . .he
handed over his spirit, so that we wept and everyone grieved his
departure."[34] The reconstruction of this section is difficult, because here
the manuscripts separate in their readings. Prieur[35] explains that, after
παρέδωκεν τὸ πνεῦμα, C and the *Epistle*, supported by the readings in
the Armenian text and the *Martyrium Prius*, have ἐπὶ τῇ εὐχαριστίᾳ
αὐτοῦ ("after his thanksgiving"). H, S, and Q, supported by the

---

[34] MacDonald, *Acts of Andrew*, 437.

[35] For general information on some of the manuscripts mentioned here, see above.
For more detailed information, see Prieur, *Acta Andreae*, 2:423–39 and 1:117.

Laudatio, the *Narratio*, and *Conuersante et docente*, have the following readings:

H, S, and Q: κλαιόντων οὖν ἡμῶν καὶ ἀνιωμένων ἀπάντων ἐπὶ τῷ χωρισμῷ αὐτοῦ

N and L: κλαιόντων ἁπάντων καὶ ἀνιωμένων ἐπὶ τῷ χωρισμῷ αὐτοῦ [in L, this is placed after ἔξοδον in *AAn* 64].[36]

Prieur notes that the *Laudatio* and the *Martyrium Prius* have different readings; he speculates that they were both used for a common, later source,[37] and thus both readings are conjoined in the *Acts of Andrew*.[38] What are we to make of this sudden move into the first person plural? One interesting parallel exists among the apocryphal acts.[39] *AJn* 155.4 presents a first person plural reference at the end of a text otherwise constructed in the third person. The passage describes John's death: "After having sealed himself in every part, standing thus, he said '(Be) thou with me, Lord Jesus Christ'; and he lay down in the trench where he had spread out his clothes; and he said to us, 'Peace (be) with you, my brethren,' and gave up his spirit rejoicing."[40] The use of the first person plural both in this text and in the *Acts of Andrew* may be a literary convention which serves to add authority to the text by giving it an eyewitness quality. This phenomenon is more puzzling in the *Acts of Andrew*, however, since the first person singular also appears suddenly at the conclusion of the text.

MacDonald and Prieur have set forth different suggestions regarding the reason for this shift of the narrative into first person plural and

[36] See ibid., 2:542–43. See also MacDonald, *Acts of Andrew*, 436–37.

[37] See his diagram (Prieur, *Acta Andreae*, 2:435).

[38] Ibid., 542 n. 5.

[39] In *APt* 21, the text shifts from third person narrative to first person plural when describing a miraculous bright light that appeared after prayer. This is interesting but does not provide a close parallel to the *AAn* 64. Consider also the irruption of the first person plural in the Syriac *Martyrdom of Narsai*. For an excellent resource for locating such phenomena in texts, see Steven M. Sheeley, *Narrative Asides in Luke-Acts* (Journal for the Study of the New Testament, Supplement Series 72; Sheffield: Sheffield Academic Press, 1992).

[40] *NTApoc*[5] 2:204.

singular. Prieur hypothesizes that the Greek *Acts of Andrew* began with a prologue in which the author explained his intention, which was to render an account of the acts of Andrew that he had witnessed, in the company of a group of disciples.[41] Prieur supports this reading by referring to the first person plural of the passage just discussed and by citing the witness of the fourth-century Philaster of Brescia, who mentions that the disciples who followed Andrew recorded his acts.[42] As mentioned earlier, Prieur asserts that the author was a philosopher, "very probably a convert who found in Christianity that which one might call 'true philosophy,'" but otherwise he does not speculate on the identity of the author.[43]

MacDonald, in contrast, expresses strong opinions concerning the shift from first person plural to singular and concerning authorship. He cites the letter of Pope Innocent I (d. ca. 417) to the priest Exuperius of Toulouse, who in the midst of difficulties with the Priscillianists had written to ask for a list of canonical writings. Innocent responds, condemning the *Acts of Andrew*, which was written "by the philosophers Xenocharides and Leonidas."[44] MacDonald asserts that we "probably should assume that the names appeared in the original." In order to resolve the conflict between dual authorship and the first person singular of *AAn* 65, MacDonald suggests that the author differs from the disciples mentioned by Philaster and from the philosophers Xenocharides and Leonidas mentioned by Innocent. The author, according to MacDonald, "seems to be locating himself as a transcriber at the end of a chain of oral tradition. That is why he prays that he has recorded accurately 'the things that were said just as they had been said'—said by his informants."[45] Here MacDonald shifts from his earlier proposal that the first portion of the book was written by either the philosopher Xenocharides or Leonidas and the second portion by the other, an

---

[41] Prieur, *Acta Andreae*, 1:38. This opinion is supported by Dennis Ronald MacDonald, *Christianizing Homer: the Odyssey, Plato, and the Acts of Andrew* (New York: Oxford University Press, 1994), 289.

[42] Prieur, *Acta Andreae*, 1:38.

[43] Ibid., 1:381.

[44] See ibid., 1:111; MacDonald, *Christianizing Homer*, 287.

[45] MacDonald, *Christianizing Homer*, 288.

explanation which supported his assertion that the *Acts of Andrew and Matthias* are connected to the Greek *Acts of Andrew*.[46]

MacDonald's proposal is indeed interesting, but I question it on two levels. First, the very mention in the manuscripts of Xenocharides and Leonidas, upon which MacDonald speculates in both his *Acts of Andrew* and his later *Christianizing Homer*, is tenuous. Prieur explains that "the mention of Andrew is missing from many manuscripts that do not depend upon each other"[47] and hypothesizes that Andrew's name may be an addition and thus unconnected to Xenocharides and Leonidas. Thus, we see that while MacDonald is right in saying that "it is difficult to imagine what might have been gained by foisting the work onto two traditional nobodies," whatever tradition links these two names to the *Acts of Andrew* is far from secure.[48] Second, while I support MacDonald's assertion that the author is not an eyewitness to the life of Andrew, I disagree with the implication of his argument: that the author is a transcriber of the oral accounts of Xenocharides and Leonidas, or that one name referred to the author and the other to the transcriber. This is too neat. Moreover, MacDonald supports this assertion by making reference to a portion of the author's prayer that "I heard what was actually said" (τῶν εἰρημένων ὡς εἴρηται).[49] As we have seen, this concern with hearing and understanding reflects larger concerns throughout the *Acts of Andrew*. In *AAn* 65, the author crystallizes the concerns regarding transmission that exist throughout the book—concerns that are not necessarily linked to a person transcribing the words of the elusive Xenocharides and Leonidas.

---

[46] MacDonald, *Acts of Andrew*, 48–50; see also the materials cited in n. 2.

[47] Prieur, *Acta Andreae*, 1:112 n. 3.

[48] MacDonald, *Christianizing Homer*, 288. MacDonald also suggests that the author is here alerting the reader to "hypertextual intentions. The 'obvious (συμφανές)' has to do with the surface reading, the 'obscure (ἀφανῶν)' refers to its transvaluation of Greek mythology and philosophy" (p. 290). Since I do not agree with his thesis that the *Acts of Andrew* is based upon Greek mythology, I question this reading of *AAn* 65. MacDonald's assessment that this passage has to do with "hypertextual intentions" is, however, a good one. He develops it further in "Is There a Privileged Reader?"

[49] Or, "I heard the things which were said as they were said [literally: it was said]." Prieur has "puissé-je avoir entendu ce qui a été dit comme cela a été dit" (*Acta Andreae*, 2:548).

AAn 65: The Construction of a Text

In both Prieur's and MacDonald's editions, *AAn* 65 is reconstructed from three Greek manuscripts (H, S, C), with reference made to the *Narratio* and the Armenian version. Both authors agree that *AAn* 65 is not a colophon; given its style and syntax as well as its theology, it is integral to the rest of the *Acts of Andrew*.[50] The Armenian version, however, building on Stratokles' speech to Aigeates in *AAn* 64, incorporates *AAn* 65 as Stratokles' final comment rather than as a conclusion from the author.[51]

According to Prieur, H and S diverge from an earlier text after the word εἰρημένων; at this point, they add their own doxology. In contrast, "a comparison with the Armenian version shows that Ann Arbor 36 [C] followed the AA [*AAn*] until the end of the work, that is to say until χαρίσματα (65, 8), and then added its doxology."[52] Although the two versions do not differ significantly, I present both here, excluding the doxology and using brackets to indicate sections where information in H and S is missing in C, or vice versa.

> H and S:
> Ἐνταῦθά που τὸ τέλος τῶν μακαρίων μου διηγημάτων ποιήσαιμι καὶ πράξεων καὶ μυστηρίων δυσφράστων ὄντων, ἵνα μὴ καὶ ἀφράστων εἴπω. [———] καὶ ἐπεύξομαι πρῶτον μὲν ἐμαυτῷ [S: ἐμαυτοῦ] ἀκοῦσαι τῶν εἰρημένων ὡς εἴρηται [———] ἔπειτα καὶ πᾶσι τοῖς διατιθεμένοις ὑπὸ τῶν εἰρημένων, κοινὴν[53] δοξολογίαν ἀναπέμψωμεν τῷ φιλανθρώπῳ θεῷ. . . .

> Here I should make an end of the blessed tales and acts and mysteries which are difficult—I should say impossible—to express. And I will pray first for myself that I heard the things that were said as they were said, then also for all who are convinced by the things that were said, that we may send forth common praise to the philanthropic God. . . .

---

[50] MacDonald, *Acts of Andrew*, 47–48; Prieur, *Acta Andreae*, 1:56–57.

[51] See Louis Leloir, "La version arménienne de la Passion d'André," *Handes Amsorya* 90 (1976): 492.

[52] Prieur, *Acta Andreae*, 1:57.

[53] Prieur reconstructs κοινωνίαν, following the Armenian.

C:

Ἐνταῦθ' ὅπου μου τὸ τέλος τῶν μακαριωτάτων [————] πράξεων
μυστηρίων δυσφράστων [————], ἵνα μὴ καὶ ἀνέκφραστον εἴπω. ἡ
κορωνὶς τελευτάτω. καὶ ἐπεύξομαι πρῶτον μὲν ἐμαυτῷ ἀκοῦσαι τῶν
εἰρημένων ὡς εἴρηται καὶ τοῦτον[54] εἰς τὸ συμφανές, εἶτα καὶ τῶν
ἀφανῶν, διανοίᾳ δὲ λοιπόν,[55] ἔπειτα καὶ πᾶσι τοῖς διατιθεμένοις ὑπὸ
τῶν εἰρημένων, κοινωνεῖν[56] ἔχειν ἐπίμαν[57] θεοῦ δὲ ἀνοίγοντος τὰς
ἀκόας τῶν ἐντυγχανόντων, ὅπως ἤλιπτὺ[58] ἄπαντα αὐτοῦ τὰ
χαρίσματα. . . .

Here is my end of the most blessed acts [and] mysteries[59] difficult—I
should say impossible—to express. Let this stroke of the pen end it.
And I pray first for myself, that I heard the things which were said as
they were said, both those which are quite manifest, and then those things
which are obscure, comprehensible to the intellect, then [I will pray]
even for all who are convinced by the things which were said, that they
may have fellowship together, as God opens the ears of those upon whom
[the message] falls, in order to make comprehensible all his gifts. . . .[60]

Clearly C manifests a fuller picture of the author, but in both texts the
authorial voice reflects the larger concerns, expressed throughout the
text, regarding words. How can one control how words are received

[54] Prieur suggests τούτων. My reconstruction of the texts from Prieur's apparatus
has been checked against the unpublished reconstruction of Jean-Daniel Kaestli. Kaestli,
too, questions whether the scribe should have written τούτων or τοῦτο.

[55] Prieur suggests ληπτῶν, following the Armenian.

[56] Prieur suggests κοινωνίαν, following the Armenian.

[57] Prieur suggests ἐπίπαν.

[58] Prieur suggests ἢ ληπτά, following the Armenian; Kaestli wonders if this should
read εἴληπται.

[59] I have no hypothesis regarding the omission of διηγημάτων from the list of
διηγημάτων, πράξεων, and μυστηρίων in H and S. I also do not think that these
words indicate any differentiation of materials within the text itself: I do not believe
that the author assumed that certain materials would be read as acts, certain as tales,
and certain as mysteries. The term μυστήρια has interesting valences, however,
especially in the Alexandrian context (I thank one of the outside readers for pointing
this out). For more on the term, see, e.g., Clement *Strom.* 5.12. Note also that the term
is applied to words in 47[15]; through the words preached, some will "observe, as in a
mirror, the mysteries concerning their proper nature."

[60] Both translations are mine, following MacDonald's.

and understood? How can one act in the manner in which the words themselves desire? Both texts go so far as to point to the community that is constituted by those who understand the *Acts of Andrew*; moreover, by use of the first person plural, H and S constitute all readers within a fellowship intimate with the author.

While the first-person authorial voice does sometimes appear at the beginning or ending of late-antiquity biographies of philosophers or other texts in praise of teachers, and while sometimes blessings and curses or instructions concerning the transmission or publication of a book are found at the conclusion of texts—the book of Revelation or the Gospel of John, for example—the *Acts of Andrew*'s concern regarding proper transmission and reception of the text is unusual. Looking to parallels, we see that Marinos, writing his *Life of Proclus* considerably later, expresses concern that by not writing about Proclus, he would fail the sage; but he also expresses his desire to become famous through writing the *Life*. Although Eunapius's *Lives of the Philosophers and Sophists* was written in the fourth century c.e., his introduction expresses similar content to *AAn* 65:

> This much, then, I place on record, and am aware that some things have perhaps escaped me, but other things have not. And in that, after expending much thought and pains so that the result might be a continuous and definite account of the lives of the most celebrated philosophers and rhetoricians, I fell short of my ambition, I have had the same experience as those who are madly and feverishly in love. For they, when they behold the beloved and the adored beauty of her visible countenance, bow their heads, too weak to fix their gaze on that which they desire, and dazzled by its rays.[61]

Here, however, the author focuses on transmitting something regarding the philosophers; the anxiety is that the person will not be properly represented. The *AAn* 65, in contrast, is concerned with the transmission of "what is said as it was said."

[61] Eunapius *Lives of the Philosophers and Sophists* 454–55, trans. Wilmer Cave Wright (LCL, 1922), 349–51.

This concern regarding proper hearing, regarding the correct understanding of the words themselves, derives in part from the model of Socrates. Prieur has argued correctly that Andrew is a kind of new Socrates, recast in a highly philosophizing Christian setting. Indeed, within the development of the concept of the hero in Greek civilization, Plato's descriptions of Socrates' death presented a new focus for the immortalization of the hero. Socrates was not immortalized through elaborate funeral games or rituals, nor is he remembered through an epic song tradition or through the laments of lyric. Rather, his words—insofar as they have been constructed by Plato—immortalize him.[62]

We also find reworkings of the Socratic tradition at a point closer to the writing of the *Acts of Andrew*. Plutarch's *De genio Socratis*, written in the late first century C.E., speculates regarding Socrates' *daimonion* (the "spirit" that guided him) and regarding how words and language worked for those led by *daimonia*, as Socrates was. During a discussion of Socrates, one character explains:

> The thoughts of daemons are luminous and shed their light on the daemonic man. Their thoughts have no need of verbs or nouns, which [humans] use as symbols in their intercourse, and thereby behold mere counterfeits and likenesses of what is present in thought, but are unaware of the original except for those persons who are illuminated, as I have said, by some special and daemonic radiance.[63]

Socrates, because he was "pure and free from passion, and commingling with the body but a little. . .was so sensitive and delicate as to respond at once to what reached him";[64] the *daimones* did not need to communicate through "blows" to the understanding but could communicate

---

[62] I refer here to Gregory Nagy, lectures, "The Concept of the Hero in Greek Civilization," Literature and Arts C-14, Harvard University, fall 1995. At the end of the *Apology*, Socrates tells the jury and his accusers that "there will be more people to test you, whom I now held back, but you did not notice it. They will be more difficult to deal with, as they will be younger, and you will resent them more" (Plato *Apology* 39d, trans. G. M. A. Grube [Indianapolis: Hackett, 1981], 42); this alludes to the continuity of the words and teachings of Socrates.

[63] Plutarch *De gen. Soc.* 589C, in *Moralia* 7:455.

[64] Ibid., 588E, in *Moralia* 7:451.

voicelessly.[65] This appeal to direct communication, as well as an allusion to the sort of "inner man" mentioned in the Greek *Acts of Andrew*, provides a slightly different but more clearly stated view of the workings of human and divine language.[66] Like Socrates, Maximilla is illuminated; she is thus able to become what the words demonstrated, since Andrew transmitted the words effectively and Maximilla received them correctly.[67]

Not only is Andrew a new Socrates; he is also a teacher and apostle like others in the Christian tradition. Although the *Acts of Andrew* differs in many ways from *The Oration and Panegyric Addressed to Origen*, the discussion of words and the concerns expressed regarding speech are similar in both. This work has been dated to approximately 238 C.E. and has been attributed to Gregory Thaumaturgus.[68] Since Gregory Thaumaturgus was a student of Origen, who taught in Alexandria, we again see a connection of the Greek *Acts of Andrew* to ideas propagated in Alexandria. As Richard Valantasis suggests, instead of reading this work for historical data regarding Origen, we should consider the rhetorical complexity of the text.[69]

---

[65] Ibid., in *Moralia* 7:453. "For speech is like a blow—when we converse with one another, the words are forced through our ears and the soul is compelled to take them in—; whereas the intelligence of the higher power guides the gifted soul, which requires no blows, by the touch of its thought."

[66] Ibid., 589F, in *Moralia* 7:459: "implying by this that he had a better guide of life in himself than a thousand teachers and attendants."

[67] This is especially interesting in view of the Adam and Eve typology set forth by Andrew in *AAn* 39. Commenting upon Gen 3:6, Philo explains, "In an allegorical sense, . . .woman is a symbol of sense, and man, of mind. Now of necessity sense comes into contact with the sense-perceptible; and by the participation of sense, things pass into the mind; for sense is moved by objects, while the mind is moved by sense" (*Quaest. Gen.* 37, trans. Ralph Marcus [LCL, 1953], 22). In this allegory, the male depends upon the female. Perhaps something similar is going on in the *Acts of Andrew*, although this is a tenuous thesis, given the geographical, temporal, and generic differences between the texts. Philo's comments, however, may also pertain to Andrew's calling Maximilla a "wise man." Maximilla, in accepting the *logoi*, becomes male, supersedes sense perception, and connects with the intellectual part of herself that is akin to the saving words.

[68] Valantasis, *Spiritual Guides of the Third Century*, 14.

[69] Ibid., 13.

The central point of the thanksgiving text is to explain a disciple's relationship with his teacher—to clarify his own spiritual development[70] and the way of instruction that Origen employed. Gregory's text, however, presents a model of relationship different from that of the *Acts of Andrew*: in the panegyric, the teacher learns directly from God and passes this on to his students; thus the teacher participates in the life of God, and the student in the life of the teacher.[71] The speaker of this panegyric does, however, express many concerns about speaking, and about words.

The speaker, after explaining that he is unable to deliver an elegant speech, explains his theory of language: "And as our words are nothing else than a kind of imagery of the dispositions of our mind we should allow those who have the gift of speech. . .to possess the liberty of painting their word-pictures."[72] Moreover, human words are mere "refuse and mud" compared to "words that are divine and pure."[73] Silence is the best course, he decides, before launching into his entire speech. Unlike the author of the *Acts of Andrew*, Thaumaturgus plays with the multivalence of *logos*, also allowing it to refer to the divine Logos.[74] Like Andrew, Origen offered the "word of salvation,"[75] and had received the gift of interpreting oracles of God to humans, "that he might understand the words of God, even as if God spake them to him, and that he might recount them to men in such wise as that they may hear them with intelligence."[76] While this model is different from that of the *Acts of Andrew*—the text is more certain of Origen's ability to transmit these salvific words—the concerns are very similar. In fact, like the javelins of words that Stratokles experiences when he hears

---

[70] Regarding this development, see ibid., 17–19. Valantasis refers his reader to Stanley F. Bonner, *Education in Ancient Rome: From the Elder Cato to the Younger Pliny* (Berkeley: University of California Press, 1977).

[71] Valantasis, *Spiritual Guides of the Third Century*, 24, 30–31.

[72] Gregory Thaumaturgus, *The Oration and Panegyric Addressed to Origen* 1, trans. S. D. F. Salmond; ed. Alexander Roberts and James Donaldson (Ante-Nicene Fathers 6; Peabody, Mass.: Hendrickson, 1994), 21.

[73] Ibid., 2 (translation, p. 23).

[74] See ibid., 4.

[75] Ibid., 6 (translation, p. 28).

[76] Ibid., 15 (translation, p. 36).

Andrew, the speaker states that "we were shot as by some sort of arrow by his discourse."[77]

Although Gregory's text is not concerned about words in quite the same way as the *Acts of Andrew*, we see here a similar emphasis upon their powerful and salvific effects. We also see that human words are easily misunderstood; certainly this is part of the anxiety underlying the discussion of words in the *Acts of Andrew*. Perhaps most importantly, Valantasis explains that the author employs various textual strategies in his speech; these strategies are evident in the varied uses of pronouns.[78] He points out that the use of the first person plural serves to incorporate readers of all times into Origen's community; it makes all readers disciples.

Conclusions: Readers and Reading

The long process of contextualizing this small passage—moving through the historical and literary milieu of the *Acts of Andrew* and through the concept of *logoi* set forth by the text itself—was intended to make explicit some of the codes of the text. Umberto Eco's *The Role of the Reader* makes clear that in order to understand a text, the reader or hearer must share certain codes with the author.[79] Otherwise, a misreading may occur, a misreading that may be interesting but that nevertheless manages at best to generate an entirely different text.

---

[77] Valantasis, *Spiritual Guides of the Third Century*, 26; βεβλημένοι μὲν ὥσπερ τινὶ βέλει τῷ παρ' αὐτοῦ λόγῳ καὶ ἐκ πρώτης ἡλικίας (6.78). The Greek text is taken from Gregoire le Thaumaturge, *Remerciement à Origène*, ed. Henri Crouzel (Sources Chrétiennes 148; Paris: Éditions du Cerf, 1969), 126.

[78] Valantasis, *Spiritual Guides of the Third Century*, 16.

[79] I am indebted to Valantasis's study (ibid.) for leading me to this text. Valantasis also uses this semiotic theory to challenge readings of his primary sources. It is interesting that MacDonald ("Is There a Privileged Reader?") also uses Eco's work to explicate the conclusion of the *Acts of Andrew*: Umberto Eco, *The Role of the Reader: Explorations in the Semiotics of Texts* (Bloomington: Indiana University Press, 1979). He concludes that *AAn* 65 alludes to the secret meaning of the text—to Andrew as a type for the hero Odysseus and to the *Acts of Andrew* (including the *Acts of Andrew and Matthias in the City of the Cannibals*; MacDonald believes this should be conjoined with the Greek *Acts of Andrew*) as an epic. MacDonald argues that these "deeper,

From *AAn* 63 to 65, the authorial voice shifts from the third person to the first person plural to the first person singular. How do these shifts in voice function? What might the purpose of such shifts be? *AAn* 63 concludes with the statement, "When he had said these things and further glorified the Lord, he handed over his spirit, so that we wept and everyone grieved his departure." These shifts into first person serve explicitly to construct an author and to incorporate that author (and the community which is constructed by the "we" who are present at the death of Andrew) into the mind of the reader and into the purposes of the text. The author here also points to his or her involvement in the transmission of the words of and about Andrew: "I will pray first for myself, that I heard what was actually said."[80]

It is necessary here to differentiate between the actual author and the inscribed author—the author as he or she constructs him or herself in the text.[81] In fact, we can move one step further and suggest that the text also constructs the author in ways that he or she might not have expected; for example, some element of anxiety may be present that the actual author seeks to cover over in his or her self-construction. In a text such as the *Acts of Andrew*, where anxiety is repeatedly expressed concerning the transmission and reception of words, the complexities of the construction of the author, and of the reader and the text itself, are especially interesting.

In his study, Eco maintains that the author is "a textual strategy establishing semantic correlations and activating the Model Reader,"[82] especially in the most extreme form of "open texts," in which "the role of its addressee (the reader, in the case of verbal texts) has. . .been

---

allegorical, 'obscure' meanings" (p. 40) have been missed throughout the history of the reuse and interpretation of the *Acts of Andrew*. I disagree with MacDonald's interpretation of the *Acts of Andrew and Matthias in the City of the Cannibals* together with the Greek *Acts of Andrew* as a Christian rewriting of Homeric epic, although there certainly may be allusions to the *Odyssey* in the *Acts of Andrew and Matthias*.

[80] The important task of the historical reconstruction of early communities that used this text is beyond the scope of this paper.

[81] See the work of Elisabeth Schüssler Fiorenza, especially *But She Said: Feminist Practices of Biblical Interpretation* (Boston: Beacon Press, 1992).

[82] Eco, *Role of the Reader*, 11.

envisaged at the moment of its generation *qua* text."[83] In the *Acts of Andrew*, we see an open text that does indeed envisage its audience at the moment of its generation. Just as Andrew's speeches are directed at a sort of model hearer—at the person who is akin to the words—the model reader is constructed as a disciple, as someone who is "convinced by what was said" and who then engages in fellowship with others who are like-minded, or akin. These are hearers or readers who understand that which is obvious and "also the obscure, comprehensible only to the intellect."

As Eco posits, however, the text does not always assume that the reader is competent: it also *creates* model readers. "The author has thus to foresee a model of the possible reader. . .supposedly able to deal interpretatively with the expressions in the same way as the author deals generatively with them."[84] The text selects a possible reader through a "specific linguistic code," through "literary style," through "specific specialization-indices," by which Eco means direct address, or generic markers such as those employed in children's books.[85] The text also builds up the competence of the reader and thus constructs the model reader by instructing the reader throughout, by encouraging the reader to reach certain conclusions or to make certain choices. In the *Acts of Andrew*, we can observe that the text as a whole may use Andrew's speeches, the conversion of Stratokles, and the actions of Maximilla as strategies for building up the competence of the model reader, who is more explicitly described in the conclusion, in *AAn* 65. Just as Maximilla became what the words showed or signified, the reader is called to be transformed by the words, to find the wise inner man within him- or herself, to allow the words of the entire text of the *Acts of Andrew* to mirror that which is proper to each reader. The model reader is thus constructed, and the reader is him- or herself discipled and asked to become a disciple, one who understands the obvious and the obscure, one who, throughout time, is akin to and in "fellowship with" Andrew and his disciples. An Andrean community is constructed within the text and reconstructed in the proper reading of the text.

[83] Ibid., 3.
[84] Ibid., 7.
[85] Ibid.

The voice present here also reconstructs the text by framing it as "blessed tales, acts, and mysteries"; the intrusion of the "I" who is writing reminds the hearer of the authorial control over the text. The author then undercuts this control, however, by making reference to a theme which we have seen expressed throughout the *Acts of Andrew*, that of the difficulty of controlling and understanding words. Although the author writes and frames the narrative, he or she also characterizes it as "difficult—or should I say impossible—to express." The first prayer is by the author and for the author, and rearticulates the difficulty of understanding and the risk of the improper reception of the words: the author prays that "I heard what was actually said, both the obvious and also the obscure, comprehensible only to the intellect."[86]

The conclusion also insists that whichever reader understands the text, that is, has a sufficient number of codes in common with the author in order merely to grasp the meaning, also must decide his or her status in regard to Andrew's community. Having read the text, are we disciples? *AAn* 65 turns and faces the reader directly, attempting to guide his or her reading. The text itself cannot completely guard against an "aberrant" reading:[87] in its allusion to certain historical and social situations, it may inscribe within itself a reading against the grain, either through its silences or through the interstices of the text—perhaps overly complex syntax, or the force of an argument, or the choice of one term and the avoidance of another. These aberrant readings are only aberrant insofar as the inscribed author is concerned, and they may in fact be extremely generative for the text itself.[88] Just as the actual author may be trans-

---

[86] Prieur states that the *Acts of Andrew* has the "goal of revealing salvation to the largest possible number of hearers" (*Acta Andreae*, 1:381).

[87] Eco, *Role of the Reader*, 8. "In the process of communication, a text is frequently interpreted against the background of codes different from those intended by the author. Some authors do not take into account such a possibility. . . . Those texts that obsessively aim at arousing a precise response on the part of more or less empirical readers. . .are in fact open to any possible 'aberrant' decoding."

[88] An example of these complicated hermeneutical problems is found in recent attempts to theorize about the situation at Corinth, for example, through reading 1 Corinthians. See Georgi, *Opponents*; Elisabeth Schüssler Fiorenza, "Rhetorical Situation and Historical Reconstruction in 1 Corinthians," *NTS* 33 (1987): 386–403; Antoinette Clark Wire, *The Corinthian Women Prophets: A Reconstruction through Paul's Rhetoric* (Minneapolis: Fortress Press, 1990).

formed in unexpected ways in the process of inscribing him- or herself in the text,[89] so the actual audience may be transformed in unexpected ways as it acquiesces to and resists the model reader and the model community set forth by the *Acts of Andrew*.

Having been faced with the strategy of incorporation employed by the "I" at the end of the *Acts of Andrew*, does the reader become a disciple or an aberrant reader? Does the reader interpret the text according to the models of the author—those of discipleship, of being akin to Andrew and his disciples—or does the reader interpret the entire *Acts of Andrew* in a way that resists this invitation to discipleship? If the strategies of the author have succeeded, the reader has been transformed by the salvific and autonomous words, has understood the words as they themselves would want, and has become "what the words signified." If that is the case, the reader participates in an ongoing project, as the author has set forth: with the proper understanding and enacting of the *logoi*, the community of Andrew—or the community of those who follow the *logoi* that Andrew strives to make clear—expands indefinitely.

---

[89] This idea was suggested to me by Helmut Koester.

Physical and Spiritual Restoration: The Role of Healing Miracles in the *Acts of Andrew*

David W. Pao

Introduction

In the *Acts of Andrew*,[1] as in other apocryphal acts, the emphasis on the dichotomy between the body and the soul has long been recognized. In a lengthy speech before the crowd, Andrew himself said:

> I entreat you who have come here together for my sake, abandon this entire life and hasten to overtake my soul which speeds toward things beyond time, beyond law, beyond speech, beyond body, beyond bitter and lawless pleasures full of every pain. (*AAn* 57)[2]

This emphasis does not, however, prevent the author of the *Acts of Andrew* (and other apocryphal acts) from portraying the apostle as a miracle worker who frequently heals the body of the sick. In the

---

[1] In this essay I shall follow the reconstruction of Jean-Marc Prieur, *Acta Andreae*, in treating the *Acts of Andrew* and the *Acts of Andrew and Matthias* as two separate works. For further information concerning the reconstruction of the text of the *Acts of Andrew*, see the discussion between Dennis R. MacDonald and Jean-Marc Prieur in MacDonald, *Apocryphal Acts of Apostles*, 9–39. Prieur has provided a further defense of his reconstruction in *Acta Andreae*, 1:32–40.

[2] For the English translation (with the corresponding chapter division) of the *Acts of Andrew*, I will use the translation of Dennis R. MacDonald, *The Acts of Andrew and the Acts of Andrew and Matthias in the City of the Cannibals* (Atlanta: Scholars Press, 1990).

surviving text of the *Acts of Andrew*,[3] more than sixteen healing stories[4] can be documented in which Andrew is portrayed as one who ministers to the "physical" needs of the people. These episodes reflect an unwillingness of the author to abandon the propagandistic value of such miracle stories.[5] Their inclusion presents problems which need to be addressed, however: How does the author of the *Acts of Andrew* solve the apparent inconsistency between the emphasis on the spiritual realm in the speeches of Andrew and the emphasis on the physical realm in the numerous healing miracles? What are some of the strategies the author uses in transforming the individual healing miracles to fit the general scheme of his work? What is the role of the healing miracles in the *Acts of Andrew* when the body and the physical realm are consistently condemned?

Such tension between attention to the physical body and the emphasis on the soteriological significance of the soul exists in the wider theological scene of early Christianity. Elizabeth Castelli offers an interesting analysis:

> The paradox of early Christianity, of course, is that its apparent rejection of the body as a shadowy and passible shell of the immortal soul is located within an ideological and practical matrix thoroughly focused

---

[3] I will concentrate on the Latin text of Gregory's *Epitome* (abbreviated *Epit.*) in discussing the various miracle stories. The Greek text of the *Passion of Andrew* will also be used, especially when examining the content of selected speeches. It will become obvious that while major speeches of the apostle Andrew are missing in Gregory's *Epitome*, the emphasis on the body-soul dualism can still be detected through the form and content of the miracle stories. For further discussion of the text of the *Acts of Andrew*, see Laura S. Nasrallah, "'She Became What the Words Signified': The Greek *Acts of Andrew*'s Construction of the Reader-Disciple," in this volume.

[4] Here, I consider "resurrection stories" as an extreme form of healing stories. Please refer to the table at the end of this essay for a list of these miracle stories.

[5] Scholars have generally agreed that miracles stories in the apocryphal acts primarily function as instruments of religious propaganda. Howard Kee (*Miracle in the Early Christian World: A Study in Sociohistorical Method* [New Haven, Conn.: Yale University Press, 1983], 287) is certainly right in suggesting that "the fundamental aim of these miracle accounts is evidential: to prove that God is behind Jesus and his messengers." Nevertheless, this does not exhaust the meaning of these numerous miracles. For a further discussion of the function of these miracles, see the section "Healing and Community," below.

on the body. Every important dimension of early Christian thought and practice is mediated through language and ideas about and the material realities of the (human or mystical) body. While it is not particularly difficult to isolate graphic quotations from the church fathers to sustain the claim that the early Christians were relentlessly anti-body, enacting the most extreme forms of Platonic dualism by embracing the spirit and casting aside the flesh, there exists the equally compelling reality that the early Christians were absolutely obsessed with the fact of human-being-in-flesh.[6]

In this essay, I shall examine one aspect of such tension as expressed in the healing miracle stories. While form-critical analyses of the miracle stories of selected apocryphal acts have been performed,[7] and the problems of miracles within the theological matrix of these texts have been examined,[8] this study seeks to examine further how healing stories are appropriated into the theological framework of the author.

First, the dualistic anthropological framework in which the author of the *Acts of Andrew* operates will be examined in the context of the cultural milieu of the early Christian centuries. In the central section, I shall discuss in detail the main strategies the author of the *Acts of Andrew* uses in incorporating the healing stories within the dualistic framework of the text. Furthermore, in order to locate the author's understanding of these healing stories in the context of the development of early Christian theology, Irenaeus's understanding of the function of miracles will also be noted. While a comprehensive study of the understanding of miracles among second-century Christian authors is beyond the scope of this essay, such a study of the two collections of writings that represent two different theological movements in the second century would be helpful. Finally, I shall conclude with a brief discussion of the function of the healing miracles in the process of the formation of the community to which the *Acts of Andrew* belongs.

---

[6] Elizabeth A. Castelli, "Mortifying the Body, Curing the Soul: Beyond Ascetic Dualism in the Life of Saint Syncletica," *Differences* 4 (1992): 137.

[7] See, for example, Robert F. Stoops, "Miracle Stories and Vision Reports in the Acts of Peter" (Ph.D. diss., Harvard University, 1982).

[8] The most recent study is that of François Bovon, "Miracles, magie et guérison dans les Actes apocryphes des apôtres," *Journal of Early Christian Studies* 3 (1995): 245–59.

Anthropological Dualism and the *Acts of Andrew*

In the *Acts of Andrew*, as in other apocryphal acts, one notes the emphasis on the importance of the ascetic life. While one may not be willing to go as far as Ross Kraemer in claiming that "in the Apocryphal Acts, Christianity is essentially defined as the acceptance of an ascetic way of life,"[9] the importance of the ascetic practices cannot be denied. In the *Acts of Andrew*, such emphasis is reflected in a statement Andrew made in his speech to Nicolaus:

> Here is what I long to receive from you: that your inner self recognize the true God, its maker and the creator of all; that it reject the earthly and crave the eternal; that it neglect the fleeting and love the everlasting; that it deny what is seen and, by contemplation, cast spiritual glances at what is not seen. (*Epit.* 16)

Again, in Andrew's prayer on behalf of Maximilla, the same emphasis can be found:

> With respect to our savage and ever boorish enemy, cause her to sleep apart from her visible husband and wed her to her inner husband, whom you above all recognize, and for whose sake the entire mystery of your plan of salvation has been accomplished. (*AAn* 16)

From these statements, the connection between the emphasis on the ascetic practice and the body-soul dualism can also be detected.[10] This body-soul dualism undergirds the text of the *Acts of Andrew*. For example, when Andrew was about to heal a sick man, Andrew said, "Now I wash your body so that it might be made well. You yourself will wash your soul" (*Epit.* 33). Such a body-soul dualism is characterized by the radical distinctions between the immaterial and the material, the permanent and the temporal, and the invisible and the visible. The

---

[9] Ross Kraemer, "The Conversion of Women to Ascetic Forms of Christianity," *Signs* 6 (1980–81): 301.

[10] Peter R. L. Brown ("Bodies and Minds: Sexuality and Renunciation in Early Christianity," in *Before Sexuality: The Construction of Erotic Experience in the Ancient World*, ed. D. M. Halperin, J. J. Winkler, and F. I. Zeitlin [Princeton: Princeton University Press, 1990], 480) notes that the origins of sexual abstinence "lay in that dark streak of discomfort with the life of the body, based on the Greek dualism of body and mind."

immaterial soul represents the inner self that is able to be enlightened by that which belongs to the eternal realm. The external body, on the other hand, is that from which the true self seeks to escape. This dualism again resurfaces in the contrast between the body that is created from perishable matter and the soul that is not. This anthropological dualism is based on a wider metaphysical framework which divides all that exists into two irreconcilable and opposing realms of existence. Under such a structure of understanding reality, an individual has to make a choice between the two realms. Identifying with one realm forces one to be radically separated and opposed to the other realm.

It is within this dualistic framework that one can appreciate the important function the words of the apostle Andrew have in the *Acts of Andrew*. In the text, the apostle takes on the role of a revealer.[11] The words of the apostle are saving words inviting the audience to flee from the material world and bind itself to the soul of the apostle "which speeds toward things. . .beyond body" (ἐπειγομένην. . .εἰς τὰ ὑπὲρ σῶμα [*AAn* 57]). Through the words of the apostle, the inner being of a person can be awakened because the words are akin (συγγενής) to the inner nature of human beings and act like a mirror in which one can recognize one's true nature (*AAn* 47). It is in this context that the author of the *Acts of Andrew* can portray Andrew as a midwife who is able to bring about self-knowledge (*AAn* 7). From this, one can see that the soteriological emphasis is placed on the soul that can be awakened by the words as spoken by the apostle. The body, on the other hand, has become an entity from which one must flee.[12]

With the emphasis on the body-soul dualism and its soteriological implications, some scholars have suggested that the *Acts of Andrew* should be located within the trajectory of the Gnostic tradition.[13] Unlike many Gnostic texts, however, the *Acts of Andrew* does not propose that the teaching of the apostle is only available to a selected few. Further-

[11] See François Bovon, "La vie des apôtres. Traditions bibliques et narrations apocryphes," in *Actes apocryphes des apôtres*, 141–58; and idem, "The Words of Life in the Acts of the Apostle Andrew," *HTR* 87 (1994): 139–54.

[12] Prieur (*Acta Andreae*, 1:288) rightly notes that in the *Acts of Andrew*, "Le corps est une prison, un tissu de liens qui soumettent l'ἄναρχος à toutes sortes de vicissitudes."

[13] See, for example, Lipsius, *Die apokryphen Apostelgeschichten*, 1:543–622.

more, the *Acts of Andrew* is not concerned with the fall of the soul and it does not offer any elaborate Gnostic cosmogony. Therefore, the dualistic framework should be attributed not to the narrow development of Gnostic theology but to the wider cultural milieu of the second century[14] in which the influence of Middle Platonism is to be recognized.[15]

Eric R. Dodds has noted that the dichotomy between the self and the body comes "from classical Greece—the most far-reaching, and perhaps the most questionable, of all her gifts to human culture."[16] In the Platonic tradition the philosopher was one who was ashamed of his body and looked forward to the moment of being freed from the flesh to a spiritual afterlife; so does Porphyry begin his *Life of Plotinus*.[17] Among the Christian circles, Origen[18] attests to the widespread practice of sexual renunciation; and Marcionites have been noted for their refusal of sacraments to married persons.[19] Such evidence reveals an emphasis on the difference between the physical and the spiritual realms of a human person.[20]

From the above discussion, one can see both the importance of the body-soul dualism in the *Acts of Andrew* and that such dualism should be located within the cultural milieu of the early Christian centuries.[21]

---

[14] Prieur, *Acta Andreae*, 1:409–12. John G. Gager ("Body-Symbols and Social Reality: Resurrection, Incarnation, and Asceticism in Early Christianity," *Religion* 12 [1982]: 356) correctly observes that the body-soul dualism "was part of the cultural koine of late antiquity itself."

[15] For the development of Middle Platonism, see John Dillon, *The Middle Platonists: 80 B.C. to A.D. 220* (Ithaca, N.Y.: Cornell University Press, 1977); and Robert M. Berchman, *From Philo to Origen: Middle Platonism in Transition* (Chico, Calif.: Scholars Press, 1984).

[16] Eric R. Dodds, *Pagan and Christian in an Age of Anxiety* (Cambridge: Cambridge University Press, 1965), 29.

[17] See the discussion in Gedaliahu G. Stroumsa, "*Caro salutis cardo*: Shaping the Person in Early Christian Thought," *HR* 30 (1990): 25–50.

[18] Origen *Contra Celsum* 7.48.

[19] Tertullian *Adv. Marc.* 1.29.

[20] It should be noted that while ascetic practices do highlight certain aspects of the relationship between the body and the soul, asceticism should not be understood as a movement which detests the body. See Susanna Elm, *"Virgins of God": The Making of Asceticism in Late Antiquity* (Oxford: Clarendon Press, 1994), 131.

[21] While this section is focused on the body-soul dualism, the importance of ascetic practices in late antiquity should be studied with more detail. See, for example, Gail P. Corrington-Streete, "Trajectories of Ascetic Behavior," in *Asceticism*, ed. Vincent L. Wimbush and Richard Valantasis (New York: Oxford University Press, 1995), 119–24.

A further discussion of the origin of the *Acts of Andrew* is beyond the scope of this study.[22]

Physical Healing and Spiritual Redemption

In a work that emphasizes the soteriological importance of the soul and the hindrance of the physical body, one would expect the *Acts of Andrew* to follow the pattern as delineated in the study of Peregrine Horden, which examines the ascetic's reaction to illness: "Treatment of a physical ailment is unnecessary; indeed it is spiritually damaging."[23] However, one finds numerous healing stories in the *Acts of Andrew*. In this section I will examine the various strategies the author of the *Acts of Andrew* uses in appropriating these healing stories into the theological structure of his work.

Since the focus of this section is on the healing stories as they appear in the text, the problem of the underlying sources and traditions will not be addressed.[24] In examining the strategies the author of the *Acts of Andrew* uses in reformulating the focus of the physical healing stories, one has to recognize that "as narratives all miracle stories carry an interpretation."[25] The interpretation of a miracle can be embedded in the narrative itself, and it can also be expressed through the framework in which these healing miracle stories are placed. In the healing stories of the *Acts of Andrew*, three strategies can consistently be detected.[26] First, in some of these stories, the healing miracle is transformed into

---

[22] For the discussion of the relationship between the *Acts of Andrew* and Middle Platonism, see Manfred Hornschuh, "Acts of Andrew," *NTApoc*³ 2:392–95.

[23] Peregrine Horden, "The Death of Ascetics: Sickness and Monasticism in the Early Byzantine Middle East," in *Monks, Hermits and the Ascetic Tradition*, ed. William J. Sheils (Oxford: Basil Blackwell, 1985), 42.

[24] Dennis R. MacDonald ("From Audita to Legenda: Oral and Written Miracle Stories," *Forum* 2 [1986]: 20) argues that "behind the *Acts of Andrew* lies no antecedent oral Andrew tradition at all," and that the "author generates narrative about the apostle not by writing down oral tales, as did the author of the Pauline Acts, but by borrowing tale-type motifs and themes from other literature."

[25] Hans Dieter Betz, "The Early Christian Miracle Story: Some Observations on the Form Critical Problem," *Semeia* 11 (1978): 70.

[26] Please refer to the table at the end of this essay on the use of various strategies in different healing stories.

an exorcism story in which the illness is portrayed as caused by the demon; therefore, the actual act of healing becomes a spiritual warfare between Andrew and the devil. The second strategy the author uses is to emphasize the ultimate goal of the physical healing—the spiritual salvation of the people. Finally, in yet another group of healing stories, the ethical aspect is highlighted. The repeated and extensive uses of these strategies allow the author of the *Acts of Andrew* to shift the focus of the miracle stories from the physical to the spiritual realm.

Physical Healing and Exorcism

In some of the healing stories, the physicality of the act of healing is de-emphasized and the focus is shifted to the struggle between the opposing spiritual forces. On one occasion in Gregory's *Epitome*, when Andrew saw a man with his wife and son, all of whom were blind, he proclaimed: "Truly this is the work of the devil, for he has blinded them in mind and body" (*Epit.* 32). While the work of the devil is high-lighted, the "spiritual blindness" of that family is also noted. Therefore, in healing them, not only did Andrew restore the light of their "physical eyes" (*corporalium oculorum*), he also invokes the authority of Jesus Christ to "unlock the darkness of [their] minds" (*Epit.* 32).

Similarly, in the same *Epitome* one finds a story in which a blind man asked Andrew to give him money for clothing and food, but Andrew replied: "I know truly that this is not the voice of a human but of the devil, who does not allow that man to regain his sight" (*Epit.* 2). Again, the power of the demon is portrayed as at least partly responsible for preventing the blind man from achieving physical health.

Finally, one may cite a story of the healing of a man who died after being attacked by seven dogs (*Epit.* 7). Raising his eyes toward heaven, Andrew said:

> Lord, I know that the attack was the work of the demons that I expelled from Nicea. I now ask you, O gracious Jesus, to revive him, lest the enemy of humankind rejoice at his destruction. (*Epit.* 7)

Here, again, the death of the man is being described as the result of the attack of the demons.

From these examples, one can see that while formally these stories cannot be classified as exorcism stories,[27] the power of the demons is understood as the primary cause of physical illness. Such connection between exorcism and healing miracles can be traced back to the canonical gospel traditions, although the connection is not as prominent there. In Mark 9:25, Jesus healed a boy by rebuking the unclean spirit: "You spirit that keeps the boy from speaking and hearing, I command you, come out of him, and never enter him again!"[28] On another occasion, after healing a woman on the sabbath, Jesus said to the Pharisees, "And ought not this woman, a daughter of Abraham whom Satan bound for eighteen long years, be set free from this bondage on the sabbath day?" (Luke 13:16). Such a connection between physical illness and the power of the demons is utilized by the author of the *Acts of Andrew* in emphasizing the importance of the spiritual realm.[29]

Physical Healing and the Salvation of the People

A more common strategy used by the author of the *Acts of Andrew* is the placing of the emphasis on the spiritual consequences of the healing miracle stories.[30] Such strategy shifts the focus from the physical benefits to the spiritual benefits of the healing miracle stories. This strategy is used in different ways. First, one finds that in Gregory's *Epitome*, after being asked to heal a boy, Andrew started "preaching at great length matters pertaining to the salvation of the people" (*Epit.* 3)[31] before

[27] See Rudolf Bultmann, *The History of the Synoptic Tradition*, trans. John Marsh (New York: Harper and Row, 1963), 223; and Gerd Theissen, *The Miracle Stories of the Early Christian Tradition*, trans. Francis McDonagh (Edinburgh: Clark, 1983), 85–90.

[28] All biblical quotations are taken from the *New Revised Standard Version* (New York: Oxford University Press, 1989).

[29] Although similar strategies appear in both the *Acts of Andrew* and early Christian gospel traditions, the pervasive use of these strategies in almost every healing story in the *Acts of Andrew* is unprecedented.

[30] Eugene V. Gallagher ("Conversion and Salvation in the Apocryphal Acts of the Apostle," *The Second Century* 8 [1991]: 16) has rightly noted that, "More than anything else, in the AAA the miracle of resurrection is portrayed as eliciting conversion." See also Paul Achtemeier, "Jesus and the Disciples as Miracle Workers in the Apocryphal New Testament," in *Aspects of Religious Propaganda in Judaism and Early Christianity,* ed. Elisabeth Schüssler Fiorenza (Notre Dame, Ind.: University of Notre Dame Press, 1976), 170–71.

[31] Here, Gregory has reduced a long speech into a single clause.

healing the boy. Such an insertion of a lengthy speech between the request for healing and the actual performance of the miracle highlights the fact that the salvation of the people is much more important than the healing of the physically ill.[32]

This strategy is employed in a second way: to state explicitly that the purpose of the performance of miracles is to convert the people. In response to a request to heal a "gravely ill" man, Andrew said, "Bring him before us, and the Lord Jesus Christ will heal him so that you may believe" (*Epit.* 13). Similarly, before bringing the boy back to life, Andrew prayed:

> O Lord, I ask that the lad's breath return, so that by his resuscitation all may turn to you from forsaken idols. May his reviving cause the salvation of all the lost, so that they may no longer be subject to death but may win eternal life by having been made yours. (*Epit.* 7)

Such explicit statements concerning the purpose of performing miracles can be found throughout the text of the *Acts of Andrew*.[33]

Finally, this strategy is expressed in statements where the limit of the material benefit of the physical healing is emphasized. This is best summarized by a question Andrew asked the crowd: "What will it profit you, men of Thessalonica, if you see this done and still do not believe?" (*Epit.* 14).

From these examples, one can see that the author has appropriated many of the healing miracle stories into the theological framework of the *Acts of Andrew* by emphasizing the spiritual effects of these miracles.[34] Again, this strategy can also be found in the early gospel traditions.[35] In several miracle stories in the synoptic tradition (for

---

[32] See also *Epit.* 16, 18c.

[33] See also *Epit.* 18c, 19, 23, 24.

[34] Werner Kahl (*New Testament Miracle Stories in Their Religious-Historical Setting* [Göttingen: Vandenhoeck und Ruprecht, 1994], 207) noted that when faith becomes the purpose of the miracle, such a miracle story becomes an "instrumental narrative program."

[35] One can, of course, trace the development of such emphasis on the spiritual benefits back to the Platonic tradition that portrays Plato as one who recognized the priority of curing the soul over healing the body. Plato also emphasized that curing the soul is the prerequisite of healing the body (*Symposium* 186 and *Timaeus* 87–91). See Morton Kelsey, *Healing and Christianity: A Classic Study* (Minneapolis: Fortress Press, 1995), 36–40.

example, Mark 2:1–12; 7:24–30; 10:46–52), the faith of the one being healed is emphasized. In the Gospel of John, however, faith is never a prerequisite for Jesus' performance of miracles. The emphasis is placed rather on the effect of the miracles as producing a certain level of faith among the people (John 4:52; 9:38; 11:45). Such an emphasis is best illustrated by the summary statement in John 20:30–31:

> Now Jesus did many other signs in the presence of his disciples, which are not written in this book. But these are written so that you may come to believe that Jesus is the Messiah, the Son of God, and that through believing you may have life in his name.[36]

Similarly, in the *Acts of Andrew*, faith is likewise never a prerequisite but always the consequence of healing miracles. This would place the *Acts of Andrew* closer to the Johannine tradition in its understanding of the significance of miracles, although the Johannine critique of faith that is built upon the performance of miracles is absent in the *Acts of Andrew*.[37] As Luise Schottroff has noted, the tension between the physical reality of the miracles of Jesus and the spiritual reality of the words of Jesus the revealer is clearly present in the Gospel of John.[38] Such a tension, as we have noted, is also present in the *Acts of Andrew*. This would explain the similar usage of the same strategy in emphasizing the spiritual effects of healing miracles in both the signs source of the Gospel of John and the *Acts of Andrew*.

Physical Healing and Ethical Exhortation

The final strategy the author of the *Acts of Andrew* uses is the highlighting of the ethical aspect. In some stories, the illness is attributed to the

---

[36] It should be noted, however, that John 20:30–31 is probably the original ending of the signs source which John uses; and the critique of faith that is based on miracles is also present in the Gospel of John. See Helmut Koester, "One Jesus and Four Primitive Gospels," in James M. Robinson and Helmut Koester, *Trajectories through Early Christianity* (Philadelphia: Fortress Press, 1971), 187–93.

[37] See John 5:18; 11:47–53; 20:29.

[38] Luise Schottroff, *Der Glaubende und die feindliche Welt. Beobachtungen zum gnostischen Dualismus und seiner Bedeutung für Paulus und das Johannesevangelium* (Wissenschaftliche Monographien zum Alten und Neuen Testament 37; Neukirchen-Vluyn: Neukirchener Verlag, 1970), 228–45.

sinful life of the subject; and a decision to turn away from the immoral lifestyle frequently becomes the condition under which the subject can be healed. Again, the ethical benefit is portrayed as far more important than the physical benefit of the actual healing. This point is well illustrated by the words Andrew spoke to a man when he healed him:

> Your grave illness is quite appropriate: you left your own marriage bed and slept with a prostitute. Arise in the name of the Lord Jesus Christ, stand up whole, and sin no more, lest you incur a worse ailment. (*Epit.* 5)

The relationship between moral life and health conditions is noted even more explicitly in Andrew's statement to the woman "swollen with dropsy":

> Lord Jesus Christ, I entreat your kind mercy that you might listen to your servant and be ready, so that if this woman returns to the lewd filth which she formerly practiced, she may by no means be healed. O Lord, by whose power future events are known, if you know that she is able to abstain from this disgrace, let her be healed at your command. (*Epit.* 5)

In Gregory's *Epitome*, one finds a variation of the use of this strategy in which the moral life of a father becomes a condition for the healing of his child. To the father, Andrew said:

> Listen mister, you beg for your son to be healed, yet at your own home you detain in shackles people with rotting flesh. If you want your prayers to come before God, first release the chains of those who suffer, so that your son too may be freed of his disability. I see that your cruelty impedes my prayers. (*Epit.* 15)

In the Gospel traditions, the connection between sin and illness is not as obvious.[39] In Mark 2:1–12 (also Matt 9:1–8 and Luke 5:17–26), a paralytic was brought to Jesus and Jesus forgave his sins. While the exact relationship between the sin of the paralytic and his illness is not

---

[39] The connection between sin and illness is well established in the Jewish tradition; see 2 Sam 12:13; 2 Chron 7:14; 30:13–20; Ps 41:5; Isa 6:10; 19:22; 38:16–17; 57:18–19; Jer 3:22; 4QPrNab; *b. Ned.* 41a.

clear, a connection between forgiveness and healing is affirmed here.[40] The connection between sin and illness is clearer in the story of the healing at Bethesda (John 5:1–15). When Jesus saw the man he healed earlier, he said, "See you have been made well! Do not sin any more, so that nothing worse happens to you" (John 5:14). Such statements are, however, qualified by John 9:3, in which a consistent correlation between sin and illness is denied.[41] Nevertheless, the plausible connection between sin and illness does remain in the texts of the canonical gospels. Such a connection is utilized by the author of the *Acts of Andrew* in expanding the focus of the healing miracles beyond the mere concern for the physical body.

From the above discussion of the three strategies, one can see that the author of the *Acts of Andrew* consistently attempts to shift the focus of the healing stories away from the physical benefits of the miracles. While healing stories in the *Acts of Andrew* describe the "treatment" of illnesses by means of miraculous power, the motif of restoration to health is never the primary focus of these stories. Without redefining the genre of these stories, one is nevertheless justified in designating all of these miracle stories as an "instrumental narrative program" in which "the liquidation of a lack related to health. . .becomes subordinate to a main [narrative program] describing the liquidation of a lack unrelated to the issue of health."[42]

The *Acts of Andrew* within the Theological Context of Second-Century Christianity

In examining the understanding of miracles in one of the apocryphal acts, it is appropriate to locate the discussion within the wider theological context of second-century Christianity.[43] In this section, Irenaeus's understanding of miracles will be discussed briefly. The writings of

---

[40] See Geza Vermes, *Jesus the Jew* (Philadelphia: Fortress Press, 1973), 68.

[41] See also Luke 13:1–5.

[42] Kahl, *New Testament Miracle Stories*, 207.

[43] I am following Prieur (*Acta Andreae*, 1:413–14) in dating the *Acts of Andrew* to the second half of the second century C.E.

Irenaeus have been selected because he is widely recognized as one of the most important figures in second-century Christianity;[44] and more importantly, because his work interacts with the works of other theological movements, especially those which affirm the body-soul dualism.

Before examining Irenaeus's comments on miracles, his anthropological presuppositions should first be noted. In contrast to those who affirm the body-soul dualism, Irenaeus insists that salvation itself is that of the flesh.[45] Irenaeus's concern for the importance of the physical body can be seen from his exegesis of Colossians 1:21–22[46] in which he emphasizes that the Lord died in a carnal body, not merely in a mystical body (against Marcion) or in a *sui generis* flesh (against the Valentinians). Furthermore, Irenaeus affirms that the reconciliation of Christ and human beings has taken place in Christ's nature according to the flesh.[47] The unity of body and soul is explicitly stated in *Adversus haereses*,[48] in which Irenaeus claims:

> Now the soul and the spirit are certainly a part of the man, but certainly not the man; for the perfect man consists in the commingling and the union of the soul receiving the spirit of the Father, and the admixture of that fleshly nature which was molded after the image of God. (*Adv. haer.* 5.6.1)

---

[44] Johannes Quasten (*Patrology*, vol. 1, *The Beginnings of Patristic Literature* [Utrecht-Antwerp: Spectrum Publishers, 1975], 287) considers Irenaeus to be the greatest Christian theologian of the second century. In singling out Irenaeus, however, I do not intend to suggest that his theology represents the totality of the theological thinking of mainstream second-century Christianity. The differences between eastern and western Christianity should not be ignored, and many differences between the *Acts of Andrew* and the writings of Irenaeus may reflect the differences between the East and the West rather than between mainstream and "heterodox" theologies.

[45] *Adv. haer.* 2.29.2; 4.18.5; 5.2.3; 5.4.1; 5.5.2; 5.6.2; 5.15.1; 5.31.2. In this section, I am indebted to Antonio Orbe, *Anthropología de San Ireneo* (Madrid: Biblioteca de Autores Cristianos, 1969).

[46] *Adv. haer.* 5.14.2–3.

[47] See, for example, *Adv. haer.* 4.20.2.

[48] In this essay, quotations from Irenaeus's writings are taken from *The Writings of the Apostolic Fathers, Justin Martyr, Irenaeus*, ed. Alexander Roberts and James Donaldson (Ante-Nicene Christian Library 1; 1870; American reprint, Grand Rapids, Mich.: Eerdmans, 1981).

Gedaliahu G. Stroumsa sees Irenaeus's anthropology as a "radical break with the Platonic conception of man and the elaboration of a new anthropology, which saw the essence of man not in his soul but in the composite of soul and body."[49] Noting the differences between the anthropological presuppositions of the author of the *Acts of Andrew* and that of Irenaeus, we shall now examine how these result in their distinct understanding of miracles.

Most of Irenaeus's comments on miracles occur in his discussion of the healings of Jesus.[50] Many of these references occur in Book Five of *Adversus haereses*, in which Irenaeus is most concerned with refuting the Gnostic disparagement of the body. Irenaeus's concern with the physical body can be seen in his emphasis on the understanding of healing as the renewal of the basic substance of the body:[51]

> He whose withered hand was healed, and all who were healed generally, did not change those parts of their bodies, which had at their birth come forth from the womb, but simply obtained these anew in a healthy condition. (*Adv. haer.* 5.12.5)

Such emphasis on the physical body is also reflected in his discussion of the purpose of the healing miracles. Unlike the author of the *Acts of Andrew*, who de-emphasizes the physical benefit of the healing events, Irenaeus argues that the very fact of Jesus' healing attests to the enduring importance of the body. This argument is best articulated in the following statement:

> For what was his object in healing [different] portions of the flesh, and restoring them to their original condition, if those parts which had been

---

[49] Stroumsa, "*Caro salutis cardo*," 42. For a discussion of the complexity of Irenaeus's anthropology, see Adalbert G. Hamman, *L'homme, image de Dieu. Anthropologie patristique* (Paris: Desclée, 1986), and Caroline W. Bynum, *The Resurrection of the Body in Western Christianity, 200–1336* (New York: Columbia University Press, 1995), 34–43.

[50] Irenaeus's discussion of the healing miracles of Jesus occurs in more than thirty-five passages in *Adv. haer.*

[51] For further discussion of Irenaeus's understanding of healing as a process of repair, see R. J. S. Barrett-Lennard, *Christian Healing after the New Testament* (New York: University Press of America, 1994), 97–98.

healed by him were not in a position to obtain salvation? For if it was merely a temporary benefit which He offered, He granted nothing of importance to those who were the subjects of His healing. (*Adv. haer.* 5.12.6)

Furthermore, Irenaeus relates the significance of healing miracles to the work of redemption that is understood as the act of a new creation:

For the Maker of all things, the Word of God, who did also from the beginning form man, when He found His handiwork impaired by wickedness, performed upon it all kinds of healing. (*Adv. haer.* 5.12.6)

From this quotation, one can see that while the author of the *Acts of Andrew* focuses on spiritual restoration, Irenaeus emphasizes "all kinds of healing," including physical healing. Irenaeus further notes that "at another time He [Jesus] did once for all restore man sound and whole in all points, preparing him perfect for Himself unto the resurrection" (*Adv. haer.* 5.12.6). Such incorporation of physical healing into the work of redemption should not be ignored.[52]

The above discussion shows how different anthropological perspectives could produce different understandings of the focus of the healing miracle stories.[53] For Irenaeus, who affirms the significance of both the body and the soul, the healing stories represent a stage in the redemptive history of humankind. For the author of the *Acts of Andrew*, who maintains the body-soul dualism, however, the healing stories have to be reappropriated and different strategies have to be employed in shifting the focus away from the physical benefits of the miracles.

[52] For a detailed discussion, see Barrett-Lennard, *Christian Healing after the New Testament*, 89–165.

[53] Instead of comparing miracle stories in the *Acts of Andrew* with statements on the theological interpretation of miracles in Irenaeus's writings, I understand that a more desirable approach is to compare the structure of miracle stories as they appear in the *Acts of Andrew* and the writings of Irenaeus. This is not possible, however, because Irenaeus does not include any full account of healing stories in his writings. G. W. H. Lampe ("Miracles and Early Christian Apologetic," in *Miracles: Cambridge Studies in Their History and Philosophy*, ed. Charles F. D. Moule [London: Mowbray, 1965], 205–18) has argued that such absence of miracle accounts reflects the fact that mainstream Christian writers do not always utilize miracle stories as apologetic tools.

Healing and Community

The significance of these healing stories for the definition of the implied community should also be noted. In other words, to consider these miracle stories merely as apologetic tools[54] fails to appreciate the importance of the role these stories play in the overall rhetorical plan of the *Acts of Andrew*. In this section, I will attempt to examine further the positive contributions the healing stories make in the construction of the theological program for the community.[55]

Recent studies on health care systems have shown that one should not consider healing as an isolated phenomenon. In examining the practice of medicine in different cultural contexts, Arthur Kleinman, the pioneer of medical anthropology, argues that healing should be considered as a cultural system embodying symbolic meanings anchored in particular patterns of social arrangements:

> The health care system, like other cultural systems, integrates the health-related components of society. These include patterns of belief about the causes of illness; norms governing choice and evaluation of treatment; socially-legitimated statuses, roles, power relationships, interaction settings and institutions.[56]

In insisting that one should view acts of healing within the web of social relationship, Kleinman concludes that "biomedical and psychiatric reductions make it impossible to study healing from [the] cultural standpoint."[57]

---

[54] See, for example, Maurice Miles ("Miracles in the Early Church," in Moule, *Miracles*, 225), who designates the use of miracles in the apocryphal acts as merely a "naïve appeal to miracle."

[55] In using the word "community" in this section of the essay, I am referring to the implied community within the symbolic universe of the *Acts of Andrew*. While a connection between such an implied community and an actual community cannot be denied, the distinction has to be maintained since a simple linear relationship between the two cannot be established.

[56] Arthur Kleinman, *Patients and Healers in the Context of Culture: An Exploration of the Borderland between Anthropology, Medicine, and Psychiatry* (Berkeley: University of California Press, 1980), 24.

[57] Ibid., 364.

It will be helpful to apply some of these insights in examining the wider significance of the discussed strategies for the definition of the community within the *Acts of Andrew*.[58] Kleinman suggests that clinical practice "creates particular social worlds" through the redefinition of the values of the community.[59] In the *Acts of Andrew*, the consistent use of various methods may also be understood as tools in creating the social world of an alternate community. Likewise, Peter Brown aptly notes that "the history of what constitutes a 'cure' in a given society is a history of that society's values."[60] In utilizing the various strategies, the author of the *Acts of Andrew* is able to redefine (or reflect) the value of the community by noting that the ultimate cure exists beyond the physical realm.[61] The body-soul dualism is thus maintained and the emphasis is now shifted to the saving words of the apostle. The healing miracles become ritual acts in which the ultimate values of the community are affirmed with the curing of the soul. These healing stories thus produce a model for the reformulation of cultural values within which the implied audience is expected to operate.

Similarly, one may also argue that the emphasis on asceticism in the *Acts of Andrew* also serves to delineate the identity of the community in relation to the larger society.[62] In this sense, both the use of the various strategies to de-emphasize the importance of the physical body and the emphasis on the importance of an ascetic life become tools for the author of the *Acts of Andrew* to construct his symbolic universe. Here, one can only agree with Brown in recognizing that the body becomes a bridge which serves to provide a contact point between the community

---

[58] I am aware of the problems of applying anthropological and sociological analyses to literary texts. Insights from anthropological and sociological studies may, however, be used in highlighting certain aspects that traditional historical-literary methods have failed to address.

[59] Kleinman, *Patients and Healers*, 34.

[60] Peter Brown, *Society and the Holy in Late Antiquity* (Berkeley: University of California Press, 1982), 142.

[61] On a society's consideration of the relationship between the causes of illness and the appropriate cure, see Robert A. Hahn, *Sickness and Healing: An Anthropological Perspective* (New Haven, Conn.: Yale University Press, 1995), 19.

[62] See, for example, Gager, "Body-Symbols and Social Reality," 347–48.

and the external world and at the same time to separate the two.[63]

Finally, not only do the healing stories redefine the identity of the community, they also serve to create a web of power relationships. In emphasizing the spiritual realm in healing miracle stories, the apostle Andrew becomes one who has the power over both the physical and spiritual welfare of the people.[64] In many cases, healing stories became the *rites de passage* through which the subject transfers his or her allegiance to the apostle Andrew.[65] In other cases where one finds competition between Andrew and others, Andrew's miracles further affirm his role as the one who can provide protection for his followers.[66]

It is clear that healing stories play a significant role in redefining the community within the world of the *Acts of Andrew*. The various strategies that the author of the *Acts of Andrew* uses in shifting the focus away from the physical realm are crucial in such a process of redefinition.

Conclusion

An examination of the healing stories in the *Acts of Andrew* allows one to see how various strategies are utilized in incorporating the healing miracles into the theological program of the author. It becomes apparent that both the healing stories and the contexts in which these stories were placed reflect the careful art of the author in transforming traditional materials to depict the life of the apostle Andrew.

---

[63] Brown, "Bodies and Minds," 485. Similarly, Mary Douglas ("Social Preconditions of Enthusiasm and Heterodoxy," in *Forms of Symbolic Action*, ed. Robert F. Spencer [Seattle: American Ethnological Society, 1969], 71) points out that "the human body is never seen as a body without at the same time being treated as an image of society."

[64] Outside of the contexts of healing miracles, Andrew is also presented with remarkable characteristics (e.g., *Epit.* 11.18, *AAn* 59.7–10). The importance of the role of Andrew as the center of drama may explain the lack of an explicit Christology in the *Acts of Andrew*. For a further discussion of the role of Andrew in the *Acts of Andrew*, see Jean-Marc Prieur, "La figure de l'apôtre dans les Actes apocryphes d'André," in *Actes apocryphes des apôtres*, 121–39.

[65] See, especially, *Epit.* 3, 7, 14, 15, 16. Bovon ("Miracles, magie et guérison," 255) notes that "le miracle est une figure, le sacrement un signe efficace."

[66] See, for example, *Epit.* 4, 18c, 22.

TABLE 1. HEALING MIRACLES IN THE *ACTS OF ANDREW*

	Problem	Request	Description of Andrew	Invocation	Action	Condition (e.g., Faith)	Setting	Reaction	Possible Opponents	Focus/ Strategy
Epit. 2	Blind	Yes	Apostle of Christ	No (but see reaction)	Touched his eyes	None	Public	Glorified God	The Devil	Power of demons
Epit. 3	Dead	Yes	Servant of God	Name of Jesus Christ	Verbal	None	Public	All believed and were baptized	None	Preached to the salvation of the people after the request to heal and before healing the boy
Epit. 5 (i)	Gravely ill	Yes	God's servant; enemy of the human race	Name of the Lord Jesus Christ	Verbal	None	Public	Believed in the Lord; required to abstain from immoral acts	None	Andrew rebuked him since his illness is the result of immoral acts
Epit. 5 (ii)	Gravely ill	Yes	None	Prayer	Verbal	Lead a moral life	Public	Believed in the Lord; required to abstain from immoral acts	None	Andrew rebuked her since her illness is the result of immoral acts
Epit. 7	Dead	None	His (God's/ Christ's) servant	Prayer; Name of Jesus Christ	Verbal	The father will give the boy to the apostle	Public	Glorified God	Demon	Power of demons; Andrew prayed that the body be healed "so that all may turn to you from forsaken idols"
Epit. 13	Gravely ill	Yes	None	No (but see reaction)	Verbal (indirect)	None	Public	Glorified God and said, "No one equals Andrew's God"	None	Andrew said, "The Lord Jesus Christ will heal him so that you may believe"

Epit. 14	Dead	Yes	The stranger who proclaims the true God; man of God	Name of Jesus Christ	Verbal	None	Public	All believed	Demon	The people said to Andrew, "be assured that if he is raised we will all believe"
Epit. 15	Crippled	Yes	Man of God; servant of God	Name of Jesus Christ	Verbal	Lead a moral life	Public	All believed as the healed boy himself healed others	None	The boy's health depends on the moral life of his father
Epit. 16	"Plagued by extreme torment"	Yes	Servant of God	None	None	Reject the earthly and crave the eternal	Public	All believed and praised him	None	Before Andrew healed the girl, he "persuaded everyone to forsake idols and to believe in the true God"
Epit. 18c (i)	Dead	None	The magician called by the proconsul	Prayer	Verbal	None	Public	Glorified God	Proconsul Varianus	Andrew asked the proconsul to "believe in the true God" before the healing
Epit. 18c (ii)	Dead	None	None	Name of Christ, prayer	Took the corpse's hand	None	Public	Magnified God	Proconsul Varianus	Andrew said, "I will revive his son in the name of Christ whom I preach, so that you might more easily believe"
Epit. 19	Dead	Yes	None	Name of Jesus Christ	Verbal	None	Public	Fell at the apostle's feet and gave thanks	Snake, called "enemy" (demon?)	Before healing the boy, Andrew said, "Our God. . .sent me here so that you might believe in him"

TABLE 1. HEALING MIRACLES IN THE *ACTS OF ANDREW* (CONTINUED)

	Problem	Request	Description of Andrew	Invocation	Action	Condition (e.g., Faith)	Setting	Reaction	Possible Opponents	Focus/ Strategy
Epit. 23	Dead	Yes	Beloved of God	Prayer; name of Jesus	Touched her head	None	Public	Reconciled with her husband	Demon	Andrew prayed that she might be healed "so that all may know that you are the Lord God"
Epit. 24 (i)	Dead	None	Servant of the true God	Prayer	Grabbed the dead man's hand	None	Public	Fell at Andrew's feet (and requested that others be saved also)	The enemy (demon?)	Andrew said, "This corpse should be resuscitated, so that we might learn what the enemy has done to him"
Epit. 24 (ii)	Dead	Yes	Servant of the true God	Prayer	Raised the hands of the corpse to heaven	None	Public	Glorified God: "None is like you, O Lord"	The enemy (demon?)	Andrew prayed that the corpses be brought forth from the sea "that they too may know that you are the true and only God"
Epit. 32	Blind	None	None	Name of Jesus Christ	Touched their eyes	None	Public	Kissed his feet, glorified and thanked God; many believed	Devil	Power of the Devil

An Inquiry into the Relationship between Community and Text: The Apocryphal *Acts of Philip* 1 and the Encratites of Asia Minor

Richard N. Slater

Introduction

The publication in 1996 of the French translation of the *Acts of Philip* according to the manuscript *Xenophontos 32* from Mount Athos, with notes and commentary, is the result of years of scholarship on this long-neglected apocryphal writing.[1] Interest in the recently rediscovered manuscript of *Xenophontos 32* had already been stimulated by the publication, in 1989, of its version of act 1 of the *Acts of Philip*.[2] A comparison with the heretofore standard text of *Vaticanus graecus 824*[3] revealed that *Xenophontos 32* contained substantial new material.

---

[1] Amsler, Bovon, and Bouvier, *Actes de l'apôtre Philippe*.

[2] Bertrand Bouvier and François Bovon, "Actes de Philippe, I, d'après un manuscrit inédit," in *Œcumenica et Patristica. Festschrift für Wilhelm Schneemelcher zum 75. Geburtstag*, ed. Damaskinos Papandreou, Wolfgang A. Bienert, and Knut Schäferdiek (Stuttgart: Kohlhammer, 1989), 367–94. See Christopher R. Matthews, "Trajectories through the Philip Tradition" (Th.D. diss.; Harvard University, 1993), 228–88; and Frédéric Amsler, "Les Actes Apocryphes de Philippe: Commentaire" (Th.D. diss.; Université de Genève: Faculté autonome de théologie protestante, 1994). For additional information on the *Acts of Philip*, see François Bovon, "Les Actes de Philippe," *ANRW* II 25/6:4431–527; idem, "Acts of Philip," *ABD* 5:312; Aurelio de Santos Otero, "Acta Philippi," in *NTApoc*[5] 2:468–73.

[3] Maximilien Bonnet, "Acta Philippi," in *AAA* 2/2:1–90.

Indeed, the differences between these two manuscripts were so great as to suggest that they might represent two very different stages in the development of the text.

Act 1 of the *Acts of Philip* is built upon the structure of a miracle story. Peculiar to the longer text of *Xenophontos 32* is a lengthy tour of hell set within the miracle story, containing a detailed list of sins, sinners, and chastisements. The narration of this tour is replete with terrifying scenes of torture and punishment, accompanied by explanatory speeches. The sounds and sights of this inferno hint at the existence of an intense conflict, never clearly described but powerfully present in the text. It seems that the author has in mind a reader familiar with this conflict, perhaps a party to the conflict, for whom no explanation is needed. Indeed, it seems as though the tour is written for the benefit of this reader, who would find in the ideals expressed by both the miracle story and the tour of hell encouragement for the struggle.

In this study I will look carefully at the two manuscript traditions of act 1 represented by *Vaticanus graecus 824* and *Xenophontos 32*, inquiring into the character of their difference and its meaning. I will endeavor to establish the thesis that the longer text of *Xenophontos 32*, with its tour of hell, demonstrates a relationship to a particular community, reflecting that community's ideals as well as its circumstance of conflict.

Textual Issues and Matters of Genre

The Miracle Story: Luke and the Acts of Philip

The miracle story of act 1 is modeled upon Luke's account of Jesus raising the only child of the widow of Nain (Luke 7:11–17).[4] The following comparison reveals the structural similarity of the two texts and shows how the author of the *Acts of Philip* adapted the miracle story model to express the ideals and address the needs of the *Acts of Philip* community.

---

[4] Bovon, "Actes de Philippe," 4475. Matthews ("Trajectories," 257) also notes the similarity of Philostratus *Vit. Ap.* 4.45.

TABLE 1. COMPARISON OF LUKE AND ACT 1 OF THE *ACTS OF PHILIP*[5]

Luke 7:11–17	*Acts of Philip* 1
v. 11: Jesus goes to Nain with disciples and a great crowd.	§ 1: Philip leaves Galilee.
v. 12: The only son of a widow is being carried out. A large crowd accompanies the widow.	§ 1: The only son of a widow is being carried out.
v. 13: Jesus has compassion and speaks: "Do not weep."	§§ 1–3: Philip, saddened, engages the widow in dialogue wherein the powerlessness of pagan gods is detailed. Philip promises to raise her son. The widow pledges to lead a life of sexual and dietary purity.
vv. 14–15:	§ 3 [4]: The widow speaks: "I believe in Jesus. . . ."
Jesus touches the bier, and speaks: "Young man, I say to you arise."	§ 4: Philip approaches the corpse and speaks: "Arise, young man, it is Jesus who raises you to his glory."
The dead young man sits up and begins to speak. (His speech is not recorded.)	*Vaticanus graecus 824*, § 4: The young man arises and speaks briefly of a visit to a prison of judgment, and the experience of torment and suffering.
	Xenophontos 32, §§ 4–17: The young man arises and speaks at great length of a visit to a place of torment and suffering. Each of eight scenes is described in great detail, replete with speeches. A squall lifts him from the place of torment and returns him to earth, where he sees Philip and his mother.
vv. 16–17: Fear seizes the crowd and they glorify God. Jesus' fame spreads.	§ 18 [5]: The young man believes and with his mother is baptized. Many are converted and baptized. The young man becomes a follower of the Apostle. All glorify God.

[5] See Matthews, "Trajectories," 258.

In both accounts the healer encounters a widow whose son has died. In act 1 of the *Acts of Philip*, the widow describes the failure of pagan gods and a clairvoyant to come to her aid and laments that she has scorned the Christians and lost her only son. Philip assures her that her experience is not peculiar, and that he will raise her son to life again "by the power of my God, Jesus Christ" (*APh* 1.2).[6] Her gratitude is rather particularly expressed, as she, a non-Christian, states that it would be better to live the ascetic life, practicing celibacy, abstaining from eating that which excites the body, such as wine and meat, eating instead bread and water (*APh* 1.2).

The miracle stories differ at several points. Jesus is accompanied by his disciples and a large crowd, while Philip appears to be alone. Luke portrays Jesus as drawing upon God's power in raising the young man from the dead, while in the *Acts of Philip* Jesus is the source of divine power.[7] The lengthy dialogue of the *Acts of Philip* differs from Luke, whose dialogue is brief. When the resuscitation has been accomplished, the young man of act 1, *Xenophontos 32*, begins to speak, narrating at length things seen in the afterworld. The revived young man in act 1, *Vaticanus graecus 824*, speaks only briefly of a prison of judgment and the experience of torments and sufferings which the human tongue is incapable of expressing (*APh* 1.4). The young man in Luke 7 is said to speak, but his words are not recorded (7:15).

Acts of Philip *1 and* Acts of Thomas *6*

The placement of the tour of hell within the miracle story involves a noticeable shift in genre. As Frédéric Amsler has shown, a similar literary structure occurs in *Acts of Thomas* 6.51–61.[8] There a young woman

---

[6] All translations in this chapter are my own, unless otherwise indicated. Since the 1989 edition, the enumeration of the paragraphs of act 1, according to the *Xenophontos 32*, has been changed for practical reasons. The enumeration here of *Xenophontos 32* is the new one from the French translation in Amsler, Bovon, and Bouvier, *Actes de l'apôtre Philippe*. The old enumeration is provided once (p. 289), in brackets, which is the one from the Greek text published by Bouvier and Bovon, "Actes de Philippe, I." The enumeration of *Vaticanus graecus 824* is that of *AAA* 2/2.

[7] Amsler, "Commentaire," 36.

[8] Ibid., 51–53.

is raised from the dead and, after her resuscitation, describes in careful detail a "dreadful and cruel" place from which she has been delivered.

In both the *Acts of Philip* and the *Acts of Thomas*, it is the statement by the resuscitated that they have seen something of another world, a world of punishments and chastisements, that invites the shift in genre from miracle story to tour of hell (*ATh* 6.54; *APh* 1.4–5). At the conclusion of the tour of hell, the text returns to the miracle story genre, and finds the revived person conversing with the apostle. The conclusion provides testimony that this witness has effected the conversion of many, and the story ends with the apostle embarking on yet another journey on behalf of the Christ (*APh* 1.18; cf. *ATh* 6.59).

The two works differ in several important ways. The principal actors in the *Acts of Philip* are a widow whose only son has died and the apostle Philip (*APh* 1.1). In the *Acts of Thomas* the actors include the apostle Thomas, a young man converted to the ascetic Christian life by Thomas, and a young woman loved by the young man but murdered by him for her unwillingness to join him in the ascetic life (*ATh* 6.51). The guide of the other-worldly tour in the *Acts of Philip* is an angel, while the guide in the *Acts of Thomas* is a dark, hateful, and exceedingly dirty man (*ATh* 6.55). The repugnant guide explains the punishments in the *Acts of Thomas*, while in the *Acts of Philip*, both the victims and the angel guide explain the punishments. The dialogue that characterizes act 1 of the *Acts of Philip* stands in contrast to the monologue of *Acts of Thomas* 6 in which the narrator gives detailed explanations, in spite of the absence of questions or comments from the young woman. The torments in the two texts are distinct, with the *Acts of Thomas* including hanging punishments (*ATh* 6.56), which are characteristic of the tours of hell genre but completely absent from the *Acts of Philip*.[9] While the *Acts of Thomas* tour includes both sins of speech and sexual sins, the *Acts of Philip* tour includes only sins of speech.[10] The element of conflict with ecclesiastical authorities, so powerfully expressed in the *Acts of Philip*, is absent from the *Acts of Thomas*.

---

[9] Martha Himmelfarb, *Tours of Hell: An Apocalyptic Form in Jewish and Christian Literature* (Philadelphia: University of Pennsylvania Press, 1983), 45–67, 82–92.

[10] See n. 31 below.

The similarity in literary structure suggests that the author/redactor of the *Acts of Philip* was familiar with the *Acts of Thomas* miracle story/ tour of hell.[11] One need not find in their structural similarity a rigid literary dependence, however, for the plots of the miracle stories and the contents of the tours bear little resemblance to each other.[12] At most, it would seem that the author of the *Acts of Philip* found in the *Acts of Thomas* a model through which an important message could be communicated to the intended readers.

Comparing the Principal Manuscripts

An issue which challenges every student of *Acts of Philip* 1 is the remarkable difference in the length and content between the two major manuscripts. As we consider the source of this variation, we must understand that rules learned for the textual criticism of canonical writings may not be relied upon for the study of apocryphal writings. In particular, the maxim *lectio breuior lectio potior* (the shorter reading is the more probable reading) must be suspended, for many apocryphal writings were abbreviated and excerpted for liturgical and commemorative purposes and edited to reduce or eliminate material offensive to orthodox editors.[13]

Examining the two texts of act 1 reveals that, with the exception of the tour of hell and the brief literary bridges that connect the tour to the miracle story, the two manuscripts are very much alike. They differ mostly in word order and variations in verb tense and form. It is the tour itself that distinguishes them and encourages inquiry into the history and development of the text. Since external witness to the text is scant, scholars have focused upon the internal evidence of the text. To date, three principal explanations have emerged: 1) the text was adapted

[11] This is not surprising, for the *Acts of Thomas* predates the *Acts of Philip* and was circulated widely among encratic sects and orthodox groups alike. H. J. W. Drijvers, "Acts of Thomas," in *NTApoc*[5] 2:323–24.

[12] Amsler, "Commentaire," 53. Amsler concludes that a literary dependence of *APh* 1 upon *ATh* 6 is improbable.

[13] The well-known abridgement of the *Acts of Andrew* by Gregory of Tours, the so-called *Epitome*, is one good example of the kind of editing to which apocryphal texts were subjected. See J.-M. Prieur, "The Acts of Andrew," in *NTApoc*[5] 2:103. See also, in this volume, François Bovon, "Byzantine Witnesses for the Apocryphal Acts of the Apostles," and "Editing the Apocryphal Acts of the Apostles."

to the changing needs of the communities; 2) ideological concerns led to censorship of the text; or 3) some combination of the above.

Christopher R. Matthews suggests that act 1 was redactionally developed over time, beginning with a simple miracle story that was subsequently expanded by filling the frame with dialogue: "Thus the frame of a miracle story became the setting for an excursus that complains about the inadequacy of gods and seers (§ 1), another that highlights the necessity of living an ascetical Christian life (§ 3), and a third that briefly (according to Bonnet's edition) alludes to the punishments that await the wicked after death (§ 4)."[14] His thesis that the community may have adapted the text as their needs changed over time[15] may find support in the work of Christine M. Thomas. Thomas argues that the concept of an original text may not have been meaningful to a scribe or copyist in antiquity: "Even if we grant the existence of an 'original text' written by a single author, we must reckon with a whole string of people who did not strive to preserve this original text, but perceived the liberty to go about rewriting it in their own peculiar fashion."[16] She further notes that a text may wear different faces at different points in its history, expressing the "shifting concerns of editors and copyists of the text over a span of time."[17] Her observations, when applied to act 1, would suggest that its redaction to include or exclude the tour of hell may well have been the result of these shifting concerns.

François Bovon argues that ideological motivations are responsible for many of the variations in apocryphal texts. In the brief introduction accompanying their publication of act 1 of the *Acts of Philip* according to the manuscript *Xenophontos 32*, Bertrand Bouvier and Bovon note that *Xenophontos 32* offers a detailed vision of the inferno that seems to have been censured in *Vaticanus graecus 824*.[18] In his study of the *Acts of Philip*, Bovon observes that portions of other acts in *Xenophontos 32* are missing; he suggests that it may have been a theological concern that prompted an unknown hand to tear folios from

[14] Matthews, "Trajectories," 256.
[15] Ibid., 263.
[16] Thomas, "The Acts of Peter," 21.
[17] Ibid., 23.
[18] Bouvier and Bovon, "Actes de Philippe, I," 367. See also Bovon, "Acts of Philip," 5:312.

the document.[19] Citing Lou H. Silberman's work on Jewish literature and Pierre Vidal-Naquet's study of Josephus, which show that "ancient historians frequently arranged and rearranged the material of their sources on the basis of doctrinal or ideological criteria," Bovon uses selections from the *Acts of Philip* to illustrate his argument that editorial modification of a text is not so much a matter of historical truth as it is an issue of ideological orientation.[20] In his discussion of other Greek texts related to the apostle Philip, Bovon evaluates a tenth-century text of Simeon Metaphrastes and describes how its report of Philip's martyrdom is editorially domesticated, in comparison with more primitive reports, by the elimination of encratism, the anger of the apostle, the presence of animals, and speculation on the cross.[21]

Frédéric Amsler considers *Vaticanus graecus 824* also to be an expurgated text dependent upon *Xenophontos 32* and censured by those whose orthodox interest was not so much the elimination of encratic traits as the suppression of the content of the tour of hell.[22] He shows how the editor of *Vaticanus graecus 824* reworked the text of *Xenophontos 32*, disrupting a carefully constructed thought built around three εἰ statements by expanding and refocusing the second statement (see table 2).[23] These εἰ statements summarize what may be learned from the tour of hell. Remnants of the εἰ statements are still evident in *Vaticanus graecus 824*, documenting the editor's dependence upon *Xenophontos 32* and revealing the editor's effort at reshaping the text by the addition of ὑπὸ τοῦ ἀνθρώπου τούτου κηρυττομένῳ ("proclaimed by this man") to the second εἰ statement. This addition modifies the reference point of the second εἰ statement so that it no longer refers to the tour of hell but to the apostle's proclamation last heard in the miracle story. The result of the editor's work, Amsler concludes, is a degrading of the text.[24]

---

[19] Bovon, "Actes de Philippe," 4471–73. See also Bovon, "Acts of Philip," 5:312.

[20] François Bovon, "The Synoptic Gospels and the Non-canonical Acts of the Apostles," *HTR* 81 (1988): 19–36.

[21] Bovon, "Actes de Philippe," 4444.

[22] Amsler, "Commentaire," 24. Amsler, Bovon, and Bouvier, *Actes de l'apôtre Philippe*, 24–25.

[23] Amsler, "Commentaire," 24.

[24] Ibid., 24–25. Amsler finds the theme of purity present throughout act 1, welding the two parts of the text in a common ideal and constituting a most impressive standard of unity.

TABLE 2. COMPARISON OF εἰ STATEMENTS

Xenophontos 32, APh 1.17 [14] (p. 391, lines 2–5)	*Vaticanus graecus 824, APh* 1.4 (p. 3, lines 16–20)
εἴ τις οὖν θελήσῃ ἑαυτὸν ἐλεῆσαι, πάντων τῶν κακῶν ἀφέξεται·	εἴ τις οὖν ἀδελφοὶ θελήσειεν ἑαυτὸν ἐλεῆσαι, πάντων τῶν κακῶν ἐκφεύξεται,
εἴ τις πιστεύσῃ τῷ θεῷ, μακαριστὸς ἔσται, καὶ	καὶ πιστεύσει τῷ θεῷ τῷ ὑπὸ τοῦ ἀνθρώπου τούτου κηρυττομένῳ, καὶ μακάριος ἔσται·
εἴ τις ὁμολογήσῃ τὸν ἀγαπητὸν Χριστόν, δοξασθήσεται.	καὶ εἴ τις ὁμολογήσει τὸν ἀγαπητὸν Χριστὸν δοξασθήσεται.

A third option for understanding the current form of act 1 should not be overlooked. If, as suggested by Matthews, the work grew through a series of redactions effected by the changing needs of the community, it is possible that a later editor, working at a time when recourse to other-worldly visions and angelic speeches was discouraged and the ascetic excesses found in the tour of hell forbidden, recognized in the miracle story an earlier form of the act. A genuine interest in returning the act to its earlier form may have allowed this editor to remove legitimately the tour of hell from act 1, returning it to its earlier form while at the same time excising material considered offensive.[25]

The Implied Author and the Implied Reader

Narrative criticism's categories of "implied author" and "implied reader" provide a useful perspective for exploring the matter of the shorter and longer versions of the text, and for gaining insight into the relation between community and text.[26] The implied author of *Vaticanus graecus 824* reveals a distinct, if complementary, interest to the implied author of *Xenophontos 32*. Both authors are concerned with 1) identifying the

[25] François Bovon suggested this option to me.

[26] Mark Alan Powell, *What Is Narrative Criticism?* (Minneapolis: Fortress Press, 1990), 5. See also Wayne Booth, *The Rhetoric of Fiction*, 2d ed. (Chicago: University of Chicago Press, 1983), 66–77; and Seymour B. Chatman, *Story and Discourse: Narrative Structure in Fiction and Film* (Ithaca, N.Y.: Cornell University Press, 1978), 147–51.

apostle Philip as a miracle worker in the spirit of Jesus of Nazareth, 2) arguing the superiority of the Christian God to non-Christian gods, and 3) testifying in the speeches of the widow and the apostle that the ascetic way is the superior way for the Christian. The implied author of *Xenophontos 32*, however, has a more urgent issue to address. Whereas the miracle story stands at the center of *Vaticanus graecus 824*, the implied author of *Xenophontos 32* places a lengthy tour of hell at its center, with the miracle story functioning as prologue and epilogue. With its apocalyptic language and symbols, speeches by angels, and visions of other-worldly torments and chastisements, this tour moves beyond mere advocacy of the ascetic life, implying that Christians who scorn the ascetic life are in danger of hell's torment. Moreover, this implied author identifies with the injured and their cause by naming specific injuries and offenses, identifying the offended by title, and connecting the offenders through symbol and veiled language to the majority church. Thus, *Xenophontos 32* reveals an implied author committed to the support of an embattled ascetic community through the use of apocalyptic material shaped so that it speaks to their circumstances.

The implied reader of the miracle story of *Vaticanus graecus 824* is not necessarily Christian. This reader is sympathetic to the widow's efforts to obtain help for her son within her religious and cultural milieu. The implied reader may well have sought similar relief without success ("What you have experienced was not peculiar, oh mother" [*APh* 1.2]). The implied reader is impressed with the power of Philip's God ("Jesus Christ, who was crucified and buried, and who was raised and who rules" [*APh* 1.2]) to raise the young man from the dead and is willing to entertain an appeal to accept the Christian ascetic's pure faith, a faith which opens the way to intimacy with God ("for God abides with the pure" [*APh* 1.3]). The implied reader is vulnerable to the implied author's evangelistic urging to abandon belief in non-Christian gods and adopt an ascetically purified Christian faith, marked by celibacy and abstinence from wine and meat.

In the tour of hell of *Xenophontos 32*, the implied reader is not only a Christian but is almost certainly a member of an ascetic community. The implied reader attaches importance to the afterlife and is comfortable with an apocalyptic genre which teaches through visions, voices, images, and angelic messengers. The implied reader understands the apocalyptic code embedded in this tour and can interpret the meaning of punishments, offenses, and warnings in the context of the life situation. Perhaps this implied reader is a member of the ascetically pure community glimpsed in the miracle story and with that community will find encouragement in the encoded message of the tour to stand firm in the midst of trial, remaining true to the pure faith.

The Tour of Hell Examined

A Summary of the Tour

In the first scene of the tour of hell (*APh* 1.5), a woman with a face like a dragon and hands that dart like the tongue of an asp is holding a fiery hook and pushing human souls toward the abyss. She is identified as one who "incites humans to slander and mock believers, to say that Christ is a seducer." The souls she pushes into the abyss are engaged in "shallow talk."

In the second scene (*APh* 1.6), a tormented man is cast into an infernal pit. His teeth are chattering as he is tortured pitilessly by an anonymous angel holding a blazing sword. His sin is that he "tyrannized many people, struck bishops and priests, and slandered them." He attributes his plight to ignorance, for he failed to believe there was judgment after death. He now receives the "just wages of his actions."

In the third scene (*APh* 1.7–8), a young man, his sides bursting, lies on a bed of embers with pus flowing from his flesh. The pus changes into fiery serpents which continuously devour him. "It was my tongue," he states, "that brought my ruin. I respected neither father, nor mother, nor priests: I even insulted a most chaste virgin. . .causing her to blush. . .so as to dishonor her in the eyes of the bystanders. . .forcing her to swear in the presence of God, near the altar." The young man being conducted on the other-worldly tour, profoundly moved, asks to speak with the eunuchs and virgins, believing that his prayers may obtain forgiveness for the tortured one. Michael dissuades him: "You can obtain nothing, because it is another who judges."

In the fourth scene (*APh* 1.9), men pelt one another with balls of fire, punishment for having in their drunkenness "spoken ill of the just and those who live in purity."

In the fifth scene (*APh* 1.10–11), the tormented person is a bald-headed man. Upon his head are heaped fiery coals. An angel further torments him, holding over him a smelter's ladle from which fire drips upon his head. His sins were the drinking of wine and in drunkenness speaking imprudently against "bishops and presbyters and eunuchs and virgins." Sympathetic to this aged man, the youth seeks to intercede with the virgins, but his request is denied. Moved again to seek respite for the tormented man, he renews his search for the virgins. Michael stops him, stating that his effort is futile, for there is no pity for those who allow themselves to be led to ruin by wine. The scene ends with an unseen force beckoning the narrator back toward the world.

In the sixth scene (*APh* 1.12), as the young man moves toward the world, he sees a dog called Cerberus devouring a man and a woman, holding their livers between his paws.[27] The young man would save them by pulling Cerberus away, but the archangel Michael stops him, saying that "they too have blasphemed against priests, elders, eunuchs, deacons, deaconesses, virgins, falsely accusing them of impurity and adultery."

The seventh scene (*APh* 1.13), is situated just outside the door of hell and concerns the attendants (λειτουργοί) at the altar. The young man asks about the chastisements which remain unseen, hidden by the hypocrisy of those who are at the altar. Michael responds saying that these attendants will receive their punishment too, for God grants no one special treatment. An immense throne, seemingly made of flowers, is visible to the young man. From the throne comes a voice like thunder, bringing charges against the attendants. They are charged with drunkenness and gossip, anger toward their fellows, the sin of slander, and hypocrisy. Michael warns the young man to beware of these attendants, who are as wolves dressed in the clothing of lambs.

At this point the story appears to have ended as the young man reenters the presence of Philip (*APh* 1.14). His concern that the devil

---

[27] Amsler, "Commentaire," 47–48. Amsler notes that the presence of Cerberus in this scene is an indicator of the Asian origin of the text.

might be playing tricks on him gives Philip the opportunity to speak briefly of the benefits of the pure life: "If you do not make yourself pure, you are exposing yourself to these chastisements. . . . If you fight the good fight, you will forever become a patron to many" (*APh* 1.15).

Just when it seems that the report of the tour is complete, the young man asks Philip if he may give one more report. In this final vision (*APh* 1.16), two men with hands tied behind their backs are being tortured in a stove, forced to drink from a cauldron of molten lead. Their sins are many. They have condemned and scorned the innocent; thinking themselves just, they have behaved as tyrants; haughty, backbiters, they have rivaled one another in drunkenness, and they have despoiled the poor. They have savored the sensual pleasures of the world and have filled the servants of God with bitterness by saying, "What have we to do with these people!" A punishment of "measure for measure" is implied in the narrator's observation that "everything that a man accomplishes in his own interest falls back here upon his own head as a result of the idle talk his impenitent tongue engaged in."[28]

A gust of wind brings the young man back (*APh* 1.17), and as he is rejoined to Philip and his mother, so the texts of *Vaticanus graecus 824* and *Xenophontos 32* are rejoined in reporting similar material. The young man and his mother are converted, baptized, and glorify God. They bestow upon Philip ample provisions for his journey. The young man follows the apostle, exalting in the miracles which Philip accomplishes.

Commentary on the Tour

The sins mentioned in this tour, and the identification of those injured by these sins, provide the kind of detail that might allow one to draw conclusions about the religious and social setting of the author's community. While noting Martha Himmelfarb's warning that tours of hell are too deeply influenced by earlier tours of hell and the canonical texts of Judaism and Christianity to be of much value,[29] I nevertheless find that a careful examination of the more prominent sins in this tour,

---

[28] Himmelfarb, *Tours of Hell*, 68–105. Himmelfarb shows that "measure for measure" sins are common to the genre.

[29] Ibid., 73.

and the identities of those injured by these sins, convincingly places the text within a particular historical era and ecclesiastical context.

TABLE 3. SINS FOUND IN ACT 1, *XENOPHONTOS 32*

Scene	Speech	Drunkenness	Persecution	Attitude
1	Slander, mockery; blasphemy of Christ; shallow talk			
2	Slander		Tyrannized people; struck bishops and presbyters	Entertained vain thoughts
3	Insulted chaste virgin; slandered purity		Dishonored virgin in eyes of bystanders	Failed to respect parents, presbyters
4	Spoke ill of the just, pure	Yes		
5	Spoke against bishops, presbyters, eunuchs, virgins; slander, false accusations	Yes		
6	Blasphemed presbyters, etc.; false accusations of impurity			
7	Gossip, slander	Yes		Reading without understanding; hypocrisy, anger
8	Scorned the innocent; backbiting	Yes	Condemned and dishonored the innocent	Tyrannical, haughty; avarice; thinking selves just

It is significant that every scene includes sins of speech, that four include the sin of drunkenness, that sins of attitude are found in four scenes, and that violence or persecution is found in three. While sexual sins are found in almost every apocalyptic tour of hell, they are conspicuously absent here.[30] This suggests that controlling sexual behavior was not an issue for the community of the *Acts of Philip*, or perhaps that it was considered of lesser consequence in the face of more pressing concerns.[31]

TABLE 4. PERSONS SINNED AGAINST IN ACT 1, *XENOPHONTOS 32*

Scene	General	Office Holders	Community Members
1			Believers
2	Many people	Bishops, presbyters	
3	Father, mother	Presbyters	Chaste virgin
4			Those who live in purity; the just
5		Bishops, presbyters, eunuchs, virgins	
6		Male and female presbyters, eunuchs, deacons, deaconesses, virgins	
8	The poor		Innocent, servants of God

Note that most of the offenses are committed against the pure, the chaste, the just, the innocent, and the leaders of the community. The hierarchical titles present in the second, third, fifth, and sixth scenes provide useful insight into the organizational life of the community.[32] They demonstrate

---

[30] Ibid., 70. Note that the "sensual pleasures" (ἡδονή) of the eighth scene do not necessarily imply sexual sin. The term is used here as a collective noun for the sins previously detailed, none of which are specifically sexual in nature. See Amsler, Bovon, and Bouvier, *Actes de l'apôtre Philippe*, 95 n. 15.

[31] Himmelfarb, *Tours of Hell*, 70. "It may be that the strong interest in sexual sins and sins of speech in the tours of hell is a result of the invisibility of those sins."

[32] Scene 2: ἐπισκόπους. . .καὶ πρεσβυτέρους.
Scene 3: πατέρα ἢ μητέρα ἢ πρεσβυτέρους. . .παρθένον σεμνοτάτην.
Scene 5: ἐπισκόπων καὶ πρεσβυτέρων καὶ εὐνούχων καὶ παρθένων.
Scene 6: πρεσβυτέρους, πρεσβύτιδας, εὐνούχους, διακόνους, διακονίσσας, παρθένους.

that the *Acts of Philip* community had developed a hierarchy similar to that of the majority church, and that it included both male and female officeholders as well as "virgins and eunuchs," a group honored by the community for their singular devotion to the sexually pure life. The presence of these titles within the lists of the offended further suggests that the struggle had engaged the leaderships of both the *Acts of Philip* community and the majority church, and that the leaders of the *Acts of Philip* community were suffering from the consequences of that struggle.

The chastisements, with few exceptions, seem to have no higher purpose than to punish evil deeds and ignorance with unending suffering and to alert the reader to the awful destiny that awaits all who commit these sins. At times the punishment seems measured according to the sin (scenes two, four, and eight), though the justice of the punishment is not always obvious. More common is the sense of incalculable suffering from which there is no release and for whose victims there is no pity. It is noteworthy that while the seventh scene would seem concerned with the greatest of sins, the abuse of the privilege of attending the altar, the attendants go unpunished.

The archangel's commentary reinforces the idea that it is the sins of speech that concern the author most.[33] The discourse of Michael is initially focused on those who publicly slander purity and who will not refute another's slander (*APh* 1.8). His second speech explains that the danger of wine is that it leads to "malicious whispering" and many similar vices (*APh* 1.11). Michael comments, finally, that there is no pity for those who "blaspheme and make false accusations of impurity" against the leaders of the community (*APh* 1.12). The speeches of Michael are supported by the voice from the throne, which speaks against "babbling and drunkenness" (*APh* 1.13), while the final speech ends with the thought, "Everything that a man accomplishes in his own interest falls back here upon his own head as a result of the idle talk his impenitent tongue engaged in" (*APh* 1.16).

The lists of sins and punishments, the accompanying speeches, and the escalating punishments that parallel the expansion of the lists as we move from scene to scene are a clever literary device, intensifying

---

[33] Amsler, Bovon, and Bouvier, *Actes de l'apôtre Philippe*, 29.

interest and strengthening the moral of the story: punishment will come to those who oppose the pure and salvation will be the reward of those who live in purity.

One hears in this tour echoes of intense conflict between the *Acts of Philip* community and the majority church.[34] In the third scene (*APh* 1.7) the sin of insulting the "most chaste virgin. . .dishonoring her in the eyes of bystanders" may speak, in veiled terms, of a struggle with religious authority in which ascetics were compelled to renounce their asceticism and make false confessions. The seventh scene (*APh* 1.13) is similarly laden with thinly veiled language attacking those who attend the altar. From the throne, a voice like thunder brings charges against these attendants of slander and hypocrisy. Such images and language, while common to the genre, nevertheless allow one room to believe that such conflict may have been a reality for the *Acts of Philip* Community.

The Relationship between Community and Text

Review of Current Scholarship

Bovon believes that the *Acts of Philip* is the work of a fourth-century monk of encratic persuasion.[35] Aurelio de Santos Otero arrives at a similar conclusion, as do Éric Junod and Jean-Daniel Kaestli, who argue that the redactor, a person directly connected to the Asian Encratite movement, drew upon other apocryphal writings as sources for the composition of this work and injected into his writing an element which is obviously encratic.[36] Amsler views act 1 as an Encratite text from the end of the fourth century or the beginning of the fifth century, of rural Asian origin. In his opinion, it appears as the desperate cry of a

---

[34] Evidence of this conflict is also found in the miracle story, where Philip states to the widow that "purity excites jealousy among humankind, for unable to live in purity or content to be water-drinkers, they persist in telling lies against those who live in purity" (*APh* 1.3). See Amsler, Bovon, and Bouvier, *Actes de l'apôtre Philippe*, 93 n. 9, who consider this an important key to the interpretation of act 1.

[35] Bovon, "Actes de Philippe," 4522.

[36] de Santos Otero, "Acta Philippi," 469. Junod and Kaestli, *L'histoire des Actes apocryphes des apôtres*, 30.

community searching for pure Christian faith that finds itself progressively marginalized. As its members are repressed in a manner totally unjustified in their eyes, they have no other weapon with which to fight back than literary fiction.[37]

Given this support for a connection between the Encratites of Asia Minor and act 1 of the *Acts of Philip*, it seems important that we inquire further. The difficulties of doing this should be obvious, for there are few textual clues to their historical and geographical location, and only their ideology is unambiguously declared. Moreover, the theory that the redaction of this text may have taken place over several centuries suggests that a formative relationship may have existed with several communities.[38]

This study will now turn to important evidence from the writings of church fathers and heresiologists, the decrees of Theodosius, canons from the Council of Gangra, and epitaphs from encratic tombs in Asia Minor. Apart from epigraphy, the evidence will be gathered from the opponents of Encratism, and thus it will be necessary to regard these writings with suspicion and to consider their assertions in light of their obvious polemical purposes.[39]

The Encratites

Our earliest testimony regarding Encratism comes from Irenaeus who, writing about 185 C.E., attributes its formulation to Tatian:

> Springing from Saturninus and Marcion, those who are called Encratites (self-controlled) preached against marriage, thus setting aside the original creation of God, and indirectly blaming Him who made them male and

---

[37] Amsler, "Commentaire," 59.

[38] Matthews, "Trajectories," 261–63.

[39] Constantine Bonis, "What Are the Heresies Combatted in the Work of Amphilochios Metropolitan of Iconium (ca 341/5–ca 395/400) 'Regarding False Asceticism'?" *Greek Orthodox Theological Review* 9 (1963): 79–86. Bonis comments: ". . .the student of the whole range of polemic literature must not forget that all of the polemic authors, from Irenaios up to Amphilochios, Ephiphanios, and Theodorites, are motivated by the conviction that, just as in the official Catholic Church there is a 'succession' of bishops, so, too, in all the heresies there is such a 'succession' whose origin is attributed, first, to the Devil himself, and, secondly, to Simon the Magician."

female for the propagation of the human race. Some of those reckoned among them have also introduced abstinence from animal food, thus proving themselves ungrateful to God, who formed all things. (*Adv. haer.* 1.28.1)[40]

Eusebius, following Irenaeus, labels Encratism "a strange and corrupting false doctrine" (*Hist. eccl.* 4.28.1). The most extensive writing against the ascetic beliefs of Tatian and the Encratites comes from Clement of Alexandria's *Stromata*. Clement is concerned to refute Tatian's judgment that marriage is a debauchery inspired by the devil. While allowing that continence is an option for the Christian which achieves great worth in the eyes of God, Clement upholds responsible marriage as a valid option for the Christian community (*Strom.* 3.79.4–7). Clement also refutes Tatian's views on meat and wine, asserting that everything created by God is good (*Strom.* 3.85).

In the latter half of the fourth century the influence of encratic belief is of sufficient import to warrant the attention of Epiphanius, bishop of Salamis and prominent heresiologist. In *Panarion* 45–47 and 61 (ca. 375–77), Epiphanius writes against the Encratites, Severians, Tatianites, and Apostolics. He attributes to each of these groups belief in a dualistic view of the origin of the world, prohibition of marriage based upon the belief that marriage is the work of the devil, abstinence from meat and wine, use of water in place of wine at the Eucharist, use of apocryphal writings, and disdain for the Old Testament. In spite of these similar beliefs, Epiphanius treats them as individual heresies.[41]

The Church's Response to the Encratites

Two letters of St. Basil (ca. 374–75), bishop of Caesarea, give some idea of the character and geographical spread of the Encratite movement

---

[40] English translation by Alexander Roberts and W. H. Rambaut, *The Writings of Irenaeus*, vol. 1 (Ante-Nicene Christian Library 5; Edinburgh: Clark, 1868), 100.

[41] The *Panarion*'s construction upon an artificial framework requiring eighty heresies for completeness may explain the large number of similar heresies bearing different names and may diminish the importance of the distinctions made between the groups. Blond states that, at the time of Epiphanius, these groups were largely indistinguishable. Georges Blond, "L' 'hérésie' encratite vers la fin du quatrième siècle," *Recherches de science religieuse* 32 (1944): 176.

of that time. His letters are a response to correspondence from Amphilochius, bishop of Iconium, who writes to ask Basil what attitude he should display toward the Encratites and similar groups. Letter 188 concerns the question of readmitting Encratite heretics to the church and assumes the existence of an Encratite hierarchy with bishops, clergy, and lay leadership. Near the end of the letter, Basil notes that the Encratites practice a "peculiar baptism of their own," defiantly rendering themselves unacceptable to the Catholic church.[42] In letter 199, Basil addresses the issue of rebaptism, suggesting that a gathering of bishops might be called to publish a canon regarding the sect. The need for such a gathering implies that the Encratite movement had become so widespread and influential as to be worrisome to the bishops. Again, in letter 236, the matter of Encratite belief is addressed. Here the issue is the Encratite challenge to the church regarding the eating of meat, which, in a particularly scatological manner, Basil repudiates. We note in these letters no mention of Tatian, for Basil regards Encratite belief as emanating from the Marcionites (letter 199).

In the fragment of the treatise attributed to Amphilochius and titled by scholars *Regarding False Asceticism*, or *Contra haereticos*, the author argues forcefully against the encratic ideals of continence and abstinence.[43] They are denounced as a diabolical stumbling block (*Contra haereticos* 3.97) intended to turn believers away from the church (*Contra haereticos* 6). Amsler shows that the point of view which Amphilochius argues against is precisely that which is advocated in the dialogue of Philip and the widow (*APh* 1.3).[44]

The Eustathians and the Council of Gangra

The Council of Gangra (ca. 340) convened to discuss the fate of Eustathius of Sebaste and his followers. The Eustathians were formally charged with heretical beliefs bearing remarkable similarity to Encratism. The Eustathians described by the twenty one canons of this

[42] For discussion of the baptismal directive, see Amsler, "Commentaire," 300–302.

[43] For further discussion of this treatise, see Amsler, "Commentaire," 57–58, 302–3; Junod and Kaestli, *L'histoire des Actes apocryphes des apôtres*, 25–27, 119–26; and Bonis, "Heresies," 79–87.

[44] Amsler, "Commentaire," 57.

council rejected marriage, esteemed vegetarianism, refused to receive communion from a married priest, scorned the meetings of the official church, looked down on the married, and proudly accentuated the righteousness of continence.[45] The Council pronounced all of these things objectionable and sinful and reproved and condemned them.[46]

In his study of the *Acts of Philip*, Erik Peterson notes a number of striking similarities between the beliefs and practices of the Eustathians condemned at Gangra and the ideals of the *Acts of Philip* community.[47] There are notable parallels with respect to rejection of marriage and the dissolution of existing marriages (*APh* 5), buildings designated συναγωγή (*APh* 7), distinctive clothing (*APh* 2), the teaching that slaves should be freed (*APh* 6), the practice of women wearing men's clothing (*APh* 8), the rejection of meat and wine (*APh* 1), the practice of not entering an impure house (*APh* 4), and contempt for the rich (*APh* 6). Peterson concludes that the practice of wearing distinct clothing and the stipulation that one enter into the homes of married people only after purification are important signs that the ascetics condemned at Gangra are related to the ascetics of the *Acts of Philip*. He is careful to note, however, that the *Acts of Philip* may not give an accurate picture of the ascetics of the fourth century, for the date of authorship has not been accurately determined, and the question of the effects of redaction upon the *Acts of Philip* must still be explored.[48]

The Decrees of Theodosius I

The collusion of the Catholic Church and imperial power to limit the growth and influence of nonconforming systems of faith is clearly documented in the *Codex Theodosianus*. Designating the beliefs of

---

[45] O. Larry Yarbrough, "Canons from the Council of Gangra," in *Ascetic Behavior in Greco-Roman Antiquity: A Sourcebook*, ed. V. L. Wimbush (Minneapolis: Fortress Press, 1990), 448–55.

[46] Bonis, "Heresies," 89. Bonis, who notes the remarkable similarity of belief between the heretics condemned at Gangra and the Encratites which troubled Amphilochius, is not convinced that they are the same group.

[47] Erik Peterson, "Die Häretiker der Philippus-Akten," *ZNW* 31 (1932): 97–111. See also Yarbrough, "Canons."

[48] Peterson, "Häretiker," 106.

heretical groups, Jews, and pagans as *superstitio*, and the majority church's faith as *uera religio*, church and state worked fervently to eradicate *superstitio*.[49] It is clear that the Encratites were regarded as falling into the category of *superstitio*, for three imperial decrees, dated 381, 382, and 383 C.E., imposed severe restrictions upon their personal rights of inheritance and the freedom of their communities to gather and practice their faith (*Codex Theodosianus* 16.5.7, 9, 11). The decrees condemned the Encratites, Hydroparastates, and Saccophores and forbade on pain of death the practice of their beliefs.[50] Theodosius II renewed these laws in 428. They seem to have been effective in eliminating encratic faith and practice, for after the fifth century no mention of Encratism can be found.[51]

The Witness of Epigraphy

A number of inscriptions discovered in the region of Laodicia of Lyconia provide evidence of the existence of groups with encratic ideals and show interesting detail of their organization. The inscriptions date from as early as the second half of the third century to the end of the fourth.[52] The evidence offered by epigraphy is of special value because its sources are the deceased ascetic believers and their spiritual or physical families, who offer a more sympathetic quality of insight into their lives and ideals.

Building upon the earlier work of William M. Calder, Henri Grégoire, William Ramsay, Franz Cumont, and others, Georges Blond assesses the data provided by inscriptions from this region known to have been heavily populated by ascetics.[53] His work has drawn my attention to certain inscriptions, which are important for our study.

[49] David Hunt, "Christianizing the Roman Empire: The Evidence of the Code," in *The Theodosian Code*, ed. Jill Harries and Ian Wood (Ithaca, N.Y.: Cornell University Press, 1993), 145.

[50] Theodosius considers all of these groups to be Manichaeans who use their distinct names to escape the prohibitions of imperial law.

[51] Georges Blond, "Encratisme," *Dictionnaire de Spiritualité* 4/1 (1960): 628–42, particularly 640.

[52] Blond, "Hérésie," 194.

[53] Ibid., 194–208.

The following inscription is found at Dinek Serai, not far from Ladik.[54] Ramsay, who visited the monument in 1901 and again in 1905, notes its deteriorated condition but offers the following translation based upon his "conjectural restoration."[55]

> By this sign (or stone) I bid the passer hail, and all who go by; but do thou show me favour, approaching, and taking pleasure in my words and learning clearly that Nestor in old times was priest in these lands [a revered presby]ter, the help of virtuous widows.

Further information is then given about the character and duties of priest Nestor:

> . . .moreover, he (was) the minister of continence (ἐνκρατίης ὁ διάκονος), excellent subordinate worker, chosen treasure of our province, the teacher of the heavenly decree to young men; and he was a trustworthy judge among men, and he sat among the governors, and a thousand nations know this.

The last lines relate to the wife of Nestor and read: "Mammeis, his wife, daughter of Telephis, the most holy of priestesses, faithful steward of continence (πιστὴν ἐνκρατίης οἰκονόμον)." Blond understands that Mammeis, having been won over to continence, joins her husband in an agreement to separate. If he is correct, this epitaph documents the presence of the same kind of preaching which so influenced the lives of the characters found in the *Acts of Philip*. One must note that Ramsay does not draw quite the same meaning, interpreting πιστὴν ἐνκρατίης οἰκονόμον as "trusty dispenser of continence," a true companion to her husband, the "minister of continence."[56] At the very least, this epitaph reveals the influence of ascetic preaching in this region and the presence of an ascetic Christian community which viewed continence as a positive Christian value.[57]

---

[54] William M. Ramsay, *Luke the Physician* (London: Hodder and Stoughton, 1908), 360–66.

[55] Ibid., 360–63.

[56] Ibid., 364–65.

[57] Blond, "Hérésie," 200.

A second inscription, published by Calder, was discovered in 1928 near Kestel, to the west of Ladik.[58] It reads:

> Mirus, son of Adventinus, one of the Encratites, while still alive and of a sound mind, has raised this tomb in memoriam, for himself and his first cousin Tati, his brother Paul and his sister Pribis. If any among the wine drinkers should place a body in this tomb, he will have to answer before God and before Jesus Christ.

This inscription is important for its specific reference to the Encratites, numbering Mirus among them, and for its warning against the burial of wine-drinkers in his tomb. While warning formulas were common enough in pagan communities, its use is exceptional in an area that is predominantly Christian.[59] Mirus, who like all Encratites refused wine even at the Eucharist, intends this tomb to be used only by members of his physical and spiritual family. Calder views it as a polite rebuff to his critics, referring them to the tribunal of God and Christ.[60]

A number of inscriptions in the region of Nevinneh, dating from 475 to 525 C.E., reveal an Encratite hierarchy similar to that of the majority church.[61] The following inscription, from a slab with two panels located in Nevinneh, makes reference to the offices of deaconess and presbyter in the Encratite community.[62] Translated, it reads:

> Aurelius Antonius, son of Mirus, with his aunt Elaphia, deaconess of the Encratites, have raised this tomb.

And,

> Elaphia, deaconess of the Encratites, I have raised this tomb to the presbyter Peter and to his son Polychronius, in memory.

---

[58] William M. Calder, "Leaves from an Anatolian Notebook," *Bulletin of the John Rylands Library* 3 (1929): 264–65.

[59] Blond, "Hérésie," 204–5.

[60] Calder, "Leaves," 264–65.

[61] This assumes that when communities adopted hierarchical names, they adopted hierarchical functions as well. See Blond, "Hérésie," 203.

[62] William M. Calder, *Monumenta Asiae Minoris Antiqua* (London: Manchester University Press, 1928), 1:xxv.

Situated in a region known to have been heavily populated by Christian ascetics, these inscriptions demonstrate the presence of ascetics who do not allow wine, who praised continence and may have interrupted marriage, and who utilized a church structure similar to that of the majority church.

Concluding Thoughts

While the quest for definitive conclusions about an original form of the text of *Acts of Philip* 1 is difficult, for reasons already mentioned, the material we have reviewed allows certain judgments to be made. I concur with the view that the longer text of act 1 of *Xenophontos 32* predates the shorter *Vaticanus graecus 824* and demonstrates in its two parts an impressive literary and theological unity. This edition of the text emerged from the experience of an embattled encratic community; it served both as a vehicle for telling their story and advocating their ideals and as a source of encouragement to the community struggling to maintain their encratic vocation.

It appears, however, that the text drew enough attention to itself to eventually attract the censorial hand of a redactor. The shorter text of *Vaticanus graecus 824* reveals the hand of this redactor whose work effects 1) a removal of the tour of hell and its condemnation, implicit and explicit, of the majority church; and 2) a reduction of the power of act 1, with its recourse to visions and angelic witness to turn Christians toward a rigorously ascetic Christian life. This shorter text remains marked by the encratic ideal and demonstrates an awareness of the longer version and its tour of hell. Nevertheless, it expresses the values of a community for whom the ascetic life is no longer an option, living in a time when the ideals of the majority church had gained the upper hand. This allows for a redaction no earlier than the mid-fifth century.

The evidence of the writings of church fathers, heresiologists, and epigraphy shows that during the latter part of the fourth and early part of the fifth centuries there were encratic communities in the region of Asia Minor living in a state of conflict with civil and religious authorities. The similarity of the ideals expressed in act 1 according to *Xenophontos 32* to those of the embattled ascetic communities and the consistent echo of conflict heard in the text of act 1 in its *Xenophontos 32* version persuade me that the editor/compiler knew firsthand the bitter conflict of these encratic Christians with the majority church and wrote to encourage and support the community and their commitment to the ascetic life.

Appendices

The *Martyrdom of the Holy Apostle Ananias* (*BHG* 75y)

François Bovon and
Evie Zachariades-Holmberg

Ananias of Damascus is remembered as one of the faithful of the first generation of Christians. According to the Acts of the Apostles (9:10–19 and 22:12–16), he healed and baptized Saul of Tarsus after the Christophany on the road to Damascus. He should not be confused with the believer from Jerusalem, who, along with his wife Saphira, was struck by divine wrath (Acts 5:1–11). The date of the saint's celebration has been established by the Orthodox Church as the first of October.[1]

The text on Ananias that follows, the recension *BHG* 75y, one of the three recensions of the *Martyrdom of Ananias* that the Bollandists have located (*BHG* 75x, 75y, and 75z), is edited here for the first time. Another account of the martyrdom of Ananias, written in the tenth century by Symeon Metaphrastes (*BHG* 76), is easily accessible in the *Patrologia Graeca* of Jacques Paul Migne.[2] An epitome of this story by Symeon (*BHG* 76a) has circulated but remains unpublished.

The *Menologion* of the emperor Basil[3] and the *Synaxarion* of the Church of Constantinople[4] also sum up the life and martyrdom of

---

[1] The Catholic Church commemorates Ananias on 25 January, the same time that the conversion of Paul is celebrated. Apparently, no Latin martyrdom of Ananias was ever composed. Under Ananias, the *BHL* 1:66 does not mention any hagiographic text.

[2] *PG* 114, 1001–9.

[3] *PG* 117, 80.

[4] *Propylaeum ad Acta Sanctorum Novembris. Synaxarium Ecclesiae Constantinopolitanae*, ed. Hippolyte Delehaye (1902; reprint, Brussels: Société des Bollandistes, 1954), col. 95.

Ananias. These texts have preserved significant biographical details, such as his inclusion among the seventy disciples of Jesus, his miracles at Damascus and Eleutheropolis, and his torture with a whip made from the tendons of an ox and the scraping of his sides with iron utensils.

The first part of the text (paragraphs 1–6) presents the person of Ananias and summarizes his encounter with Paul after the Christophany on the road to Damascus. The second part (paragraphs 7–23)—the longest—tells the story of Ananias's martyrdom. It is a classic story of a Roman governor, Lucianus, whose initial investigation and trial of the Christians leads to Ananias's condemnation and death. The conclusion of the narrative mentions the saint's compatriots from a town called Anani who are anxious to take his mortal remains with them to bury "in his paternal inheritance" (paragraph 22). It is also in this concluding part that the author of the narrative presents himself, mentioning the role that he has played and even giving his name, Barsapthas (paragraph 22).

These last paragraphs are of particular interest: Was Anani a real city in Syria or was it an imaginary one based upon the name of the saint? If it was actual, should we imagine a local cult of the martyr behind the gesture of the inhabitants of Anani? And, should we inquire into the relationship between Damascus and Anani and establish if there was any tension between the two cities over Ananias's relics?

With the help of the *Bibliotheca Hagiographica Graeca* and its *Auctarium* and *Novum Auctarium*,[5] the hagiographic manuscript catalogue of the Bollandists, and several catalogues of Greek manuscripts, we can establish a list of nineteen manuscripts for the three recensions of the *Martyrdom of Ananias*.[6] We hope in the future to provide a critical edition of all three recensions. In this article, however, we will focus on one unedited recension, *BHG* 75y, and on one single manuscript,

---

[5] *BHG* 75x–76a (vol. 1, pp. 23–24); *BHG: Auctarium* 75x–76a (p. 20) and *BHG: Novum Auctarium* 75x–76a (p. 19).

[6] These nineteen, by recension, are:

BHG 75x   Ann Arbor, *36*, fourteenth–fifteenth century
Milan, Ambrosiana, *graecus 377 (F 144 sup.)*, eleventh–twelfth century
Ochrid, *4* (Mošin *76*), tenth century
Paris, Bibliothèque Nationale, Coislin, *121*, anno 1342
Rome, Chisiana, R.VI.39, twelfth century
Vaticanus graecus 866, eleventh–twelfth century
Vaticanus graecus 1631, eleventh–twelfth century

Weimar, *Q 729* (codex Froehner), a parchment of the eleventh century belonging to the category Albert Ehrhard entitled "Textsammlungen für Apostelfeste"[7] and containing the texts listed in table 1.

TABLE 1

Folios	Text
1ʳ–70ᵛ	*Acts of John* by Pseudo-Prochorus (*BHG* 916–917z)
71ʳ–82ᵛ	An encomium on St. John by Andrew of Creta (*BHG* 932j or 932k?)
82ᵛ–101ᵛ	*Acts of Peter and Paul* by Pseudo-Marcellus, shorter or longer version? (*BHG* 1490 or 1491?)
101ᵛ–114ᵛ	*Martyrdom of James, the brother of the Lord* (*BHG* 766)
114ᵛ–131ᵛ	*Martyrdom and travels of Matthias the Apostle* (*BHG* 1224d)
132ʳ–134ᵛ	*Death of St. Luke* (*BHG* 992b)
134ᵛ–150ᵛ	*Travels and martyrdom of Andrew, Narratio* (*BHG* 99)
150ᵛ–155ʳ	*Martyrdom of Mark the Evangelist* (*BHG* 1036)
155ʳ–158ᵛ	An encomium on the Twelve Apostles by St. John Chrysostom (*BHG* 159 or 160i?)
158ᵛ–162ʳ	*Martyrdom of the Holy Apostle Ananias* (*BHG* 75y)
162ʳ–172ᵛ	*Life of Paul the Ascetic of Thebes* by St. Jerome (*BHG* 1466)
173ʳ–180ʳ	*Acts and martyrdom of Bartholomew* (unknown until now; BHG: *Novum Auctarium* 226z)

BHG 75y   Argyrocastro, *5* (the manuscript may be lost or destroyed)
        Athens, National Library, *1027*, twelfth century
        Athens, National Library, *2319*, fifteenth century
        Milan, Ambrosiana, *graecus 213 (C 123 sup.)*, eleventh–twelfth century
        Oxford, Bodleian, Clark, *43*, twelfth century
        Saint Petersburg (Leningrad), *graecus 213*, twelfth century
        Weimar, *Q 729*, eleventh century
BHG 75z   Athos, Karakallou, *6 (olim 8)*, now *48*, tenth–eleventh century
        Athos, Pantocrator, *40*, eleventh century
        Milan, Ambrosiana, *graecus 259 (D 92 sup.)*, eleventh century
        Parisinus graecus 1468, eleventh century

N. Bees, "Κατάλογος τῶν χειρογράφων κωδίκων τῆς ᾿Αγιώτατος Μητροπόλεως ᾿Αργυροκάστρου," ᾿Επετηρὶς τοῦ Μεσαιωνικοῦ ᾿Αρχείου 4 (1951-1952), 135, mentions the manuscript from Argyrocastro, which he saw in 1940–41. The *Martyrdom of Ananias* occupies the fifth position in the manuscript. The manuscript Cambridge, *Add. 3047*, sixteenth century, also contains the *Martyrdom of Ananias*, but we do not know as yet which one of the three recensions it is transmitting.

    [7] Compare Jacques Noret, "Manuscrits grecs à Weimar (Fonds W. Froehner) et archives Max Bonnet," *AnBoll* 87 (1969): 81, n. 3.

We have subdivided the text into numbered paragraphs and inserted quotation marks around spoken words for greater readability. Following the Nestle-Aland edition of the New Testament (for example, Acts 1:12), we have chosen to use the soft breathing for the Semitic form of the word Jerusalem (line 11: Ἰερουσαλήμ), rather than the hard breathing of the Greek form (Ἱεροσόλυμα; for example, Luke 13:22). The same is true for Ἀνανίας (Nestle[27] has Ἁνανίας). In contrast to Δαμασκός (lines 10 and 12), Ἀνανί (line 103) does not get declined. Despite the tendency in the Byzantine period to use the future indicative (rather than the subjunctive aorist) after ἵνα, we have changed the manuscript to read, more correctly, ἵνα. . .ἰάσωμαι instead of ἵνα. . .ἰάσομαι (line 55).

There are no complicated textual problems, but we should mention that on line 103, the word συγκωμῆται (translated as "fellow citizens")—which we have read behind the word συγκομεισταί—is a compound of ὁ κωμήτης ("the villager"). Aside from the fact that the word appearing in the manuscript, συγκομεισταί, has the accent in the wrong place, the second σ, which is erroneous, is probably due to confusion with κομίζω. The manuscript Athos, Karakallou, *6(8)*, now *48*, f. 34ʳ (recension *BHG* 75z) has the periphrasis οἱ ἀπὸ τῆς κώμης αὐτοῦ ("those from his village").

In the apparatus we do not include the numerous spelling mistakes (for example, ἐξέφνης for ἐξαίφνης and περιίστραψεν for περιήστραψεν, lines 12–13).

The *Martyrdom of the Holy Apostle Ananias* (*BHG* 75y)

Manuscript

A   Weimar, *Q 729* (codex Froehner; *BHG* 75y)
A^{pc} A *post correctionem*

Martyrdom of the holy apostle Ananias

1 After the ascension of our Lord Jesus Christ and the journey up to heaven to his own father, the great among apostles and martyrs, Ananias, the so noble and considerable and most translucent illuminator appeared to us, coming from his country, the region of the people of Damascus, performing many signs and marvels among the people. **2** And there was in those days a certain Saul, a man from Tarsus, breathing out threats and slaughter against all the disciples of Christ, so that he went to the high priest and asked from him letters to Damascus, so that if he should encounter any men and women of the way, he might lead them bound to Jerusalem. **3** And it happened that while he was traveling and approaching Damascus, suddenly a light from heaven flashed around him. And when he fell to the ground, he heard a voice saying to him: "Saul, Saul, why do you persecute me?" And he said: "Who are you, Lord?" And the Lord said: "I am Jesus, whom you persecute. But arise and enter the city, and you will find a man named Ananias, who will make you see again." **4** And the Lord appeared to Ananias and said: "Ananias, arise, go to the street which is called Straight and seek in the house of Simon Judas a man by the name of Saul." **5** And Ananias departed and entered the house and placed his hands upon him and said: "Brother Saul, the Lord has sent me, the one who appeared to you on the road, in order that you might see again and be filled with the Holy Spirit." **6** And immediately scales fell from his eyes and he regained his sight, rose, and was baptized. **7** While Saint Ananias was accomplishing these things and performing many signs, the governor in those regions of the East, Lucianus, who was eager to eradicate the race of the Christians, heard about it and made a search against the servants of God. But the devil, with his servants, was wounded, and after he fell he

---

Before the title we read: "The first of the month of October."
Lines 6–7   Acts 5:12 (σημεῖα καὶ τέρατα πολλὰ ἐν τῷ λαῷ).
Lines 7–25   Acts 9:10–18; 22:6–16; 26:12–18.

f. 158ᵛ μαρτύριον τοῦ ἁγίου ἀποστόλου Ἀνανίου

1 μετὰ τὴν ἀνάληψιν τοῦ κυρίου ἡμῶν Ἰησοῦ Χριστοῦ καὶ τὴν πρὸς τὸν οὐρανὸν ἄνοδον τὴν πρὸς τὸν ἴδιον πατέρα, ἀνέτειλεν ἡμῖν καὶ ὁ μέγας ἐν ἀποστόλοις καὶ μάρτυσιν Ἀνανίας ὁ τοιοῦτος καὶ τηλικοῦτος διαυγέστατος φωστήρ, πατρίδος μὲν ἐκ τῆς τῶν 5 Δαμασκηνῶν χώρας ὁρμώμενος, σημεῖα καὶ τέρατα πολλὰ ποιῶν ἐν τῷ λαῷ. **2** ἐγένετο δὲ ἐν ταῖς ἡμέραις ἐκείναις Σαῦλός τις ἀνὴρ Ταρσαῖος, ἐμπνέων ἀπειλῆς καὶ φόνου εἰς πάντας τοὺς μαθητὰς τοῦ
f. 159ʳ Χριστοῦ, ὥστε προσελθεῖν τῷ ἀρχιιερεῖ καὶ αἰτῆσαι παρ' αὐτοῦ ἐπιστολὰς εἰς Δαμασκόν, ὅπως, ἂν εὕρῃ τινὰς ἐν τῇ ὁδῷ ἄνδρας τε 10 καὶ γυναῖκας, δεδεμένους ἀγάγῃ εἰς Ἰερουσαλήμ. **3** ἐν δὲ τῷ πορεύεσθαι αὐτὸν ἐγένετο ἐγγίζειν αὐτὸν τῇ Δαμασκῷ, καὶ ἐξαίφνης περιήστραψεν αὐτὸν φῶς ἐκ τοῦ οὐρανοῦ. καὶ πεσὼν ἐπὶ τὴν γῆν ἤκουσεν φωνὴν λέγουσαν αὐτῷ· "Σαῦλε, Σαῦλε, τί με διώκεις;" εἶπεν δέ· "τίς εἶ, κύριε;" ὁ δὲ κύριος εἶπεν· "ἐγώ εἰμι Ἰησοῦς, ὃν σὺ 15 διώκεις. ἀλλὰ ἀνάστηθι καὶ εἴσελθε εἰς τὴν πόλιν, καὶ εὑρήσεις ἄνδρα ὀνόματι Ἀνανίαν, ὅστις σε ποιήσει ἀναβλέψαι." **4** ἐμφανισθεὶς δὲ ὁ κύριος τῷ Ἀνανίᾳ εἶπεν· "Ἀνανία, ἀναστὰς πορεύθητι ἐπὶ τὴν ῥύμην τὴν καλουμένην Εὐθεῖαν καὶ ζήτησον ἐν οἰκίᾳ Σίμωνος Ἰούδα Σαῦλον ὀνόματι." **5** ἀπελθὼν δὲ ὁ Ἀνανίας 20 εἰσῆλθεν εἰς τὴν οἰκίαν καὶ ἐπιθεὶς ἐπ' αὐτὸν τὰς χεῖρας εἶπεν· "Σαοὺλ ἀδελφέ, ὁ κύριος ἀπέσταλκέν με, ὁ ὀφθείς σοι ἐν τῇ ὁδῷ, ὅπως ἀναβλέψῃς καὶ πλησθῇς πνεύματος ἁγίου." **6** εὐθέως ἀπεσπάσθησαν ἀπὸ τῶν ὀφθαλμῶν αὐτοῦ ὡσεὶ λεπίδες, ἀνέβλεψέν
f. 159ᵛ τε καὶ ἀναστὰς ἐβαπτίσθη. **7** ταῦτα αὐτοῦ ἐκτελοῦντος | τοῦ ἁγίου 25 Ἀνανίου καὶ σημεῖα πολλὰ ποιοῦντος, ἀκούσας ὁ ἡγεμὼν Λουκιανὸς ἐν τοῖς μέρεσιν τῆς Ἀνατολῆς, ὁ καὶ σπεύδων ἐξᾶραι τὸ τῶν χριστιανῶν γένος, ζήτησιν ἐποιήσατο κατὰ τῶν δούλων τοῦ θεοῦ. ἀλλ' ὁ μὲν διάβολος σὺν τοῖς ὑπηρέταις αὐτοῦ ἐτραυματίσθη

A
1 ante titulum: ꝩ ὀκτωβριω α΄ A pro μηνὶ Ὀκτωβρίῳ α΄ ‖ 8 Ταρσαῖος: ταρσέως A legend. Ταρσεύς? ‖ 10 ἂν: legend. ἐὰν? ‖ 11 τῷ: τὸ A ‖ 14 αὐτῷ: αὐτὸν A ‖ 20 Σίμωνος: σήμωνος A delevit Aᵖᶜ ‖ 23 πλησθῇς: πλησθεῖς A ‖ 27 Λουκιανὸς: λούκιος A cf. line 33 et passim.

burst open. The workers of the truth, however, produced wheat of piety as good earth, according to what is written, bearing fruit from their labors in abundance. **8** Hence the most impious and most unlawful Lucianus initiated a persecution against the Christians, and he set up such a decree saying: "Whoever is found naming Christ and worshiping the crucified one, I order such a person to be handed over for terrible chastisements and bitter punishments. But whoever sacrifices to the gods will be worthy of great honors and gifts." **9** And during those days Saint Ananias found himself in that country healing the brothers there, for the Lord was with him, providing through him the healing for those who were sick. Then, therefore, the worshipers of the madness of idols and assistants of the devil, after they arrested the servant of Christ Ananias, brought him before the seat of Lucianus, the governor. **10** And the governor, turning toward him, said: "Are you the one who loathes the sacrifices of the gods and deceives the people preaching another living god? Now then, man, I see that you are admirable in your appearance and wise in your sagacity. Listen to me and come to the gods, and do not destroy yourself, tormented by me." **11** Saint Ananias answered saying: "I do not worship those who are not gods, but our Lord Jesus Christ the true God, who became for us true light and we have seen with our eyes, and our hands touched, and delivered us from the error of idols, and led us toward his own father. **12** And before these days when I was in the city of Damascus, he himself commanded me, that I heal Saul in his name. Hence let us declare the living God worthy and good and not worship unclean demons." **13** Lucianus said:

Lines 39–40   the Lord is with him; see Judg 6:12; Luke 1:28, etc.
Line 40   summaries of healing; see, for example Matt 4:23.
Line 49   criticism of idols; see, for example, Isa 44:6–23 and 1 Cor 8:4–6.
Lines 50–52   see John 1:9 (τὸ φῶς τὸ ἀληθινόν); 1 John 1:1–2 (ὃ ἑωράκαμεν τοῖς ὀφθαλμοῖς ἡμῶν. . .καὶ αἱ χεῖρες ἡμῶν ἐψηλάφησαν).
Line 52   he saved us from the error of idols; see Col 1:13; 1 Thess 1:9–10; and Rom 11:26 (quoting Isa 59:20).
Line 53   guiding to the Father; see Eph 2:8; 1 Pet 3:18.

καὶ πεσὼν ἐλάκησεν. οἱ δὲ τῆς ἀληθείας ἐργάται καρποφορήσαντες 30
σῖτα εὐσεβείας ὡς γῆ ἀγαθὴ κατὰ τὸ γεγραμμένον εἰς
πολυπλασιασμὸν τοὺς πόνους αὐτῶν ἐκαρποφόρουν. **8** ὅθεν ὁ
ἀσεβέστατος καὶ παρανομώτατος Λουκιανὸς διωγμὸν ἐποίησεν
κατὰ τῶν χριστιανῶν, καὶ δόγμα ἐξέθετο τοιοῦτον λέγων· "ὅστις ἂν
εὑρεθῇ Χριστὸν ὀνομάζων καὶ σέβεται τῷ ἐσταυρωμένῳ, δειναῖς 35
κολάσεσιν καὶ πικραῖς τιμωρίαις τοῦτον κελεύω παραδοθῆναι. ὃς
δ᾽ ἂν θύσῃ τοῖς θεοῖς, τιμῶν μεγάλων καὶ δωρεῶν ἀξιωθήσεται."
9 ἐν δὲ ταῖς ἡμέραις ἐκείναις εὑρεθεὶς ὁ ἅγιος Ἀνανίας κατὰ τὴν
χώραν ἐκείνην θεραπεύων τοὺς ἐκεῖσε ἀδελφούς, ἦν γὰρ ὁ κύριος
μετ᾽ αὐτοῦ παρέχων δι᾽ αὐτοῦ τὴν ἴασιν τοῖς ἀσθενοῦσιν. τότε οὖν 40
f. 160ʳ   οἱ τῆς εἰδωλομανίας θρησκευταὶ | καὶ τοῦ διαβόλου ὑπηρέται
κρατήσαντες τὸν τοῦ Χριστοῦ θεράποντα Ἀνανίαν ἤνεγκαν αὐτὸν
ἔμπροσθεν τοῦ βήματος Λουκιανοῦ τοῦ ἡγεμόνος. **10** καὶ προσχὼν
αὐτῷ ὁ ἡγεμὼν ἔφη· "σὺ εἶ ὁ τὰς θυσίας τῶν θεῶν βδελυσσόμενος
καὶ ἀπατῶν τοὺς ἀνθρώπους κηρύττων ἕτερον θεὸν ζῶντα; νῦν οὖν, 45
ὦ ἄνθρωπε, ὁρῶ ὅτι θαυμαστὸς εἶ ἐν τῇ ἰδέᾳ σου καὶ σοφὸς ἐν τῇ
συνέσει σου. ἄκουσόν μου καὶ πρόσελθε τοῖς θεοῖς, καὶ μὴ σεαυτὸν
ἀπολέσῃς παρ᾽ ἐμοῦ αἰκιζόμενος." **11** ἀπεκρίθη ὁ ἅγιος Ἀνανίας
λέγων· "ἐγὼ οὐ προσκυνῶ τοῖς μὴ οὖσι θεοῖς, ἀλλὰ τὸν κύριον ἡμῶν
Ἰησοῦν Χριστὸν τὸν ἀληθινὸν θεόν, ὃς ἐγένετο ἡμῖν φῶς ἀληθινὸν 50
καὶ ἑωράκαμεν τοῖς ὀφθαλμοῖς ἡμῶν, καὶ αἱ χεῖρες ἡμῶν
ἐψηλάφησαν. καὶ ἀπὸ τῆς πλάνης τῶν εἰδώλων ἐρύσατο ἡμᾶς, καὶ
πρὸς τὸν ἑαυτοῦ πατέρα προσήγαγεν ἡμᾶς. **12** καὶ γὰρ πρὸ τούτων
τῶν ἡμερῶν ὄντα με ἐν Δαμασκῷ τῇ πόλει, αὐτὸς ἐνετείλατό μοι,
ἵνα ἐν τῷ ὀνόματι αὐτοῦ ἰάσωμαι τὸν Σαῦλον. ὅθεν ἄξιον καὶ καλὸν 55
εἴπωμεν θεὸν ζῶντα καὶ μὴ προσκυνεῖν δαίμοσιν ἀκαθάρτοις."

A

33 Λουκιανὸς: λούκιος A λουκιανὸς Aᵖᶜ ‖ 34 λέγων: legend. λέγον? ‖ 35 σέβεται:
legend. σεβόμενος? ‖ τῷ ἐσταυρωμένῳ: legend. τὸν ἐσταυρωμένον? cf. line 62 ‖
46 θαυμαστὸς: θαυμαστῶς A ‖ 50 ὃς: ὡς A ‖ 54 ὄντα με: legend. ὄντος μου uel ὄντι
μοι? ‖ 55 ἰάσωμαι: ἰάσομαι A.

"Renounce the one whom you called god. For he will not help you in anything. For if you do this, you will be released from many punishments." **14** Then the blessed Ananias answered: "I do not renounce my God, by no means. And those that are called gods by you happen to be blocks of stone, works of human hands, I curse and reject them as dumb and senseless and all those who respect them." **15** And stretching out his hands to heaven he said: "Lord Jesus Christ, Son of God the blessed Father, listen to my prayer and make me worthy of your blessed apostles in the future age. And in the same way you saved Saul by your light, save me from the hands of this most impious one who opposes the truth, so that he may not do his will upon me. And do not deprive me of the kingdom of heaven, the one prepared for all who do your will, and for those who love your way of truth and keep your commandments." **16** And after he finished the prayer, the governor ordered that he be beaten with a whip made from the tendons of an ox while the herald was shouting: "Obey the governor." And after those who were beating stopped, the governor said to the saint: "And now spare your body and soul and renounce the one whom you call god. And if you are not willing," he said, "more bitter torments will be brought to you." Then the blessed Ananias answered and said: "I told you first and I do not stop telling you, that I do not renounce my God, nor do I worship useless and defiled idols." **17** Then the governor ordered that his sides be scraped. And the righteous one, raising his eyes to heaven, was praying, bearing this terrible punishment. **18** Again Lucianus says to him: "Until what time will you disdain the commands of the emperor and not worship the gods which the whole world worships?" **19** And the saint

Lines 60–61   the idols as works of human hands; see Isa 44:9–17.
Lines 68–69   the Kingdom of heaven prepared for those who keep your commandments; see Col 1:13 and 1 Cor 2:9.

f. 160ᵛ **13** Λουκιανὸς εἰπών· "ὃν ἔφης θεὸν ἄρνησαι. οὐ|δὲν γάρ σε
ὠφελήσει. τοῦτο γὰρ ποιῶν πολλῶν τιμωριῶν ἀπαλλαγῆς." **14** τότε
ὁ μακάριος Ἀνανίας ἀπεκρίθη· "τὸν θεόν μου οὐκ ἀρνοῦμαι, μὴ
γένοιτο. τοὺς δὲ λεγομένους ὑφ᾽ ὑμῶν θεούς, στῆλαι τυγχάνουσι,   60
ἔργα χειρῶν ἀνθρώπων, οὓς κωφὰ καὶ ἀναίσθητα καταρῶμαι καὶ
ἀποβάλλομαι καὶ πᾶσι τοῖς σεβομένοις αὐτά." **15** καὶ ἐκτείνας τὰς
χεῖρας εἰς τὸν οὐρανὸν εἶπεν· "κύριε Ἰησοῦ Χριστέ, υἱὲ τοῦ θεοῦ
τοῦ εὐλογημένου πατρός, εἰσάκουσον τῆς προσευχῆς μου καὶ ἄξιόν
με ποίησον τῶν μακαρίων σου ἀποστόλων ἐν τῷ μέλλοντι αἰῶνι.   65
καὶ ὃν τρόπον ἔσωσας Σαῦλον ἐν τῷ φωτί σου, σῶσόν με ἐκ τῶν
χειρῶν τοῦ ἀσεβεστάτου τούτου ἐναντιουμένου τῇ ἀληθείᾳ, ἵνα μὴ
ποιήσῃ τὸ θέλημα αὐτοῦ εἰς ἐμέ. καὶ μὴ ἀποστερήσῃς με τῆς
βασιλείας τῶν οὐρανῶν τῆς ἡτοιμασμένης πᾶσιν τοῖς ποιοῦσιν τὸ
θέλημά σου, καὶ τοῖς ἀγαπῶσιν τὴν ὁδόν σου τῆς ἀληθείας καὶ   70
φυλάττουσιν τὰς ἐντολάς σου." **16** καὶ μετὰ τὸ πληρῶσαι τὴν εὐχὴν
ἐκέλευσεν ὁ ἡγεμὼν βουνεύροις αὐτὸν τύπτεσθαι τοῦ κήρυκος
ἐπιβοῶντος· "πείσθητι τῷ ἡγεμόνι." καὶ μετὰ τὸ παύσασθαι τοὺς
τύπτοντας εἶπεν ὁ ἡγεμὼν πρὸς τὸν ἅγιον· "κἂν ἄρτι φεῖσαι τοῦ |
f. 161ʳ σώματός σου καὶ τῆς ψυχῆς σου καὶ ἄρνησαι ὃν λέγεις θεόν. εἰ δὲ   75
μὴ θελήσῃς," εἶπεν, "ἀχθήσονταί σοι πικρότεραι βάσανοι." τότε
ἀποκριθεὶς ὁ μακάριος Ἀνανίας εἶπεν· "εἶπόν σοι καὶ πρῶτον καὶ
λέγειν οὐ παύομαι, ὅτι τὸν θεόν μου οὐκ ἀρνοῦμαι, οὐδὲ προσκυνῶ
ἀνωφελέσιν καὶ μιαροῖς εἰδώλοις." **17** τότε ὁ ἡγεμὼν ἐκέλευσεν
ξυσθῆναι αὐτοῦ τὰς πλευράς, ὁ δὲ δίκαιος τοὺς ὀφθαλμοὺς   80
ἀνατείνας εἰς τὸν οὐρανὸν προσηύχετο ὑπομένων τὴν δεινὴν
τιμωρίαν ταύτην. **18** πάλιν λέγει αὐτῷ Λουκιανός· "ἕως πότε
ἐξουθενεῖς τὰ προστάγματα τοῦ αὐτοκράτορος καὶ οὐ προσκυνεῖς
τοὺς θεούς, οὓς προσκυνεῖ ὅλος ὁ κόσμος;" **19** ἀποκριθεὶς δὲ ὁ

A
57 εἰπών: legend. εἶπεν? ‖ ἄρνησαι: ἄρνησον A cf. line 75 ‖ 58 ἀπαλλαγῆς:
ἀπαλλαγεῖς A legend. ἀπαλλαγήσῃ? ‖ 62 πᾶσι τοῖς σεβομένοις: legend. πάντας
τοὺς σεβομένους? ‖ 68 ποιήσῃ: ποιήσει A ‖ 76 πικρότεραι: πικρότεροι A ‖
79 ἀνωφελέσιν: ἀνοφελεῖς A ‖ 81 ὑπομένων: ὑπομένον A ‖ 83 ἐξουθενεῖς: ἐξουθενὴς
A ‖ προσκυνεῖς: προσκυνῆς A ‖ 84 ἀποκριθεὶς: ἀποκριθὴς A.

answered and said: "Gods who did not make the heaven and the earth, let them perish. As for me, neither am I afraid of the commands of your emperor nor of your threats. Therefore do what you wish, enemy of the truth. **20** You heard once and twice from me, that I worship but one God who is Father, and his only begotten Son and his Holy Spirit which made the heaven and the earth and all in them. In whom I believed and he gave me the strength on this day to stand before you. For your will and that of your demons which you worship, I will never do, for I exist as a slave of Christ. Therefore why do you cause yourself troubles? You already heard the things concerning me, do what you wish." **21** And the governor, filled with anger, ordered all the people of the town to take Saint Ananias and stone him outside the city. And after they seized him, they led him to the place. And the blessed one said in a loud voice: "Lord Jesus Christ, in your hands I place my spirit." And they made him stand in the middle, and stoned him. And thus he delivered his holy soul in peace. **22** And after Saint Ananias reached his final perfection and all withdrew from him, his fellow citizens from the small town Anani came and, after taking his body, they buried it in his paternal inheritance. And I, Barsapthas, wrote his notes and placed them near the remains of this apostle and athlete Ananias, so that they serve as a model and a beneficial guide and a desirable mirror for all those who hope in the promise of our Savior Jesus Christ. **23** Thus the holy apostle and martyr Ananias comes to an end the first of the month of October, in Christ Jesus our Lord. To him belongs the glory and the power together with the Father and the all-holy Spirit now and forever and to the ages, amen.

Lines 85 and 90–91   the God who made the sky and the earth; see Matt 10:25 and parallels and Col 1:16.

Line 94   Rom 1:1 et passim (δοῦλος Χριστοῦ).

Line 95   Luke 4:28 (καὶ ἐπλήσθησαν πάντες θυμοῦ).

Lines 97 and 100   stoning outside the city; see Acts 7:58.

Line 98   Acts 12:17 (εἰς ἕτερον τόπον).

Line 98   in a loud voice; see Matt 27:46 and parallels; Acts 7:57 and 8:7.

Lines 98–101   "to deliver one's spirit in the hands of God" and "to deliver one's soul in peace"; see Ps 31(30):6; Luke 23:46; Acts 7:59.

Lines 103–4   receiving the body and burying it; see Matt 14:12 (for John the Baptist).

ἅγιος εἶπεν· "θεοί, οἳ τὸν οὐρανὸν καὶ τὴν γῆν οὐκ ἐποίησαν, 85
ἀπολέσθωσαν. ἐγὼ γὰρ οὔτε τὰ προστάγματα τοῦ αὐτοκράτορός σου
οὔτε τὰς ἀπειλάς σου πτοοῦμαι. τὸ λοιπὸν ὃ βούλῃ, ἐχθρὲ τῆς
ἀληθείας, ποίει. **20** ἤκουσας ἅπαξ καὶ δὶς παρ᾽ ἐμοῦ, ὅτι οὐ
προσκυνῶ πλὴν ἑνὶ θεῷ, ὅς ἐστιν πατήρ, καὶ τῷ μονογενεῖ αὐτοῦ
υἱῷ καὶ τῷ πνεύματι αὐτοῦ τῷ ἁγίῳ τῷ ποιήσαντι τὸν οὐρανὸν καὶ 90
f. 161ᵛ τὴν γῆν καὶ πάντα τὰ ἐν αὐτοῖς. | εἰς ὃν ἐπίστευσα καὶ αὐτὸς ἔδωκέν
μοι δύναμιν ἐν τῇ ἡμέρᾳ ταύτῃ στῆναι ἔμπροσθέν σου. τὸ γὰρ
θέλημά σου καὶ τῶν δαιμόνων ὧν σὺ προσκυνεῖς οὐ μὴ ποιήσω, ἐγὼ
γὰρ δοῦλος Χριστοῦ ὑπάρχω. τὸ λοιπὸν τί κόπους παρέχεις σεαυτῷ;
ἤδη τὰ κατ᾽ ἐμὲ ἤκουσας· ὃ βούλῃ πρᾶττε." **21** καὶ θυμοῦ πλησθεὶς 95
ὁ ἡγεμὼν ἐκέλευσεν τὸν δῆμον ἅπαντα λαβεῖν τὸν ἅγιον Ἀνανίαν
καὶ πέραν τῆς πόλεως λιθοβολῆσαι· οἱ δὲ λαβόντες αὐτὸν ἀπήγαγον
ἐπὶ τὸν τόπον. ὁ δὲ μακάριος μεγάλῃ τῇ φωνῇ εἶπεν· "κύριε Ἰησοῦ
Χριστέ, εἰς χεῖράς σου παρατίθημι τὸ πνεῦμά μου." καὶ ἔστησαν
αὐτὸν ἐπὶ τὸ μέσον καὶ ἐλιθοβόλησαν αὐτόν. καὶ οὕτως τὴν ψυχὴν 100
αὐτοῦ τὴν ἁγίαν παρέδωκεν ἐν εἰρήνῃ. **22** μετὰ δὲ τὸ τελειωθῆναι
τὸν ἅγιον Ἀνανίαν καὶ ἀναχωρῆσαι ἀπ᾽ αὐτοῦ πάντας, ἦλθον οἱ
συγκωμῆται αὐτοῦ ἐξ Ἀνανὶ τῆς κώμης καὶ λαβόντες τὸ σῶμα αὐτοῦ
ἔθαψαν αὐτὸ εἰς τὴν κληρονομίαν τὴν πατρικὴν αὐτοῦ. ἐγὼ δὲ
Βαρσάπθας ἔγραψα τὰ ὑπομνήματα αὐτοῦ καὶ ἔθηκα πρὸς τὸ 105
f. 162ʳ λείψανον τοῦ ἀποστόλου καὶ ἀθλη|τοῦ τούτου Ἀνανίου, ἵνα γένηται
εἰς ὑπογραμμὸν καὶ εἰς τύπον ὠφελείας καὶ ἔσοπτρον ἐπιθυμητὸν
πᾶσι τοῖς ἐλπίζουσιν ἐπὶ τῇ ἐπαγγελίᾳ τοῦ σωτῆρος ἡμῶν Ἰησοῦ
Χριστοῦ. **23** τελειοῦται δὲ ὁ ἅγιος ἀπόστολος καὶ μάρτυς Ἀνανίας
μηνὶ Ὀκτωβρίῳ αʹ ἐν Χριστῷ Ἰησοῦ τῷ κυρίῳ ἡμῶν. αὐτῷ ἡ δόξα 110
καὶ τὸ κράτος σὺν τῷ πατρὶ καὶ τῷ παναγίῳ πνεύματι νῦν καὶ ἀεὶ
εἰς τοὺς αἰῶνας, ἀμήν.

A
87 βούλῃ: βούλλῃ A ‖ ἐχθρὲ: ἐχθραὶ A ‖ 93 σὺ: σοὶ A ‖ 103 συγκωμῆται:
συγκομεισταὶ A diff. legimus ‖ τὸ: τῷ A ‖ 104 αὐτὸ: αὐτῷ A ‖ 105 ἔθηκα: ἔθηκαν A
ἔθηκα Aᵖᶜ.

Commentary

The Greek Language

The text is written in an unrefined variety of Koine Greek with occasional pretensions toward a higher style (for example, two participles in the genitive absolute: ταῦτα αὐτοῦ ἐκτελοῦντος τοῦ ἁγίου ᾿Ανανίου καὶ σημεῖα πολλὰ ποιοῦντος [lines 25–26]). In this short phrase there is already a redundant expression, αὐτοῦ. . .τοῦ ἁγίου ᾿Ανανίου (unless the word "αὐτοῦ" is used in its adverbial meaning, "there").

The grammar and syntax are not always correct. Lines 38–39 do not form a complete sentence. Line 54 should not read ὄντα με, but ὄντος μου—the genitive absolute—or ὄντι μοι, in order to agree with ἐνετείλατό μοι. The use of the accusative here is one of the indications of the development of the language into demotic Greek, where, besides the genitive of possession and the nominative of the subject and predicate, practically everything else is expressed in the accusative. Line 58 should read ἀπαλλαγήσῃ, but ἀπαλλαγῆς (aorist subjunctive) can be used instead of a future indicative; line 60 should read οἱ δὲ λεγόμενοι ὑφ᾿ ὑμῶν θεοί. Line 62 should read πάντας τοὺς σεβομένους instead of πᾶσι τοῖς σεβομένοις. On line 79 we read ἀνωφελέσι whereas the manuscript has ἀνωφελεῖς. This last form shows the development toward Modern Greek, where there is no dative case or third declension, except for the plural of some words. On line 84, οὓς προσκυνεῖ ὅλος ὁ κόσμος has a syntax bordering on that of Modern Greek.

In spite of the fact that the vocabulary is for the most part elementary, there are instances where the author employs rare and older words, such as διαυγέστατος (line 5, the superlative of διαυγής, -ές, "translucent," "brilliant"; the superlative is already found in Aristotle); ἐλάκησεν (line 30, the aorist of λάσκω, "to crack," "to crash," "to pierce," "to tear," and, eventually, "to resound," "to burst"; this verb is used in the canonical Acts [1:18], referring to the death of Judas, with the meaning "to burst open"); βδελύσσομαι (line 44: here the present participle βδελυσσόμενος, "to feel nausea," "to feel sick," "to loath," which is already attested in Xenophon, is also used in the New Testament with the meaning of "being loathsome," "being abominable"); αἰκιζόμενος (line 48, from αἰκίζω, "to treat injuriously," "to torment," in the passive "to be tormented"); τὸ βούνευρον (line 72, it is not listed in Liddell-Scott-Jones but it is found in Lampe:[8] "tendons of an ox" to make into some kind of a whip); ξυσθῆναι (line 80, the aorist infinitive passive of the verb ξύω; it is already attested in Homer and its use as a reflexive ["to scrach oneself"] is a medical term); line 84, "the whole world" or—another translation—"the whole people."

The use of rare vocabulary in describing torture is appropriate to the genre of martyrdom. The expression εἰς ὑπογραμμὸν καὶ εἰς τύπον (line 107) is very similar to the Modern Greek phrase τύπος καὶ ὑπογραμμός, indicating a perfect model. Finally, how should the expression ἐν τῇ ἰδέᾳ σου (line 46) be translated? It most probably refers to external appearances and not to an interior, intellectual form or idea. In spite of the scarcity of these words in New Testament Greek, the majority of them, with the exception of αἰκιζόμενος (line 48), are used in puristic Greek (the high form of Modern Greek).

On lines 38–40 we encounter a phrase without a principal verb that contains two present participles (θεραπεύων and παρέχων) separated by an insertion ("for the Lord was with him"). It is interesting to compare lines 7–25 to Acts 9:1–19. The text of our manuscript at this point is taken almost verbatim from the canonical Acts, with only minor adjustments having been made in order to present the healing incident of Saul, while still concentrating on the story of Ananias.[9] These minor adjustments in the syntax reveal the subtle differences between the careful and proportioned use of Greek in Acts and that in the present text. In Acts 9:1–2, the narrative uses two participles and one indicative, while the *Martyrdom of Ananias* uses one indicative, one participle, and two infinitives with ὥστε in order to express the same ideas. Acts 9:17 reads: ἀπῆλθεν δὲ Ἀνανίας καὶ εἰσῆλθεν εἰς τὴν οἰκίαν καὶ ἐπιθεὶς ἐπ᾿ αὐτὸν τὰς χεῖρας εἶπεν. . . . The *Martyrdom* (lines 20–21) reads: ἀπελθὼν δὲ ὁ Ἀνανίας εἰσῆλθεν εἰς τὴν οἰκίαν καὶ ἐπιθεὶς ἐπ᾿ αὐτὸν τὰς χεῖρας εἶπεν. . . . It seems that the author of this text was

---

[8] *A Patristic Greek Lexicon*, ed. G. H. W. Lampe (Oxford: Clarendon Press, 1968), s.v.
[9] For a short comparison between our text and the canonical Acts, see below, pp. 328–29.

striving for variety, but in doing so he sacrificed some of the directness and intensity of expression of the original in Acts. In addition to these examples, the occasional placement of the direct object of a verb in participle form or in the indicative after the verb—instead of before, as is the classical Attic custom, followed by Acts—as well as the use of vocabulary which is obviously later (for example, line 18, ἐμφανισθείς instead of the usual ὀφθείς; line 24, ἀπεσπάσθησαν instead of ἀπέπεσαν as in Acts) indicate a late date of composition for this text.

Analysis of the Text

In the heading (line 1 and in the apparatus) the date of the martyrdom (1 October) and title of the piece (μαρτύριον) are mentioned. The emphasis is on the second, nonbiblical part of the narrative, namely, the martyrdom. Note also within the title the naming of Ananias as ἀπόστολος. This man belongs to the first generation, and the *Synaxarion* of the Church of Constantinople makes him one of the seventy apostles of Jesus.[10]

The first part (lines 2–25, paragraphs 1–6) is itself subdivided into two sections. The first briefly presents Ananias, his origins, and his ministry, while the second evokes his meeting with Saul of Tarsus.

In the beginning of the first section (lines 2–7, paragraph 1), the sanctification of Ananias, there is no reference to another human being, Saul of Tarsus, nor to a historical event, Pentecost, but only to Christ and the Ascension. It is important that the latter is indicated by two substantives which occur concurrently (ἀνάλημψις and ἄνοδος). Ananias is not first presented according to his Jewish background, but according to his Christian existence. As is proper with regard to a celebration of a saint, the author covers Ananias with laudatory titles: he is "the great among apostles and martyrs"; he is the "most translucent illuminator" (allowing the light of Christ "to pass through," we suppose, which is indicated on line 50, paragraph 11; here, the adjective could also mean "brilliant"). The word φωστήρ (line 5), referring to the faithful, dates to the beginning of Christianity (Phil 2:15, see Matt 5:14).

---

[10] Compare Delehaye, *Synaxarion*, 95.

This great apostle has "dawned," "risen," translated "appeared" (ἀνατέλλω) (line 3), like a star, "to us": this "us" corresponds structurally to the "us" in the beginning of the gospel of Luke[11] (the events that happened, ἐν ἡμῖν, Luke 1:1).[12] It is the pronoun that defines, not a generation, such as the first one, but a community of sacred origins. The star has risen. In prosaic terms, this means that Ananias has headed out of the region of Damascus in order to fulfill a ministry of signs and miracles among the people (once he had become a Christian).

In the second section (lines 7–25, paragraphs 2–6), one particular story emerges—that of Saul (his name is more often rendered Σαῦλος, except when Ananias addresses him and uses the Semitic form Σαούλ, which reminds us that they are supposed to be speaking in Hebrew or Aramaic). The name "Paul" does not appear. To begin with, we do not know where the action takes place: Ananias is no longer in the region of Damascus, nor is Saul any longer in Tarsus. Damascus is mentioned, but only in relation to the letters and to the prisoners who were going to be brought there. The text, however, makes it clear next (lines 11–17, paragraph 3) that Saul is approaching Damascus. A Christophany occurs, accompanied by a celestial voice ("Saul, Saul, why do you persecute me?") and by a dialogue ("Who are you, Lord?" "I am Jesus, whom you persecute," followed by the command, "But arise and enter the city," and the promise, "and you will find. . .").

In paragraph 4 (lines 18–20) another Christophany is mentioned, this time to Ananias, who is entrusted with a mission. In paragraph 5 (lines 20–23) Ananias meets Saul, places his hands on him, and communicates three pieces of salvific information: 1) the Lord has sent him; 2) this Lord is the same one who appeared to Saul on the road; 3) this all took place in order that Saul might see and be filled with the Holy Spirit. In paragraph 6 (lines 23–25) these prophesies and promises are realized. Saul regains his eyesight and is baptized (for the author, the sacrament of baptism probably includes the effusion of the Holy Spirit).

---

[11] See François Bovon, *L'Évangile selon saint Luc (1, 1–9, 50)* (Commentaire du Nouveau Testament 3a; Geneva: Labor et Fides, 1991), 38.

[12] Even though he shows greater respect for the periods, Livy does not have a very different view in his *Ab urbe condita, Praefatio.*

The second part (lines 25–101, paragraphs 7–21), the longer of the two parts, contains the actual account of the martyrdom of Ananias. Saul is henceforth forgotten. A new character is introduced. Initially he is called Λούκιος (line 27, paragraph 7). Later on he is called Λουκιανός. On line 33 (paragraph 8), where this character appears for the second time, the scribe had first written Λούκιος, but then corrected it to Λουκιανός (one can see very well the correction, and the accent on the first syllable Λου- is still visible). His name is Λουκιανός in Symeon Metaphrastes, as it is in the *Synaxarion* of the Church of Constantinople and the *Menologion* of the emperor Basil. The Roman *Martyrologion* calls him Licinius.[13] In this edition we call him Λουκιανός, Lucianus, throughout.

This governor[14] of the East (line 27, paragraph 7) organizes what is initially called a search (ζήτησις, line 28). It fails because of the quality of the Christians (lines 25–32, paragraph 7). The governor makes another attempt, this time launching a persecution (διωγμός, line 33), introduced by a decree (δόγμα, line 34), the content of which is given to us (lines 34–37, paragraph 8). Before this threat, the ministry of Ananias, which always follows the same pattern of healing rather than preaching, is reprised (lines 38–40, paragraph 9).

The confrontation with the governor is inevitable from this point on. Ananias is arrested (lines 40–43, paragraph 9) and the first dialogue between him and Lucianus constitutes the first round, as it were, of this match, which unfolds as follows: The benevolent governor wishes, so he says, to protect Ananias from himself (lines 43–48, paragraph 10). Ananias answers by beginning a polemic against the false gods in the name of the revelation of Jesus Christ who has led his followers to his Father (lines 48–53, paragraph 11). In order to describe Jesus Christ, the author uses the prologue of the first chapter of the first epistle of John (1 John 1:1–4). Passing again from the general to the particular, he evokes the conversion of Saul of Tarsus (lines 53–55, paragraph 12) before concluding (lines 55–56, paragraph 12). There then follows the

[13] Compare *PG* 114, 1001, n. 1.
[14] Is he known from other sources?

answer of the governor and the response of Ananias, each reminding the other of their arguments (lines 57–58, paragraph 13, and lines 58–62, paragraph 14). The peak of this first round is marked by a prayer by Ananias, which is typical of a believer at the point of suffering martyrdom (lines 63–71, paragraph 15). His prayer contains a double request: save me (as you have saved Saul, creating a parallel between the two) and provide for me the kingdom above. Two points of interest should be noted: the title of God as "the blessed Father" (line 64); and the expression "make me worthy of your blessed apostles" (lines 64–65). The governor's answer is hostile: he threatens Ananias with whips[15] and renews his initial proposal (lines 71–76, paragraph 16). The first round ends with Ananias's words, in which he persists and remains firm in his position (lines 76–79, paragraph 16).

τότε (line 79) marks the beginning of the second round, which is shorter but follows a structure similar to the first, although in the opposite order (the torture is placed in the beginning: they flay his sides; the prayer is indicated but without any mention of its content; the dialogue takes place with a long plea by Ananias [lines 79–95, paragraphs 17–20]).

The third and final round (lines 95–101, paragraph 21) begins with the wrathful governor summoning the people for a stoning similar to Stephen's in Acts 7:54–60 (like the protomartyr, Ananias delivers his spirit into the hands of Christ during a last prayer "outside the city" [line 97] "upon the place" [ἐπὶ τὸν τόπον, line 98, see, concerning Peter, εἰς ἕτερον τόπον, "to another place," Acts 12:17]). The governor, furious, no longer addresses Ananias, and Ananias speaks only to his Lord in a final prayer (lines 98–99). This is the third prayer of the martyr (there is one in each round).

In the conclusion (lines 101–12, paragraphs 22–23), after the saint has "reached his final perfection" (lines 101–2, paragraph 22), the mob, the hostile and profane presence, departs. The compatriots of the saint, the favorable and sacred presence, arrive. What is the meaning of the expression: εἰς τὴν κληρονομίαν τὴν πατρικὴν αὐτοῦ (line 104,

---

[15] The whips will remain in Christian memory; see above, p. 310.

paragraph 22)? Will his own inherit his body? Is there a real geographical interest or an artificial one? Where is Anani? Is it a real or an imaginary place?[16]

Is Barsapthas a Semitic name? Is it known from other sources? What do we know about the author? He has written, and submitted his writing, with an objective in mind, namely, to provide an example of a model for others (lines 101–9, paragraph 22).

The counterpart to the title (lines 109–12, paragraph 23) again gives the date of the martyrdom and the doxology.

The Relation of the Text to the Canonical Acts of the Apostles

As we know, the conversion of Paul is narrated three times in the canonical Acts of the Apostles: the narrative itself (Acts 9) is recalled and summarized in two later discourses of the apostle in chapter 22 before the Sanhedrin and in chapter 26 before the governor Festus, King Agrippa, and Berenice.[17]

The recension of the *Martyrdom of Ananias* published here adapts and quotes the narrative of Acts 9. The parallels to the canonical Acts found in the *Martyrdom* text are presented in table 2.

---

[16] In a personal letter, 17 May 1998, Alain Desreumaux wrote that he found no mention of Anani in any of the several atlases and other reference tools he checked.

[17] In the first narrative Ananias is presented as a Christian from Damascus (Acts 9:10a). Then the Lord appears to him (Acts 9:10b). Ananias answers the call (Acts 9:10c). The Lord then pronounces a long command (Acts 9:11–12), which Ananias first refuses (Acts 9:13–14). The commission is repeated by the Lord (Acts 9:15–16) and finally accepted by Ananias (Acts 9:17a). The Christian from Damascus meets then with Saul, cures him, and baptizes him (Acts 9:17b–18). In the second narrative, which is part of one of Paul's biographical speeches, the story of Ananias is shortened: it contains a description of Ananias (Acts 22:12), a mention of his successful meeting with Saul (Acts 22:13), followed by Ananias's speech to him (Acts 22:14–16). In Acts 22, one notices the absence of the first dialogue between the Lord and Ananias (Acts 9:10b–c) and the transformation of Jesus' speech (Acts 9:15–16) into a report by Ananias (Acts 22:14–16; Acts 9:11–14 simply disappears in Acts 22). See Gerhard Lohfink, *Paulus vor Damaskus. Arbeitsweisen der neueren Bibelwissenschaft dargestellt an den Texten Apg 9:1–19; 22:3–21; 26:9–18* (Stuttgarter Bibelstudien 4; Stuttgart: Katholisches Bibelwerk, 1965).

TABLE 2

Portion of the *Martyrdom*	Relation to Acts
Paragraph 1 (lines 3–6)	Information taken from Acts 9:10a
Paragraph 2 (lines 7–11)	Quotation of Acts 9:1–2
Paragraph 3 (lines 11–16a)	Quotation of Acts 9:3–6a (the details contained in lines 16b–17 are more precise than Acts 9:6b)
Paragraph 4 (lines 18–20)	Quotation of Acts 9:11 (with an allusion to Acts 9:10b)
Paragraph 5 (lines 20–23)	Quotation of Acts 9:17
Paragraph 6 (lines 23–25)	Quotation of Acts 9:18

Verses 7–10 and verses 12–16 of Acts 9, with their subtleties, have been omitted. There is practically no influence of the parallels of Acts 22 and 26 on the *Martyrdom*.

We note that Ochrid, *4* (*BHG* 75x) and Karakallou, *6(8)*, now *48* (*BHG* 75z), do not contain the narrative of Saul's conversion and his baptism by Ananias (in our narrative, paragraphs 1–6). Concerning the narrative of the Martyrdom itself (second part), it would be interesting to compare its structure to the narratives of ancient and medieval martyrdoms.[18]

Conclusion

Even if the *Martyrdom of the Holy Apostle Ananias* is late and takes the form of a hagiographic document, it should not be neglected by scholars interested in early Christian apocryphal literature. Since Ananias is a figure from the origins of Christianity mentioned in the New Testament, his story, particularly his martyrdom, found a place in the Church's calendar and his relics probably received veneration at a certain site. The construction of a sacred time, as well as the construction

---

[18] Compare Hippolyte Delehaye, *Les passions des martyrs et les genres littéraires* (Subsidia hagiographica 13B; Brussels: Société des Bollandistes, 1921); or Alain Bourreau, *La Légende dorée: le système narratif de Jacques de Voragine († 1298)* (Histoire; Paris: Cerf, 1984).

of a sacred space, preserved his memory. The first of October became the date of his feast. Syria, Damascus, and the small town of Anani, if an actual place, constituted his field of missionary activity, episcopal responsibility, and everlasting rest. The creation of such a story certainly does not coincide with the first wave of apocryphal narratives on the apostles, where the stories of their travels and esoteric teachings were particularly remembered. It does, however, fit well into the second wave, in a time when the relation to the canon (here the Acts of the Apostles) has become inescapable, the relation to the institution established (Ananias as the first bishop of Damascus), and the celebration of the martyrdom of the holy man fixed at a precise moment in the religious calendar and a precise place on the map of Christianity (somewhere in Syria).

Bibliographic Notes

Acta sanctorum Ianuarii, 2, Antwerpen, 1643, 613–15, 1151.

Clugnet, Léon. "Ananie," *Dictionnaire d'histoire et de géographie ecclésiastiques*, vol. 2, col. 1431–32. Paris: Letouzey et Ané, 1914.

Halkin, François. "Ananie de Damas," *Δίπτυχα* 4 (Athens, 1986): 178–82.

Lattanzi, Ugo. "Anania," *Bibliotheca Sanctorum*, edited by the Istituto Giovanni XXIII nella Pontificia Università Lateranense, col. 1037. Rome, 1961.

Mayr, Vincent. "Ananias of Damaskus," *Lexikon der christlichen Ikonographie*, vol. 5, col. 129. Freiburg im Breisgau, 1973.

Noret, Jacques. "Manuscrits grecs à Weimar (Fonds W. Froehner) et archives Max Bonnet," *AnBoll* 87 (1969): 79–83.

Wikenhauser, Alfred. "Ananias," *Lexikon für Theologie und Kirche*, vol. 1, col. 486–87. Freiburg im Breisgau, 1957.

Very little on Ananias is in Lipsius, *Die apokryphen Apostelgeschichten*: Ananias is mentioned in the *Abeille*, a work of Salomon of Bassorah (a Syrian author of the first half of the thirteenth century; see *Anecdota Oxoniensia*, ed. Ernst A. Wallis [Semitic Studies 1/2; Oxford, 1886], pp. 103ff. of the Syriac and pp. 115ff. of the English translation); he appears in the list of the seventy; he is absent from the *Chronicon Paschale*, but he is present in the text Dorotheos B and in one by

Hippolytus.[19] Lipsius adds that Ananias is sometimes mentioned in the *Menologia* on the date of 30 June and in some manuscripts of the *Menologion* of the emperor Basil (*Parisinus graecus 1587* and *Parisinus graecus 1588*, both twelfth century): both mention Ananias, placing him between the evangelist Philip and Joseph the Just (also called Barsabas).[20]

Besides the commentaries on the canonical Acts of the Apostles, there is an article by Sten Lundgren concerning Ananias as he appears in Acts 9 and 22, entitled "Ananias and the Calling of Paul in Acts," *Studia Theologica* 25 (1971): 117–22. In opposition to Hans Conzelmann (and before him Ferdinand Christian Baur), Lundgren believes that the episode of Ananias does not function to assure the continuation between the first and second generation of Christianity (Paul being a "Bindeglied" and Ananias representing the church of Luke's time). According to Lundgren, Ananias's function is certainly active although limited: he heals and baptizes Paul.

An analysis of the index sanctorum of the *Analecta Bollandiana*[21] and the last volumes of this periodical (1969–1997) has not revealed any big surprises. Two things may be mentioned. There exists a version of the *Martyrdom of Ananias* in old Slavonic[22] of the recension *BHG* 75y, that is, the one presented here, of which eight manuscripts have been located; and the one article by François Halkin ("Ananie de Damas"), which gives the edition of one manuscript—the oldest—of the recension *BHG* 75x (Ochrid, *4*, ff. 164–66; tenth century), a French translation, and a few lines of introduction.

---

[19] Lipsius, *Die apokryphen Apostelgeschichten* 1:203.

[20] Ibid., 1:205.

[21] See François Halkin, *Analecta Bollandiana. Inventaire hagiographique des tomes 1–100 (1882–1982)* (Brussels: Société des Bollandistes, 1983), 29, which does not indicate any article on the apostle Ananias.

[22] See Aurelio de Santos Otero, *Die handschriftliche Überlieferung der altslavischen Apokryphen*, vol. 1 (Berlin: de Gruyter, 1978), 138–39.

The *Memorial of Saint John the Theologian* (*BHG* 919fb)

Yuko Taniguchi, François Bovon, and Athanasios Antonopoulos

Introduction

A Publication of a New Text on John the Theologian

When Yuko Taniguchi first encountered a photocopied version of two Greek folios at the Andover-Harvard Theological Library, it was difficult to imagine where this project would lead.[1] At that stage, the original folios, which had been in the "Gregory Archive," had already been identified as the missing parts of the Georgius Gospels,[2] manuscript 727 of the University of Chicago, and had been given to that library,[3] where the complete codex of the Georgius Gospels is now preserved.[4]

---

[1] Patrick Tiller had suggested that Taniguchi search some unpublished manuscripts in the "Gregory Archive" at the Andover-Harvard Theological Library in the spring of 1993.

[2] The family of Caspar René Gregory (1846–1917) gave his collection to the Andover-Harvard Theological Library in 1985. The whole codex had previously belonged to the Russian Archaeological Institute; Gregory saw the codex in 1906. The date and the manner by which Gregory acquired the folios are uncertain.

[3] Department of Special Collections, Joseph Regenstein Library, the University of Chicago.

[4] At the request of the Andover-Harvard Theological Library, Barbara Aland of the Institut für Neutestamentliche Textforschung, Westfälische Wilhelms Universität, in Münster, Germany, identified the folios, determining that they fill the missing part of manuscript 727 of the University of Chicago. Immediately after the identification in 1988, the Andover-Harvard Library gave the original folios to the University of Chicago Library.

When work on the folios began, the handwriting of Luke 24:44–53 was easy to read, but a prefatory part of the Gospel of John, called the *Memorial* (ὑπόμνημα) *of Saint John the Theologian*, contained so many abbreviations and difficult writings that it was barely decipherable. François Bovon then joined in reading the *Memorial*.[5] When the transcription and translation of the folios were nearly finished, Bovon and Taniguchi visited the University of Chicago library to look at the whole manuscript of the Georgius Gospels. Later, Athanasios Antonopoulos assisted in this project. He helped particularly with the historical and philological notes. Jean-Daniel Kaestli of the University of Lausanne provided a critical response to the first draft of the transcription. He also procured for us microfilms of two manuscripts which contain the same text, Athos, Vatopedi *901* and Athos, Vatopedi *905*, thus providing us with the opportunity to improve our critical edition of the manuscript. Evie Zachariades-Holmberg and Christine Thomas helped with the translation, and many other people have provided assistance with this project over the years.

Description of Manuscript 727 of the University of Chicago

The Georgius Gospels codex was written for lectionary purposes. The codex is composed of Eusebius's letter to Carpianus; Eusebius's canon tables preceding the Gospels; the four Gospels, each with a preface (ὑπόθεσις or ὑπόμνημα) and a table of chapter titles (κεφάλαια); and the original lectionary tables for *Synaxarion* and *Menologion* following the Gospel of John. The document must have been written by the scribe Theodoros Hagiopetrites around 1300 and bound around 1600.[6]

This manuscript carries the number *2266* in the official list of New Testament manuscripts, according to the Caspar René Gregory system.[7]

---

[5] In this essay, we refer to our particular text as the *Memorial*; however, the other prefatory texts are referred to in general as prologues.

[6] For more detailed information, see R. W. Allison, "Description of Manuscript *727*" (Chicago: University of Chicago Library, 1971, photocopy).

[7] Since the identification of the manuscript as the one missing from the Russian Archaeological Institute, the original Gregory number, *2266*, has replaced the Gregory number *2410*, listed by Kenneth Willis Clark, *A Descriptive Catalogue of Greek New Testament Manuscripts in America* (Chicago: University of Chicago Press, 1937). See Kurt Aland, *Kurzgefasste Liste der griechischen Handschriften des Neuen Testaments*, 2d ed. (Arbeiten zur neutestamentlichen Textforschung 1; Berlin: de Gruyter, 1994), 1:177.

This codex, *Gregory 2266*, is similar in format to the manuscript *Gregory 412*. Curiously, the preface, or prologue, to the Gospel of John is also missing from *Gregory 412*, as it was from our manuscript.[8] Because of the loss of the same pages, the omission of these folios could be intentional,[9] but the exact reasons for and circumstances of the excision in each codex remain unknown. At the University of Chicago Library, we observed that the folios have not been rebound into the manuscript of the Georgius Gospels but have been placed in a separate envelope with the manuscript.

The Identity of the Text

Our text should probably be identified with *BHG* 919fb. Among the many Greek hagiographic texts on John the Theologian, it is closest to *BHG* 919f, but it differs in the following ways: the final words of the two texts are different; and, while our text, *BHG* 919fb, includes a quotation from Dionysius the Areopagite's letter to John, *BHG* 919f does not cite the letter.[10]

Nearly a century ago, Hermann von Soden collected some ancient prefaces and prologues to the Gospels, but his collection does not allow any real parallel story to our text on John.[11] In the Chicago manuscript *727* (*Gregory 2266*), the prefaces to the synoptic Gospels are similar, "with minor variants," to the prefaces given the number *120* by von Soden.[12] To our knowledge, no edition of our text on the Gospel of John has ever been published.

The Search for Other Manuscripts

We have located five witnesses of our text, whereas François Halkin lists only two: the *Sinaiticus graecus 267* and the Venice, *Marcianus*

---

[8] As for other similar codices, Hermann von Soden considers *Gregory 412* and *1394*, which he cites as *419* and *1415*, to be exactly identical. Hermann von Soden, *Die Schriften des Neuen Testaments in ihrer ältesten erreichbaren Textgestalt* (2 vols. in 4; Berlin: Alexander Duncker, 1902), 1/2:783.

[9] Allison, "Description of Manuscript *727*," footnotes on pages 4–5.

[10] See *BHG: Novum Auctarium*, p. 113.

[11] von Soden, *Schriften des Neuen Testaments*, 1/1:300–327.

[12] Allison, "Description of Manuscript *727*," 4. On number *120*, see von Soden, *Schriften des Neuen Testaments*, 1/1:314–15.

graecus 1.20, both mentioned in the *Bibliotheca Hagiographica Graeca*. The three new manuscripts, Chicago, University *727*, Athos, Vatopedi *901*, and Athos, Vatopedi *905*, should be added to the list. We present here a critical edition of all these witnesses.

Definition and Genre of the Prologue

Other prologues, such as the "old Gospel Prologues," have received some attention from scholars examining the early formation of the New Testament canon.[13] Otherwise, few studies of prologues exist, probably because they are considered irrelevant to any inquiry into the life of the historical John or the lives of any other evangelists. Such prologues, however, offer valuable insight into the traditions of the beloved apostle.

Unfortunately, the term "prologue" has not yet been clearly defined. The manuscripts themselves have various titles for the prefatory text, including ὑπόθεσις ("preface"), ὑπόμνημα ("memorial"), προοίμιον ("introduction"), πρόλογος ("introductory speech"), πρόγραμμα ("public notice"), and δήλωσις ("explanation").[14] Von Soden does not himself make any clear distinction among these. It is appropriate to categorize, in broad terms, two types of preface: one is a summary of the gospel and the other is a note on the life of the author.[15]

In manuscript *727* of the University of Chicago, only the prefatory text associated with the Gospel of John is called a "memorial" (ὑπόμνημα).[16] The other three prefatory parts, attached to the Synoptics, are each called a "preface" (ὑπόθεσις). They are shorter than the *Memorial* (ὑπόμνημα) *of Saint John the Theologian* and mainly summarize the content of each Gospel, with a brief reference to the evangelists. The *Memorial* (ὑπόμνημα), however, does not summarize the content of the Gospel, consisting instead of a brief description of

---

[13] Jürgen Regul, *Die antimarcionitischen Evangelienprologe* (Freiburg im Breisgau: Herder, 1969). See also *Synopsis Quattuor Evangeliorum*, ed. Kurt Aland, 13th ed. (Stuttgart: Deutsche Bibelgesellschaft, 1985), 532.

[14] von Soden, *Schriften des Neuen Testaments*, 1/1:300–301.

[15] André Feuillet, "Prologues et sommaires de la Bible," *Dictionnaire de la Bible Supplément* (Paris: Letouzey et Ané, 1972), 8:688–92.

[16] We confirmed this observation when we examined the manuscript at the University of Chicago Library. Kenneth Willis Clark refers to any prefatory sections of the Gospels as a preface (ὑπόθεσις), but this designation is not correct. See Clark, *Descriptive Catalogue*, 265.

the author's life and of the accomplishment of writing the Gospel. A more elaborate definition of a prologue and a more in-depth examination into its nature is required, but we cannot provide that here.

The Text Summarized

After the Ascension of Christ, John leaves Palestine and arrives in Ephesus. Because of his success as a missionary, he is slandered by the Greeks to the emperor Domitian. Although the text is not clear about John's itinerary, he is eventually exiled to the island of Patmos. Dionysius the Areopagite then sends a letter from Athens to John in Patmos. In his letter, Dionysius encourages John and foretells his return to Asia. After Dionysius is martyred by Domitian, John is indeed released from exile by the emperor Trajan. However, the people of Patmos try to persuade John to stay with them. As they are unsuccessful, the people ask for the words of John in place of his personal presence. After a period of fasting, John takes his disciple Prochorus with him to a mountain. Receiving a divine revelation, John dictates the words of God to his disciple Prochorus, who cannot discern the word of God in the thundering sounds. Afterwards, John descends the mountain with a complete Gospel. Although the people of the island still do not want John to leave, he departs for Ephesus. In the end, the Gospel is spread to all believers.

Some Observations on the Memorial

The *Memorial* mentions two individuals from the canonical Acts of the Apostles who are significant: Dionysius the Areopagite (Acts 17:34) and Prochorus (Acts 6:5). It is possible to detect two independent traditions, based on the roles of these two figures in the *Memorial*. Because the story of Dionysius is independent from the story of Prochorus and is not directly involved in the process of writing the Fourth Gospel, it may belong to a tradition which has been added to the one of the narrative. One possible function of the story of Dionysius in the *Memorial* is to provide a historical framework for the text. Also, some elements of mysticism attributed to Dionysius the Areopagite may have influenced the formation of our document. The story of Prochorus, which can be considered as the core of the *Memorial*, may stem from the *Acts of John* by Pseudo-Prochorus.

The Tradition of Prochorus

In the New Testament, Acts 6:5, Prochorus is named as one of the seven leaders. He may have been a Jew either in the Diaspora or in Palestine; he was, in any case, a Greek-speaking Jew whose leadership was conferred upon him along with the other six leaders in Acts.[17] There is no indication of how Prochorus became John's significant disciple.

The *Acts of John* by Pseudo-Prochorus was written around the fifth century. The story can be divided into four parts. First, the author depicts John's journey from Jerusalem to Ephesus. At the same time, Prochorus, one of the seventy disciples, is sent to accompany John and to help him. Second, John and Prochorus start their missionary work by performing miracles in the city of Ephesus (including travel to Rome and the miracle of the boiling oil). Third, they are exiled to Patmos. On Patmos John, accompanied by Prochorus, converts many and performs miracles. John eventually dictates the Fourth Gospel to Prochorus on Patmos. After two unsuccessful pleas of the islanders for John to remain on Patmos, John and Prochorus leave for Ephesus. Fourth, the story ends with John's death and burial in Ephesus.[18]

Although the *Memorial* adds several characters and motives, the scenes concerning the writing of the Fourth Gospel in each text are almost identical.[19] Both texts, the *Acts of John* by Pseudo-Prochorus and the *Memorial*, have an aetiological character. Both agree that the Fourth Gospel was written to replace John's teaching in his absence. The tradition of Patmos as the birthplace of the Fourth Gospel is accepted by each text. The depiction of John's dictation to Prochorus is the same.

It is very likely that the writer, and even the readers, of the *Memorial* presuppose the story of the *Acts of John* by Pseudo-Prochorus. For

[17] According to one legend, Prochorus became a bishop of Nicomedia and was martyred at Antioch. See Jon Paulien, "Prochoros," *ABD* 5:473.

[18] *Acta Joannis*, ed. Theodor Zahn (Erlangen: Deichert, 1880). See Junod and Kaestli, *Acta Iohannis*, 2:743–44; R. Alan Culpepper, *John, The Son of Zebedee: The Life of a Legend* (Columbia: University of South Carolina Press, 1994), 206–22.

[19] It has been proposed that one function of apocryphal literature may be to support the authority of canonical literature; see François Bovon, "Réception apocryphe de l'*Évangile de Luc* et lecture orthodoxe des Actes apocryphes des apôtres," *Apocrypha* 8 (1997): 137–46.

example, in the *Memorial*, Prochorus suddenly appears only when John needs to dictate his Gospel to someone, and he disappears as abruptly, with no explanation, after the Gospel is completed. Nevertheless, the writer of the *Memorial* modifies the *Acts of John* by Pseudo-Prochorus in order to emphasize the writer's agenda.

First, whereas the *Acts of John* by Pseudo-Prochorus does not mention John's birthplace or upbringing, focusing instead on his missionary activities, his death, and his burial, the *Memorial*, by contrast, briefly describes John's life up until he finished the Gospel and is then silent about the rest of John's life. The *Memorial*, it would appear, is interested in the life of John only as it illuminates the Fourth Gospel.

Second, the *Acts of John* by Pseudo-Prochorus vaguely indicates the date of the writing of the Fourth Gospel, stating only that Trajan (curiously not Domitian) orders the exile of John to Patmos and that the next emperor, whose name is not given, releases him from exile.[20] The *Memorial*, obsessed with naming emperors, indicates, however, that Domitian deports John and Trajan releases him from exile. With such specific information, the *Memorial* places the formation of the Fourth Gospel within the framework of Roman history.

Third, the *Acts of John* by Pseudo-Prochorus focuses on details in order to lend credence to the story: John sends Prochorus from the mountain back to the city to acquire ink and papyrus. It takes two days and six hours to write down the Gospel on the mountain. After going down from the mountain, John commands Prochorus to transcribe the Gospel from papyrus to parchment. After completing the transcription, Prochorus reads the Gospel aloud in front of the people. Finally, John instructs the people to keep the parchment Gospel on Patmos and to send the papyrus to Ephesus. In contrast, the *Memorial* leans toward mystical explanations. John frees his mind from "the sense perception." John can stand during the manifestation of God, because "love casts away fear."[21] The appearances of Moses and Samuel in the *Memorial*

---

[20] Zahn, *Acta Joannis*, 45–46, 150–51.

[21] The only comparison in the Septuagint to John standing "erect" (ὄρθιος) before God appears in 1 Sam 28:14, when the dead prophet Samuel appears before King Saul during an act of necromancy. Mention of Samuel in the *Memorial* may indicate a later interpretation of his appearance before Saul.

lend the Fourth Gospel the stature of the Torah and the books of the prophets. As to the expression of the divine words, the *Acts of John* by Pseudo-Prochorus portrays the first words of the Fourth Gospel as coming from John's mouth. The *Memorial*, however, carefully depicts the words of the Gospel first as the direct thundering sound of God; only through John can Prochorus hear the thundering sounds as human words.

These brief observations hint at the historical shift in the perception of John. In the *Acts of John* by Pseudo-Prochorus, the writing of the Gospel is but one of the significant missionary activities John undertakes; it is not the climax of the entire story of the Apostle. John the Apostle returns to Ephesus and continues his missionary activities there until his death. In the *Memorial*, John is the theologian who interprets the indiscernible words of God to Prochorus, the scribe. Although the *Memorial* describes John's return to Ephesus, the implication is that, with the completion of the writing of the Gospel, missionary activity in the name of God, the dispensation of the Gospel, has been continuing until the present.

The Tradition of Dionysius

Pseudo-Dionysius, a late-fifth- or early-six-century Neoplatonic mystic in Syria, is attested under the name of "Dionysius the Areopagite," a man who was converted to Christianity by Paul at the Areopagus in Acts 17:34.[22] According to Eusebius, this Dionysius of the canonical Acts was the first bishop of Athens (*Hist. eccl.* 4.23.3). Eusebius attributes this information to another Dionysius, who was the bishop of Corinth in the second century (*Hist. eccl.* 3.4.6–11). However, little is known of the actual writer of the *Corpus Dionysiacum* in the fifth century.

The letter quoted in the *Memorial* is the last in a collection of ten letters from Pseudo-Dionysius that are addressed to different people. This tenth letter is the only one addressed to the apostle John. The historical context in the letter, though fictitious, agrees with and expands upon the information provided by Eusebius. Dionysius the Areopagite,

[22] Frank E. Wheeler, "Dionysius," *ABD* 2:201. For more on Pseudo-Dionysius, see Adolf Martin Ritter, *Pseudo-Dionysius Areopagita. Über die mystische Theologie und Briefe* (Bibliothek der griechischen Literatur 40; Stuttgart: Anton Hiersemann, 1994).

who was a contemporary of John, must have been very old when he wrote the letter. The scholiast John of Scythopolis conjectured that Dionysius must have been "around ninety" when he wrote the letter.[23] The chronological order of the emperors and the age Eusebius attributes to Dionysius are therefore in agreement with the descriptions in the *Memorial*. Furthermore, the prophecy of John's return from exile after Domitian's death, which is attested in Pseudo-Dionysius's letter, fits with the story written in the *Memorial* as well as with Eusebius's account (*Hist. eccl.* 3.23.1).

The minor alterations in the *Memorial*'s quotation of the beginning of the letter may suggest some modification of the Dionysius tradition, though the quotation of the conclusion of the letter is nearly identical. In the beginning of the letter as quoted in the *Memorial*, Dionysius greets "your holy soul" instead of "you [John]," as in the *Corpus Dionysiacum*. Also, because of the different prepositions and different number, instead of "more particular than for the many (παρὰ τοὺς πολλοὺς ἰδιαίτερον)," in the *Corpus Dionysiacum*, the *Memorial*'s phrasing is "concerning the many who are closer to you (περὶ τοὺς πολλοὺς ἰδιαιτέρους)." Finally, the *Memorial* summarizes the phrase "truly beloved, beloved of him who is really to be yearned for, sought after, and very greatly loved (ἀληθῶς ἠγαπημένε, τῷ ὄντως ἐρατῷ καὶ ἐφετῷ καὶ ἀγαπητῷ λίαν ἠγαπημένε)" as "truly beloved by Christ (ἀληθῶς ἠγαπημένε Χριστῷ)."[24]

Conclusion

Although the role of Dionysius is not directly connected to the writing of the the Fourth Gospel in the *Memorial*, the names of Dionysius and Prochorus are significant because of their close relationship to the

---

[23] Paul Rorem, *Pseudo-Dionysius: A Commentary on the Texts and an Introduction to Their Influence* (Oxford: Oxford University Press, 1993), 27–29.

[24] For the Greek text of Pseudo-Dionysius's letter, see *Corpus Dionysiacum. Pseudo-Dionysius Areopagita*, vol. 2, ed. Günter Heil and Adolf Martin Ritter (Patristische Texte und Studien 36; Berlin: de Gruyter, 1991), 208–10. For the English translation, see *Pseudo-Dionysius: The Complete Works*, trans. Colm Luibheid (New York: Paulist Press, 1987). We are grateful to Enrico Norelli of Geneva who recognized the text and gave us this information.

canonical Acts, even though from a critical and historical point of view it is impossible to trace these individuals. Later, legends arose around these figures. They were declared bishops or martyrs and might have been locally prominent. Pseudepigraphical texts were attributed to them: the *Acts of John* to Prochorus and a whole corpus to Dionysius. Interestingly, in both cases the pseudonymous writings occurred around the fifth century. References to these two traditions were finally combined into the *Memorial*.

As with most rediscovered texts, study of the *Memorial* raises important questions. The purpose, nature, and function of the *Memorial* all need to be explored, especially in light of its relationship with the Fourth Gospel in canon. The definition of the genre of the prologue, in general, requires more extensive thought, and study of the prologue, still a neglected area, needs more attention.

The *Memorial of Saint John the Theologian* (*BHG* 919fb)

Manuscripts

A Chicago, University *727* (e *2266*), 2 folios between f. 195 and f. 196, *olim* Andover-Harvard Theological Library
B Athos, Vatopedi *901*, ff. 198ᵛ–200ʳ
C Athos, Vatopedi *905*, ff. 285ᵛ–87ᵛ
D Venice, *Marcianus graecus 1.20*, ff. 194ᵛ–96ʳ
Dᵖᶜ D *post correctionem*
S *Sinaiticus graecus 267*, ff. 81ᵛ–82ᵛ

Memorial of Saint John the Theologian

This evangelist is, by birth, from a small village, from Bethsaida of Galilee, but he received a not inconsiderable Greek education. After he leaves Palestine, following the Ascension of the Lord, he stays in Asia and remains in Ephesus. After he has overturned the idols there, and has sown the seeds of piety, he is slandered by the Greeks to Domitian,

Line 3   Together with Capernaum and Nazareth, Bethsaida is mentioned in many instances in the New Testament (as Matt 11:21; Luke 9:10; 10:13). It was the place of Jesus' journey by boat (Mark 6:45), and where he performed the miracles of the healing of the blind man (Mark 8:22–26) and the feeding of the multitudes (Luke 9:10). Bethsaida was also the home of the apostle Philip (John 1:44; 12:21) and the birthplace of the brothers and later apostles Peter and Andrew. The city was probably located two miles north of the mouth of the Jordan (the east side of the river, present-day Et Tell), and not on Lake Gennesaret (present-day El-Araj). It should be identified with Julias, according to Josephus (*Ant.* 18.2.2). The city participated in the Jewish revolt against Roman rule, 66–73 C.E. In Byzantine times, Bethsaida was apparently abandoned. Interest in the city has increased in recent years, because of archaeological findings. See Barnabé Meistermann, *Capharnaum et Bethsaïde, suivi d'une étude sur l'âge de la synagogue de tell Houm* (Paris: Auguste Picard, 1921); Michael Avi-Yonah, "Bethsaida," *IDB* 1:396–97; Heinz-Wolfgang Kuhn and Rami Arav, "The Bethsaida Excavations: Historical and Archaeological Approaches," in *The Future of Early Christianity: Essays in Honor of Helmut Koester*, ed. Birger A. Pearson et al. (Minneapolis: Fortress Press, 1991), 77–106.

Line 4   Once referred to as the country of the Philistines, Palestine designates the Mediterranean coast from Joppa to Gaza. From 139 C.E., the term was used by the Romans as a new name for the province of Judaea. Later, it came to refer to the entire eastern coast of the Mediterranean Sea. See Josephus *Ant.* 1, 13; Wendelin Klaer and Bo Reicke, "Palästina," in *Biblisch-historisches Handwörterbuch*, ed. Bo Reicke and Leonhard Rost, 4 vols. (Göttingen: Vandenhoeck und Ruprecht, 1962–1979), 3:1365–80; Peter Machinist et al., "Palestine," *ABD* 5:69–126.

Lines 4–5   The text presupposes the sending of the apostles by Christ after his resurrection and prior to his Ascension, mentioned in Matt 28:16–20, Luke 24:44–48, and Acts 1:1–11 and narrated in some apocryphal stories, *Acts of Thomas* 1 or *Acts of Philip* 8, 1(94). See Jean-Daniel Kaestli, "Les scènes d'attribution des champs de mission

ὑπόμνημα εἰς τὸν ἅγιον Ἰωάννην τὸν θεολόγον

οὗτος ὁ εὐαγγελιστὴς πατρίδος μὲν ἦν ἤτοι κώμης εὐτελοῦς ἀπὸ
Βηθσαϊδὰ τῆς Γαλιλαίας, Ἑλληνικῆς δὲ παιδείας μετεῖχεν οὐδὲ
βραχύ. τὴν οὖν Παλαιστίνην ἀπολιπὼν μετὰ τὴν τοῦ κυρίου
ἀνάληψιν, τῇ Ἀσίᾳ ἐπιδημεῖ καὶ τῇ Ἐφέσῳ ἐφίσταται. καὶ τὰ ἐκεῖσε   5
εἴδωλα καταστρέψας καὶ τὴν εὐσέβειαν ἐγκατασπείρας ὑπὸ τῶν

ABCDS
1 ἅγιον Ἰωάννην A C S: ἅγιον ἀπόστολον Ἰωάννην B D ‖ 6 ἐγκατασπείρας A C D
S: ἐγκατεσπείρας B.

et de départ de l'apôtre dans les Actes apocryphes," in *Actes apocryphes des apôtres*,
246–64.
   Line 5   Ephesus, one of the port cities of Ionia (Asia Minor), was a major political,
religious, and commercial center in antiquity. The city was known for its temple of
Artemis, which has been considered one of the Seven Wonders of the Ancient World.
Ephesus was also the capital of the wealthy and influential province of Asia during the
Roman imperial period. The city had a long tradition in the arts and sciences and was
a significant cultural center. The book of Acts provides information about the city
during the first century. Ephesus was also an important center of early Christianity;
Paul's ministry is specifically connected with Ephesus. See Acts 18:19, 21, 24; 19:1,
17, 26, 35; 20:16, 17; 1 Cor 15:32. Clive Foss, *Ephesus after Antiquity: A Late Antique,
Byzantine, and Turkish City* (Cambridge/New York: Cambridge University Press, 1979);
Richard Oster, "Ephesus, Ephesians," *EEChr* 1:373–75; Daphne Athas, *Entering
Ephesus* (Sag Harbor, N.Y.: Second Chance Press, 1991); Selahattin Erdemgil, *Ephesus*
(Istanbul: Net, 1993); Peter Scherrer, ed., *Ephesos. Der neue Führer: 100 Jahre
österreichische Ausgrabungen 1895–1995* (Vienna: Österreichisches Archäologisches
Institut in Verbindung mit dem Efes Müzesi Selçuk, 1995); *Ephesos Metropolis of
Asia: An Interdisciplinary Approach to Its Archaeology, Religion, and Culture*, ed.
Helmut Koester (Valley Forge, Pa.: Trinity Press International, 1995).
   Lines 5–6   The destruction of idols by Christ or his apostles is a traditional motif
in the apocryphal literature. See *Pseudo-Matthew* 22:2–24; *Acts of John* 37–45; and
Acts of Paul, pp. 35–39 of PHeid. François Bovon, "Le Dieu de Luc," *La parole de
grâce (Mélanges Augustin George). Recherches de science religieuse* 69 (1981): 297–98.

Vespasian's son, who is in power after Titus. Hence he sails from Asia toward Europe, and he leaves for exile on the island of Patmos. While he happens to be there, the wonderful Dionysius, who is about ninety

Line 7   Domitian (Titus Flavius Domitianus), Roman emperor of the Flavian dynasty from 81 to 96 C.E., was the second son of Vespasian and Flavia Domitilla. His administration included various reforms of a domestic nature. The book of Revelation, especially 2:13–14 and 20:4, provides us with information on the martydoms under Domitian, in Asia Minor. It was at this time that John, the author of Revelation, was exiled on the island of Patmos. On 18 September 96, Domitian was murdered and succeeded by Nerva (96–98 C.E.). See Paul Keresztes, "The Jews, the Christians, and the Emperor Domitian," *Vigiliae Christianae* 27 (1973): 1–28; Hermann Bengtson, *Die Flavier: Vespasian, Titus, Domitian: Geschichte eines römischen Kaiserhauses* (Munich: Beck, 1979); John B. Campbell, "Domitian," *OCD*, 491; Brian W. Jones, *The Emperor Domitian* (London/New York: Routledge, 1992).

Line 7   The use of the dative τῷ Οὐεσπασιανῷ here is surprising. One expects the genitive: Vespasian's son. Vespasian (Titus Flavius Sabinus Vespasianus), Roman emperor from 69 until 79 C.E. and founder of the Flavian dynasty, was born 17 November 9 B.C.E. in Sabine Reate and was the son of Flavius Sabinus and Vespasia Polla. During his ten-year rule, he increased taxation and sent the Roman army to Scotland. He also began construction of several monuments, among them the famous Colosseum. His most important contribution was the restoration of peace and stability to the empire following the civil war of 68–69 C.E. and the Jewish revolt of 66–73. Vespasian died 23 June 79 C.E. Guy E. F. Chilver and Barbara M. Levick, "Vespasian (Titus Flavius Vespasianus)," *OCD*, 1590–91.

Line 7   Titus (Titus Flavius Sabinus Vespasianus) was Roman emperor from 79 until 81 C.E. The elder son of the emperor Vespasian and Flavia Domitilla, he was born 30 December 39, in Rome. He served in Germany and Britain, and in 70 C.E., as a leader of the Roman army in Palestine, he captured and destroyed Jerusalem. In commemoration of his victory against the Jews, it is probably his brother Domitian who erected the Arch of Titus. On the same occasion, his father appointed him praetorian prefect. Titus succeeded his father in June 79 and, as emperor, he erected several monuments, among them the baths, and he completed the construction of the Colosseum. Nothing is known about his attitude toward Christians. Titus died in Rome on 13 September 81. John B. Campbell, "Titus," *OCD*, 1532–33; Brian W. Jones, *The Emperor Titus* (London: Croom Helm; New York: St. Martin's Press, 1984); Brian W. Jones, "Titus," *ABD* 6:580–81; Michael P. McHugh, "Titus," *EEChr* 2:1135; Leandro Navarra, "Titus," *EEC* 2:843.

Line 8   Asia, or Asia Minor, is the western portion of Turkey, extending from the Bosporus along the Aegean coast. Asia Minor and its most famous cities—Miletus, Ephesus, Laodicea—are mentioned in the New Testament, especially in connection with the apostle Paul's missionary journey, as well as in the book of Revelation. In the fourth century C.E., as part of the Eastern Roman Empire, with its capital, Byzantium (Constantinople), this region played a significant role. During the fifth century three

Ἑλλήνων διαβάλλεται Δομετιανῷ τῷ Οὐεσπασιανῷ, ὃς μετὰ Τῖτον 7
εἶχε τὸ κράτος. ὅθεν καὶ ἀπὸ τῆς Ἀσίας ἐπὶ τὴν Εὐρώπην ἀνάγει
καὶ εἰς ὑπερορίαν ἀπάγει ἐν Πάτμῳ τῇ νήσῳ. ἔνθα δὴ καὶ τυγχάνοντι

A B C D S
7 Δομετιανῷ A B C D: δομετίω S ‖ Οὐεσπασιανῷ: οὐέσπασιανῶ B S οὐεσπασιανῶ
D A ut uid. uel οὐεσπασιανοῦ   οὐέσπεσιανοῦ C ‖ 9 ὑπερορίαν ἀπάγει A C D S:
ὑπερορίἀπαγει B.

---

major councils were held in Asia Minor: the Council of Ephesus (431); the so-called
Robber Council of Ephesus (449); and the Council of Chalcedon (451). See 1 Macc
11:13; 12:39; 13:32; 2 Macc 3:3; 10:24; 3 Macc 3:14; 2 Esd 15:46; 16:14; Acts 2:9;
6:9; 16:6; 19:10, 22, 26, 31; 20:4, 16, 18; 21:27; 24:18; 27:2; 1 Cor 16:19; 2 Cor 1:8; 2
Tim 1:15; 1 Pet 1:1; Rev 1:4; Donald F. Easton and Stephen Mitchell, "Asia Minor,"
OCD, 190–91; David Magie, *Roman Rule in Asia Minor to the End of the Third Century
after Christ* (Salem, N.H.: Ayer, 1988); Frederik W. Norris, "Asia Minor," *EEChr* 1:132–
34; Clive Foss, "Asia Minor," *ODB* 1:205–7; Daria De Bernardi Ferrero and Marina
Falla Castelfranchi, "Asia Minor," *EEC* 1:85–89.

Line 9   The island of Patmos is located in the northwestern part of the Dodecanese
Islands, between the islands of Ikaria and Leros, near Asia Minor. Thucydides, Strabo,
and Pliny all mention Patmos. According to Strabo, "Nearby are both Patmos and the
Corassiae; these are situated to the west of Ikaria (island), and Ikaria to the west of
Samos (island). . .and the islands just mentioned—the Corassiae and Patmos and Leros."
(Strabo *Geographia* 10.5.13; translation by H. L. Jones [LCL, 1931]). During the Roman
imperial period, Patmos became a place of exile for political prisoners. Thus, during
the reign of Domitian, John, the author of Revelation, was exiled on Patmos (Rev 1:9–
10). According to a legendary tradition, in the Monastery of the Apocalypse, and
especially in the Cave of St. Anne, John is said to have dictated the Book of Revelation
to his disciple Prochorus. In 1088, Christodoulos Letrinos, the Bithynian abbot, received
permission from the Byzantine emperor, Alexios I Comnenos, to found a monastery at
Patmos, in honor of Saint John the Theologian. The text of the present manuscript
seems to presuppose that Patmos belongs to Europe. See Victor Guérin, Josiah Brewer,
and John Warner Barber, *Description de l'île de Patmos et de l'île de Samos* (Paris:
Auguste Durand, 1856); Anna Marava-Chatzenikolaou, *Patmos* (Athens: Aster, 1972);
Henri Dominique Saffrey, "Relire l'Apocalypse à Patmos," *Revue Biblique* 82 (1975):
385–417; Timothy E. Gregory and Nancy Patterson Ševčenko, "Patmos," *ODB* 3:1596–
97; Scott T. Carroll, "Patmos," *ABD* 5:178–79.

Lines 9 and 23   The word ὑπερορία derives from the verb ὑπερορίζω, "go beyond
the frontier," "cross the border," "banish." In our text, ὑπερορία means the country
beyond one's own frontiers, a foreign country, or country for exile.

Line 9: καὶ τυγχάνοντι   This is a strange use of the dative. This word would
usually be in the genitive absolute: ἔνθα δὴ καὶ τυγχάνοντος αὐτοῦ.

years old, sends the following from Athens: "I greet your holy soul, beloved, this will be by me to you concerning the many who are closer to you. Rejoice, therefore, truly beloved by Christ." And next he adds this, saying something admirable: "If Christ is true, the unrighteous ones expel the disciples, too, from the cities, and assigning to themselves the things of which they are worthy, and separating, and keeping themselves, the accursed ones, away from the holy things." Then, with regard to the future things also, he indicates this: "You will be set free from prison in Patmos and you will sail back to the Asian land. And you will accomplish there the messages of the good God and you will pass them on to those after you." After this Dionysius is perfected in martyrdom by Domitian. Then, Nerva comes to power after Domitian,

Line 10   Dionysius the Areopagite is supposed to have lived in Athens in the first century C.E. and was a member of the Athenian Areopagus. Acts 17:34 informs us of his conversion to Christianity by Paul. According to the tradition, he was the first bishop of Athens and was martyred during the reign of Emperor Domitian. The *Synaxarion of Constantinople*, 102.8–14, even provides a brief description of Dionysius: "He was of moderate height, emaciated, with white and sallow skin, flatness, with puckered eyebrows, sunken eyes, always deep in thought, with large ears, abundant gray hair, a moderately cleft upper lip, a straggly beard, a slight pot-belly and long slender fingers" (*ODB* 1:629). See Acts 17:33–34; *BHG* 554–58m and *BHG: Novum Auctarium* 554–58s; Andrew W. Lintott, "Dionysius the Areopagite," *OCD*, 477–78; Andrew Louth, *Denys the Areopagite* (London: Chapman; Wilton, Conn.: Morehouse-Barlow, 1989); James A. Brooks, "Dionysius the Areopagite, Pseudo-," *EEChr* 1:335; Alexander Kazhdan and Nancy Patterson Ševčenko, "Dionysios the Areopagite," *ODB* 1:629; Salvatore Lilla, "Dionysius the Areopagite, Pseudo-," *EEC* 1:238–40; and Frank E. Wheeler, "Dionysius," *ABD* 2:201.

Lines 11–20   The author of our ὑπόμνημα quotes here part of a letter attributed in the manuscript tradition to Dionysius the Areopagite. See above, pp. 340–41.

Lines 14–17   These lines are very difficult to understand.

Lines 20–21   Symeon Metaphrastes has provided significant detail in his description of the martyrdom of Dionysius the Areopagite in his *Menologion*, *BHG* 555 (*PG* 115, 1032–49).

Line 21   Nerva (Marcus Cocceius), Roman emperor from 96 until 98 C.E., was born in Narnia, Umbria. After Domitian's assassination in 96 C.E., he was elected emperor. During his administration, he reduced the costs of the government and created an economic welfare policy especially directed toward poor citizens. He was succeeded by Trajan. See John B. Campbell, "Nerva, Marcus Cocceius," *OCD*, 1038–39.

Line 22   Trajan (Marcus Ulpius Trajanus), the first Roman emperor of Spanish

καὶ ὁ θαυμαστὸς Διονύσιος περίπου τὸ ἐνενηκοστὸν ἤδη τῆς ἡλικίας 10
ὢν ἔτος ἐξ ᾽Αθηνῶν ἐπιστέλλει τοιάδε· προσαγορεύω σου τὴν ἱερὰν
ψυχὴν ἠγαπημένε καὶ ἔσται μοι τοῦτο πρὸς σὲ περὶ τοὺς πολλοὺς
ἰδιαιτέρους. χαῖρε τοίνυν ἀληθῶς ἠγαπημένε Χριστῷ. ἐξῆς δὲ καὶ
ταῦτα προστίθησι τὶ θαυμαστὸν λέγων· εἰ Χριστὸς ἀληθεύει, καὶ
τοὺς μαθητὰς οἱ ἄδικοι τῶν πόλεων ἐξελαύνουσιν, αὐτοὶ τὰ κατ᾽ 15
ἀξίαν ἑαυτῶν ἀπονέμοντες καὶ τῶν ἁγίων οἱ ἐναγεῖς
ἀποδιαστελλόμενοι καὶ ἀποφοιτῶντες. εἶτα καὶ περὶ τῶν μελλόντων,
ταῦτα ἐπισημαίνεται ὅτι καὶ τῆς ἐν Πάτμῳ φυλακῆς ἀφεθήσῃ καὶ
εἰς τὴν ᾽Ασιάτιδα γῆν ἐπανήξεις. καὶ δράσεις ἐκεῖ τοῦ ἀγαθοῦ θεοῦ
μηνύματα καὶ τοῖς μετὰ σὲ παραδώσεις. μετὰ ταῦτα Διονύσιος μὲν 20
ἐτελειώθη τῷ μαρτυρίῳ παρὰ Δομετιανῷ. Νερούας δὲ μετὰ
Δομετιανὸν τὴν ἀρχὴν διαδέχεται καὶ μετὰ Νερούαν Τραϊανός, ὑφ᾽

A B C D S
10 τὸ A B C S: τὸν D ‖ 11 προσαγορεύω A C D S: προσαγορεύσω B ‖ 12 ἠγαπημένε
B C S: A et D ut uid. uel ἠγαπημένην ‖ περὶ A C: παρὰ B D S ‖ 13 ἰδιαιτέρους A B
C D: ἰδιαίτερον S ‖ ἐξῆς B D S: ἐξεῖς A et C diff. legimus ‖ 14 προστίθησι C:
πρὸστίθησι S B προστίθηϊ D προστίθη A diff. legimus ‖ 15 ἐξελαύνουσιν B D S:
ἐξελαύνουσι A C ‖ 16 ἑαυτῶν A: ἑαυτοῖς B C D S ‖ 17 εἶτα A B C D: εἶτα S diff.
legimus ‖ 17–18 καὶ περὶ τῶν μελλόντων, ταῦτα A B C D: omit. S ‖ περὶ: B C D, A ut
uid. ‖ 18 ἀφεθήσῃ: ἀφεθήσῃ A B D S ἀφεθήσει C diff. legimus ‖ 20 μηνύματα nos:
μιμήμτ A μίμητ᾽ B μίμηματα C D μιμήματα S ‖ 21 Δομετιανῷ A D: δομετϊανοῦ B C S.

descent, reigned from 98 to 117 C.E. He was born on 18 September 53 C.E. in Spain. He participated in the Roman campaigns against Spain, Germany, and Syria. After Nerva's death, and with the Roman army's support, Trajan was elected emperor. During his administration he reduced taxes, constructed roads, bridges, canals, harbors (Centum Cellae), and public monuments (Trajan's Column in the Forum of Trajan) throughout the empire. He also led campaigns against the Dacians (101–2, 105–6) and the Parthians (113–17). He died in 117 C.E. in the Roman province of Cilicia (Asia Minor) and was succeeded by Hadrian. Trajan is most noted for his major expansion of the empire. He has had "good press" among Christians because of the Pliny correspondence. See John B. Campbell, "Trajan (Marcus Ulpius Traianus)," *OCD*, 1543–44; Brian W. Jones, "Trajan," *ABD* 6:639–40. Jean Beaujeu, *La religion romaine à l'apogée de l'empire*, vol. 1: *La politique religieuse des Antonins* (Paris: Société d'édition Les Belles Lettres, 1955); Julian Bennett, *Trajan: Optimus Princeps: A Life and Times* (London/New York: Routledge, 1997); Eugen Cizek, *L'époque de Trajan: Circonstances politiques et problemes idéologiques* (Paris: Société d'édition Les Belles Lettres, 1983).

and after Nerva, Trajan, by whom an edict goes out to those in exile calling them all back. And the edict comes also to John in Patmos. Though he feels the desire to leave, the Patmians ask him not to go. And because they cannot convince him, they ask to possess his writings in his place. And he, after agreeing, first commands himself to fast, and the very same for everyone else, as well as separation from evil things. Then, after John takes Prochorus along with him, he reaches the mountain ridge, in order that the former should interpret what comes from God, and the latter, what comes from the former. Then, he stands as straight as Samuel, and he stretches forth both his hands like Moses and he frees his mind from the sense perception and brings it wholly up to the desired one. What happens then? Horrible thunderings and fearful things and lightning continuously rending the sky, exactly as at the time of Moses. Then, face down and as if without breath, Prochorus is not able to withstand such spectacles. But John stands steadfast, because love casts away fear. And after a while the thunder articulates itself as a voice and it sounds forth extremely strongly: "In the beginning was the word, and the word was with God, and God was the word." Prochorus

Line 24   The word ἀνάκλησις derives from the verb ἀνακαλέω, which means "to call up," "to call again," "to recall." In our text, the word ἀνάκλησις means "calling on," "salutation." Also, it is a technical term in Roman law.

Line 25   The word ἔφεσις derives from the verb ἐφίεμαι, which means "aiming at a thing," or "appetite." In this text, the word ἔφεσις means "desire." But the text is uncertain and the original reading may have been Ἔφεσον.

Line 27   The word ἀσιτία derives from the verb ἀσιτέω, meaning "abstain from food," or "abstain from forbidden food," "fast." See Acts 27:21, 33.

Line 30   The verb στηλόω means here "to set up as a monument" or "to stand firm."

Lines 30–31: στηλοῦται κατὰ τὸν Σαμουὴλ ὄρθιος   See 1 Kings 17:16 (LXX): ἐστηλώθη τεσσαράκοντα ἡμέρας. See also 1 Sam 28:14 (LXX): Samuel appears, ὄρθιος.

Line 32   τῶν αἰσθήσεων, literally, "from the sense perception things," is not easily translated.

Lines 33 and 42   The word δεῖμα derives from the verb δείδω, one of whose meanings is "to fear." In our text, δείματα means "fear," "affright," or "an object of fear," "a terror," "horror."

Line 34   The adjective πρηνής means "with his face downwards," "head-foremost." It indicates in our text the position of the human body. See also Acts 1:18.

οὗ γράμματα ἧκε πρὸς τοὺς ἐν ὑπερορίᾳ πάντας ἀνακαλούμενα. ἧκε
καὶ ἐν Πάτμῳ πρὸς Ἰωάννην ἀνάκλησις. καὶ ὁ μὲν παραπλεῖν ἔγνω
τὴν ἔφεσιν, οἱ δὲ Πάτμιοι οὐ μεθήσειν ἔλεγον. ὡς δὲ πείθειν οὐκ   25
εἶχον, αἰτοῦνται τοὺς αὐτοῦ λόγους ἀντ᾽ αὐτοῦ κατέχειν. ὁ δὲ
πεισθεὶς πρῶτα μὲν ἀσιτίαν ἑαυτῷ παραγγέλλει, τοῖς δ᾽ ἄλλοις αὐτό
τε τοῦτο καὶ τὴν τῶν κακῶν ἀλλοτρίωσιν. εἶτα παραλαβὼν τὸν
Πρόχορον τῆς ἀκρώρας ἐφάπτεται ἵνα ὁ μὲν τὰ παρὰ θεοῦ, ὁ δὲ τὰ
ἐκείνου διασημαίνηται. ἔπειτα στηλοῦται κατὰ τὸν Σαμουὴλ   30
ὄρθιος, κατὰ δὲ Μωσέα τὼ χεῖρε διεσχημάτισται καὶ τὸν νοῦν
ἐξελὼν τῶν αἰσθήσεων ὅλον ἀναφέρει πρὸς τὸν ποθούμενον. τί οὖν
τὸ ἐντεῦθεν; βρονταὶ φρικώδεις καὶ δείματα καὶ ἀστραπαὶ συνεχῶς
ἀπορρηγνύμεναι καθάπερ ἐπὶ Μωσέως εἶτα πρηνὴς καὶ οἰονεὶ
ἄπνους, ὁ Πρόχορος τοιούτοις οὐκ ἐνεγκὼν ἐνδιατρίβειν θεάμασιν.   35
αὐτὸς δὲ ἀμετάτρεπτος ἵσταται πόρρω τῆς ἀγάπης τὸ δέος βαλούσης.
εἰς φωνὴν δὲ ὀψέ πως ἡ βροντὴ διαρθροῦται καὶ τρανότατα ὑπηχεῖ
τὸ ἐν ἀρχῇ ἦν ὁ λόγος καὶ ὁ λόγος ἦν πρὸς τὸν θεόν, καὶ θεὸς ἦν ὁ
λόγος. πλησίον τῆς θεωρημοσύνης ὁ Πρόχορος. τὸ μὲν φῶς διορῶν,

A B C D S
25 ἔφεσιν A: ἔφεσον B C D S ‖ Πάτμιοι B C S: πάτμοι A D ‖ 27 πρῶτα A C D S:
πρῶτον B ‖ ἑαυτῷ A B D S: ἑαυτοῖς C ‖ 28 τὴν τῶν A B C S: τῶν D ‖ παραλαβὼν S:
ἐπιλαβὼν A B C D ‖ 29 ἀκρώρας A D: ἀκρωρίας B C S ‖ 30 διασημαίνηται nos:
διασημήνηται A B C S διασημείνηται D ‖ στηλοῦται B C D S: A ut uid. uel
στηλούμενος ‖ 31 τὼ χεῖρε A B C D: τῶ χεῖρε uel τῇ χεῖρε S ‖ 32 ἐξελὼν: legend
ἐξελθών? ‖ αἰσθήσεων B C D S αἰσθητῶν A diff. legimus ‖ 34 ἀπορρηγνύμεναι A B
C D: ἐπιρρηγνήμεναι S ‖ πρηνὴς καὶ A: πρινὴς μεν καὶ B D S πρηνοὶς μὲν καὶ C ‖
35 ὁ Πρόχορος A B C D S: ὁ Dᵖᶜ ‖ τοιούτοις A B D S: τούτοις C ‖ 36 ἵσταται A uel
ἵστατο?: ἵστατο B C D S ‖ βαλούσης A C S: βαλλούσης B D ‖ 37 τρανότατα: A et
D ut uid. uel τρανότης? τρανώτερον B S τρανότερον C ‖ 38 τὸ A B C D: τὸ δὲ S ‖ 39
θεωρημοσύνης A: θεορημοσύνης S θεορρημοσύνης B C D.

Line 35   The adjective ἄπνους derives from the verb ἀ-πνέω and in our text means
a person "without breath" or "lifeless."

Lines 38–39   This is a quotation of John 1:1.

is near the vision of God. Though he sees the light, he hears nothing (the theologian is the tongue of the thunder), and the initiate, after he has recovered from fear, inscribes with a trembling hand what happens there until the Gospel is completed. Then, the fearful events subside and the heavenly things are revealed to those upon the earth. Later, John descends from the mountain having been handed the law, just like Moses, the one who saw God, is handed the tablets, which he gives to those who have requested it, and he leaves for Ephesus even though the islanders are unwilling. And the Gospel has been dispersed to all those who believe, for our benefit and to the glory of Christ our God.

Line 40   The word μύστης has the following aspects: 1) one who is initiated into the mysteries; 2) one to whom spiritual truth has been revealed; 3) one who is a spiritual being; 4) one who has full knowledge of the meaning of the scriptures; 5) one who is privy to a secret; 6) one who is being initiated. See *A Patristic Greek Lexicon*, ed. G. W. H. Lampe (Oxford: Clarendon Press, 1976), s.v. μύστης.

Lines 42–43   The author may presuppose John 3:12: "If I tell you about earthly things and you do not believe, how can you believe if I tell you about heavenly things?"

ἀκούων δὲ οὐδενὸς (γλῶσσα τῆς βροντῆς ὁ θεολόγος) καὶ ὁ μύστης   40
τοῦ δέους ἀνενεγκών, ὑπὸ τρεμούσῃ χειρὶ τὰ ἐκεῖ διαχαράττει ἕως
ἀπηρτίσθη τὸ εὐαγγέλιον. ἔπειτα ὑποχωροῦν μὲν τὰ δείματα τοῖς δ'
ἐπὶ γῆς ἀνακαλύπτεται τὰ οὐράνια. ὀψὲ καὶ ἀπὸ τοῦ ὄρους κάτεισιν
ὁ Ἰωάννης τὸν νόμον ἐγχειρισθεὶς ὡς ὁ θεόπτης τὰς πλάκας Μωσῆς
ὃν δοὺς τοῖς αἰτησαμένοις. αὐτὸς μὲν καὶ ἀκόντων τῶν νησιωτῶν   45
παρέπλει τὴν Ἔφεσον. τὸ δὲ εὐαγγέλιον διεδόθη εἰς πάντας τοὺς
πιστεύοντας εἰς ὠφέλειαν ἡμῶν. καὶ εἰς δόξαν Χριστοῦ τοῦ θεοῦ
ἡμῶν.

A B C D S
40 τῆς A B D S: τοῖς C ‖ ὁ θεολόγος A C D S: θεολόγος B ‖ 41 ἐκεῖ A: ἐκεῖθεν B C D
S ‖ 42 ἀπηρτίσθη A C D S: ἀπηρτήθη B ‖ ὑποχωροῦν A D: ὑποχωροῦσι B C S ‖
δείματα A C D S: δείγματα B ‖ 42–43 τοῖς δ' ἐπὶ γῆς A C D S: τοῖς ἐπὶγῆς B ‖ 44 ὁ
Ἰωάννης A B C D: ἰωάννης S ‖ 45 ὃν δοὺς A B D S: ὃ ἡδοὺς C ‖ ἀκόντων A B C D:
κόντων S ‖ νησιωτῶν A C S: νησιτῶν B D ‖ 46 διεδόθη A B D S: ἐδόθη C ‖ 48 ἡμῶν
A B D S: ἡμῶν ἀμήν C.

Bibliography

Amsler, Frédéric, François Bovon, and Bertrand Bouvier, eds. *Actes de l'apôtre Philippe. Introduction, traductions et notes.* Apocryphes 8. Turnhout: Brepols, 1996.

Bauer, Johannes Baptist. *Die neutestamentlichen Apokryphen.* Die Welt der Bibel 21. Düsseldorf: Patmos, 1968.

Bedjan, Paul. *Acta Martyrum et Sanctorum*, vol. 1. 1890. Reprint, Hildesheim: Olms, 1968.

Bieler, Ludwig. *ΘΕΙΟΣ ΑΝΗΡ. Das Bild des "göttlichen Menschen" in Spätantike und Frühchristentum.* 2 vols. 1935–36. Reprint, 2 vols. in 1; Darmstadt: Wissenschaftliche Buchgesellschaft, 1976.

Blumenthal, Martin. *Formen und Motive in den apokryphen Apostelgeschichten.* Texte und Untersuchungen zur Geschichte der altchristlichen Literatur 48/1. Leipzig: Hinrichs, 1933.

Bornkamm, Günther. *Mythos und Legende in den apokryphen Thomasakten. Beiträge zur Geschichte der Gnosis und zur Vorgeschichte des Manichäismus.* Forschungen zur Religion und Literatur des Alten und Neuen Testaments 49. Göttingen: Vandenhoeck und Ruprecht, 1933.

Bovon, François. *New Testament Traditions and Apocryphal Narratives.* Trans. Jane Haapiseva-Hunter. Princeton Theological Monograph Series 36. Allison Park, Pa.: Pickwick Publications, 1995.

Bovon, François, et al. *Les Actes apocryphes des apôtres. Christianisme et monde païen.* Publications de la Faculté de théologie de l'Université de Genève 4. Geneva: Labor et Fides, 1981.

Bovon, François, and Pierre Geoltrain, eds. *Écrits apocryphes chrétiens*, vol. 1. Bibliothèque de la Pléiade 442. Paris: Gallimard, 1997.

Bremmer, Jan N., ed. *The Apocryphal Acts of John*. Studies on the Apocryphal Acts of the Apostles 1. Kampen: Kok Pharos, 1995.

———. *The Apocryphal Acts of Paul and Thecla*. Studies on the Apocryphal Acts of the Apostles 2. Kampen: Kok Pharos, 1996.

———. *The Apocryphal Acts of Peter: Magic, Miracles, and Gnosticism*. Studies on the Apocryphal Acts of the Apostles 3. Leuven: Peeters, 1998.

Brock, Ann Graham, "Genre of the *Acts of Paul*: One Tradition Enhancing Another." *Apocrypha* 5 (1994):119–36.

Brown, Peter. *The Body and Society: Men, Women, and Sexual Renunciation in Early Christianity*. Lectures on the History of Religions, n.s., 13. New York: Columbia University Press, 1988.

———. *The Cult of the Saints: Its Rise and Function in Latin Christianity*. Haskell Lectures on History of Religions, n.s., 2. Chicago: University of Chicago Press, 1981.

Budge, E. A. Wallis. *The Contendings of the Apostles*. 2 vols. 1899–1901. Reprint, Amsterdam: APA, Philo, 1976.

Burrus, Virginia. *Chastity as Autonomy: Women in the Stories of the Apocryphal Acts*. Studies in Women and Religion 23. Lewiston, N.Y.: Mellen Press, 1987.

Charlesworth, James H., with James R. Mueller. *The New Testament Apocrypha and Pseudepigrapha: A Guide to Publications, with Excurses on Apocalypses*. American Theological Library Association Bibliography Series 17. Chicago: ATLA; Metuchen, N.J.: Scarecrow Press, 1987.

Cooper, Kate. *The Virgin and the Bride: Idealized Womanhood in Late Antiquity*. Cambridge, Mass.: Harvard University Press, 1996.

Dagron, Gilbert, with Marie Dupré La Tour. *Vie et miracles de sainte Thècle. Texte grec, traduction et commentaire*. Subsidia hagiographica 62. Brussels: Société des Bollandistes, 1978.

Davies, Stevan L. *The Revolt of the Widows: The Social World of the Apocryphal Acts*. Carbondale: Southern Illinois University Press; London: Feffer and Simons, 1980.

de Santos Otero, Aurelio. *Die handschriftliche Überlieferung der altslavischen Apokryphen*. 2 vols. Patristische Texte und Studien 20 and 23. Berlin/New York: de Gruyter, 1978–81.

————. *Los Evangelios Apocrifos. Colección de textos griegos y latinos, versión crítica, estudios introductorios, comentarios e ilustraciones.* Biblioteca de autores cristianos 148. 6th ed. Madrid: La Editorial Catolica, 1988.

Desreumaux, Alain. *Histoire du roi Abgar et de Jésus*. Apocryphes 3. Turnhout: Brepols, 1993.

Dvornik, Francis. *The Idea of Apostolicity in Byzantium and the Legend of the Apostle Andrew*. Dumbarton Oaks Studies 4. Cambridge, Mass.: Harvard University Press, 1958.

Ehrhard, Albert. *Überlieferung und Bestand der hagiographischen und homiletischen Literatur der griechischen Kirche von den Anfängen bis zum Ende des 16. Jahrhunderts*. 3 vols. Texte und Untersuchungen zur Geschichte der altchristlichen Literatur 50–52. Leipzig: Hinrichs, 1937–52.

Elliott, James K., ed. *The Apocryphal New Testament: A Collection of Apocryphal Christian Literature in an English Translation*. Oxford: Clarendon Press, 1993.

Elm, Susanna. *Virgins of God: The Making of Asceticism in Late Antiquity*. Oxford Classical Monographs. Oxford/New York: Oxford University Press, 1994.

Erbetta, Mario. *Gli Apocrifi del Nuovo Testamento*, vol. 2, *Atti e Legende*. Turin: Marietti, 1966.

Fabricius, Johann Albert. *Codex Apocryphus Novi Testamenti*. 2d ed. 3 vols. in 2. Hamburg: Schiller, 1719–43.

Festugière, André Jean. *Les Actes apocryphes de Jean et de Thomas. Traduction française et notes critiques*. Cahiers d'Orientalisme 6. Geneva: Cramer, 1983.

Ficker, Gerhard. *Die Petrusakten. Beiträge zu ihrem Verständnis.* Leipzig: Barth, 1903.

Flamion, Joseph. "Les Actes apocryphes de Pierre." *Revue d'histoire ecclésiastique* 9 (1908): 233–54, 465–90; 10 (1909): 5–29, 215–77; 11 (1910): 5–28, 223–56, 447–70, 675–92; 12 (1911): 209–30, 437–50.

————. *Les Actes Apocryphes de l'Apôtre André. Les Actes d'André et de Mathias, de Pierre et André et les textes apparentés.* Recueil de travaux publiés par les membres des conférences d'histoire et de philologie 33. Louvain: Université de Louvain, 1911.

Francis, James A. *Subversive Virtue: Asceticism and Authority in the Second Century Pagan World.* University Park: Pennsylvania State University Press, 1995.

Gamperl, J. "Die Johannesakten." Diss., Vienna, 1965.

Geerard, Maurice. *Clavis Apocryphorum Novi Testamenti.* Corpus Christianorum. Turnhout: Brepols, 1992.

Hennecke, Edgar, ed. *Handbuch zu den neutestamentlichen Apokryphen.* Tübingen: Mohr (Siebeck), 1904.

Hennecke, Edgar, and Wilhelm Schneemelcher. *Neutestamentliche Apokryphen in deutscher Übersetzung.* 3d ed. 2 vols. Tübingen: Mohr (Siebeck), 1959–64.

Herbert, Máire, and Martin McNamara. *Irish Biblical Apocrypha: Selected Texts in Translation.* Edinburgh: Clark, 1989.

Hernández, Jose Antonio Artés. "Estudios sobre la lengua de los Hechos apocrifos de Pedro y Pable." 2 vols. Diss., Murcia, 1994.

James, Montague Rhodes. *The Apocryphal New Testament Being the Apocryphal Gospels, Acts, Epistles, and Apocalypses with Other Narratives and Fragments Newly Translated.* Corrected ed. Oxford: Clarendon Press, 1953.

Jeremias, Joachim. *Unbekannte Jesusworte.* Abhandlungen zur Theologie des Alten und Neuen Testaments 16. Zurich: Zwingli, 1948.

Junod, Éric, and Jean-Daniel Kaestli. *Acta Iohannis.* 2 vols. Corpus Christianorum. Series Apocryphorum 1–2. Turnhout: Brepols, 1983.

———. *L'histoire des Actes apocryphes des apôtres du IIIe au IXe siècle. Le cas des Actes de Jean.* Cahiers de la Revue de théologie et de philosophie 7. Geneva/Lausanne/Neuchâtel: Revue de théologie et de philosophie, 1982.

Kaestli, Jean-Daniel, and Daniel Marguerat, eds. *Le mystère apocryphe. Introduction à une littérature méconnue.* Essais Bibliques 26. Geneva: Labor et Fides, 1995.

Klijn, Albertus Frederik Johannes. *The Acts of Thomas.* Supplements to Novum Testamentum 5. Leiden: Brill, 1962.

———. *Jewish-Christian Gospel Tradition.* Leiden: Brill, 1992.

Koester, Helmut, and François Bovon. *Genèse de l'écriture chrétienne.* Mémoires premières. Turnhout: Brepols, 1991.

Kurcikize, C., ed. *Kartuli versiebi apokripebisa mocikulta sesaxeb: IX–XI ss. xelnacerta mixedvit. Teksti gamosacemad moamzada, gamokvleva da leksikoni daurto.* Tbilisi: Sakartvelos SSR mecnierebata akademiis gamomcemloba, 1959. (This is a critical edition of the Georgian versions of the Apocryphal Acts of the Apostles.)

Lalleman, Pieter J. *The Acts of John: A Two-Stage Initiation into Johannine Gnosticism.* Studies on the Apocryphal Acts of the Apostles 4. Leuven: Peeters, 1998.

Landes, Richard, and Catherine Paupert. *Naissance d'apôtre. La Vie de saint Martial de Limoges.* Mémoires premières. Turnhout: Brepols, 1991.

Leloir, Louis. *Écrits apocryphes sur les apôtres. Traduction de l'édition arménienne de Venise.* 2 vols. Corpus Christianorum. Series Apocryphorum 3–4. Turnhout: Brepols, 1986–92.

Lipinski, Matthias. *Konkordanz zu den Thomasakten.* Bonner Biblische Beiträge 67. Frankfurt am Main: Athenäum, 1988.

Lipsius, Richard Adelbert. *Die apokryphen Apostelgeschichten und Apostellegenden. Ein Beitrag zur altchristlichen Literaturgeschichte.* 2 vols. in 3 and supplement. 1883–90. Reprint, Amsterdam: Philo, 1976.

Lipsius, Richard Adelbert, and Maximilien Bonnet. *Acta Apostolorum Apocrypha*. 2 vols. in 3. 1891–1903. Reprint, Hildesheim: Olms, 1990.

MacDonald, Dennis Ronald. *The Acts of Andrew and the Acts of Andrew and Matthias in the City of the Cannibals*. Society of Biblical Literature. Texts and Translations 33. Christian Apocrypha 1. Atlanta: Scholars Press, 1990.

———. *Christianizing Homer:* The Odyssey, *Plato, and* The Acts of Andrew. New York/Oxford: Oxford University Press, 1994.

———. *The Legend and the Apostle: The Battle for Paul in Story and Canon.* Philadelphia: Westminster Press, 1983.

———, ed. *The Apocryphal Acts of Apostles. Semeia* 38. Decatur, Ga.: Scholars Press, 1986.

McNamara, Martin. *The Apocrypha in the Irish Church*. Dublin: Institute for Advanced Studies, 1975.

Matthews, Christopher R. "Trajectories through the Philip Tradition." Th.D. diss., Harvard University, 1993.

Moraldi, Luigi. *Apocrifi del Nuovo Testamento*, vol. 2. Classici delle religioni 24. Sezione 5: Le altre confessioni cristiane. Turin: Unione tipografico-editrice torinese, 1971.

Morard, Françoise. "La légende copte de Simon et Théonoé." *Langues orientales anciennes. Philologie et linguistique* 4 (1993):139–83.

New Testament Apocrypha. Revised Edition of the Collection Initiated by Edgar Hennecke, edited by Wilhelm Schneemelcher. English translation edited by R. McL. Wilson. 2 vols. Louisville: Westminster/John Knox Press, 1991–92.

Norelli, Enrico, et al. *Ascensio Isaiae*. 2 vols. Corpus Christianorum. Series Apocryphorum 7–8. Turnhout: Brepols, 1995.

Pervo, Richard I. *Profit with Delight: The Literary Genre of the Acts of the Apostles*. Philadelphia: Fortress Press, 1987.

Peterson, Peter M. *Andrew, Brother of Simon Peter: His History and Legends*. Supplements to Novum Testamentum 1. Leiden: Brill, 1958.

Phillips, George. *Labubna bar Sennak: Mallepanuta d-Addai Shelila: The Doctrine of Addai the Apostle: Now First Edited in a Complete Form in the Original Syriac with an English Translation and Notes.* London: Trubner, 1876.

Piontek, Ferdinand. *Die katholische Kirche und die häretischen Apostelgeschichten bis zum Ausgange des 6. Jahrhunderts. Ein Beitrag zur Literaturgeschichte.* Breslau: Nischkoursky, 1908.

Plümacher, Eckhard. "Apokryphe Apostelakten." In *Paulys Realencyclopädie der classischen Altertumswissenschaft*, ed. Georg Wissowa et al., cols. 11–70. Supplementband 15. Munich: Druckenmüller, 1978.

Poirier, Paul-Hubert. *L'Hymne de la perle des Actes de Thomas. Introduction, texte, traduction, commentaire.* Homo religiosus 8. Louvain-la-Neuve. Pierier, 1981.

Prieur, Jean-Marc. *Acta Andreae.* 2 vols. Corpus Christianorum. Series Apocryphorum 5–6. Turnhout: Brepols, 1989.

———. *Actes de l'apôtre André. Présentation et traduction du latin, du copte et du grec.* Apocryphes 7. Turnhout: Brepols, 1995.

Rordorf, Willy. *Lex orandi—Lex credendi. Gesammelte Aufsätze zum 60. Geburtstag.* Paradosis 36. Fribourg, Switzerland: Universitätsverlag, 1993.

Schmidt, Carl. *Acta Pauli aus der Heidelberger koptischen Papyrushandschrift Nr. 1.* 2d ed. 1905. Reprint, Hildesheim: Olms, 1965.

———. *Die alten Petrusakten im Zusammenhang der apokryphen Apostelliteratur. Nebst einem neuentdeckten Fragment.* Texte und Untersuchungen zur Geschichte der altchristlichen Literatur 24/1. Leipzig: Hinrichs, 1903.

———. *ΠΡΑΞΕΙΣ ΠΑΥΛΟΥ. Acta Pauli nach dem Papyrus der Hamburger Staats- und Universitäts-Bibliothek*, unter der Mitarbeit von Wilhelm Schubart. Veröffentlichen aus der Hamburger Staats- und Universitäts-Bibliothek 2. Glückstadt/Hamburg: Augustin, 1936.

Schmidt, Karl Ludwig. *Kanonische und apokryphe Evangelien und Apostelgeschichten.* Abhandlungen zur Theologie des Alten und Neuen Testaments 5. Basel: Majer, 1944.

Schneemelcher, Wilhelm. *Gesammelte Aufsätze zum Neuen Testament und zur Patristik*. Analecta Vlatadon 22. Thessaloniki: Patriarchal Institute for Patristic Studies, 1974.

———. *Neutestamentliche Apokryphen in deutscher Übersetzung*. 5. Auflage der von Edgar Hennecke begründeten Sammlung. 2 vols. Tübingen: Mohr (Siebeck), 1987–89.

Schneider, Paul G. *The Mystery of the Acts of John: An Interpretation of the Hymn and the Dance in the Light of the Acts' Theology*. Distinguished Dissertation Series 1. San Francisco: Mellen Research University Press, 1991.

Sirker-Wicklaus, Gerlinde. *Untersuchungen zu den Johannesakten. Untersuchungen zur Struktur, zur theologischen Tendenz und zum kirchengeschichtlichen Hintergrund der Acta Johannis*. Beiträge zur Religionsgeschichte 2. Witterschlick-Bonn: Wehle, 1988.

Smith Lewis, Agnes. *Acta Mythologica Apostolorum*. Horae Semiticae 3. London: Clay, 1904.

———. *The Mythological Acts of the Apostles*. Horae Semiticae 4. London: Clay, 1904.

Söder, Rosa. *Die apokryphen Apostelgeschichten und die romanhafte Literatur der Antike*. 1932. Reprint, Stuttgart: Kohlhammer, 1969.

Stoops, Robert F. "Miracle Stories and Vision Reports in the Acts of Peter." Ph.D. diss., Harvard University, 1983.

Sturhahn, Carl Luitpold. *Die Christologie der ältesten apokryphen Apostelakten. Ein Beitrag zur Frühgeschichte des altchristlichen Dogmas*. 2 vols. Göttingen: Vandenhoeck und Ruprecht, 1952. Microfilm.

Thilo, Johann Karl. *Codex apocryphus Novi Testamenti*, vol. 1. Leipzig: Vogel, 1832.

Thomas, Christine M. "The Acts of Peter, the Ancient Novel, and Early Christian History." Ph.D. diss., Harvard University, 1995.

van Kampen, Lieuwe. *Apostelverhalen: Doel en compositie van de oudtse apokriefe Handelingen der apostelen. Stories about the Apostles: Intent and Composition of the Oldest Apocryphal Acts of the Apostles (with a summary in English)*. Sliedrecht: Merweboek, 1990.

von Gebhardt, Oskar Leopold. *Passio S. Theclae virginis. Die lateinischen Übersetzungen der Acta Pauli et Theclae.* Texte und Untersuchungen zur Geschichte der altchristlichen Literatur 22/2. Leipzig: Hinrichs, 1902.

Vouaux, Léon. *Les Actes de Paul et ses lettres apocryphes. Introduction, textes, traduction et commentaire.* Les Apocryphes du Nouveau Testament. Paris: Letouzey et Ané, 1913.

————. *Les Actes de Pierre. Introduction, textes, traduction et commentaire.* Les Apocryphes du Nouveau Testament. Paris: Letouzey et Ané, 1922.

Wilson, Robert McL. "Apokryphen II: Apokryphen des Neuen Testaments." In *Theologische Realenzyklopädie* 3, pp. 317–62. Berlin/New York: de Gruyter, 1978.

Wright, William, ed. *Apocryphal Acts of the Apostles. Edited from Syriac Manuscripts in the British Museum and Other Libraries.* 2 vols. 1871. Reprint, 2 vols. in 1. Hildesheim/New York: Olms, 1990.

Zahn, Theodor. *Acta Ioannis.* 1880. Reprint, Hildesheim: Gertsenberg, 1975.

Index of Biblical References

Index of Early Christian Apocrypha

Index of Ancient Texts and Authors

General Index

Accidence, in apocryphal texts, 103–4
Achaia, 236
Acta Martyrum, 82
Acta Sanctorum, 69–70
Adam, 212*n*, 243, 252*n*
    Andrew as, 48*n*
    naming of animals by, 211
Adamik, Tamás, 207*n*
Addai, 182*n*
Adventinus, 304
Aegeates (Aigeates), in *Acts of Andrew*,
    109, 237, 242–43, 248
AELAC. *See* Association pour l'étude
    de la littérature apocryphe
    chrétienne (AELAC)
Agrippa, 61
    in *Acts of Peter*, 50, 51, 53, 54, 55,
    151, 163
    in *Martyrdom of the Holy Apostles
    Peter and Paul*, 52
Agrippa, King, 328
Akolouthia, 88*n*
Aland, Barbara, 333*n*
Albinus, 61
    in *Acts of Peter*, 50, 51, 54, 155*n*
Alexander, in *Acts of Paul*, 154, 156,
    163, 163*n*
Alexander (nephew of Philo), on
    rationality in animals, 214–15,
    215*n*
Alexander, Loveday, 105
Alexandria
    authorship of *Acts of Andrew* in, 236

conflicts between cults of Christ and
    Sarapis at, 76–77
Mark the Evangelist at, 67–68, 69,
    70–71, 84
Alexandrian Greeks, in *Acts of Mark*,
    67–68
"Alexandrian School," 128*n*
Alexios I Comnenus, Emperor, 347*n*
Alphaeus, 91, 96, 96*n*
Ambiguities, in Arabic language, 80–81
Ambrose, 216*n*
Ambrosiana library (Milan), 16–17, 18
Ammaniake, Mark the Evangelist at, 80
Ammia, in *Acts of Paul*, 208
Ammon, in magic spells, 189
Amsler, Frédéric, 2, 35*n*, 284–85, 288,
    288*n*, 292*n*, 297–98, 300
Anacoluthon, 43
Analecta Bollandiana, 7, 14, 15, 331
Anani, 310, 320, 328, 328*n*, 330
Ananias of Damascus, 328*n*
    martyrdom of, 309–12, 314–21,
    322–31
Andover-Harvard Theological Library,
    *Memorial of Saint John the
    Theologian* at, 333–34
Andrew, 48*n*, 95, 106, 108–11, 117*n*, 344*n*
    crucifixion of, 240–41
    healing miracles of, 259–80
    homilies on, 92
    manuscripts about, 140–41, 233–58
    as revealer, 263
    as Socrates, 251–52